DK EYEWITNESS

W9-AID-555

TOP 10
BARCELONA

Top 10 Barcelona Highlights

Welcome to Barcelona.................5
Exploring Barcelona 6
Barcelona Highlights 10
Sagrada Família..........................12
La Rambla...................................16
Barcelona Cathedral...................18
Museu Nacional d'Art
    de Catalunya........................20
Parc Güell...................................22
La Pedrera..................................26
Fundació Joan Miró 28
Museu Picasso 30
Palau de la Música Catalana.......32
Museu d'Art Contemporani
    and Centre de Cultura
    Contemporània.....................34

The Top 10 of Everything

Moments in History 38
Churches and Chapels 40
Museums and Galleries 42
Modernista Buildings 44
Public Squares...........................46
Parks and Beaches.....................48
Off the Beaten Track..................50
Children's Attractions 52
Performing Arts and
    Music Venues........................54
Photo Spots 58
Outdoor Bars.............................60
Restaurants and Tapas Bars.......62
Cafés and Light Bites.................64
Shopping Destinations................66
Markets.....................................68
Barcelona for Free 70
Festivals and Events 72

CONTENTS

Barcelona Area by Area

Barri Gòtic and La Ribera............**76**

El Raval..**86**

Montjuïc......................................**94**

The Seafront................................**100**

Eixample.....................................**106**

Gràcia, Tibidabo and
    Zona Alta.............................**116**

Beyond Barcelona......................**124**

Streetsmart

Getting Around...........................**134**

Practical Information.................**138**

Places to Stay............................**142**

General Index.............................**150**

Acknowledgments.....................**156**

Phrase Book................................**158**

Within each Top 10 list in this book, no hierarchy of quality or popularity is implied. All 10 are, in the editor's opinion, of roughly equal merit.

Title page, front cover and spine *The striking mosaic-covered Gran Plaça Circular, Park Güell* ***Back cover, clockwise from top left*** *Ceiling of Palau de la Musica Catalana; Barceloneta Beach; outdoor restaurants, Plaça Reial; Park Güell; Museu Nacional d'Art de Catalunya*

The rapid rate at which the world is changing is constantly keeping the DK Eyewitness team on our toes. While we've worked hard to ensure that this edition of Barcelona is accurate and up-to-date, we know that opening hours alter, standards shift, prices fluctuate, places close and new ones pop up in their stead. So, if you notice we've got something wrong or left something out, we want to hear about it. Please get in touch at **travelguides@dk.com**

Welcome to
Barcelona

On the shores of the Mediterranean, the Catalan capital sizzles with creativity. Dramatic Modernista structures stand amid grand medieval quarters in an aesthetic juxtaposition of old and new. Across town, cutting-edge design, a vibrant art scene and delectable cuisine serve up a feast for the senses. With DK Eyewitness Top 10 Barcelona, it's yours to explore.

For all its apparent big-city bustle, Barcelona is a place to linger, whether on the palm-shaded seafront, over coffee in a medieval square or picnicking at **Park Güell** or in a **Montjuïc** garden. The best way to experience the city is on foot, getting lost in the labyrinthine alleyways of **Barri Gòtic** or taking time to notice the details – ceramic garlands, wrought-iron balustrades, vibrant tiles – on the **Eixample** Modernista mansions. The streets are full of **public art**, from Haring murals to Lichtenstein sculptures, and there are a host of fantastic **museums** dedicated to Picasso, Miró, contemporary art and more.

Modern Catalan cuisine is both innovative and daring, and alongside molecular gastronomy in award-winning restaurants, you'll also find some places serving fabulous local produce the way they've done for generations. At the colourful local festivals you'll get an insight into what makes Barcelona so different from the rest of Spain. Instead of flamenco dancing, you can admire the locals as they dance the *sardana* or watch the giants and fatheads process through the streets.

Whether you're coming for a weekend or a week, our Top 10 guide brings together the best of everything that the city has to offer, from Gaudí's finest masterpieces, the **Sagrada Família** and **Casa Batlló**, to the 18th-century maze in **Parc del Laberint d'Horta**. The guide has useful tips throughout, from seeking out what's free to places off the beaten track, plus nine easy-to-follow itineraries, designed to tie together a clutch of sights in a short space of time. Add inspiring photography and detailed maps, and you've got the essential pocket-sized travel companion. **Enjoy the book, and enjoy Barcelona**.

Clockwise from top: **Museu Nacional d'Art de Catalunya, stained-glass dome at the Palau de la Música Catalana, La Pedrera's chimneys, entrance to Park Güell, Casa Batlló's windows, maze at the Parc del Laberint d'Horta, plaza outside Basílica de la Mercè, Barri Gòtic**

Exploring Barcelona

You'll be utterly spoiled for choice for things to see and do in Barcelona, which is packed with historical buildings, parks, museums and beaches. Whether you're coming for a weekend, or want to get to know the city better, these two- and four-day itineraries will help you make the most of your visit.

Two Days in Barcelona

Day ❶

MORNING

Stroll along Barcelona's most celebrated avenue, **La Rambla** *(see pp16–17)*, then dive into the warren of medieval streets that makes up the **Barri Gòtic** *(see pp76–9)* and visit **Barcelona Cathedral** *(see pp18–19)*.

AFTERNOON

Continue your exploration of Barcelona's historic heart with a wander around the Born neighbourhood. Visit the **Museu Picasso** *(see pp30–31)*, then see if you can get tickets for an evening performance at the lavish Modernista **Palau de la Música Catalana** *(see pp32–3)*.

Day ❷

MORNING

Spend the morning marvelling at Gaudí's incredible **Sagrada Família** *(see pp12–15)*, but make sure you've booked tickets online in advance to avoid the long queues.

AFTERNOON

Ride the funicular up the green hill of **Montjuïc** *(see pp94–7)* to the **Fundació Joan Miró** *(see pp28–9)*, a stunning modern building that is home to a spectacular collection of Miró's work.

Four Days in Barcelona

Day ❶

MORNING

Make the day's first stop the playful, whimsical **Park Güell** *(see pp22–3)*, a UNESCO World Heritage Site.

AFTERNOON

Head south to the city's most iconic building, the **Sagrada Família** *(see pp12–15)*, then take in the **Museu**

The vibrant **Mercat de la Boqueria** is one of Europe's largest markets for fresh produce, cheese and meat.

Picasso *(see pp30–31)*, set in a complex of five interconnected Gothic palaces. Book tickets online in advance to avoid queues at these attractions.

Day ❷

MORNING

Take a stroll along **La Rambla** *(see pp16–17)*, ducking into the **Mercat de la Boqueria** *(see p68)* to admire the dizzying range of produce. Then meander through the medieval lanes of the **Barri Gòtic** *(see pp76–9)* to find **Barcelona Cathedral** *(see pp18–19)*.

AFTERNOON

Take in the boutiques of the elegant **Passeig de Gràcia** *(see p66)*, then visit one of Gaudí's most remarkable buildings, **La Pedrera** *(see pp26–7)*. Here you'll visit a restored apartment and the famous undulating rooftop.

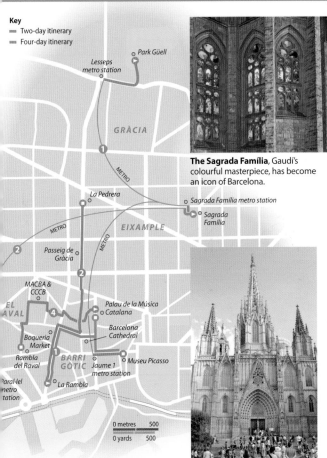

Key
— Two-day itinerary
— Four-day itinerary

Park Güell

*Lesseps
metro station*

GRÀCIA

METRO

The Sagrada Família, Gaudí's
colourful masterpiece, has become
an icon of Barcelona.

La Pedrera

Sagrada Família metro station

*Sagrada
Família*

METRO

EIXAMPLE

*Passeig de
Gràcia*

METRO

*MACBA &
CCCB*

EL
AVAL

*Palau de la Música
Catalana*

*Barcelona
Cathedral*

*Boqueria
Market*

*Rambla
del Raval*

BARRI
GÒTIC

*Jaume 1
metro station*

Museu Picasso

*Paral·lel
netro
tation*

La Rambla

0 metres   500
0 yards   500

Day ❸
MORNING
Relax in one of the many gardens
on **Montjuïc** (see pp94–7), perhaps
the charming **Jardins Laribel** or the
leafy groves of **Jardins de Miramar**
(see p98), before visiting the **Fundació
Joan Miró** (see pp28–9), one of the
world's largest Miró collections.
AFTERNOON
You'd need more than an afternoon
to see every gallery at the **Museu
Nacional d'Art de Catalunya** (see
pp20–21), but the Romanesque and
Gothic collections are a must. In the
evening, enjoy the sound and light
show at the **Font Màgica** (see p95).

**Barcelona's 13th-century
cathedral** has a magnificent
façade and a quiet cloister.

Day ❹
MORNING
Take a tour of the **Palau de la Música
Catalana** (see pp32–3), a breathtaking
Modernista masterpiece with an eye-
popping auditorium.
AFTERNOON
Check out the contemporary art
at the **Museu d'Art Contemporani
(MACBA)** and **Centre de Cultura
Contemporània (CCCB)** (see pp34–5),
then relax over a coffee on the nearby
Rambla del Raval (see p88).

Top 10 Barcelona Highlights

The soaring, tree-like columns
of the Sagrada Família's nave

Barcelona Highlights	10	La Pedrera	26
Sagrada Família	12	Fundació Joan Miró	28
La Rambla	16	Museu Picasso	30
Barcelona Cathedral	18	Palau de la Música Catalana	32
Museu Nacional d'Art de Catalunya	20	Museu d'Art Contemporani and Centre de Cultura Contemporània	34
Park Güell	22		

Barcelona Highlights

One of the busiest ports of the Mediterranean, Barcelona has it all. With beautiful Modernista buildings, atmospheric medieval streets, enchanting squares, beaches and treasure-filled museums, this awe-inspiring city will keep you coming back for more.

Sagrada Família ①

Gaudí's otherworldly *pièce de résistance* is the enduring symbol of the city and its Modernista legacy. Of the 18 planned spires, 12 jut into the sky (see pp12–15).

② La Rambla

Barcelona's centrepiece, this thriving pedestrian thoroughfare cuts a wide swathe through the old town, from Plaça de Catalunya to the glittering Mediterranean Sea (see pp16–17).

③ Barcelona Cathedral

Dominating the heart of the old town is this magnificent Gothic cathedral, with a soaring, elaborate façade and a graceful, sun-dappled cloister containing palm trees and white geese (see pp18–19).

Museu Nacional d'Art de Catalunya ④

The stately Palau Nacional is home to the Museu Nacional d'Art de Catalunya (MNAC). Its extensive collections boast some of the world's finest Romanesque art, rescued from churches around Catalonia during the 1920s (see pp20–21).

⑤ Park Güell

With its whimsical dragon, fairy-tale pavilions and sinuous bench offering dramatic city views, this magical hillside park is indubitably the work of Gaudí (see pp22–3).

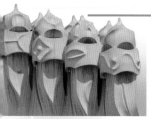

6 La Pedrera

Unmistakably Gaudí, this Modernista marvel seems to grow from the very pavement itself. Its curving façade is fluid and alive, and mosaic chimneys keep watch over the rooftop like shrewd-eyed knights *(see pp26–7)*.

7 Fundació Joan Miró

An incomparable blend of art and architecture, this museum showcases the work of Joan Miró, one of Catalonia's greatest 20th-century artists. Paintings, sculptures, drawings and textiles repre-sent 60 prolific years *(see pp28–9)*.

8 Museu Picasso

Housed in a medieval palace com-plex, this museum charts Picasso's rise to fame through an extensive collection of his early works, including many masterful portraits that he painted at the young age of 13 *(see pp30–31)*.

Palau de la Música Catalana 9

No mere concert hall, the aptly-named Palace of Catalan Music is one of the finest, and most exemplary, Modernista buildings in Barcelona *(see pp32–3)*.

10 Museu d'Art Contemporani and Centre de Cultura Contemporània

The city's gleaming contemporary art museum and its cutting-edge cultural centre have sparked an urban revival in the El Raval area *(see pp34–5)*.

TOP 10 ⭐ Sagrada Família

Nothing prepares you for the impact of the Sagrada Família. A *tour de force* of the imagination, Antoni Gaudí's church has provoked endless controversy. It also offers visitors the unique chance to watch a wonder of the world in the making. Over the last 90 years, at incalculable cost, sculptors and architects have continued to build Gaudí's dream. It was hoped the project would be complete by 2026, the 100th anniversary of Gaudí's death, however the pandemic in 2020 has delayed work.

1 Spiral Staircases
These helicoidal stone stairways **(above)**, which wind up the bell towers, look like snail shells.

2 Nave
The immense central body of the church **(below)**, now complete, is made up of leaning, tree-like columns with branches that are inspired by a banana tree spreading out across the ceiling; the overall effect is that of a beautiful stone forest.

3 Nativity Façade
Gaudí's love of nature is visible in this façade **(above)**. Up to 100 plant and animal species are sculpted in stone, and the two main columns are supported by turtles.

4 Apse
Adorned with serpents, four large snails and lizards, this was the first section to be completed by Gaudí. Here, the stained glass graduates in tones beautifully.

Sagrada Família Floorplan

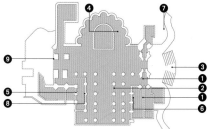

5 Hanging Model

This contraption is testimony to Gaudí's ingenuity. He made the 3D device – using multiple chains and tiny weighted sacks of lead pellets – as a model for the arches and vaulted ceilings of the Colonia Güell crypt. No one in the history of architecture had ever designed a building like this.

6 Spires

Gaudí's plan originally detailed a total of 18 spires. For a closer look at the mosaic tiling and gargoyles on the existing spires, take the lift up inside the bell tower. The views are equally spectacular.

7 Rosario's Claustro

In the only cloister to be finished by Gaudí, the imagery is thought to be inspired by the anarchist riots that began in 1909 (see pp38–9). The Devil's temptation of man is depicted by the sculpture of a serpent wound around a rebel.

8 Crypt Museum

Gaudí now lies in the crypt (below), and his tomb is visible from the museum. Using audio-visual exhibits, the museum provides a lot of information about the construction of the church. The highlight is the maquette workshop, producing scale models for the ongoing work.

9 Passion Façade

Created between 1954 and 2002, this Josep Subirachs façade represents the sacrifice and pain of Jesus. The difference between the Gothic feel of Subirachs' style and the intricacy of Gaudí's work has been controversial.

10 Unfinished Business

The church buzzes with activity even today. You will see sculptors dangle from spires, stonemasons carve huge slabs of stone and cranes and scaffolding litter the site. Watching the construction in progress allows visitors to grasp the monumental scale of the project.

NEED TO KNOW

MAP G2 Entrances: C/Marina (for groups only) and C/Sardenya ■ 93 207 30 31 ■ www.sagradafamilia.org

Open 9am–6pm daily (to 7pm Mar & Oct, 8pm Apr–Sep)

Adm €27, including audio guide; €28 for combined ticket with Casa-Museu Gaudí, including audio guide; access to towers closed.

■ Advance online booking is strongly recommended. Check website for full details of guided tours.

■ Sit in a terrace bar on Av Gaudí and drink in the view of Gaudí's masterpiece illuminated at night.

■ For the best photos, get here before 8am: the light on the Nativity Façade is excellent and the tour buses haven't yet arrived.

■ In the cryptogram on the Passion Façade, the numbers add up to the age of Christ at his death.

Sight Guide
The main entrance is on C/Marina, in front of the Nativity Façade, along with gift shops. There is a lift in each façade (stairs are not open to the public). The museum is near the entrance on C/Sardenya. 12 of the 18 planned towers are built and are open to the public, but these are not accessible for those with specific requirements.

Key Sagrada Família Dates

1 **1882**
The first stone of the Sagrada Família is officially laid, with architect Francesc del Villar heading the project. Villar soon resigns after disagreements with the church's religious founders.

2 **1883**
The young, up-and-coming Antoni Gaudí is commissioned as the principal architect. He goes on to devote the next 40 years of his life to the project: by the end he even lives on the premises.

3 **1889**
The church crypt is completed, ringed by a series of chapels, one of which is later to house Gaudí's tomb.

4 **1904**
The final touches are made to the Nativity Façade, which depicts Jesus, Mary and Joseph amid a chorus of angels.

5 **1925**
The first of the 18 planned bell towers, measuring 100 m (328 ft) in height, is finished.

6 **1926**
On 10 June, Gaudí is killed by a tram while crossing the street near his beloved church. No one recognizes the city's most famous architect.

Sculpture, Passion Façade

7 **1936**
The military uprising and the advent of the Spanish Civil War brings construction of the Sagrada Família to a halt for some 20 years. During this period, Gaudí's studio and the crypt in the Sagrada Família are burned by revolutionaries, who despise the Catholic church for siding with the nationalists.

8 **1987–1990**
Sculptor and painter Josep Maria Subirachs (b 1927) takes to living in the Sagrada Família just as his famous predecessor did. Subirachs completes the statuary of the Passion Façade. His angular, severe and striking sculptures draw both criticism and praise.

9 **2000**
On 31 December, the nave is at long last declared complete.

10 **2010–2021**
The central nave of the church is complete, and in November 2010 Pope Benedict XVI consecrated it as a basilica. The Lion of Judah, among other things, was added to the Passion Façade in 2018, marking its completion. The construction, as Gaudí intended, continues today and relies on public subscriptions. The basilica's second-tallest tower, the tower of the Virgin Mary, will be completed in 2021.

Stained-glass windows in the apse

ANTONI GAUDÍ

Gaudí (1852–1926)

A flag bearer for the Modernista movement of the late 19th century, Antoni Gaudí is Barcelona's most famous architect. A strong Catalan nationalist and a devout Catholic, he led an almost monastic life, consumed by his architectural vision and living in virtual poverty for most of his life. In 2003 the Vatican opened the beatification process for Gaudí, which is the first step towards declaring his sainthood. Gaudí's extraordinary legacy dominates the architectural map of Barcelona. His name itself comes from the Catalan verb *gaudir*, meaning "to enjoy", and an enormous sense of exuberance and playfulness pervades his work. As was characteristic of *Modernisme*, nature prevails, not only in the decorative motifs, but also in the very structure of Gaudí's buildings. His highly innovative style is also characterized by intricate wrought-iron gates and balconies and *trencadís* tiling.

TOP 10
GAUDÍ SIGHTS IN BARCELONA

1 **Sagrada Família**

2 **La Pedrera** (1910)
see pp26–7

3 **Park Güell** (1900)
see pp22–3

4 **Casa Batlló** (1905)
see p45

5 **Palau Güell** (1890)
see p87

6 **Torre Bellesguard** (1875)

7 **Finca Güell** (1887)

8 **Casa Calvet** (1899)

9 **Col·legi de les Teresianes** (1890)

10 **Casa Vicens** (1885)

Casa Batlló's many chimneys are adorned with tiled designs. These usually unremarkable parts of a building have become authentic examples of Gaudí's caprice.

TOP 10 ⭐ La Rambla

One of the city's best-loved sights, the historic La Rambla avenue splits the Old Town in half as it stretches from Plaça de Catalunya to Port Vell. Lined with a host of enticing shops, charming cafés and tiny tapas bars, and teeming with locals, tourists and performance artists, this far-reaching street has long been a lively hub of exuberant activity. There may be no better place in the country to indulge in the Spanish ritual of the *paseo* (stroll) than on this wide, tree-shaded pedestrian street that snakes through the heart of the city.

1 Gran Teatre del Liceu

The city's grand opera house **(right)**, founded in 1847, brought Catalan opera stars such as Montserrat Caballé to the world. Twice gutted by fire, it *(see p54)* has been fully restored.

2 Mercat de la Boqueria

A cacophonous shrine to food, this cavernous market *(see p68)* has it all, from stacks of fruit to suckling pigs and fresh lobsters.

3 Arts Santa Mònica

Once the haunt of rosary beads and prayers, this former 17th-century monastery was reborn in the 1980s as a contemporary art centre, thanks to government funding. This 'Centre de la Creativitat' lays special emphasis on encouraging creativity in Catalunya and promoting homegrown talent. Exhibitions here range from large-scale video installations to photography.

Visitors on La Rambla

4 Flower Stalls

La Rambla is teeming with life and things to distract the eye, but the true Rambla old-timers are the flower stalls flanking the pedestrian walkway, many run by the same families for decades.

5 Monument a Colom

Pointing resolutely out to sea, this 1888 bronze statue *(see p102)* of Christopher Columbus **(left)** commemorates his return to Spain after his famed journey to the Americas. An elevator whisks visitors to the top of the column for stunning views.

6 Font de Canaletes

Ensure that you come back to the city by sipping water from this 19th-century fountain **(right)**. It is inscribed with the legend that those who drink from it "will fall in love with Barcelona and always return".

⑦ Palau de la Virreina

This Neo-Classical palace was built by the viceroy of Peru in 1778. Today, the Palace of the Viceroy's Wife is home to the Centre de la Imatge, and hosts art exhibitions and cultural events.

⑧ Miró Mosaic

On the walkway on La Rambla is a colourful floor mosaic *(see p71)* by Catalan artist Joan Miró. Symbolizing the cosmos, it incorporates his signature abstract shapes and primary colours which unfold at your feet.

La Rambla

NEED TO KNOW

Gran Teatre del Liceu:
MAP L4; La Rambla 51–59; 93 485 99 31; Guided tours in English available daily, times vary; adm; www.liceu barcelona.cat

Mercat de La Boqueria:
MAP L3; La Rambla 91; open 8am–8:30pm Mon–Sat; www.boqueria.info

Arts Santa Mònica:
MAP L5; La Rambla 7; 93 567 11 10; open 11am–9pm Tue–Sat, 11am–7pm Sun (to 8pm Nov–Mar); artssantamonica.gencat. cat/ca

Palau de la Virreina:
MAP L3; 93 316 10 00;

La Rambla 99: open 11am–8pm Tue–Sun; ajuntament.barcelona. cat/lavirreina/en

Església de Betlem:
MAP L3; C/Xuclà 2; 93 318 38 23; open 8:30am–1:30pm & 6–9pm daily; www.mdbetlem.net

■ Kick back at the Cafè de l'Òpera at No. 74 *(see p64)* and soak up the La Rambla ambience with a cool *granissat* (crushed ice drink) in hand.

■ La Rambla is rife with pickpockets – be careful with your belongings, especially your wallets and cameras.

⑨ Bruno Quadras Building

Once an umbrella factory, this playful, late 19th-century building boasts several Oriental motifs. Its exterior is festooned with umbrellas and an ornate Chinese Dragon statue **(above)**.

⑩ Església de Betlem

From a time when the Catholic Church was rolling in pesetas (and power), this hulking 17th-century church *(see p41)* is a seminal reminder of when La Rambla was more religious than risqué.

Barcelona Cathedral

From its Gothic cloister and Baroque chapels to its splendid 19th-century façade, the cathedral, dating from 1298, is an amalgam of architectural styles, each one paying homage to a period in Spain's religious history. Records show that an early Christian baptistry was established here in the 6th century, later replaced by a Romanesque basilica in the 11th century, which gave way to the current Gothic cathedral. This living monument still functions as the Barri Gòtic's spiritual hub.

1 Main Façade
The 19th-century façade **(below)** has the entrance, flanked by twin towers, Modernista stained-glass windows and 100 carved angels. The restoration process took 8 years and was completed in 2011.

2 Choir Stalls
The lavish choir stalls (1340), crowned with wooden spires, are decorated with colourful coats of arms by artist Joan de Borgonya.

3 Cloister
Graced with a fountain, palm trees and roaming geese, the cloister dates back to the 14th century. The mossy fountain is presided over by a small iron statue of Sant Jordi – St George *(see p41)*.

4 Nave and Organ
The immense nave **(above)** is supported by slender columns and features a raised high altar. The 16th-century organ looming over the interior fills the space with music during services.

Crypt of Santa Eulàlia 5
In the centre of the crypt lies the graceful 1327 alabaster sarcophagus **(right)** of Santa Eulàlia, Barcelona's first patron saint. Reliefs depict her martyrdom.

6 Capella de Sant Benet

Honouring Sant Benet, the patron saint of Europe, this chapel showcases the 15th-century altarpiece *Transfiguration of the Lord* by illustrious Catalan artist Bernat Martorell.

7 Capella de Santa Llúcia

This lovely Romanesque chapel is dedicated to Santa Llúcia, the patron saint of eyes and vision *(see p41)*. On her saint's day (13 December), the blind come to pray at her chapel.

Barcelona Cathedral Floorplan

8 Capella del Santíssim i Crist de Lepant

This 15th-century chapel features the Crist de Lepant **(right)** which, legend has it, guided the Christian fleet in the 16th-century Battle of Lepanto against the Ottoman Turks, who could not then advance to Europe.

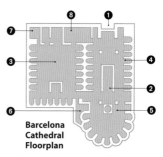

9 Pia Almoina and Gaudí Exhibition Centre

The 11th-century Pia Almoina, once a rest house for pilgrims and the poor, houses the Gaudí Exhibition Centre where interactive exhibits showcase Gaudí's life and works.

10 Casa de l'Ardiaca

Originally built in the 12th century, the Archdeacon's House is located near what was once the Bishop's Gate in the city's Roman walls. Expanded over the centuries, it now includes a lovely leafy patio with a fountain.

NEED TO KNOW

MAP M3 ■ Pl de la Seu; 93 342 82 62 ■ Open 10:30am–2pm & 4–7pm Mon–Fri, 10:30am–5:30pm Sat ■ Adm choir and rooftops (via lift) €3 each, for cathedral floor & cloister €7 donation (see website for timings) ■ www.catedralbcn.org

Gaudí Exhibition Centre: **MAP N3** ■ Av de la Catedral 4; closed due to COVID-19; adm €15

Casa de l'Ardiaca: **MAP M3** ■ C/Santa Llúcia 1; open 9am–8:45pm Mon–Fri (to 1pm Sat); Jul–Aug: 9am–7:30pm Mon–Fri

■ Dress modestly to visit the cathedral (covered shoulders; no shorts).

■ Choral/organ concerts are usually held monthly; information is available at the Pia Almoina.

■ Watch *Sardanes*, Catalonia's regional dance, performed in Plaça de la Seu at 6pm on Saturdays and at noon on Sundays.

Cathedral Guide

The main entrance is the main portal on Plaça de la Seu. As you enter, to the left you will find a series of chapels, the organ and elevators that go up to the roof. The Gaudí Exhibition Centre is located to the left of the main entrance; Casa de l'Ardiaca is to the right.

TOP 10 ⭐ Museu Nacional d'Art de Catalunya

Holding one of the most important medieval art collections in the world, the Museu Nacional d'Art de Catalunya (MNAC) is housed in the majestic Palau Nacional, built in 1929. A highlight is the Romanesque art section, which consists of the painted interiors of Pyrenean churches dating from the 11th and 12th centuries. Other collections include works by Catalan artists from the early 19th century to the present day.

1 The Madonna of the Councillors

Commissioned by the city council in 1443, this work by Lluís Dalmau is rich in political symbolism, with the head councillors, saints and martyrs kneeling before an enthroned Virgin.

2 Murals: Santa Maria de Taüll

The well-preserved interior of Santa Maria de Taüll (c 1123) gives an idea of how colourful the Romanesque churches must have been. There are scenes from Jesus's early life, with John the Baptist and the Wise Men.

3 Cambó Bequest

Catalan politician Francesc Cambó (1876–1974) left his huge art collection to Catalonia; two large galleries contain works from the 16th to early 19th centuries, including Tiepolo's 1756 *The Minuet* **(above)**.

4 Thyssen-Bornemisza Collection

A small but fine selection from Baron Thyssen-Bornemisza's extensive collection. Among the magnificent paintings are Fra Angelico's sublime *Madonna of Humility* (1433–5) and a charmingly domestic *Madonna and Child* (c 1618) by Rubens **(left)**.

5 Frescoes: Sant Climent de Taüll

The interior of Sant Climent de Taüll is a melange of French, Byzantine and Italian influences. The apse is dominated by *Christ in Majesty* **(below)** and the symbols of the four Evangelists and the Virgin, with the apostles beneath.

7 Woman with Hat and Fur Collar

Picasso's extraordinary depiction of his lover Maria-Thérèse Walter shows him moving beyond Cubism and Surrealism into a new personal language, soon to be known simply as the "Picasso style".

9 Confidant from the Batlló House

Among the fine Modernista furnishings are some exquisite pieces by Antoni Gaudí, including an undulating wooden chair designed to encourage confidences between friends.

6 Ramon Casas and Pere Romeu on a Tandem

This painting **(above)** depicts the painter Casas and his friend Romeu, with whom he began the bohemian Barri Gòtic tavern Els Quatre Gats.

8 Crucifix of Batlló Majesty

This mid-12th century wooden carving is a depiction of Christ on the cross with open eyes and no signs of suffering, as he has defeated death.

Museu Nacional d'Art de Catalunya Floorplan

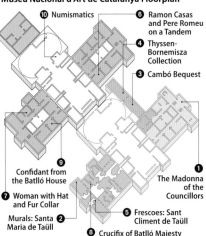

⑩ Numismatics
⑥ Ramon Casas and Pere Romeu on a Tandem
④ Thyssen-Bornemisza Collection
③ Cambó Bequest

⑨ Confidant from the Batlló House
⑦ Woman with Hat and Fur Collar
Murals: Santa Maria de Taüll ②
① The Madonna of the Councillors
⑤ Frescoes: Sant Climent de Taüll
⑧ Crucifix of Batlló Majesty

10 Numismatics

The public numismatic collection at the MNAC dates back to the 6th century BC and features medals, early paper money, 15th-century Italian bills as well as coins **(above)** including the ones from the Greek colony of Empúries which had its own mint from the 5th century BC.

Key to Floorplan

- Romanesque Art Gallery
- Modern Art; Drawings, Prints and Posters
- Gothic Art Gallery
- Renaissance and Baroque Art
- Library

NEED TO KNOW

MAP B4 ■ Palau Nacional, Parc de Montjuïc ■ www. museunacional.cat/en

Open 10am–6pm Tue–Sat (to 8pm May–Sep), 10am–3pm Sun; timings for roof terrace vary, check website.

Adm €12 (valid for 2 days in a month); free on Sat from 3pm and first Sun of the month; free for under 16s & over 65s; roof terrace €2

Free guided tours first Sun of the month (except Aug; Catalan noon, Spanish 12:15pm), by appointment

■ The terrace outside the front entrance of the museum has panoramic views over the city.

Gallery Guide

The Cambó Bequest, with Zurbarán's and Goya's works, and the Thyssen-Bornemisza Collection, with works from the Gothic to the Rococo, are on the ground floor, as are the Romanesque works. On the first floor are the modern art galleries and the photography and numismatics collections.

🔟 ⭐ Park Güell

Built between 1900 and 1914, Park Güell was conceived as an English-style garden city, which were becoming popular in the early 20th century. Gaudí's patron, Eusebi Güell, envisaged elegant, artistic villas, gardens and public spaces. However, the project failed. The space was sold to the city and, in 1926, reopened as a public park where Gaudí had let his imagination run riot on the pavilions, stairways, the main square with its sinuous tiled bench and the tiled columns of the marketplace.

4 Casa del Guarda

The porter's lodge, one of two fairy-tale pavilions that guard the park entrance **(right)**, is now an outpost of MUHBA, the Barcelona History Museum (see p78). It contains an exhibition dedicated to the history of Park Güell.

1 Sala Hipòstila

Jujol was one of Gaudí's most gifted collaborators, responsible for decorating the 84 columns **(above)** of the park's marketplace, creating vivid ceiling mosaics from shards of broken tiles.

2 Tiled Bench

An enormous bench, which functions as a balustrade, ripples around the edge of Plaça de la Natura. Artists ranging from Miró to Dalí were inspired by its beautiful abstract designs created from colourful broken tiles.

3 Jardins d'Àustria

These beautifully manicured gardens are modern, laid out in the 1970s on what was originally destined to be a plot for a mansion. They are especially lovely in the spring.

5 L'Escalinata del Drac

A fountain runs along the length of this impressive, lavishly-tiled staircase, which is topped with whimsical creatures. The most famous of these is the enormous multicoloured dragon, which has become the symbol of Barcelona.

6 Viaducts

Gaudí created three viaducts **(below)** to serve as carriageways through Park Güell. Set into the steep slopes, and supported by archways and columns in the shape of waves or trees, they appear to emerge organically from the hill.

7 Plaça de la Natura

The park's main square offers panoramic views across the city, and is fringed by a remarkable tiled bench. The square was originally called the Greek Theatre and was intended for open-air shows, with the audience watching from the surrounding terraces.

⑨ Pòrtic de la Bugadera

One of the park's many pathways, this is known as the Portico of the Laundress after the woman bearing a basket of washing on her head **(left)**, which is carved into an arch.

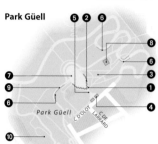

Park Güell

UNFULFILLED IDEAS

Sadly, many of Gaudí's ideas for Park Güell were never realized owing to the economic failure of Eusebi Güell's garden city. Among the most daring of these ideas was his design for an enormous entrance gate, which he intended to be swung open by a pair of gigantic mechanical gazelles.

⑩ Turó de les Tres Creus

Three crosses crown the very top of the hill, marking the spot where Gaudí and Güell, both intensely religious men, intended to build Park Güell's chapel. The climb to the top is well worth it in order to enjoy the spectacular city views.

⑧ Casa-Museu Gaudí

One of only two houses to be built in Park Güell, this became Gaudí's home and contains original furnishings and memorabilia. It is located outside the Monumental Zone.

NEED TO KNOW

MAP C1 ■ C/d'Olot s/n
■ parkguell.barcelona

Open Jan–Mar: 9:30am–6:15pm daily; Apr: 9:30am–8:30pm daily; Jun–Aug: 9:30am–9:30pm daily; Sep & Oct: 9:30am–8:30pm daily; Nov & Dec: 9:30am–6:15pm daily; last entry 1 hr before closing

Adm to Monumental Zone €10; free for under 6s, €7 under 12s; the rest of the park is free of charge; Casa del Guarda included with park ticket; separate ticket required in advance for Casa-Museu Gaudí, open Sat & Sun, adm €5.50

■ There are very few options to eat around the Park Güell, so it's a good idea to bring a picnic. There are a couple of picnic areas with tables available.

■ Note that visits to the Monumental Area are timed. Ensure that you do not miss your slot as the schedules are not flexible.

■ There are three small playgrounds with swings and slides, perfect to let little ones blow off some steam.

■ The entrance ticket, available online or at the automatic ticket machine at the entrance.

Following pages *Elegant Neo-Classical buildings and towering palm trees on Plaça Reial*

TOP 10 ⭐ La Pedrera

Completed in 1912, this fantastic, undulating apartment block with its out-of-this-world roof is one of the most emblematic of all Gaudí's works. Casa Milà, also known as La Pedrera ("the stone quarry"), was Gaudí's last great civic work before he dedicated himself to the Sagrada Família. What makes it so magical is that every detail bears the hallmark of Gaudí's visionary genius. Now restored to its former glory, La Pedrera contains the Espai Gaudí, an exhibition hall, courtyards, a roof terrace and the Pedrera Apartment.

① Façade and Balconies
Defying the laws of gravity, La Pedrera's irreverent curved walls are held in place by undulating horizontal beams attached to invisible girders. Intricate wrought-iron balconies **(below)** are an example of the artisan skill so integral to *Modernisme*.

④ Roof
The strikingly surreal rooftop sculpture park has chimneys resembling medieval warriors and huge ventilator ducts twisted into bizarre organic forms **(below)**, not to mention superb views over the Eixample.

② Espai Gaudí
A series of drawings, photos, maquettes and multimedia displays help visitors grasp Gaudí's architectural wizardry. The museum is housed in the breathtaking vaulted attic, with its 270 catenary brick arches forming atmospheric skeletal corridors.

⑥ Temporary Exhibition Hall
This interesting gallery space is run by the Catalunya-La Pedrera Foundation and hosts regular free art exhibitions. It has displayed works by Francis Bacon, Salvador Dalí and Marc Chagall among others. The ceiling here looks as if it has been coated with whisked egg whites.

③ Interior Courtyard: Carrer Provença
A brigade of guides take the multitude of visitors through here each day. A closer inspection of this first courtyard reveals its beautiful mosaics and multicoloured wall paintings lining a swirling, fairy-tale staircase.

⑤ Gates
The mastery in imagining the huge wrought-iron gates **(right)** reveals the influence of Gaudí's predecessors – four generations of artisan metal workers. The use of iron is integral to many of Gaudí's edifices.

⑧ La Pedrera Apartment

This Modernista flat **(left)** with period furnishings is a reconstruction of a typical Barcelona bourgeois flat of the late 19th century. It provides an engaging contrast between the more sedate middle-class conservatism of the era and the undeniable wackiness of the outer building itself.

Visitors exploring the unusual roof of La Pedrera

⑦ Interior Courtyard: Passeig de Gràcia

Like the first courtyard, this too has a grand, ornate staircase **(below)**. This one is decorated with a stunning, floral ceiling painting.

⑨ Auditorium

The auditorium, located in the former coach house, hosts regular events such as jazz and contemporary concerts. The adjacent garden offers visitors a glimpse of greenery.

NEED TO KNOW

MAP E2 ▪ Pg de Gràcia 92 ▪ 93 214 2576 ▪ www.la pedrera.com

Open 9am–8:30pm daily (to 6:30pm Nov–Feb, 8:30pm at Christmas time); times for evening guided tours and temporary exhibits vary

Adm €27 (€24 online); audio guides in several languages included; reserve ahead

▪ Check the website for current activities and temporary exhibitions.

▪ Explore La Pedrera with nocturnal and early morning tours, or opt for a combined guided tour where you can experience the sight day and night.

▪ Tickets for the popular night-time sound and light show can be booked online for €34 (night visit and dinner €59).

Sight Guide
The Espai Gaudí, the Pedrera Apartment, the Passeig de Gràcia and Carrer Provença Courtyards, the Exhibition Room and the roof are open to visitors. A lift goes up to the apartment, Espai Gaudí and the roof. The courtyards, staircases, café and shop are accessible from the entrance on the corner of Pg de Gràcia and C/Provença.

⑩ La Pedrera Shop and Café

A wide range of Gaudí-related memorabilia includes replicas of the warrior chimneys in ceramic and bronze.

TOP 10 ⭐ Fundació Joan Miró

Founded in 1975 by Joan Miró himself, who wanted it to be a contemporary arts centre, this is now a superb tribute to a man whose legacy as an artist and a Catalan is visible across the city. The museum holds more than 14,000 of his paintings, sketches and sculptures, tracing Miró's evolution from an innovative Surrealist in the 1920s to one of the world's most challenging modern artists in the 1960s.

1 Tapis de la Fundació

This immense, richly coloured tapestry **(below)** represents the culmination of Miró's work with textiles, which began during the 1970s. The work framed the characteristic colour palette of Miró's output.

The façade of Fundació Joan Miró

2 Pages Catala al Car de Lluna

The figurative painting *Catalan Peasant by Moonlight* **(right)** dates from the late 1960s and highlights two of Miró's favourite themes: the earth and the night. The figure of the peasant, a very simple collage of colour, is barely decipherable, as the crescent moon merges with his sickle and the night sky takes on the rich green tones of the earth.

3 L'Estel Matinal

This is one of 23 paintings known as the Constellation Series. The *Morning Star's* intro-spective quality reflects Miró's state of mind at the outbreak of World War II, when he was hiding in Normandy. Spindly shapes of birds, women, heavenly bodies, lines and planes of colour are suspended in an undefined space.

4 Home i Dona Davant un Munt d'Excrement

Tortured and misshapen semi-abstract figures try to embrace against a black sky. Miró's pessi-mism at the time of *Man and Woman in Front of a Pile of Excrement* would soon be confirmed by the outbreak of the Civil War.

10 Terrace Garden

More of Miró's sculptures are randomly scattered on a spacious terrace (left), from which you can appreciate the Rationalist architecture of Josep Lluís Sert's geometric building. The 3-m (10-ft) tall *Caress of a Bird* (1967) dominates the terrace.

7 Font de Mercuri

Alexander Calder donated the *Mercury Fountain* to the Fundació as a mark of his friendship with Miró. The work was an anti-fascist tribute, conceived in memory of the attack on the town of Almadén.

9 Sculpture Room

This room (below) focuses on Miró's sculptures from the 1940s to the 1950s, when he experimented with ceramic, bronze and, later, painted media and found objects. Notable works include *Sun Bird* and *Moon Bird* (both 1946–9).

8 Espai 13

This space showcases the experimental work of new artists from around the world. The exhibitions, based on a single theme each year, are usually radical and often use new technologies.

5 Sèrie Barcelona

The Fundació holds the only complete set of prints of this series of 50 black-and-white lithographs. This important collection is only occasionally on display.

6 Visiting Exhibitions

Over the years, a number of temporary exhibitions, which are usually held in the Fundació's west wing, have included retrospectives of high-profile artists such as Mark Rothko, Andy Warhol, René Magritte and Fernand Léger.

NEED TO KNOW

MAP B4 ■ Av Miramar, Parc de Montjuïc ■ 93 443 94 70 ■ www.fmiro bcn.org

Open 10am–6pm Tue–Sat (to 8pm Apr–Oct), 10am–9pm Thu (to 8pm Sat, 3pm Sun)

Adm €13, concessions €7; Espai 13 €3; multimedia guide €5; temporary exhibitions €7

■ The restaurant-café has a garden terrace with indoor and outdoor seating and is one of the area's best dining options.

■ In summer, live experimental music is showcased in the auditorium, usually on Thursday nights (but check beforehand).

■ The gift shop has an original range of Miróesque curiosities, from tablecloths to champagne glasses.

Katsuta Collection

The Foundation's collections have been supplemented with 34 important artworks loaned out by Kazumasa Katsuta, a Japanese businessman who owns the world's largest private collection of Miró's works.

TOP 10 ⭐ Museu Picasso

Pay homage to the 20th century's most acclaimed artist at this treasure-filled museum. Highlighting Pablo Picasso's (1881–1973) formative years, the museum boasts the world's largest collection of his early works. At the tender age of 10, Picasso was already revealing remarkable artistic tendencies. In 1895 he moved to Barcelona where he blossomed as an artist. From precocious sketches and powerful family portraits to Blue- and Rose-period works, the museum offers visitors the rare chance to discover the artist as he was discovering himself.

1 Home amb boina
This portrait reveals brush strokes – and a subject matter – that are far beyond a 13-year-old child. No puppies or cats for the young Picasso; instead, he painted the portraits of the oldest men in the village. He signed this work P Ruiz, because at this time he was still using his father's last name.

4 L'Espera (Margot) and La Nana
Picasso's *Margot* is an evocative painting portraying a call girl as she waits for her next customer, while *La Nana* **(left)** captures the defiant expression and stance of a heavily rouged dwarf dancer.

5 El Foll
The Madman is a fine example of Picasso's Blue period. This artistic phase, which lasted from 1901 to 1904, was characterized by melancholic themes and monochromatic, sombre colours.

2 Autoretrat amb perruca
At 14, Picasso painted *Self-portrait with Wig*, a whimsical depiction of how he might have looked during the time of his artistic hero, Velázquez.

3 Ciència i Caritat
One of Picasso's first publicly exhibited paintings was *Science and Charity*. Picasso's father posed as the doctor.

6 Menu de Els Quatre Gats
Picasso's premier Barcelona exhibition was held in 1900 at the Barri Gòtic café and centre of *Modernisme*, Els Quatre Gats. The artist's first commission was the pen-and-ink drawing **(left)** of himself and a group of artist friends, which graced the menu cover of this bohemian hang-out.

8 Arlequí

A lifting of spirits led to Picasso's Neo-Classical period, typified by paintings like *Arlequí* or *The Harlequin* **(left)**, which celebrated the light-hearted liberty of circus performers.

7 Las Meninas Series

Picasso's reverence for Velázquez culminated in this remarkable series of paintings **(below)**, based on the Velázquez painting *Las Meninas*.

9 Home assegnt

Works such as *Seated Man* **(above)** confirmed Picasso's status as the greatest Analytic Cubist painter of the 20th century.

10 Cavall banyegat

The anguished horse in this painting later appears in Picasso's large mural *Guernica*, which reveals the horrors of war. This work gives viewers the chance to observe the process that went into the creation of one of Picasso's most famous paintings.

NEED TO KNOW

MAP P4 ■ C/Montcada 15–23 ■ www.museu picasso.bcn.cat

Open 11am–9pm Tue–Sun

Adm €12; temporary exhibitions €7; free first Sunday of the month (permanent collections) and 5–9pm every Thursday

Guided tours in English are available at 3pm on Wednesday, at 7pm on Thursday and at 11am on Sunday; adm €6 plus price of ticket

■ The Museu Picasso is housed in a Gothic palace complex, replete with leafy courtyards, all of which can be explored.

■ The café has outdoor tables in summer and offers a changing menu of daily lunch specials.

Gallery Guide

The museum is housed in five interconnected medieval palaces featuring stone archways and pretty courtyards. The permanent collection is arranged chronologically on the first and second floors of the first three palaces. The last two host temporary exhibitions on the first and second floors.

TOP 10 ⭐ Palau de la Música Catalana

Barcelona's Modernista movement reached its aesthetic peak in Lluís Domènech i Montaner's magnificent 1908 concert hall. The lavish façade is ringed by mosaic pillars, and each part of the foyer in Domènech's "garden of music", from banisters to pillars, has a floral motif. The concert hall, whose height is the same as its breadth, is a celebration of natural forms, capped by a stained-glass dome that floods the space with sunlight.

1 Stained-Glass Ceiling
Topping the concert hall is a breathtaking, stained-glass inverted dome ceiling **(below)**. By day, sunlight streams through the fiery red and orange stained glass, illuminating the hall.

4 Stained-Glass Windows
Blurring the boundaries between the outdoors and the interior, the architect encircled this concert hall with vast stained-glass windows decorated with floral designs that let in sunlight and reveal the changing time of day.

2 Rehearsal Hall of the Orfeó Català
This semicircular, acoustically sound rehearsal room is a smaller version of the massive concert hall one floor above. At its centre is an inlaid foundation stone that commemorates the construction of the Palau.

5 Horse Sculptures
Charging from the ceiling are sculptor Eusebi Aranu's winged horses, infusing the concert hall with movement and verve. Also depicted is a representation of Wagner's chariot ride of the Valkyries, led by galloping horses that leap towards the stage.

6 Façade
The towering façade **(above)** reveals Modernista delights on every level. An elaborate mosaic represents the Orfeó Català choral society, founded in 1891.

Stage 3
The semicircular stage **(right)** swarms with activity – even when no one's performing. Eighteen mosaic and terracotta muses spring from the backdrop, playing everything from the harp to the castanets.

7 Busts
A bust of Catalan composer Josep Anselm Clavé (1824–74) marks the Palau's commitment to Catalan music. Facing him across the concert hall, a stern, unruly-haired Beethoven **(left)** represents the hall's classical and international repertoire.

8 Foyer and Bar
Modernista architects worked with stone, wood, ceramic, marble and glass, all of which Domènech used liberally, most notably in the opulent foyer.

9 Lluís Millet Hall
Named after Catalan composer Lluís Millet, this immaculately-preserved lounge boasts gorgeous stained-glass windows. On the main balcony outside are rows of stunning mosaic pillars, each with a different design.

10 Concert and Dance Series
Over 500 concerts and dance shows are staged each year, and seeing a show here is a thrilling experience **(right)**. For symphonic concerts, keep an eye out for the Palau 100 Series; for choral concerts, look out for the Orfeó Català series.

NEED TO KNOW

MAP N2 ■ Sant Pere Més Alt ■ 90 247 54 85 ■ www. palaumusica.cat

Guided tours daily, every 30 mins 10am–3:30pm (Easter & Jul: to 6pm; Aug: 9am–6pm); advance booking recommended; mini recital available

Adm €15, €20 (guided visit); free for under 10s

■ Café Palau offers free live music performances on its terrace. Check the website for details.

■ The Palau shop sells items inspired by the building's architecture and it also has a section devoted to children.

■ Buy tickets online, or from the box office at Sant Pere Més Alt *(open 10am–3:30pm daily)*.

ORFEÓ CATALÀ

The famous choral group, Orfeó Català, for whom the concert hall was originally built, performs here regularly and holds a concert on 26 December every year. Book in advance.

TOP10 ★ Museu d'Art Contemporani and Centre de Cultura Contemporània

Barcelona's sleek contemporary art museum stands in bold contrast to its surroundings. The Museu d'Art Contemporani (MACBA), together with the Centre de Cultura Contemporània (CCCB) nearby, has provided a focal point for the city since 1995 and has played an integral part in the rejuvenation of El Raval. MACBA's permanent collection includes big-name Spanish and international artists, while the CCCB serves as a cutting-edge exploration of contemporary culture.

Façade **1**

American architect Richard Meier's stark, white, geometrical façade **(right)** makes a startling impression against the dull and industrial-toned backdrop of this working-class neighbourhood. On the front side, hundreds of panes of glass reflect the skateboarders who gather here daily.

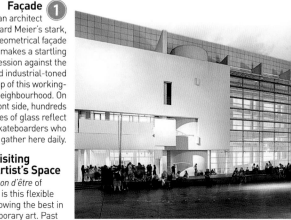

2 Visiting Artist's Space

The *raison d'être* of MACBA is this flexible area showing the best in contemporary art. Past exhibitions have included Zush and acclaimed painter Dieter Roth.

3 Revolving Permanent Collection

The permanent collection comprises more than 2,000 modern artworks, 10 per cent of which are on show at any one time. All major contemporary artistic trends are represented. This 1974 work **(below)** by Eduardo Arranz Bravo is titled *Homea*.

4 Interior Corridors

Space and light are omnipresent in the museum's bare white walkways that hover between floors **(left)**. Look through the glass panels onto the Plaça dels Àngels for myriad images before you even enter the gallery spaces.

8 A Sudden Awakening
One of the only pieces of art on permanent display is Antoni Tàpies' deconstructed bed (1992–3), with its bedding flung across the wall in disarray **(left)**. Its presence to the right of the main entrance underlines the late Tàpies' importance in the world of Catalan modern art.

5 Capella MACBA
One of the few surviving Renaissance chapels in Barcelona has been converted for use as MACBA's temporary exhibition space *(see p87)*. It is located in a former convent across the Plaça dels Àngels.

9 Thinking and Reading Spaces
Pleasant and unusual features of MACBA are the white leather sofas between the galleries. Usually next to a shelf of relevant books and a set of headphones, these quiet spaces provide the perfect resting spot to contemplate – and learn more about – the art.

10 Temporary Exhibitions/CCCB
Exhibitions at the CCCB tend to be more theme-based than artist-specific. It hosts the World Press Photo exhibition in spring and numerous literary festivals throughout the year. Home to several fascinating avant-garde art exhibits, the CCCB is always at the forefront of the latest cultural trends.

El Pati de les Dones/CCCB 6
This courtyard **(right)** off Carrer Montalegre forms part of the neighbouring CCCB. An ultramodern prismatic screen acts as a mirror reflecting the medieval courtyard, giving visitors a magical juxtaposition of different architectural styles.

7 Plaça Joan Coromines
The contrast between the modern MACBA, the University building, the Tuscan-style CCCB and the 19th-century mock-Romanesque church make this square one of the city's most enchanting. It is home to the terrace restaurants of MACBA and CCCB.

NEED TO KNOW

MACBA: **MAP K2**; Pl dels Àngels; 93 481 33 68; open 10am–8pm Mon, Wed–Sat, 10am–3pm Sun; adm €11 (€10 online); concessions €8.80; free for under 14s; www.macba.cat/en

CCCB: **MAP K1**; C/ Montalegre 5; 93 306 41 00; open 11am–8pm Tue–Sun; adm €6 for 1 show, €8 for 2 shows; concessions €4 for 1 show, €6 for 2 shows; free for under 12s; free every Sunday 3–8pm; www.cccb.org

■ Pause at the nearby Doña Rosa café *(C/Ferlandina)*, which offers a range of modern Mediterranean food to a hip crowd, or at CCCB's delightful Terracccita Bar.

■ MACBA offers tours in sign language as well as adapted tours for the visually impaired.

Sights Guide
Although they share the Plaça Joan Coromines, MACBA and CCCB have separate entrances. Both multilevel galleries have flexible display spaces. MACBA has rest areas dotted among the galleries on all floors, allowing you to take breaks as you explore.

The Top 10
of Everything

Moments in History	38
Churches and Chapels	40
Museums and Galleries	42

**Art Nouveau façade of Casa Vicens,
embellished with bright graphic tiles**

Modernista Buildings	44		Outdoor Bars	60
Public Squares	46		Restaurants and Tapas Bars	62
Parks and Beaches	48		Cafés and Light Bites	64
Off the Beaten Track	50		Shopping Destinations	66
Children's Attractions	52		Markets	68
Performing Arts and Music Venues	54		Barcelona for Free	70
Photo Spots	58		Festivals and Events	72

🔟 Moments in History

1 3rd Century BC: The Founding of a City

Barcino, as the city was first known, was founded in the 3rd century BC by Carthaginian Hamilcar Barca. It was taken by the Romans in 218 BC but played second fiddle in the region to the provincial capital of Tarragona.

2 4th–11th Centuries: Early Invasions

As the Roman Empire began to fall apart in the 5th century, Visigoths from the Toulouse area took over the city. They were followed in the 8th century by the Moors, who moved up through the Iberian peninsula at great speed. Around AD 800, Charlemagne conquered the area with the help of the Pyrenean counts, bringing it back under the control of the Franks.

Exhibition poster, 1929

3 12th–16th Centuries: The Middle Ages

During this period, Barcelona was the capital of a Catalan empire that stretched across the Mediterranean. The city's fortune was built on commerce, but as neighbouring Castile expanded into the New World, trading patterns shifted and the Catalan dynasty faltered. Barcelona fell into decline and came under Castilian domination.

4 1638–1652: Catalan Revolt

In reaction to the oppressive policies set out in Madrid, now ruled by the Austrian Habsburgs, various local factions, known as *Els Segadors*, rebelled. Fighting began in 1640 and dragged on until 1652, when the Catalans and their French allies were finally defeated.

5 19th Century: Industry and Prosperity

Booming industry and trade with the Americas brought activity to the city. Immigrants poured in from the countryside, laying the foundations of prosperity but also seeds of unrest. The old city walls came down, broad Eixample avenues were laid out and workers crowded into the old city neighbourhoods left behind by the middle classes.

6 1888–1929: The Renaixença

The International Exhibitions of 1888 and 1929 sparked a Catalan renaissance. Modernista mansions came up and the nationalists oversaw a revival of Catalan culture.

7 1909–1931: The Revolutionary Years

Discontent was brewing among workers, Catalan nationalists, communists, Spanish fascists, royalists, anarchists and republicans. In 1909, protests against the Moroccan war turned into a brutal riot, the *Setmana Tràgica* (Tragic Week). Lurching towards Civil War, Catalonia suffered under a dictatorship before being declared a republic in 1931.

8 1936–1975: Civil War and Franco

At the outbreak of war in 1936, Barcelona's workers and militants managed to fend off General Franco's troops for a while. The city was taken by Fascist forces in 1939, prompting a wave of repression, particularly of the Catalan language, which was banned in schools.

Franco addressing a rally, 1939

9 1975–1980s: Transition to Democracy

Franco's death in 1975 paved the way for democracy. The Catalan language was rehabilitated and the region was granted autonomy. The first Catalan government was elected in 1980.

10 1992–Present Day: The Olympics and Beyond

Barcelona was catapulted onto the world stage in 1992 with the highly successful Olympic Games. In 2015, the Junts pel Sí ('Together for Yes') coalition won the regional elections. In 2017, they held an independence referendum that had a 43 per cent turnout and the "yes" side won. However, this was decreed illegal by Spain and saw many politicians put in jail. The struggle continues.

Opening ceremony, 1992 Olympics

TOP 10 HISTORICAL FIGURES

Ferdinand the Catholic

1 Guifré the Hairy
The first Count of Barcelona (d 897), seen as Catalonia's founding father.

2 Ramon Berenguer IV
He united Catalonia and joined it with Aragon by marrying the Aragonese princess Petronilla in 1137.

3 Jaume I the Conqueror
This 13th-century warrior-king conquered the Balearics and Valencia, laying the foundations for the empire.

4 Ramon Llull
Mallorcan philosopher and missionary, Llull (d 1316) is the greatest figure in medieval Catalan literature.

5 Ferdinand the Catholic
King of Aragon and Catalonia (d 1516), he married Isabella of Castile, paving the way for the formation of a united Spain and the end of Catalan independence.

6 Francesca Bonnemaison
A supporter of women's education, she established Europe's first women-only library in Barcelona in 1909.

7 Antoni Gaudí
An idiosyncratic and devout Modernista architect, Gaudí was responsible for Barcelona's most famous monuments.

8 Francesc Macià
This socialist nationalist politician proclaimed the birth of the Catalan Republic in 1931 and Catalan regional autonomy in 1932.

9 Lluís Companys
Catalan president during the Civil War. Exiled in France, he was arrested by the Gestapo in 1940 and returned to Franco, who had him executed.

10 Ada Colau
A street activist turned politician, Colau is now the mayor of Barcelona.

🔟 Churches and Chapels

1 Barcelona Cathedral

Barcelona's magnificent Gothic cathedral *(see pp18–19)* boasts an eye-catching façade and a peaceful cloister.

2 Església de Santa Maria del Mar

The elegant church *(see pp78–9)* of Santa Maria del Mar (1329–83) is one of the finest examples of Catalan Gothic, a style characterized by simplicity. A spectacular stained-glass rose window illuminates the lofty interior.

Rose window, Església de Santa Maria del Mar

3 Temple Expiatori del Sagrat Cor

MAP B1 ■ Pl del Tibidabo ■ 93 417 56 86 ■ Open 11am–9pm daily ■ Adm for lifts

Mount Tibidabo is an appropriate perch for this over-the-top Neo-Gothic church *(see p119)*, topped with a large golden statue of Christ with arms outstretched. The name Tibidabo comes from the words *tibidabo*, meaning "I shall give you", said to have been uttered by the Devil in his temptation of Christ. Zealously serving the devoted, the priest here celebrates the Eucharist throughout the day.

Temple Expiatori del Sagrat Cor

4 Església de Sant Pau del Camp

Founded as a Benedictine monastery in the 9th century by Guifre II, a count of Barcelona, this church *(see p89)* was rebuilt the following century. Its sculpted façade and intimate cloister with rounded arches exemplify the Romanesque style.

5 Església de Sant Pere de les Puel·les

MAP P2 ■ Pl de Sant Pere ■ Open for Mass: 7pm Mon–Fri, 5pm Sat, 11am & 12:30pm Sun

Built in 801 as a chapel for troops stationed in Barcelona, this *església* later became a spiritual retreat for young noblewomen. The church was rebuilt in the 1100s and is notable for its Romanesque central cupola and a series of capitals with carved leaves. Look out for two stone tablets depicting a Greek cross, which are from the original chapel.

6 Capela de Sant Miquel and Església al Monestir de Pedralbes

Accessed through an arch set in ancient walls, the lovely Monestir de Pedralbes *(see p117)*, founded in 1327, still has the air of a closed community. Inside is a Gothic cloister and the Capela de Sant Miquel, decorated with murals by Catalan artist Ferrer Bassa in 1346. The adjoining Gothic church contains the alabaster tomb of Queen Elisenda, the monastery's founder. On the church side, her effigy wears royal robes and on the other, a nun's habit.

7 Església de Santa Maria del Pi

MAP L3 ■ Pl del Pi ■ Closed due to COVID-19

This lovely Gothic church with its ornate stained-glass windows graces the Plaça del Pi (see p47). The rose window is one of the largest in Catalonia.

8 Capella de Santa Àgata

MAP N3 ■ Pl del Rei ■ Open 10am–2pm & 3–8pm Tue–Sun ■ Adm (free 3–8pm Sun)

Within the beautiful Palau Reial is the medieval Capella de Santa Àgata, which can only be entered as part of a visit to the Museu d'Història de Barcelona (see p78). The 15th-century altarpiece is by Jaume Huguet.

9 Capella de Sant Jordi

MAP M4 ■ Pl Sant Jaume ■ Closed due to COVID-19

Inside the Palau de la Generalitat (see p77) is this fine 15th-century chapel, dedicated to the patron saint of Catalonia.

Interior of the Església de Betlem

10 Església de Betlem

La Rambla (see pp16–17) was once dotted with religious buildings, most dating to the 17th and 18th centuries. This Baroque *església* is one of the major functioning churches from this period. Immensely popular around Christmas, it hosts one of the largest displays of *pessebres* (manger scenes) in the world.

TOP 10 CATALAN SAINTS AND VIRGINS

The famous Virgin of Montserrat

1 Virgin of Montserrat
The famous "Black Virgin" is a patron saint of Catalonia, along with Sant Jordi.

2 Sant Jordi
Catalonia's patron saint is St George, whose dragon-slaying prowess is depicted all over the city.

3 Virgin Mercè
The Virgin of Mercè became a patron saint of the city in 1687, and shares the honour with Santa Eulàlia. Festes de la Mercè (see p73) is the most raucous festival in town.

4 Santa Eulàlia
Santa Eulàlia is Barcelona's co-patron saint (with La Mercè). She was martyred by the Romans in around AD 300.

5 Santa Elena
Legend has it that St Helena converted to Christianity after finding Christ's cross in Jerusalem in AD 346.

6 Santa Llúcia
The patron saint of eyes and vision is celebrated on 13 December, when the blind come to worship at the Santa Llúcia chapel in Barcelona Cathedral (see pp18–19).

7 Sant Cristòfor
Cars are blessed on the feast day of Sant Cristòfor, patron saint of travellers, at a tiny chapel on C/Regomir (see p80).

8 Sant Antoni de Padua
On 13 June, those seeking a husband or wife pray to the patron saint of love.

9 Santa Rita
Those searching for miracles pray to Santa Rita, deliverer of the impossible.

10 Sant Joan
The night of St John (see p72) is celebrated with bonfires and fireworks.

⭐10 Museums and Galleries

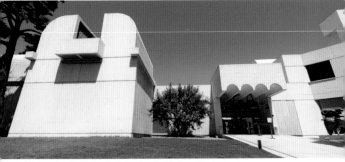

The modern buildings of the Fundació Joan Miró

1 Fundació Joan Miró

The airy, high-ceilinged galleries of this splendid museum *(see pp28–9)* are a fitting home for the bold, abstract works of Joan Miró, one of Catalonia's most acclaimed 20th-century artists.

2 Museu Nacional d'Art de Catalunya

Discover Catalonia's Romanesque and Gothic heritage at this impressive museum *(see pp20–21)*, housed in the 1929 Palau Nacional. Highlights include striking medieval frescoes and a collection of Modernista furnishings and artworks.

3 Museu Picasso

Witness the budding – and meteoric rise – of Picasso's artistic genius at this unique museum *(see pp30–31)*, one of the world's largest collections of the painter's early works.

4 Museu d'Art Contemporani & Centre de Cultura Contemporània

Inaugurated in 1995, MACBA is Barcelona's centre for modern art. Combined with the neighbouring CCCB, the two buildings form an artistic and cultural hub in the heart of El Raval *(see pp34–5)*.

Both regularly host temporary exhibitions: the MACBA showcases contemporary artists; the CCCB is more theme-based.

5 Fundació Tàpies

Works by Catalan artist Antoni Tàpies are showcased in this graceful Modernista building *(see p108)*. Venture inside to discover Tàpies' rich repertoire, from early collage works to large abstract paintings, many alluding to political and social themes.

6 Museu d'Història de Barcelona (MUHBA)

Explore the medieval Palau Reial and wander among the splendid remains of Barcelona's Roman walls and waterways at the city's history museum. The museum is partly housed in the 15th-century Casa Padellàs on the impressive medieval Plaça del Rei.

FC Barcelona badge

7 Museu del FC Barcelona

This shrine to the city's football club draws a mind-boggling number of fans. Trophies, posters and other memorabilia celebrate the club's 100-year history. Also visit the adjacent Camp Nou Stadium *(see p118)*.

8 Museu Frederic Marès

Catalan sculptor Frederic Marès (1893–1991) was a passionate and eclectic collector. Housed here, under one roof, are many remarkable finds amassed during his travels (see p78). Among the vast array of historical objects on display are Romanesque and Gothic religious art and sculptures, plus everything from dolls and fans to pipes and walking sticks.

9 Museu Marítim

The formidable seafaring history of Barcelona is showcased in the cavernous, 13th-century Drassanes Reials (Royal Shipyards). The collection (see p87), which ranges from the Middle Ages to the 19th century, includes a full-scale replica of the *Real*, the flagship galley of Don Juan of Austria, who led the Christians to victory against the Turks at the Battle of Lepanto in 1571. Also on display are model ships, maps and navigational instruments.

Medieval warship, Museu Marítim

10 CosmoCaixa Museu de la Ciència

Exhibits covering the whole history of science, from the Big Bang to the computer age, are housed in this modern museum (see p118). Highlights include an interactive tour of the geological history of our planet, an area of real Amazonian rainforest, and a planetarium. There are also temporary displays on environmental issues and family activities.

TOP 10 QUIRKY MUSEUMS AND MONUMENTS

Wax models at the Museu de Cera

1 Museu de Cera
MAP L5 = Ptge de la Banca 7
Home to over 350 wax figures, from Marilyn Monroe to Franco and Gaudí.

2 Hash, Marihuana and Hemp Museum
MAP E5 = C/Ample 35
This cannabis museum is set in a magnificent Modernista building.

3 Centre d'Interpretació del Call
MAP M4 = Pl de Manuel Ribé
Artifacts from Barcelona's medieval Jewish community can be found here.

4 Museu Etnològic i de Cultures del Món
See objects of artistic and cultural heritage from the people of Africa, Asia, America and Oceania here (see p79).

5 Museu dels Autòmates
MAP B1 = Parc d'Atraccions del Tibidabo
A colourful museum of human and animal automatons.

6 Museu de la Xocolata
MAP P4 = C/Comerç 36
A celebration of chocolate; enjoy interactive exhibits, edible city models and tastings.

7 Museu del Disseny
MAP H3 = Pl de les Glòries Catalanes
A design museum covering clothes, architecture, objects and graphic design.

8 Museu del Perfum
MAP E2 = Pg de Gràcia 39
The museum displays perfume bottles from Roman times to the present.

9 Cap de Barcelona
MAP N5 = Pg de Colom
Pop artist Roy Lichtenstein's "Barcelona Head", created for the 1992 Olympics.

10 Peix
MAP G5 = Port Olímpic
Frank Gehry's huge shimmering goldfish sculpture (1992).

⭐10 Modernista Buildings

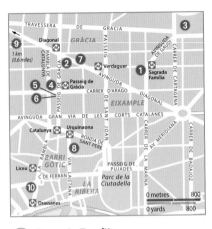

project *(see p107)* was planned around two avenues running at 45-degree angles to the Eixample streets. Started by Domènech i Montaner in 1905 and completed by his son in 1930, the Hospital de la Santa Creu i de Sant Pau's pavilions are lavishly embellished with mosaics, stained glass, and sculptures by Eusebi Arnau. The octagonal columns with floral capitals are inspired by those in the Monestir de Santes Creus *(see p128)*, to the south of Barcelona.

1 Sagrada Família
Dizzying spires and intricate sculptures adorn Gaudí's magical masterpiece *(see pp12–15)*. Construction began at the height of *Modernisme*, but is still in progress more than a century later.

2 La Pedrera
This amazing apartment block, with its curving façade and bizarre rooftop, has all of Gaudí's architectural trademarks *(see pp26–7)*. Especially characteristic are the building's wrought-iron balconies and the ceramic mosaics decorating the entrance halls.

3 Sant Pau Recinte Modernista
In defiant contrast to the Eixample's symmetrical grid-like pattern, this ambitious

4 Fundació Tàpies
With a Rationalist, plain façade alleviated only by its Mudéjar-style brickwork, this building *(see p108)*, dating from 1886, was home to the publishing house Montaner i Simón. It bears the distinction of being the first Modernista work to be designed by Domènech i Montaner, which explains why it has so few of the ornate decorative touches that distinguish his later works. Today it is home to the Fundació Tàpies, and is dominated by an enormous sculpture by the Catalan artist.

5 Casa Batlló
■ MAP E2 ■ Pg de Gràcia 43
■ Open 9am–9pm daily ■ Adm (audio guide) ■ www.casabatllo.es

Illustrating Gaudí's nationalist sentiments, Casa Batlló, on La

Hospital de la Santa Creu i de Sant Pau

Colourful exterior of Casa Batlló

Mansana de la Discòrdia *(see p107)*, is a representation of the Sant Jordi story *(see p41)*. The roof is the dragon's back; the balconies, in the form of carnival masks, are the skulls of the dragon's victims. The façade exemplifies Gaudí's remarkable use of colour and texture.

6 Casa Amatller
MAP E2 ▪ Pg de Gràcia 41
▪ Open 10am–6pm daily; guided and audio tours only ▪ Adm ▪ www.amatller.org

The top of Casa Amatller's façade bursts into a brilliant display of blue, cream and pink tiles with burgundy florets. Architect Puig i Cadafalch's exaggerated decorative use of ceramics is typical of *Modernisme*. Tours include the Modernista apartment and a slide show in Amatller's former photography studio *(see p107)*, and describe the neo-medieval vestibule.

7 Casa de les Punxes (Casa Terrades)
Av Diagonal 420 ▪ Closed due to COVID-19 ▪ Adm ▪ www.casadelespunxes.com

Taking *Modernisme*'s Gothic and medieval obsessions to extremes that others seldom dared, Puig i Cadafalch created this imposing, castle-like structure between 1903 and 1905 *(see p108)*. Given the nickname Casa de les Punxes or "House of Spines" because of the sharp, needle-like spires that rise up from its conical turrets, the building's real name is Casa Terrades, for its

original owners. The flamboyant spires contrast with a façade that is sparsely decorated.

8 Palau de la Música Catalana
Domènech i Montaner's magnificent concert hall is a joyous celebration of Catalan music *(see pp32–3)*. Ablaze with mosaic friezes, stained glass, ceramics and sculptures, it displays Modernista style in its full glory. The work of Miquel Blay on the façade is rated as one of the best examples of Modernista sculpture in Barcelona.

9 Casa Vicens
A UNESCO World Heritage Site, Casa Vicens *(see p119)* was the first home designed by Antoni Gaudí. The façade is an explosion of colour, at once austere and flamboyant, with Neo-Mudéjar elements and sgraffito floral motifs. The building now functions as a cultural centre. Inside, you will find perfectly preserved residential rooms with original furniture and paintings. Down in the coal cellar is a fascinating underground bookshop.

10 Palau Güell
The use of parabolic arches here *(see p87)* to orchestrate space is an example of Gaudí's experiments with structure. He also used unusual building materials, such as ebony and rare South American woods.

Arched interiors of Palau Güell

🔟 Public Squares

Stately Plaça Reial, surrounded by Neo-Classical buildings and palm trees

1 Plaça Reial

The arcaded Plaça Reial *(see p78)*, in the heart of the Barri Gòtic, is unique among Barcelona's public squares due to its old-world charm, gritty urbanization and Neo-Classical flair. It is home not only to fascinating Gaudí lampposts and majestic mid-19th-century buildings, but also to a slew of buzzing bars and cafés, and an entertaining and colourful crowd of inner-city Barcelona denizens.

2 Plaça de Catalunya
MAP M1

Barcelona's nerve centre is the huge Plaça de Catalunya, a lively hub from which the city's activity seems to radiate. This square is most visitors' first real glimpse of

Barcelona. The airport bus stops here, as do RENFE trains and countless metro and bus lines, including most night buses. The square's commercial swagger is evident all around, headed by Spain's omnipresent department store, El Corte Inglés *(see p66)*. Pigeons flutter chaotically at the square's centre and travellers wander about. The main tourist information office is located here. Concerts are held in the square during festivals.

3 Plaça del Rei
MAP N4

One of the city's best-preserved medieval squares, the Barri Gòtic's Plaça del Rei is ringed by grand historic buildings. Among them is the 14th-century Palau Reial *(see p78)*, which houses the Saló del Tinell, a spacious Catalan Gothic throne room and banqueting hall.

4 Plaça de Sant Jaume

Laden with power and history, this is the administrative heart *(see p77)* of modern-day Barcelona. The *plaça* is flanked by the city's two key government buildings, the stately Palau de la Generalitat and the 15th-century Ajuntament.

Plaça de Catalunya

5 Plaça de la Vila de Gràcia
MAP F1

The progressive, bohemian area of Gràcia, a former village annexed by Barcelona in 1897, still exudes a small-town ambience where socializing with the neighbours means heading for the nearest *plaça*. Topping the list is this atmospheric square, with an impressive clock tower rising at its centre. Bustling outdoor cafés draw buskers and a sociable crowd.

6 Plaça de Sant Josep Oriol and Plaça del Pi
MAP M3 & M4

Old-world charm meets modern café culture in the Barri Gòtic's leafy Plaça de Sant Josep Oriol and Plaça del Pi, named after the pine trees (*pi* in Catalan) that shade its nooks and crannies. The lovely Gothic church of Santa Maria del Pi (*see p41*) is set between the two squares.

7 Plaça Comercial
MAP P4

The buzzing Passeig del Born culminates in Plaça Comercial, an inviting square dotted with cafés and bars. It faces the 19th-century Born Market (*see p78*), which has been transformed into a cultural centre and exhibition space.

8 Plaça de Santa Maria
MAP N5

The magnificent Església de Santa Maria del Mar (*see p78*) imbues its namesake *plaça*, in the El Born district, featuring a certain spiritual

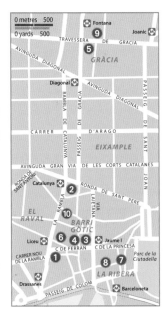

Cafés on Plaça de Santa Maria

calm. Bask in its Gothic ambience, people watch, and soak up the sun at one of the outdoor terrace cafés.

9 Plaça del Sol
MAP F1

Tucked within the cosy grid of Gràcia, this square, popularly called Plaça del Encants, is surrounded by handsome 19th-century buildings. As evening descends, it transforms into one of the most lively spots for after-dark festivities, and you can join all the *Barcelonins* who come here to mingle on the outdoor terraces.

10 Plaça de la Vila de Madrid
MAP M2

Mere steps from the busy La Rambla (*see pp16–17*) is this spacious *plaça*, graced with the remains of a Roman necropolis. A remnant of Roman Barcino, the square sat just beyond the boundaries of the walled Roman city. A row of unadorned 2nd to 4th-century tombs was discovered here in 1957. The complete remains can be viewed from street level.

Parks and Beaches

1 Parc de Cervantes

Av Diagonal 708 ■ Open 10am–dusk daily

Built in 1964 to celebrate 25 years of Franco's rule, this beautiful park on the outskirts of Barcelona would have been more appropriately named Park of the Roses. There are over 11,000 rose bushes of 245 varieties; when in bloom, their scent pervades the entire park. People pour in at weekends, but the park is blissfully deserted during the week.

2 Park Güell

The twisting pathways and avenues of columned arches of Park Güell *(see pp22–3)* blend in with the lush hillside, playfully fusing nature and fantasy to create an urban paradise. From the esplanade, with its stunning mosaic bench, visitors have spectacular views of the city and of the fairy-tale gatehouses below.

3 Jardins del Palau de Pedralbes

Av Diagonal 686 ■ Open 10am–dusk daily

These picturesque, perfectly manicured gardens lie right in front of the former Palau Reial (royal palace) of Pedralbes. Under an enormous eucalyptus tree, near a small bamboo forest, stands the Fountain of Hercules designed by Gaudí. Discovered only in 1984, the fountain features a wrought-iron dragon-head spout.

Cascada fountain, Parc de la Ciutadella

4 Parc de la Ciutadella

The largest landscaped park in Barcelona *(see p101)* offers a refreshingly green, tranquil antidote to city life. Once the location of the 18th-century military citadel, this lovely, serene 19th-century park is now home to the city zoo, the Catalan parliament, a placid boating lake and a variety of works by Catalan sculptors as well as modern artists. It also has the extravagant Cascada Monumental, a two-tiered fountain, which Gaudí helped design.

Vibrant mosaic at Park Güell

5 Parc del Laberint d'Horta

Dating back to 1791, these enchanting gardens are among the city's oldest. Situated above the city, where the air is cooler and cleaner, the park includes themed

Parc del Laberint d'Horta

gardens, water-falls and a small canal *(see p118)*. The highlight is the vast maze with a statue of Eros at its centre. There is a picnic area and a children's playground at the entrance to the gardens.

6 Parc de Joan Miró
MAP B2 ■ C/Tarragona 74 ■ Open 10am–11pm daily

Also known as Parc de l'Escorxador, this park in Eixample was built on the site of a 19th-century slaughter-house *(escorxador)*. Dominating the paved upper level of the park is Miró's striking 22-m (72-ft) sculpture, *Dona i Ocell (Woman and Bird)*, created in 1983. There are several play areas for kids and a couple of kiosk cafés.

7 Parc de l'Espanya Industrial
C/Muntadas 37 ■ Open 10am–midnight daily

Located on the site of a former textile factory, this modern park was built in 1986 by Basque architect Luis Peña Ganchegui. It is an appealing recreational space, with 10 lighthouse-style viewing towers lined along one side of the boating lake and an enormous cast-iron dragon that doubles as a slide. There is a good terrace bar with a playground for kids.

8 City Beaches
The beaches of Barcelona were once insalubrious areas to be avoided. With the 1992 Olympics they underwent a radical face-lift. Today, the stretches of the Port Olímpic and Barceloneta are a people magnet *(see p101)*. A short hop on the metro from the city centre, the beaches are regularly cleaned and the facilities include showers, toilets, play areas for kids, volleyball nets and an open-air gym. Boats and surfboards can be hired. Be aware, though, that bag snatching is endemic in these areas.

Enjoying watersports at Castelldefels

9 Castelldefels
Train to Platja de Castelldefels from Estació de Sants or Passeig de Gràcia

Just 20 km (12 miles) south of the city are 5 km (3 miles) of wide sandy beaches with shallow waters, ideal for watersports. Beach bars entice weekend sun worshippers out of the afternoon sun for long, lazy seafood lunches and jugs of sangria. Wind-surfers are available for hire.

10 Premià de Mar and El Masnou
Train to Premià or El Masnou from Plaça de Catalunya or Estació de Sants

Arguably the best set of beaches within easy reach of Barcelona, just 20 km (12 miles) to the north of the city, these two adjoining beaches lure locals and visitors alike with golden sand and clear, blue waters.

🔟 Off the Beaten Track

Dragon, Güell Pavilions gate

1 Güell Pavilions
MAP B2 ▪ Av Pedralbes 7
▪ 93 317 76 52 ▪ Open 10am–4pm
daily; call ahead for guided visits
(Spanish and Catalan only) ▪ Adm

Gaudí designed the gatehouses
and stable, known collectively as
the Güell Pavilions *(see p78)*,
for his patron Eusebi Güell
in the 1880s. You can admire
the enormous dragon,
inspired by the myth of the
Garden of the Hesperides,
which lunges out of the
wrought-iron gate, and
visit the complex as part
of a guided tour.

2 Jardins de la Rambla de Sants
MAP A2 ▪ C/d'Antoni de Capmany s/n

This elevated park, which stretches
for almost a kilometre from the
Plaça de Sants to the La Bordeta
district, is built above a disused
railway track. It provides a peaceful
stroll, with some refreshing bursts
of greenery, in amongst the high-
rise apartment blocks and old
factory buildings.

3 El Refugi 307
MAP C5 ▪ C/Nou de la Rambla
175 ▪ 93 256 21 22 ▪ Guided tours at
10:30am in English on Sun, and by
appointment ▪ Adm ▪ ajuntament.
barcelona.cat/museuhistoria

More than a thousand underground
shelters were built beneath the city
during the Spanish Civil War, when
Barcelona was being bombed by the
nationalist forces. Shelter 307, with
400 m (1,312 ft) of tunnels, contained
an infirmary, a toilet, a water fountain,
a fireplace and a children's room. It
is now part of the Museu d'Història
de Barcelona *(see p78)* and provides
a glimpse into the torment endured
by city residents during the war.

4 Mercat de la Llibertat
Pl Llibertat 27 ▪ 93 217 09 95
▪ Open 8:30am–8:30pm Mon–Fri (to
3pm Sat); timings of stalls may vary

The Mercat de la Llibertat in Gràcia
was built in 1888 and is notable
for its beautiful wrought-iron and
ceramic decoration. As well as a
fabulous range of fresh produce,
it also boasts some excellent stalls
selling everything from original
photographs to fashions.

5 Parc del Laberint d'Horta

These lovely 18th-century
gardens *(see p118)* are filled
with classical statuary, little
pavilions and ornamental
ponds, but it is the fabulous and surprisingly tricky
maze at their heart that is
the big draw.

Pavilion, Parc del Laberint d'Horta

6 Bunkers del Carmel
MAP C1 ▪ C/del Turó de la
Rovira s/n

Barcelona has a handful of disused
bunkers – a reminder of the aerial
attacks that took place during the
long Spanish civil war. Chiselled into
the side of a hill in the working-class
El Carmel district, the roof of this
bunker acts as a viewing platform.

It's become a popular place to enjoy a few beers and contemplate the city's skyline as the sun goes down.

7 Basílica de la Puríssima Concepció

MAP F2 ▪ C/d'Aragó 299 ▪ Open 7:30am–1pm & 5–9pm Mon–Fri (to 8pm Aug); 7:30am–2pm & 5–9pm Sun ▪ www.parroquia concepciobcn.org

Dating back to the 13th century, this basilica was originally part of the Santa Maria de Jonqueres monastery. It was moved stone by stone to its current site in the 19th century. Head for the charming Gothic cloister, which is filled with greenery and birdsong, and bordered by slender 15th-century columns. The basilica regularly hosts concerts.

8 Convent de Sant Agustí

MAP F4 ▪ Pl l'Academia s/n, C/Comerç 36 ▪ 93 256 50 17 ▪ Open 9am–10pm Mon–Fri, 10am–2pm & 4–9pm Sat ▪ Café: lunchtime Tue–Sat

The 15th-century Convent de Sant Agustí is now a cultural centre, with a lovely little café underneath the arches of what remains of the cloister. Relaxed and family-friendly, it is a great place to spend an afternoon.

9 Plaça Osca

MAP B2

This lovely, leafy old square in the Sants neighbourhood is flanked by cafés and bars, with tables spilling out onto the pavements. Rarely frequented by tourists but increasingly popular with trendy locals, it boasts a clutch of great spots to enjoy artisan beers and organic tapas.

10 Parc de Cervantes

Every spring, hundreds of people converge on the gardens in the Parc de Cervantes *(see p48)* to admire the blooms of 11,000 rose bushes of 245 varieties. Grassy lawns extend around the rose gardens, dotted with picnic areas and children's playgrounds.

The lush lawns and rose bushes of the Parc de Cervantes

TOP10 **Children's Attractions**

Enjoying a thrilling ride at the Parc d'Atraccions del Tibidabo

1 Parc d'Atraccions del Tibidabo

With its old-fashioned rides, the only surviving funfair in the city is a delight *(see p117)*. The attractions include a roller coaster, a House of Horrors, bumper cars, a Ferris wheel and the Museu dels Autòmates *(see p43)*, with animatronics of all shapes and sizes. There's also a puppet show, picnic areas, playgrounds and plenty of bars and restaurants.

2 La Rambla

Your shoulders will be aching from carrying the kids high above the crowds by the time you reach the end of Barcelona's main boulevard *(see pp16–17)*. Fire eaters, buskers, human statues dressed up as Greek goddesses – you name it and it's likely to be keeping the hordes entertained on La Rambla.

3 Museu Marítim

Ancient maps showing monster-filled seas, restored fishing boats and a collection of ships' figureheads give a taste of the city's maritime history *(see p87)*. Well worth a look is the full-size Spanish galleon complete with sound and light effects. Set in the vast former medieval shipyards, the Drassanes, this museum is an absolute must for any budding sea captain.

4 Parc de l'Oreneta
MAP A1 ■ Tren de l'Oreneta: www.trenoreneta.com

This delightful, shaded park has paths winding up the hillside, lots of play parks and picnic areas, as well as a paddock where kids can take pony rides. Perhaps the best of all is the miniature train (Tren de l'Oreneta), which makes a 650-m (2,130 ft) lap around the park from a tiny station.

Parc del Laberint d'Horta maze

5 Parc del Laberint d'Horta

The main feature of this exceptionally beautiful park *(see p118)* is the huge hedge maze where children can live out all of their *Alice in Wonderland* fantasies. Unfulfilled expectations of Mad Hatters are made up for by a play area and a bar for grown-ups. The park is usually busy on Sundays.

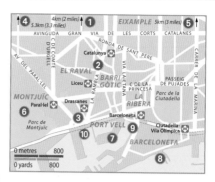

6 Telefèric de Montjuïc

MAP C5 ■ Parc de Montjuïc ■ Open daily; Jan–Feb & Nov–Dec: 10am–6pm; Mar–May & Oct: 10am–7pm; Jun–Sep: 10am–9pm ■ Adm ■ www.telefericdemontjuic.cat

Instead of taking the nerve-jangling cable-car ride across the port, try these smaller, lower-altitude cable-car trips if you have children with you. The ride to the Montjuïc summit also has the added appeal of the castle (see p95) at the top, with cannons for the kids to clamber on.

7 L'Aquàrium de Barcelona

MAP E6 ■ Moll d'Espanya ■ Open from 10am daily; closing times vary from 7:30pm to 9:30pm depending on month and day ■ Adm ■ www.aquariumbcn.com

One of Europe's biggest aquariums, this underwater kingdom is made up of 21 enormous tanks brimming with nearly 400 marine species. The highlight of a visit here is the Oceanari, where a walk-through glass tunnel will bring you face to face with three huge grey sharks named Drake, Morgan and Maverick, lurking in 4.5 million litres (990,000 gallons) of water.

8 City Beaches

For kids, there's more to going to the beach in Barcelona than just splashing in warm waters and frolicking in the sand. The Port Vell and Port Olímpic *platges* (beaches) offer a good choice of well-equipped play areas to keep the little ones entertained (see p101). Numerous bars and restaurants make finding refreshment easy too.

9 Museu d'Història de Catalunya

This museum traces Catalonia's history through a range of interactive exhibits (see p101). Visitors can dress up as medieval knights and gallop around on wooden horses. Very popular with Catalan school groups, the museum is enjoyable for visitors of all ages. In addition to its stock of children's activities, it hosts an exciting story hour every Saturday wherein Catalan legends are re-enacted.

10 Boat Trips

The city's "swallow boats", Las Golondrinas (see p102), make regular trips out of the port, providing a fun excursion for older children. Younger kids will probably prefer messing about in a rowing boat on the lake at the Parc de la Ciutadella (see p48).

Boating on the Ciutadella lake

TOP10 Performing Arts and Music Venues

Palau de la Música Catalana

1 Palau de la Música Catalana

Domenèch i Montaner's Modernista gem regularly serves up the best in jazz and classical music *(see pp32–3)*. It has lost some of its prestige to L'Auditori, but it still hosts some performances for Barcelona's Guitar Festival and also attracts visiting musicians.

2 El Molino
Vila i Vila 99 (Av Paral·lel) ▪ 93 205 51 11 ▪ Adm ▪ www.elmolinobcn.com

El Molino has been a musical theatre-bar since 1907. It hosts live music, cabaret shows, flamenco and tango performances. Shows can be booked through the website.

3 Teatre Grec
The most atmospheric and magical of all Barcelona's venues, this open-air amphitheatre, situated amid thick, verdant forest, makes an incredible setting for ballet, music or theatre *(see p96)*. Originally a quarry, it was converted in 1929 in preparation for the International Exhibition. It is open daily except during the summertime El Grec arts festival.

El Molino theatre

4 L'Auditori
MAP G1 ▪ C/Lepant 150 ▪ 93 247 93 00 ▪ www.auditori.cat

Located near the Teatre Nacional, this large auditorium is home to the Orquestra Simfònica de Barcelona and also houses the Museum of Music. Acoustics and visibility are excellent. In addition to classical music, it hosts regular jazz concerts.

5 Gran Teatre del Liceu
Phoenix-like, the Liceu *(see p16)* has risen from the ashes of two devastating fires since its founding in 1847 to become one of Europe's leading opera houses. Originally designed to house the Music Conservatory, it now also hosts ballet productions and symphony concerts. It is known for sterling performances by home-grown talent including one of the famed "three tenors", José Carreras.

6 Harlem Jazz Club
The legendary Harlem Jazz Club *(see p83)* in Barrí Gòtic is one of the city's longest surviving jazz and blues clubs. As well as presenting great artistes, the admission charge usually includes a drink, and some shows are free.

Saxophonist at the Harlem Jazz Club

(7) Mercat de les Flors
MAP B4 ■ C/Lleida 59 ■ 93 256 26 00 ■ www.mercatflors.cat

The venue of choice for dance and performance theatre groups such as La Fura dels Baus and Comediants, whose incredible mixture of circus and drama is easily accessible to non-Catalan speakers.

(8) Razzmatazz
This is one of the city's most famous venues (see p104). Hosting concerts several nights a week, the club's five areas offer a wide range of musical styles.

Vampire Weekend at Razzmatazz

(9) Sala Apolo
MAP K4 ■ C/Nou de la Rambla 113 ■ 93 441 40 01 ■ www.sala-apolo.com

A vintage dance hall with panelled bars and velvet-covered balconies, this place has reinvented itself as one of Barcelona's best nightclubs. It attracts the latest acts in music, from indie, garage and pop rock (Mondays), to reggae, soul, world music and dubstep (Thursdays).

(10) JazzSí Club – Taller de Musics
MAP J2 ■ Requesens 2 ■ 93 329 00 20 ■ Adm ■ www.tallerdemusics.com/jazzsi-club

Connected to the local music school, the JazzSí Club offers music lessons, workshops as well as daily concerts. Jazz, Cuban, flamenco or rock performances take place in the small, split-level venue between 7:30 (6:30 on Sun) and 9pm. Dinner is available from Monday to Friday.

TOP 10 VERSIÓN ORIGINAL CINEMAS AND FESTIVALS

Interior of the Filmoteca cinema

1 Filmoteca
The Catalan government's film and media archive and cinema that has three VO screenings daily.

2 Verdi
MAP B2 ■ C/Verdi 32 ■ 93 238 79 90 ■ www.cines-verdi.com
An original VO cinema with five screens.

3 Icària Yelmo Cineplex
MAP H5 ■ C/Salvador Espriu 61 ■ 90 222 09 22 ■ www.yelmocines.es
With 15 screens, this cineplex shows VO films, many of them for children.

4 Festival de Cine Documental Musical In-Edit
www.in-edit.org
This international festival celebrates music and film.

5 Festival Internacional de Cinema Fantàstic de Catalunya
Sitges ■ sitgesfilmfestival.com
A festival dedicated to VO fantasy films.

6 Zumzeig Cine Cooperativa
C/Béjar 53 ■ 93 546 14 11 ■ www.zumzeigcine.coop
This cinema screens independent films.

7 Cinemes Texas
MAP F1 ■ C/Bailen 205 ■ 93 348 47 70 ■ www.cinemestexas.cat
A modern cinema that shows VO films.

8 Sala Phenomena Experience
MAP G1 ■ C/Sant Antoni Maria Claret 168 ■ www.phenomena-experience.com
State-of-the-art cinema, one of the largest in Spain, for VO films.

9 Renoir Floridablanca
MAP C3 ■ C/Floridablanca 135 ■ 93 228 93 93 ■ www.cinesrenoir.com
Vintage projectors are on display at this theatre screening international films.

10 Sala Montjuïc
MAP B6 ■ www.salamontjuic.org
This outdoor cinema near the castle shows cult films in summer.

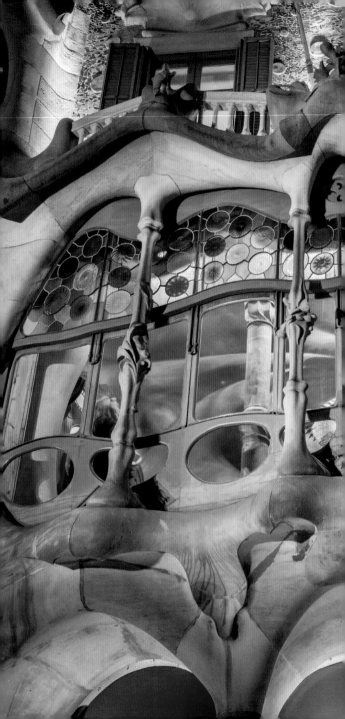

⭐10 Photo Spots

① Font Màgica

You can take some extraordinary photos of Barcelona's enchanting and exuberant "Magic Fountain" *(see p70)*, which is linked by a long, choreographed line of smaller fountains, all the way up to the Palau Nacional *(see p95)*. Set your shutter speed for a long exposure to get fluid, draping shots of the cascading water. At night, the fountain lights up with brilliant colour.

② Rooftop of the Barcelona Cathedral

For a bird's-eye view of the impressive narrow lanes and alleys of Barri Gòtic *(see pp76–79)*, climb up to the roof terrace of the Barcelona Cathedral *(see pp18–19)*, where gargoyles and the carved stone of the central spire vie for attention.

③ Park Güell

Gaudí's fairy-tale imagination was let loose on this spectacular park *(see pp22–3)*. The colourfully tiled salamander at the entrance staircase and the stunning panorama from the sinuous bench on the main square are the classic postcard views. There are scores of other exquisite details that will catch every photographer's eye.

Plaça de Sant Felip Neri at dusk

④ Plaça de Sant Felip Neri

The labyrinthine alleys and squares that make up Barri Gòtic *(see pp76–79)* are a photographer's dream. The little Plaça de Sant Felip Neri *(see p80)*, with its charming church and simple stone fountain, provides a beautiful set piece for a photo. It also features numerous historical elements that make it attractive.

⑤ Museu d'Història de Catalunya

The café on the top floor of the Museu d'Història de Catalunya *(see p101)* offers dazzling views over the yacht-filled Port Vell *(see p92)* and up to the slopes of Montjuïc *(see p125)*. It is a good idea to come at dusk to capture some of the best photos of Barcelona.

Previous pages The flowing lines of Gaudí's remarkable Casa Batlló

6 Castell de Montjuïc

This castle's bastions *(see p95)* enjoy one of the best vantage points over the entire city and offer incredible, panoramic views, which enable you to place several landmarks in the same frame. For a photo of a different side to the city, take some shots of the multicoloured shipping containers in the port.

7 Museu d'Art Contemporani

Barcelona's contemporary art museum, MACBA *(see pp34–5)*, is a striking white building over-looking a huge, modern square which has become a mecca for skateboarders. Their swift moves make for great action shots.

8 Beaches

It's hard to get a bad picture of the beaches *(see p101)*, in Barcelona whether you are visiting in the heat of summer or the relative calm of winter. A dawn shot of the tall, diaphanous sculpture, *The Wounded Star*, by Rebecca Horn on Barceloneta Beach is always a winner.

9 Tibidabo Ferris Wheel

Catch a ride on the charming and historic Ferris wheel at the Tibidabo funfair

The colourful Ferris wheel at Tibidabo

(see p117) to recreate a classic Barcelona shot: the pretty, rainbow-coloured cars juxtaposed against the sights of the entire city laid out at your feet.

10 Bunkers del Carmel
MAP E6

There are wonderful panoramic views to be had from these bunkers *(see pp50–51)* that date back to the Spanish Civil War. Tucked away in a quiet suburb, this is the per-fect spot for a view of the city lights as the sun sets. In fact, these are now one of the city's most photographed viewpoints.

Visitors admiring the city from Bunkers del Carmel

🔟 Outdoor Bars

Diners outside Bar Kasparo

1 Bar Kasparo

This laid-back outdoor bar *(see p92)* serves a varied menu of fresh international fare made with a modern twist. Must-try dishes here include chicken curry and Greek salad. With outdoor seating in a quiet, traffic-free square, this bar is great for whiling away time. By day this is a popular spot with families, thanks to the play area it overlooks, but after the sun dips beneath the horizon a bar-like vibe takes over, fuelled by beer and cider.

2 Antic Teatre Café-Bar

Tucked away in a minuscule alley, this leafy outdoor bar *(see p83)* is attached to a theatre and is a popular meeting place for actors and musicians. Perfect for a quiet coffee during the day, the bar has a relaxed atmosphere. Once night falls, it is transformed into a magical secret garden. Sit on the terrace or in the garden, and enjoy a glass of wine.

3 La Caseta del Migdia

Situated in the pine forest behind Montjuïc Castle, this is a summer-only bar *(see p99)*. Fabulous views, ice-cold beers and the occasional live jazz concert or DJ session make this an irresistible spot to escape the heat on sultry summer nights and watch the sunset.

4 El Jardí

The Gothic courtyard of a medieval hospital *(see p89)* provides a beautiful backdrop to this outdoor café, which is a quiet oasis in the heart of El Raval. The tables are arranged around a pretty garden, strung with fairy lights. It's a great spot for winding down with a cocktail after a day of sightseeing.

Cosy and whimsical setting of El Jardí

5 Bar Calders

Carrer del Parlament is packed with trendy boutiques and eateries, but Bar Calders (see p99) stands out for its charming terrace, tasty tapas and delightful staff. It's one of the best places in the city for a vermut (see p65) and a dish of olives.

6 Torre Rosa

Located in the courtyard of a pink-hued centenary villa, this bar (see p122) provides the perfect summer retreat, away from the hustle and bustle of the city. Come here to enjoy expertly mixed cocktails under the cool shade of palm trees – as the locals do.

7 Cotton Hotel Terrace

Housed in a listed landmark building, now a luxury hotel, this enormous terrace bar (see p111) is furnished with plush chairs and sofas that are shaded by numerous luxuriant plants. It's a fashionable address to enjoy wines, excellent cocktails and upmarket tapas.

8 Jardín del Alma

It's hard to believe that you are in the middle of a metropolitan city once you step into this beautiful and deeply romantic garden retreat. Jardín del Alma (see p111) forms part of the elegant Alma Barcelona Hotel (see p142). Come here for fine wines, cocktails, as well as quite a few exquisite tapas, and stay for the ambience.

9 Fragments Cafè

A friendly local café located in one of the loveliest squares in the city, Fragments Café (see p123) is not the place to eat in a hurry. Take your time and and enjoy your meal in the pretty, plant-filled

garden at the back, where you can dine by candle light on balmy summer evenings.

10 Bus Terraza

A London double decker bus pulled up by the seafront has become one of Barcelona's hottest spots. There are always queues to get into this colourful garden terrace (see p104). Sink into one of the comfortable deckchairs or loungers, and enjoy DJ sets and live music with your cocktail.

DJ booth at Bus Terraza

TOP 10 Restaurants and Tapas Bars

The unpretentious interior of La Taverna del Clínic

1 La Taverna del Clínic

Slightly off the beaten track, this ordinary-looking tavern *(see p113)* offers inventive, though pricey tapas, accompanied by a great array of wines. Arrive early or be prepared to wait for a table.

2 Igueldo

Basque cuisine, prepared with flair and originality, is served here in elegant surroundings *(see p113)*. Dishes include pig's trotters stuffed with *morcilla* (black pudding) and dried peach purée, or *zamburiñas*, a small scallop from the Atlantic. There is also a tapas bar at the entrance.

3 El Asador d'Aranda

This palatial restaurant *(see p123)*, perched high above the city on Tibidabo, is popular with businesspeople and dishes up the best in Castilian cuisine. Sizable starters include *pica pica*, a tasty array of sausages, peppers and hams. The restaurant's signature main dish is *lechazo* (young lamb), roasted in a wood-fired oven.

4 Green Spot

Voted one of the best vegetarian restaurants in Spain, Green Spot *(see p105)* will also appeal to non-vegetarians. The contemporary cuisine, served in a spacious and stylish setting, is based on locally sourced, mainly organic produce. The dishes incorporate flavours from around the world.

5 Windsor

The modern Catalan *haute cuisine* dishes served in this elegant restaurant *(see p113)* are based on seasonal local produce. Tasting menus feature *suquet de rape* (monkfish stew) and suckling lamb.

The bar area at Windsor

6 Alkimia
MAP D3 ■ Ronda de San Antoni 41 ■ 93 207 61 15 ■ Closed Sat–Mon ■ €€

Jordi Vilà has won countless awards and a Michelin star for his innovative New Catalan cuisine, taking time-honoured dishes and giving them an artful twist. This restaurant inside the Cervecería Moritz offers a suitably spectacular setting.

7 Cinc Sentits
This elegant Michelin-starred restaurant *(see p113)* is known for its inventive cuisine. The tasting menu by chef Jordi Artal can be paired with specially-chosen wines. The set-price lunch menu on weekdays is a bargain.

8 Pez Vela
Pg del Mare Nostrum 19/21 ■ 93 221 63 17 ■ €€

Contemporary decor and fresh Mediterranean cuisine coupled with some of the best sea views in the city make this a great spot for a special meal. Pez Vela is located underneath the W Barcelona hotel *(see p143)*.

9 Tickets Bar
Run by El Bulli's founders, this Michelin-starred place *(see p99)* serves inventive tapas such as tuna belly with ham and caviar, and Manchego cheese ice cream with bacon, mustard and cucumber. The vibrant quirky decor reminds one of an amusement park and vintage circus. This aesthetic is complemented by colourful accents and theatre lights.

10 Disfrutar
Avant-garde cuisine prepared by former El Bulli chefs is served here. The restaurant *(see p113)* has a well-lit, whitewashed interior that was designed as a homage to the fishing villages of Costa Brava. It also has a charming terrace. Enjoy unconventional dishes such as a *gazpacho* sandwich (sourdough with feta spread and raw vegetables) or Moroccan-style pigeon in their relaxed and modern setting.

TOP 10 TAPAS DISHES

Calamars a la Romana

1 Calamars
A savoury seafood option is *calamars a la romana* (deep-fried battered squid) or *calamars a la planxa* (grilled squid).

2 Patates Braves
This traditional tapas favourite consists of fried potatoes topped with a spicy sauce. Equally tasty are *patates* heaped with aioli (garlic and olive oil sauce).

3 Pa amb Tomàquet
A key part of any traditional tapas spread is this bread topped with tomato and olive oil.

4 Croquetes
These tasty fried morsels, usually prepared with cod, ham or chicken in a béchamel sauce, are all-time favourites.

5 Musclos o Escopinyes
Sample Barcelona's fruits of the sea with tapas of tasty mussels or cockles.

6 Truita de Patates
The most common tapas dish is this thick potato omelette, often topped with aioli (*allioli* in Catalan).

7 Ensaladilla Russa
"Russian salad" includes potatoes, onions, tuna (and often peas, carrots and other vegetables) all generously enveloped in mayonnaise.

8 Gambes a l'Allet
An appetizing dish of prawns fried in garlic and olive oil.

9 Pernil Serrà
Cured ham is a Spanish obsession. The best, and most expensive, is Extremadura's speciality, Jabugo.

10 Fuet
Embotits (Catalan sausages) include the ever-popular *fuet*, a dry, flavourful variety most famously produced in the Catalonian town of Vic.

For a key to restaurant price ranges see p85

⏏️ Cafés and Light Bites

1 Café Bliss
Hidden away down a tiny side street in one of the loveliest Gothic squares in the old city is the delightful Café Bliss (see p84). There is a bright terrace, comfortable, inviting sofas as well as a range of international magazines and newspapers to browse through. It is perfect for coffee, cakes, light meals or even a romantic drink in the evening.

The smart interior of Bar Lobo

2 Café de l'Òpera
MAP L4 ▪ La Rambla 74 ▪ www.cafeoperabcn.com

Unwind in an elegant setting at this late 19th-century café while being tended to by vested *cambrers* (waiters). This former *xocolateria* (confectionery café) – named after the Liceu opera house opposite – serves fine gooey delights such as *xurros amb xocolata* (strips of fried dough with thick chocolate). It's the perfect little nook for people-watching on La Rambla.

3 Bar Lobo
MAP Q4 ▪ C/Pintor Fortuny 3 ▪ 93 481 53 46

This chic café is a superb brunch spot during the day, but it really comes alive in the evenings. From Thursday to Saturday it opens until 1:30am for drinks. The terrace is very popular.

4 Laie Llibreria Cafè
Tuck into a generous buffet of rice, pasta, greens, chicken and more at this charming, long-running Eixample café-bookshop (see p112). You can also opt for the well-priced vegetarian menu, which includes soup, salad and a main dish.

5 Federal Café
MAP D4 ▪ C/Parlament 39 ▪ Closed Sun D ▪ www.federalcafe. es/barcelona

The airy Federal Café is a local hipster hang-out serving amazing coffee, brunch and light meals, as well as cocktails in the evening. There is also a romantic little roof terrace, free Wi-Fi and English-language magazines to flick through.

6 El Filferro
Bright and airy, this café (see p105) only has room for a few tables inside, with several more located out on the sunny square which is popular with families as it conveniently overlooks a playground. Fresh, creative Mediterranean dishes as well as tapas are served all day.

Café de l'Òpera on La Rambla

7 **Alsur Café**
MAP F3 ■ C/Roger de Llúria 23
■ 93 624 15 77 ■ www.alsurcafe.com

Its nonstop kitchen serves brunch, tapas, homemade cakes, sandwiches and salads. Free Wi-Fi, big windows and a warm atmosphere make it an ideal place to work or read the newspaper. There's also a branch in the El Born district and one in front of the Palau de la Música.

8 **En Aparté**
A light-filled café *(see p84)* serving a good selection of French cheeses and cold meats accompanied by French wines. The crème brûlée is a must and the fixed price lunch menu is good value. There are tables outside overlooking the square.

9 **Granja Dulcinea**
MAP L3 ■ C/Petritxol 2 ■ www.granjadulcinea.com

The *xocolateries* and *granjes* on Carrer Petritxol *(see p80)* have been satiating sugar cravings for decades. Among them is this old-fashioned café with to-die-for delights from *xurros amb xocolata* to strawberries and whipped cream. In summer, refreshing *orxates* and *granissats* are on the menu.

Pastries at Granja Dulcinea

10 **La Tartela**
MAP B3 ■ C/Llanca 32
■ Closed Sun D & Mon

A pretty little spot near Plaça Espanya serving cakes, quiches, lasagna and outstanding coffee. It has a few pavement tables and great service.

TOP 10 CAFÉ DRINKS

A cup of strong *cigaló*

1 Cigaló
For coffee with a bite, try a *cigaló (carajillo)*, which has a shot of either *conyac* (cognac), whisky or *ron* (rum).

2 Tallat and Cafè Sol
A *tallat* is a small cup of coffee with a dash of milk. A *cafè sol* is just plain coffee. In the summer, opt for either one *amb gel* (with ice).

3 Cafè amb llet
Traditionally enjoyed in the morning, *cafè amb llet* is a large milky coffee.

4 Orxata
This sweet, milky-white drink made from the tiger nut is a local summer time favourite.

5 Granissat
Slake your thirst with a cool *granissat*, a crushed-ice drink that is usually lemon-flavoured.

6 Aigua
Stay hydrated with *aigua mineral* (mineral water) – *amb gas* is sparkling, *sense gas*, still.

7 Cacaolat
A chocolate-milk concoction, which is one of Spain's most popular sweet drink exports.

8 Una Canya and Una Clara
Una canya is roughly a quarter litre of *cervesa de barril* (draught beer). *Una clara* is the same size but made up of equal parts beer and fizzy lemonade.

9 Cava
Catalonia's answer to champagne is its home-grown *cava* – Freixenet and Codorníu are the most famous brands.

10 Vermut
Fortified wine served with a spritz of soda water. Going out for the *vermutada* is a popular ritual for the locals.

🔟 Shopping Destinations

2 Carrer Girona
MAP P1

Those looking for fashion bargains should head to Carrer Girona (metro Tetuan), which is lined with designer and high-street outlet stores. Most of these offer women's fashions including streetwear from brands such as Mango, evening wear and shoes from Catalan designers Etxart & Panno, and upmarket designs from the likes of Javier Simorra.

3 Plaça de Catalunya and Carrer Pelai
MAP L/M1 ■ El Corte Inglés: Pl de Catalunya 14; open 9:30am–9:30pm Mon–Sat ■ El Triangle: C/Pelai 39; open 9:30am–9pm Mon–Sat (to 10pm Jun–Sep)

The city's bustling centrepiece is also its commercial crossroads, flanked by the department store El Corte Inglés and the shopping mall El Triangle, which includes FNAC (books, CDs, videos) and Séphora (perfumes and cosmetics). Lined with shops, the nearby Carrer Pelai is said to have more pedestrian traffic than any other shopping street in Spain.

4 Maremagnum
MAP N5 ■ Muelle de España 5 ■ Open 10am–9pm daily

This shopping and entertainment centre is located right on the water's edge, and is open every day of the

1 Passeig de Gràcia
MAP E3

Set right in the heart of the city, Barcelona's grand avenue of lavish Modernista buildings is fittingly home to some of the city's premier fashion and design stores. From the international big league (Chanel, Gucci, Dior, Stella McCartney) to Spain's heavy hitters (Camper, Loewe, Zara, Bimba y Lola, Mango), it's all here. The wide boulevards either side feature more designer shopping, notably Carrer Consell de Cent, which is also dotted with many art galleries, and Carrers Mallorca, València and Roselló.

Top design and fashion stores on Passeig de Gràcia

Visitors at the Maremagnum centre

year. All of the main clothing chains can be found here, along with a good variety of cafés and restaurants.

5 Portal de l'Àngel
MAP M2

Once a Roman thoroughfare leading into the walled city of Barcino, today the pedestrian street of Portal de l'Àngel is traversed by hordes of shoppers toting bulging bags. The street is chock-full of shoe, clothing, jewellery and accessory shops.

6 Rambla de Catalunya
MAP E2

The genteel, classier extension of La Rambla, this well-maintained street (see p109) offers a refreshing change from its cousin's more downmarket carnival atmosphere. Chic shops and cafés pepper the street's length from Plaça de Catalunya to Diagonal. Here you'll find everything from fine footwear and leather bags to linens and decorative lamps.

7 Carrer Portaferrissa
MAP M3

Offering an eclectic range of items, from zebra platform shoes to belly-button rings and pastel baby T-shirts, this street's other name could well be Carrer "Trendy". In addition to all the usual high-street chains – from H&M to Mango and NafNaf – along this strip you'll find El Mercadillo, crammed with hip little shops selling spiked belts, frameless sunglasses, surf wear and the like. After stocking

up on fashion, stop for a box of prettily wrapped chocolates at Fargas on the nearby Carrer del Pi (No. 16).

8 Gràcia
MAP F1

Old bookstores, family-run grocery stores and independent boutiques selling trendy, often vintage, fashion, homewares and accessories cluster along Carrer Astúries (and its side streets) and along Travessera de Gràcia. A string of contemporary clothing and shoe shops also line Gran de Gràcia.

9 El Born
MAP P4

Amid El Born's web of streets are all sorts of art and design shops (see p78). Passeig del Born and Carrer Rec are dotted with innovative little galleries (from sculpture to interior design), plus clothing and shoe boutiques. The best area for original fashion and accessories.

Handbag store, Avinguda Diagonal

10 Avinguda Diagonal
MAP D1

Big and brash, the traffic-choked Avinguda Diagonal is hard to miss – a cacophonous avenue that cuts diagonally across the entire city. It is a premier shopping street, particularly west of Passeig de Gràcia to its culmination in L'Illa mall and the huge El Corte Inglés department store close to Plaça Maria Cristina. Lining this long stretch is a host of high-end clothing and shoe stores – including Armani, Loewe and Hugo Boss – as well as a large number of interior design shops, jewellery and watch purveyors, and more.

Markets

1 Book and Coin Market at Mercat de Sant Antoni

MAP D2 ■ C/Comte d'Urgell ■ Open 8am–2:30pm Sun ■ www.dominicalde santantoni.com

For book lovers, there's no better way to spend Sunday morning than browsing at this market in Sant Antoni. You'll find a mind-boggling assortment of weathered paperbacks, ancient tomes, stacks of old magazines, comics, postcards and lots more, from coins to videos.

2 Fira de Santa Llúcia

MAP N3 ■ Pl de la Seu ■ Open 1–23 Dec: 10am–8pm (times may vary) daily ■ www.firadesanta llucia.cat

The festive season is officially under way when local artisans set up shop outside the cathedral for the annual Christmas fair. Well worth a visit, if only to peruse the *caganers*, miniature figures squatting to *fer caca* (take a poop). Uniquely Catalan, the *caganers* are usually hidden away at the back of nativity scenes. This unusual celebration of the scatological also appears in other Christmas traditions.

3 Els Encants

Trading beneath metal canopies, Els Encants (see p108) is one of Europe's oldest flea markets,

Stalls at Els Encants flea market

dating back to the 14th century. It sells everything from second-hand clothes, electrical appliances and toys to used books. Discerning shoppers can fit out an entire kitchen from the array of pots and pans available. Bargain-hunters should come early.

Produce at Mercat de la Boqueria

4 Mercat de la Boqueria

The most famous food market in Barcelona is conveniently located on La Rambla (see pp16–17). Freshness reigns supreme and shoppers are spoiled for choice, with hundreds of stalls selling everything from vine-ripened tomatoes and haunches of beef to aromatic seafood and wedges of Manchego cheese. Be sure to stop by one of the atmospheric counter bars here. These are ideal for a quick lunch stop or a coffee break.

5 Fira Artesana

MAP M3 ■ Pl del Pi ■ Open 10am–10pm first & third Fri, Sat & Sun of the month

The Plaça del Pi (see p47) brims with natural and organic foods during the Fira Artesana, when artisanal food producers bring their goods to this corner of the Barri Gòtic. The market specializes in homemade cheeses and honey – from clear clover honey from the Pyrenees to nutty concoctions from Reus.

6 Fira de Filatelia i Numismàtica

MAP L4 ■ Pl Reial ■ Open 9am–2:30pm Sun

Arranged around the elegant Plaça Reial (see p78), this stamp and coin market draws avid collectors from across town. The newest collectors' items are phone cards and old *xapes de cava* (cava bottle cork foils). When the market ends – and the local police go to lunch – a makeshift flea market takes over. Old folks and immigrants from the *barri* haul out their antique wares – old lamps, clothing, junk – and lay it out for sale on the ground.

7 Mercat de Barceloneta

MAP F6 ■ Pl Font 1, Barceloneta ■ Open 7am–3pm Mon–Thu & Sat, 7am–8pm Fri ■ www.mercatsbcn.cat

The striking Barceloneta market overlooks an expansive square. In addition to colourful produce stalls, there is a good selection of bars and bakeries here.

8 Mercat dels Antiquaris

MAP N3 ■ Pl de la Seu ■ Open 10am–8pm Thu (except Aug) ■ www.mercatgoticbcn.com

Antiques aficionados and collectors contentedly rummage through vintage jewellery, watches, candelabras, embroidery and bric-a-brac at this long-running antiques market in front of the cathedral.

9 Mercat del Art de la Plaça de Sant Josep Oriol

MAP M4 ■ Pl de Sant Josep Oriol ■ Open 11am–8:30pm Sat, 10am–3pm Sun

At weekends, local artists flock to this Barri Gòtic square to set up their easels and sell their art. You'll find a range including watercolours of Catalan landscapes to oil paintings of churches and castles.

10 Mercat de Santa Caterina

MAP N3 ■ Av Francesc Cambó 16 ■ Open 7:30am–3:30pm Mon, Wed & Sat, 7:30am–8:30pm Tue, Thu & Fri ■ www.mercatsantacaterina.com

Each *barri* has its own food market with tempting displays but this one boasts a spectacular setting. The building was designed by Catalan architect Enric Miralles (1995–2000).

The striking Mercat de Santa Caterina

🔟 Barcelona for Free

Relaxing on a Barcelona beach

1 Beaches
Barcelona boasts 10 beaches, stretching for over 4.5 km (3 miles) along the coast. Between Easter and October they are dotted with *xiringuitos* selling drinks and snacks, and have lifeguards, sun lounger rental and even a beach library.

2 Sunday Afternoons at City Museums
ajuntament.barcelona.cat/museus/diumengestarda

All city-run museums offer free admission at least one afternoon a month, usually the first Saturday or Sunday of the month, and several, including the Museu de Catalunya, Museu del Disseny, Centre de Cultura Contemporánea de Barcelona (CCCB), Museu de la Història de Barcelona (MUHBA) and Museu Blau (main site of the Museu de Ciències Naturals), are free Sunday afternoon from 3pm. A full list of these can be found on the Barcelona Turisme website.

3 Font Màgica
The Magic Fountain *(see p95)* thrills with its wonderful sound and light shows – a balletic synchronicity in which multicoloured jets of water leap to different soundtracks and soar in elegant rows all the way up to the MNAC on the hill behind. The programme, ranging from classical to Disney tunes, is on the Barcelona Turisme website. The Piromusical, a huge firework, music and laser show that is Festes de la Mercè's closing event, also takes place here.

4 Música als Parcs
City parks host free summer concerts during the annual Música als Parcs programme. Musicians from around the world perform jazz, classical and contemporary music. The Parc de la Ciutadella is the main venue, but several other parks are also involved. Check the Barcelona Turisme website for full listings.

5 La Capella
MAP K3 ■ C/Hospital 56
■ Opening times vary, check website ■ lacapella.barcelona

The chapel at the Antic Hospital de la Santa Creu *(see p89)* has been converted into a fantastic art space hosting exhibitions of contemporary works by up-and-coming artists.

6 Festes
Every neighbourhood has its own *festa major* (various dates, Jun–Sep), ranging from the bacchanalian romp in Gràcia to the more modest celebrations of Poble Sec. You will see various Catalan traditions, from *castells* (human towers) to *correfocs* (fire-running) – and all for free. One of the biggest festivals is the Festes de la Mercè *(see p73)*.

Fireworks at the Festes de la Mercè

7 Spectacular Panoramas

With its wealth of *miradors* (viewpoints), Barcelona offers ample opportunity to contemplate the city's beauty. Relax over a glass of fizzing cava at Bunkers del Carmel *(see p50)* and enjoy views of the dazzling lights as the sun sets. Or head up to Mount Tibidabo, better known as 'the magic mountain', which is equally popular for the sublime vistas it offers.

8 Carretera de les Aigües

Running along the side of the Collserola park *(see p119)*, this path is popular with mountain-bikers and runners, and offers spectacular views across the city and out to sea. Getting there is fun too: take the FGC train to Peu de la Funicular, then ride the funicular up to the *carretera* stop.

The surrealist *Head of Barcelona*

9 Street Art

The streets are filled with art by world-renowned artists including Botero's *Cat* on the Rambla del Raval; Lichtenstein's *Head of Barcelona* and Mariscal's *Gambrinus* at the city port; Gehry's glittering *Fish* by the sea; and Miró's *Woman and Bird* in the Parc de Joan Miró *(see p49)* and mosaic at the Mercat de la Boqueria *(see p68)*.

10 Open House Barcelona

48hopenhousebarcelona.org
Peek into private homes, exciting new buildings and historic monuments during the city's annual Open House weekend. Many buildings not usually open to the public can be visited, including the Arc de Triomf and the Ateneu cultural centre.

TOP 10 BUDGET TIPS

The Montjuïc parks

1 Pack a picnic of tasty local produce and head to the Montjuïc parks (the Parc Jacint Mossen Cinto with its lily ponds and shady nooks is a particular favourite) or to the beaches to dine for a fraction of the price of a restaurant.

2 If you know you're going to be visiting a lot of museums and using the public transport system, invest in the Barcelona Card, which starts at €36 for 72 hours.

3 The Art Ticket, which allows entry to six major art museums for €35 is an excellent deal for culture buffs.

4 Every summer, you can watch free film screenings on the beach.

5 Several theatres and cinemas offer reduced prices on *Dia del Espectador*, usually Monday, Tuesday or Wednesday, or for the day's first performance (usually around 4pm).

6 At weekday lunchtimes, many restaurants serve a good-value *menú del migdia* with two or three courses, a glass of wine and perhaps a coffee.

7 The best travel option is the T-Casual, a travel card valid for 10 journeys in zones 1 to 6 and the airport train (not for the airport metro).

8 Some university residences, such as the Residència Àgora BCN and the Residència Erasmus, offer cheap beds during the summer break.

9 For fashion bargains, hit the outlet stores on Carrer Girona, near the Gran Via. Brands include Mango, Etxart & Panno and Nice Things.

10 All products offered by Barcelona's tourist service, from the Bus Turístic to walking tours, are sold at a discount (usually 10 percent) on its website.

🔟 Festivals and Events

Performer at the Carnival in Sitges

① Colourful Carnivals

Barcelona's week-long carnival season kicks off on Dijous Gras (last Thursday before Lent) with a parade up the Rambla. Led by the carnival king and queen, it culminates in a confetti battle. The buzzing beach town of Sitges *(see p127)* has the biggest celebration, with over-the-top floats carrying performers.

② Llum BCN

In February, Barcelona's festival of light transforms the revitalized former warehouse district of Poble Nou. The buildings, galleries and squares flicker with light sculptures, installations and shows in a stunning display.

③ El Dia de Sant Jordi

On 23 April, the day of Sant Jordi *(see p41)*, men and women exchange books and roses, sold at open-air stalls across the city. The rose petals symbolize the blood of the slain dragon, while the books are a tribute to Cervantes and Shakespeare, who both died on 23 April 1616.

④ Summer Arrives

In celebration of St John and the start of summer, 23 June is Catalonians' night to play with fire – and play they do, with gusto. Fireworks streak through the night sky and bonfires are set ablaze on beaches and in towns throughout the region.

⑤ LGBT+ Events

www.pridebarcelona.org
■ www.circuitfestival.net/Barcelona

Barcelona has a lively LGBT+ scene, with specialist bookshops, hip boutiques and chic clubs that pulsate into the early hours. In June, the city celebrates Pride with fabulous floats, concerts and a full programme of talks and activities. The Circuit Festival in August is a sizzling event, where people flock to Barcelona's beaches for this huge LGBT+ party.

⑥ Castells

The tradition of building *castells* (human towers) in Catalonia dates back to the 18th century. In June, trained *castellers* stand on each others' shoulders to create a human castle – the highest tower takes the prize. *Castells* are often performed in Plaça Sant Jaume.

⑦ Neighbourhood Festivals

Barcelona is a city that enjoys a party. During the summer months every neighbourhood has some form of celebration. The best known *festa major* is in Gràcia in mid-August, famous for its extravagantly decorated streets and outdoor concerts. Other neighbourhood festivals include Poble Sec in July and Sants in August, both of which feature traditional parades and *correfocs* (fire-running).

Festa Major de Gràcia celebrations

8 Festes de la Mercè
www.barcelona.cat/lamerce

Barcelona's main festival is a riotous week-long celebration in honour of La Mercè, a co-patron saint of the city (see p41). The night sky lights up with fireworks, outdoor concerts are held, and there are parades of *gegants* and *capgrossos* (giants and fatheads). Don't miss the *correfoc* (fire-running), when fire-spitting dragons career through the streets.

Gegants, Festes de la Mercè

9 The Big Screen
www.sitgesfilmfestival.com

Every October Barcelona hosts the glamorous Sitges Film Festival, the world's biggest celebration of fantasy and horror productions. Outdoor cinema is offered during the summer, with the *Gandules* (deckchairs) festival featuring arthouse films.

10 Christmas Celebrations

The Nadal (Christmas) season begins on 1 December with festive artisan fairs. Fira de Santa Llúcia, Barcelona's oldest Christmas market, sees stalls set up around Catedral de Barcelona selling handmade gifts. On 5 January is the spectacular Cavalcada de Reis (Parade of the Three Kings). The kings arrive by ship into the city's harbour and then parade through streets lined with children. In Spain, the kings bring the children their presents on this magical night.

TOP 10 MUSIC, THEATRE AND ART FESTIVALS

Revellers at the Festival del Sónar

1 Guitar BCN
www.guitarbcn.com
International guitar festival organized by Spanish music promoters, The Project.

2 Jazz Terrassa
www.jazzterrassa.org
This internationally renowned festival offers jazz concerts in venues around the village of Terrassa.

3 Ciutat Flamenco
www.ciutatflamenco.com
A week of outstanding flamenco music at the Mercat de les Flors.

4 Primavera Sound
www.primaverasound.com
A pop, rock and underground dance music festival featuring many big-names.

5 Festival del Sónar
www.sonar.es
This festival is an explosion of music and the latest in audiovisual production.

6 Grec Festival Barcelona
www.barcelona.cat/grec
Barcelona's largest music, theatre and dance festival.

7 Música als Parcs
www.facebook.com/MusicaParcs
A collection of free classical music and jazz concerts held in the city's parks.

8 Festival Jardins Pedralbes
www.festivalpedralbes.com
International names in rock and pop perform in the lovely Parc de Pedralbes.

9 Festival de Música Antiga
www.auditori.cat
Concerts of early music held at outdoor venues in the Barri Gòtic and L'Auditori.

10 Festival Internacional de Jazz de Barcelona
www.jazz.barcelona
Jazz festival with experimental music and big-names, held all over the city.

Barcelona
Area by Area

A view of Barcelona, with the
Sagrada Família in the background

Barri Gòtic and La Ribera	**76**	Eixample	**106**
El Raval	**86**	Gràcia, Tibidabo and Zona Alta	**116**
Montjuïc	**94**		
The Seafront	**100**	Beyond Barcelona	**124**

 Barri Gòtic and La Ribera

Mosaic, Palau de la Música Catalana

Starting as the Roman settlement of Barcino, the city grew over the years, culminating in a building boom in the 14th and 15th centuries. Barri Gòtic is a beautifully preserved neighbourhood of Gothic buildings, lively squares and atmospheric alleys, with the cathedral at its religious and social heart a reminder of its medieval heyday. Extending east of Barri Gòtic is the ancient *barri* of La Ribera, with lovely Carrer Montcada and the Museu Picasso.

BARRI GÒTIC AND LA RIBERA

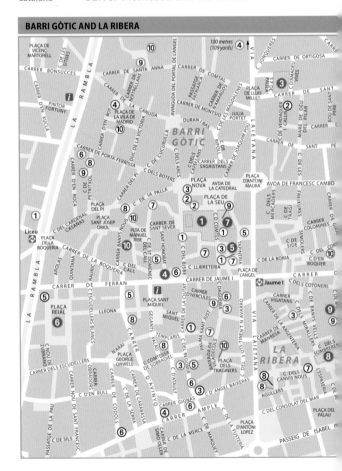

① Barcelona Cathedral

Soaring over the Barri Gòtic is Barcelona's mighty cathedral (see pp18–19), which dates from 1298.

② Museu Picasso

Discover the youthful output (see pp30–31) of one of the most revered artists of the 20th century.

③ Palau de la Música Catalana

The city's most prestigious concert hall (see pp32–3) is a breathtaking monument to both la música Catalana and the Modernista aesthetic.

①	**Top 10 Sights** see pp76–9
①	**Restaurants and Tapas Bars** see p85
①	**Shops** see p82
①	**The Best of the Rest** see p80
①	**Remains of Roman Barcino** see p81
①	**Cafés and Light Eats** see p84
①	**Cocktail and Conversation Spots** see p83

Façade of the Palau de la Generalitat

④ Plaça de Sant Jaume

MAP M4 ■ Palau de la Generalitat: 012; open 10:30am–1:30pm second & fourth Sat & Sun of the month for guided tours, reserve ahead; presidencia.gencat.cat/ca/ambits_d_actuacio/historia_generalitat_i_palau/visites ■ Ajuntament: open 10am–1:30pm Sun for guided tours (English at 10am)

The site at which the Plaça de Sant Jaume (see p46) lies today was once the nucleus of Roman Barcino. With these roots, it seems fitting that the square is home to Barcelona's two most important government buildings – the Palau de la Generalitat (the seat of Catalonian parliament) and the Ajuntament (city hall). Look out for the detailed carved relief of Sant Jordi, Catalonia's patron saint, on the 15th-century Generalitat façade. Within is the beautiful 1434 Capella de Sant Jordi (see p41). A highlight of the Gothic 15th-century Ajuntament is the Saló de Cent, from where the Council of One Hundred, Barcelona's first form of government, ruled from 1372 to 1714. Also worth exploring is the Pati dels Tarongers, a lovely arcaded courtyard planted with orange trees and overlooked by interesting gargoyles.

EL BORN

If you're hankering for a proper martini or some alternative jazz, then look no further than El Born, a sleepy-turned-hip neighbourhood "reborn" several years ago. Students and artists moved in, attracted by cheap rents and airy warehouses, fostering an arty vibe that now blends in with the area's old-time aura. Experimental design shops share the narrow streets with traditional balconied buildings festooned with laundry hung out to dry. Passeig de Born, lined with bars and cafés, leads onto the inviting Plaça Comercial, where the cavernous Born Market (in operation 1870–1970) has been converted into a cultural centre and exhibition space.

Three Graces fountain, Plaça Reial

5 Museu d'Història de Barcelona (MUHBA)

MAP M4 ▪ Pl del Rei ▪ Open 10am–2pm & 3–8pm Tue–Sun ▪ Adm; free first Sun of the month, every Sun after 3pm ▪ ajuntament. barcelona.cat/museuhistoria

The medieval Plaça del Rei (see p46) contains the core site of the Museu d'Història de Barcelona, encompassing remains ranging from Roman Barcino to the Middle Ages. These include Casa Padellàs (see p42) and the Palau Reial, which contains the Capella de Santa Àgata (see p41) and the Saló del Tinell, a massive arched hall where Ferdinand and Isabel met Columbus after his 1492 voyage to the Americas. The museum also has one of the largest underground excavations of Roman ruins on display in Europe (see p81), including a 3rd-century garum factory and winery.

6 Plaça Reial

MAP L4

Late 19th-century elegance meets sangria-drinking café society in the arcaded Plaça Reial, one of the city's most entertaining squares (see p46). The Modernista lampposts

were designed by Gaudí in 1879, and at its centre is a wrought-iron fountain representing the Three Graces. The palm-lined square has a cluster of restaurants, bars and cafés that are constantly busy.

7 Museu Frederic Marès

MAP N3 ▪ Pl de Sant Iu 5–6 ▪ Open 10am–7pm Tue–Sat, 11am–8pm Sun ▪ Adm; free first Sun of the month, every Sun after 3pm ▪ www.museumares.bcn.cat

This fascinating museum houses the collection of wealthy Catalan sculptor Frederic Marès. No mere hobby collector, the astute (and obsessive) Marès amassed holdings that a modern museum curator would die for. Among them is an array of religious icons and statues, dating from Roman times to the present, and the curious "Museu Sentimental", which displays everything from ancient watches to fans and dolls. Also worth a visit during summer is Cafè d'Estiu (see p84), a sunny spot for a break on the museum's patio.

Museu Frederic Marès

8 Església de Santa Maria del Mar

MAP P5 ▪ Pl de Santa Maria 1 ▪ Open 9am–12pm & 5–8:30pm Mon–Sat, 10am–2pm & 5–8:30pm Sun ▪ Timings for guided tours in English vary; check website ▪ Adm for guided tours ▪ santamariadelmar barcelona.org

The spacious, breathtaking interior of this 14th-century church (see p40), designed by architect Berenguer de Montagut, is a premier example of the austere Catalan Gothic style. The church is dedicated to St Mary of the Sea, the patron saint of sailors, and an ancient model ship hangs near one of the statues of the Virgin. Dubbed "the people's church", this is a popular spot for exchanging wedding vows.

9 Museu Etnològic i de Cultures del Món

MAP P4 ■ C/Montcada 14 ■ Open 10am–8:30pm daily ■ Adm; free first Sun of the month, every Sun after 3pm ■ www.barcelona.cat/museu-etnologic-culturesmon

The Museum of World Cultures, in the 16th-century Nadal and Marqués de Lliò palaces, showcases the cultures of Asia, Africa, America and Oceania. Highlights include Hindu sculptures, Japanese paintings, Nazca ceramics, brass plaques from Benin and indigenous Australian art.

Museu Etnològic i de Cultures del Món

10 El Call

MAP M4 ■ Singagoga Major: C/Marlet 2; 93 317 07 90; adm ■ Centre d'Interpretació del Call: Plaçeta del Manuel Ribé s/n; 93 256 21 22; adm

El Call was home to one of Spain's largest Jewish communities until their expulsion in the 15th century. A few of the original buildings have survived, although a small synagogue (now restored), believed to be one of the oldest in Europe, is on Carrer de Marlet. There is also an interpretation centre dedicated to El Call, run by the city's history museum.

A STROLL THROUGH ROMAN BARCELONA

Avinguda Portal de l'Àngel · Plaça de la Vila de Madrid · Barcelona Cathedral · Plaça del Rei · Plaça de Ramon Berenguer el Gran · Café-Bar L'Antiquari · Temple d'August · Museu d'Història de Barcelona · Plaça de Sant Jaume · Jaume I metro station · Bliss · Pati Llimona

▶ MORNING

Start at the Jaume I metro stop. Walk up Via Laietana to the **Plaça de Ramon Berenguer el Gran** *(see p80)*, which is backed by an impressive stretch of Roman walls. Return to the metro and turn right onto C/Jaume I to get to the **Plaça de Sant Jaume**, the site of the old Roman forum. Leading off to the left is C/Ciutat, which becomes C/Regomir: at No. 3 is **Pati Llimona** *(see p80)*, with an extensive section of Roman walls, one of the four main gateways into the city and the ruins of some thermal baths. There's a good, inexpensive café at Pati Llimona, or you can enjoy a light lunch at **Bliss** *(Plaça de Sant Just)*.

AFTERNOON

Return to the Plaça de Sant Jaume and cross it into tiny C/Paradís, where you'll find vestiges of the **Temple d'August**, a MUHBA site. At the end of the street, turn right and make for the **Plaça del Rei** *(see p46)*. Stop for coffee at the **Café-Bar L'Antiquari** *(see p84)* before visiting the **Museu d'Història de Barcelona** (MUHBA), where you can explore the remains of Roman Barcino. Walk back to C/Comtes, which flanks **Barcelona Cathedral** *(see pp18–19)*, turn right and cross Plaça Nova to C/Arcs, which leads to Avinguda Portal de l'Àngel. Turn left down C/Canuda to reach the **Plaça de la Vila de Madrid** *(see p47)*, where several Roman sarcophagi, found outside the walls according to Roman tradition, are arranged along an old Roman road.

See map on pp76–7 ←

The Best of the Rest

Neo-Gothic bridge, Carrer del Bisbe

the 17th-century Palau Dalmases with its Gothic chapel, which hosts flamenco performances.

5 Plaça de Ramon Berenguer el Gran
MAP N3

This square boasts one of the largest preserved sections of Barcelona's impressive Roman walls.

6 Carrer Regomir and Carrer del Correu Vell
MAP M5

Find splendid Roman remains on Carrer Regomir, most notably in the medieval Pati Llimona. Two Roman towers can be seen on nearby Carrer del Correu Vell, and there are ruins of Roman walls on the Plaça Traginers.

1 Carrer del Bisbe
MAP M3

Medieval Carrer del Bisbe is flanked by the Gothic Cases dels Canonges (House of Canons) and the Palau de la Generalitat *(see p77)*. Connecting the two is an eye-catching 1928 Neo-Gothic arched stone bridge.

2 Carrer de Santa Llúcia
MAP M3

This medieval street is home to the Casa de l'Ardiaca *(see p19)*, which features a pretty patio, palm trees and a fountain.

3 Capella de Sant Cristòfol
MAP M4 ■ C/Regomir 6–8

This chapel dedicated to Sant Cristòfor, the patron saint of travellers, dates from 1503, although it was remodeled in the 1890s. Drivers bring their cars to the chapel annually on the saint's feast day (25 July) to be blessed.

4 Carrer Montcada
MAP P4

The "palace row" of La Ribera is lined with Gothic architectural gems, including the 15th-century Palau Aguilar, which is now home to the Museu Picasso *(see pp30–31)*, and

7 Plaça de Sant Felip Neri
MAP M3

Sunlight filters through tall trees in this hidden oasis of calm. The *plaça (see p58)* is home to the Museu del Calçat, which showcases footwear.

8 Carrer Petritxol
MAP L3

This medieval street is lined with *granges* and *xocolateries* (cafés and chocolate shops). The famous Sala Parés art gallery, which once exhibited Picasso, Casas as well as other Catalan artists, is also located here.

9 Església de Sant Just i Sant Pastor
MAP M4 ■ Pl de Sant Just s/n ■ 93 301 74 33 ■ basilicasantjust.cat

This Gothic church, completed in 1342, has sculptures dating back to the 9th century and 5th-century Visigothic baptismal fonts.

10 Església de Santa Anna
MAP M2 ■ C/Santa Anna 29 ■ 93 301 35 76

Mere paces from La Rambla is the unexpected tranquillity of this Romanesque church with its leafy 15th-century Gothic cloister.

Remains of Roman Barcino

1 MUHBA
Spread beneath MUHBA *(see p78)* are the extensive remains of Barcino, the Roman settlement that grew into Barcelona. Some sections are remarkably intact, including roads still indented with cart ruts and laundry vats still stained with dye.

2 City Entrance Gate
MAP M3 ■ Plaça Nova & Carrer del Bisbe
Towers flanking the entrance to Carrer del Bisbe are the remnants of the only surviving entrance gate to the Roman city, the 4th-century Porta Praetoria.

3 Aqueduct
MAP M3 ■ Plaça Nova & Carrer del Bisbe
Opposite the Porta Praetoria is an archway, part of a reconstructed aqueduct, which would have been one of the several that brought water into the city. In front of it is Joan Brossa's visual poem *Barcino*.

4 Via Sepulcral Romana
MAP M2 ■ Plaça Vila de Madrid ■ Open 11am–2pm Tue, 11am–7pm Sun ■ Adm ■ www.ajuntament. barcelona.cat/museuhistoria
The Romans buried their dead in tombs outside the city walls. Several sarcophagi survive in this necropolis, dating from 1st–3rd centuries, and are visible from the walkway spanning the Plaça Vila de Madrid.

Visitors at Via Sepulcral Romana

5 Portal del Mar and Baths
MAP M4 ■ Pati Llimona Civic Centre: C/Regomir 3 ■ Open 10am–2pm & 4–6pm Mon–Fri ■ www.pat llimona.net
Travellers and goods brought by ship would pass this gate to enter the city. A bath was obligatory for these travellers and the remnants of the baths can still be seen next to the gate.

6 Forum
MAP M4 ■ Plaça Sant Jaume
This large square was the forum and meeting point of the Roman settlement's main arteries: the *cardus* and the *decumanus*.

7 Temple d'August
MAP M4 ■ C/Paradís s/n ■ ajuntament.barcelona.cat/ museuhistoria
An alley just off the Plaça Sant Jaume leads to a quartet of 9-m- (30-ft-) high columns, the only remains of the once-imposing Temple of Augustus from 1st century BC.

8 Roman Domus
MAP M4 ■ C/Avinyó 15 ■ Open 10am–2pm & 4–7pm daily ■ Adm ■ ajuntament.barcelona.cat/museu historia/en
This Roman house dates between 1st–4th centuries and was discovered in 2004. Parts of the original wall paintings and mosaics can still be seen.

9 Walls and Moat
MAP N3 ■ Plaça de Ramón Berenguer el Gran
One of the best-preserved sections of the Roman walls is studded with towers, which have been incorporated into the Plaça de Ramon Berenguer el Gran *(see p78)*.

10 Defence Towers
MAP E5 ■ Plaça Traginers
Dating back to the 4th century, this tall, circular watchtower is one of the 78 defensive constructions that once formed part of the Roman walls.

See map on pp76–7➔

Shops

① Escribà Confiteria i Fleca

MAP L3 ▪ La Rambla 83
▪ www.escriba.es

If the glistening pastries and towering chocolate creations aren't enough of a lure, then the Modernista storefront certainly is. Buy goodies to go or enjoy them in the café.

② La Manual Alpargatera

MAP M4 ▪ C/Avinyó 7
▪ Closed Sun ▪ www.
lamanualalpargatera.es

Shoes from La Manual Alpargatera

Notable personalities, including Pope John Paul II, Jack Nicholson and Salvador Dalí, have shopped for *alpargatas* and espadrilles at this famous store.

③ Colmado

MAP P5 ▪ C/Brosoli 5
▪ colmadoshop.com

This small boutique has a carefully curated selection of clothing and accessories from stylish labels such as Costa, Heinui and Wolf & Moon.

④ Sombreria Mil

MAP N1 ▪ C/Fontanella 20
▪ Closed Sun ▪ www.sombreria mil.com

This century-old hat shop offers a fine range of headwear (including the traditional Catalan beret) for men and women.

⑤ Beatriz Furest

MAP P5 ▪ C/Esparteria 1
▪ Closed Sun ▪ www.beatrizfurest.com

Handcrafted bags and purses by Barcelonian designer Beatriz Furest are sold in this small, chic boutique.

⑥ Casa Colomina

MAP M3 ▪ C/Cucurulla 2
▪ www.casacolomina.es

Sink your teeth into the Spanish nougat-and-almond speciality *torró*. Casa Colomina, established in 1908, offers a tantalizing array, including chocolate and marzipan varieties.

⑦ Cereria Subirà

MAP N4 ▪ Baixada Llibreteria 7
▪ Closed Sun ▪ www.cereriasubira.cat

Founded in 1761, this is the city's oldest shop crammed with every kind of candle imaginable.

⑧ Vila Viniteca

C/Agullers 7 ▪ Closed Sun ▪ www.vilaviniteca.es

This is one of the city's best wine merchants stocking a range of wines and spirits. An adjoining shop sells quality Spanish delicacies, including hams, cheeses and olive oil.

⑨ Guantería Alonso

MAP M2 ▪ C/Santa Anna 27
▪ Closed Sun ▪ www.tiendacenter.com

This long-established shop is the place to visit for colourful hand-painted fans, handmade gloves, delicately embroidered mantillas and other traditional Spanish accessories.

⑩ L'Arca

MAP M3 ▪ C/Banys Nous 20
▪ larcabarcelona.com

Find amazing antique clothing, from flapper dresses to boned corsets, silk shawls, puff-sleeved shirts and antique wedding dresses here.

Vintage silk shawl at L'Arca

Cocktail and Conversation Spots

1 Bar L'Ascensor
MAP M4 ■ C/Bellafila 3 ■ 93 318 53 47 ■ Open 5:30pm–1:30am Sun–Thu (to 2:30am Fri & Sat)

An old-fashioned, dark-wood elevator serves as the entrance to this dimly lit, convivial bar popular with a cocktail-swilling crowd.

2 Antic Teatre
MAP N2 ■ C/ Verdaguer i Callís 12 ■ Open 10am–11:30pm Mon–Fri, 5–11:30pm Sat & Sun ■ www.antic teatre.com

This bohemian café-bar (see p60) is set in the courtyard of a small theatre. Sit at one of the tables, shaded by trees, for coffee or drinks.

The living-room decor at Milk

3 Milk
MAP M5 ■ C/Gignàs 21 ■ 93 268 09 22 ■ Open 9am–midnight Mon, Thu & Sun (to 4pm Tue & Wed), 9am–1am Fri & Sat

Decorated like a luxurious living room, Milk serves a lovely brunch (from 9am to 4:30pm), lunch and dinner daily.

4 Las Cuevas de los Rajahs
MAP E5 ■ C/ d'en Cignas 2 ■ Open 7pm–3am Tue–Sun ■ www. lascuevasbar.com

With Neo-Gothic paraphernalia, this bar is set in a cave-like space and offers cocktails, beers and wine.

5 Glaciar
MAP L4 ■ Pl Reial 3 ■ 93 302 11 63 ■ Open 10–2am daily

At this atmospheric café-bar, try to grab a spot on the terrace for a front-row view of activities on the plaça.

The 1980s-style Polaroids bar

6 Polaroids
MAP M5 ■ C/Còdols 29 ■ Open 7pm–2:30am daily

A bar with 80s-style decor and retro music, Polaroids offers well-priced drinks that come with free popcorn. Try to arrive early as this place is always packed.

7 La Vinya del Senyor
MAP N5 ■ Pl Santa Maria 5 ■ 93 310 33 79 ■ Opening times vary

Wine lovers from all over the city come here to sample a rich array of Spanish and international varieties.

8 Collage Art & Cocktail Social Club
MAP N5 ■ C/Consellers 4 ■ Open 8pm–3am daily

Enjoy unique original cocktails at good prices at this spot. The lounge upstairs hosts pocket-size painting exhibitions.

9 Paradiso
MAP F5 ■ C/ de Riera Palau 4 ■ Open 7am–2:30am daily

This cocktail den is accessed via a gourmet sandwich bar (you need to ask to be let in). The drinks are artistically presented.

10 Mudanzas
MAP P5 ■ C/Vidrieria 15 ■ 933 19 11 37 ■ Open 10am–2:30am daily

With black-and-white tiled floors, and circular marble tables, Mudanzas has a fun, laid-back vibe.

See map on pp76–7

Cafés and Light Eats

1 Cafè d'Estiu
MAP N3 ▪ Pl de Sant Iu 5–6
▪ 93 310 30 14 ▪ Closed Nov–Mar

This terrace café on the patio of the Museu Frederic Marès *(see p78)* is replete with stone pillars, climbing ivy and orange trees. Your museum ticket entitles you to a discount.

2 Demásie
MAP F5 ▪ C/de la Princesa 28
▪ 93 269 11 80 ▪ www. demasie.es

With a bright yellow interior and benches to sit, this bakery serves amazing cakes and cookies. Fresh juices and cold-pressed coffee make this the perfect place for a stopover.

3 Cafè-Bar L'Antiquari
MAP N4 ▪ C/Veguer 13
▪ 93 461 95 89

By day, sit by the window and enjoy views of the medieval old town. By night, sip cocktails in the Baroque-inspired upstairs lounge.

4 Elsa y Fred
MAP F4 & Q2 ▪ C/Rec Comtal 11
▪ 93 501 66 11 ▪ www.elsayfred.es

With its leather armchairs and big windows, this is the perfect place to enjoy a long, lazy brunch, with dishes ranging from classic *patates braves* to salmon sushi.

5 Tetería Salterio
MAP M4 ▪ C/Sant Domenec del Call 4 ▪ 93 302 50 28 ▪ Closed Mon–Fri D

Enjoy tea and sweet Arab cakes. Don't miss the *sardo*, an Oriental-style pizza with a variety of fillings.

6 Café Bliss
MAP N4 ▪ Pl Sant Just ▪ 93 268 10 22

Stop at this delightful café *(see p64)* while exploring the Barri Gòtic. It offers divine cakes, light meals, snacks and coffee. Ask for an outside table in summer.

7 En Apartè
MAP P2 ▪ C/Lluís el Piadós 2
▪ 93 269 13 35 ▪ www.enaparte.es

With outside tables overlooking the square, this relaxed café *(see p65)* offers French dishes and wines, good coffee and brunch.

8 Caelum
MAP M3 ▪ C/Palla 8
▪ 93 302 69 93

Up the stairs of this shop you will find preserves and other foods, all made in Spain's convents and monasteries. Sample the delicacies downstairs at the site of the 15th-century baths.

9 La Granja Pallaresa
MAP L3 ▪ C/Petritxol 11
▪ 93 302 20 36 ▪ Closed L daily

This family-run *xocolateria* has long been serving up thick, dark hot chocolate with *xurros* (fried, sugary dough strips) for dunking.

10 Bar del Pla
MAP P4 ▪ C/Montcada 2
▪ 93 268 30 03 ▪ Closed Sun

Savour Spanish tapas with a French twist here. Try the pig's trotters with *foie gras* or the squid ink croquettes.

Entrance to the popular Bar del Pla

Restaurants and Tapas Bars

1 Bar Mundial
MAP P3 ■ Pl de Sant Agustí Vell 1 ■ 93 319 90 56 ■ Closed Mon ■ €

Opened in 1925 and still boasting the original marble tables, this classic tapas bar is one of the best. The menu changes constantly.

2 Cal Pep
MAP P5 ■ Pl de les Olles 8 ■ 93 310 79 61 ■ Closed Sun, Mon L, last three weeks of Aug ■ €€

Taste a variety of delicious tapas, including the finest seafood, at this busy, established eatery.

3 Cafè de l'Acàdemia
MAP N4 ■ C/Lledó 1 ■ 93 319 82 53 ■ Closed Sat, Sun, Aug ■ €€

Located in an 18th-century building, this excellent restaurant serves superb modern Catalan cuisine and top-notch desserts.

4 Casa Delfín
MAP F5 ■ Passeig del Born 36 ■ 93 319 30 88 ■ €€

This pretty bistro uses seasonal produce in imaginative dishes and tapas. The fried artichokes with *romesco* sauce are a must.

5 Llamber
MAP F4 & P4 ■ C/Fusina 5 ■ 93 319 62 50 ■ €€

Enjoy modern Spanish cuisine made with fresh seasonal produce, including homegrown vegetables and Mediterranean red prawns, in a cool, loft-style interior with exposed brickwork and warm woodwork. Also on offer is a wine menu with 30 wines by the glass and 150 by the bottle.

6 Agut
MAP M5 ■ C/Gignàs 16 ■ 93 315 17 09 ■ Closed Sun D, Tue–Thu D & Mon, 1 week in Jan, Aug ■ €€

Established in 1924, this friendly family restaurant has been delighting patrons with excellent Catalan cuisine at reasonable prices.

PRICE CATEGORIES

For a three-course meal for one with half a bottle of wine (or equivalent meal), including taxes and extra charges.

€ under €35   €€ €35–50   €€€ over €50

7 Bodega La Palma
MAP M4 ■ Palma de Sant Just 7 ■ 93 315 06 56 ■ Closed Sun ■ €

This bohemian restaurant in a former wine cellar offers a delicious choice of tapas, including stuffed Piquillo peppers.

The elegant interior of Rasoterra

8 Rasoterra
MAP M4 ■ C/Palau 5 ■ 93 318 69 26 ■ Closed Mon, Tue–Fri L ■ €€

Proponents of the slow food movement, the owners of this stylish, loft-style restaurant serve delicious vegetarian and vegan dishes along with organic wines and beer.

9 El Xampanyet
MAP P4 ■ C/Montcada 22 ■ 93 319 70 03 ■ Closed Sun & Mon ■ €

An old-fashioned bar popular for its *cava* and range of simple tapas.

10 Govinda
MAP M2 ■ Pl Vila de Madrid 4 ■ 93 318 77 29 ■ Closed Sat D & Sun ■ €

This simple eatery serves up vegetarian Indian main dishes and delectable desserts, but no alcohol.

See map on pp76–7

⟨TOP 10⟩ El Raval

The sleek Museu d'Art Contemporani (MACBA) sits near ramshackle tenements; Asian groceries sell spices next to what were once Europe's most decadent brothels; art galleries share narrow streets with smoky old bars – this is a traditional working-class neighbourhood in flux. Since the 1990s it has been undergoing an enthusiastic urban renewal. Although the area has become a magnet for the city's young and hip crowd, it has still got plenty of edge.

Chimney, Palau Güell

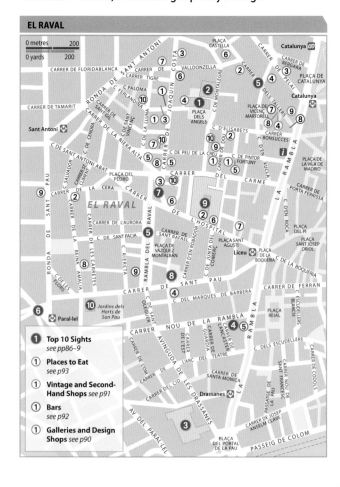

EL RAVAL

- **1** Top 10 Sights
  see pp86–9
- **①** Places to Eat
  see p93
- **①** Vintage and Second-
  Hand Shops see p91
- **①** Bars
  see p92
- **①** Galleries and Design
  Shops see p90

The stark white exterior of MACBA

1 Museu d'Art Contemporani (MACBA)

This dramatic, glass-fronted building was designed by American architect Richard Meier. An eclectic array of work by big-name Spanish and international artists is gathered in this contemporary art mecca *(see pp34–5)*. Excellent temporary exhibitions display everything from mixed media to sculpture and photography. Opposite stands the Gothic-style 16th-century Convent dels Àngels, built by Bartomeu Roig for the Dominican Tertiary Sisters. This is now used by Capella MACBA for temporary exhibitions, but long-term plans are to extend the galleries and exhibit some of MACBA's collection here permanently.

2 Centre de Cultura Contemporània (CCCB)

Housed in the 18th-century Casa de la Caritat, the CCCB is a focal point for the city's thriving contemporary art scene *(see pp34–5)*. It hosts innovative art exhibitions, literature festivals, film screenings and lectures. A medieval courtyard is dazzlingly offset by a massive angled glass wall, artfully designed to reflect the city's skyline.

3 Museu Marítim

MAP K6 ■ Av de les Drassanes ■ Open 10am–8pm daily ■ Adm, free from 3pm Sun ■ Santa Eulàlia sailing: trip times vary ■ www.mmb.cat

Barcelona's seafaring legacy comes to life at this museum *(see p43)*, located in the beautifully-restored Gothic shipyards. Admire the dramatic Gothic arches, where the royal ships were once built, and the full-scale replica of the *Real*, a 16th-century fighting galley. You can also explore the *Santa Eulàlia (see p102)*, a 1918 schooner moored at the Moll de la Fusta, and even take a sailing trip in her around the seafront (check website for timings and advance booking).

4 Palau Güell

MAP L4 ■ C/Nou de la Rambla 3–5 ■ Open 10am–2pm & 4–8pm Tue–Sun (to 5:30pm Nov–Mar); last entry 1 hr before closing ■ Adm ■ www.palauguell.cat

In 1886, Count Güell asked Gaudí to build him a mansion that would set him apart from his neighbours. The result is the Palau Güell, one of Gaudí's earliest commissions. The interior is darker and less playful than his later works, but stained-glass panels and windows make the most of the light. The rooms are arranged around a huge central salon topped with a domed ceiling. The charming roof terrace hints at the glorious rooftops like La Pedrera.

Sumptuous interior of Palau Güell

5 La Rambla del Raval
MAP K4

This pedestrian walkway, lined with palm trees, started as an attempt by city planners to spark a similar environment to that of the famed La Rambla *(see pp16–17)*. The striking, conical Barceló Hotel, with its panoramic rooftop terrace, and the sleek Filmoteca, a film archive complete with café and cinema, are signs of the area's gentrification. Halfway down the street, Botero's huge, plump bronze *Cat* usually has several neighbourhood kids crawling over its back. Trendy bars and cafés mean the Rambla del Raval rivals its more famous cousin for snacking and people-watching.

6 Avinguda Paral·lel
MAP B3–D5

This long avenue was home to the city's liveliest theatre and cabaret halls at the turn of the 20th century, and, despite being badly bombed in the Civil War, it remains the centre of the theatre district. The area is currently undergoing a resurgence, spearheaded by the restoration of the landmark El Molino music hall, which dates from 1898 and is once again a venue for concerts and shows *(see p54)*. The street hosts a number of festivals

Buildings on Avinguda Paral·lel

and there are plans to turn the century-old Teatro Arnau into a museum of the performing arts.

Shop on Carrer de la Riera Baixa

7 Carrers dels Tallers and de la Riera Baixa
MAP L1 & K3

Looking for vintage blue-and-white French navy tops once favoured by the likes of Picasso or bootleg CDs of Madonna's European tour? Along Carrers dels Tallers and de la Riera Baixa in the heart of El Raval are several vintage music and clothing shops selling everything from vinyl records and the latest CDs to original Hawaiian shirts. On Saturdays, Carrer de la Riera Baixa has its own market (open 11am–9pm), when its stores display their wares on the street.

8 Filmoteca
MAP K4 ■ Pl de Salvador Seguí 1–9 ■ 93 567 10 70 ■ www.filmoteca.cat

The Filmoteca – the Catalan film archive – occupies a huge, sleek contemporary building just off the Rambla del Raval and has played a large part in the ongoing regeneration of this neighbourhood. It has two screening rooms and shows a varied and interesting programme. This includes film cycles dedicated to the finest directors from around the world, documentaries, Catalan

films, and special events for kids.
It's extremely popular, not least
because prices are very reasonable.
There is also a great café which has
a library, a documentation centre and
an in-demand outdoor terrace. On
the first Sunday of the month, a flea
market is held in the square outside.

⑨ Antic Hospital de la Santa Creu

MAP K3 ■ Entrances on C/Carme
and at C/Hospital 56 ■ Courtyard
open 9am–8pm daily

This Gothic hospital complex, now
home to the National Library and
various cultural organizations, dates
from 1401 and is a reminder of the
neighbourhood's medieval past *(see
p90)*. Visitors can wander in a pleasant garden surrounded by Gothic
pillars, but a reader's card is needed
for admission to the library. The
chapel has been converted into a
wonderful contemporary art space.

⑩ Església de Sant Pau del Camp

MAP J4 ■ C/Sant Pau 101 ■ Open
9:30am–noon & 3:30–6:30pm Mon–
Fri, 9:30am–12:30pm Sat; Mass 8pm
Sat, noon Sun

Deep in the heart of El Raval is this
Romanesque church *(see p40)*, one
of the oldest in Barcelona. Originally
founded as a Benedictine monastery
in the 9th century and subsequently
rebuilt, this ancient church boasts
12th-century cloister.

Església de Sant Pau del Camp

A RAMBLE IN EL RAVAL

 MORNING

Choose an exhibition that appeals
at either **MACBA** or the **CCCB**
(see p87), the city's two most
important institutions of contemporary art and culture, which sit
right next to each other. Watch
the skateboarders on the **Plaça
dels Àngels** or relax in the café
overlooking the courtyard. Take
C/Joaquin Costa down to the
Rambla del Raval where you can
stroll beneath the palm trees and
admire Fernando Botero's **Cat**.
The Rambla is crammed with
cafés and restaurants: pick one
for lunch, or head to the popular
café in the **Filmoteca**, located
just off the Rambla.

AFTERNOON

At the bottom of the Rambla,
turn right on C/Sant Pau towards
the charming Romanesque monastery of **Església Sant Pau del
Camp**. Admire the simple church
and its miniature cloister with
delicately-carved columns. Then
walk back along C/Sant Pau,
turning right when you reach
the Rambla, then left on C/Nou
de la Rambla. At no. 3 stands
Gaudí's remarkable **Palau Güell**
(see p87), an extravagant mansion
that was one of his first commissions for the Güells. It has been
beautifully restored, with its lavish salons and charming rooftop
open to visitors. Kick off the
evening with an absinthe at
one of Barcelona's oldest bars,
the **Marsella** *(see p92)*, before
heading to the nearby **Bar Muy
Buenas** *(see p92)*, which boasts
restored Modernista decor.

See map on p86 ←

Galleries and Design Shops

1 Galeria dels Àngels
MAP L2 ■ C/Pintor Fortuny 27
■ Open 10:30am–7pm Mon–Fri
■ angelsbarcelona.com

Works of emerging and established
artists are showcased at this painting,
photography and sculpture gallery.

2 Miscelanea
MAP K5 ■ C/Dr Dou 16
■ Open Sep–Jul: 4:30–11pm
Tue–Sun (to midnight Fri &
Sat) ■ www.
miscelanea.info

Miscelanea is an
artists' project. It
is a multifunctional
space, with a gallery
for exhibitions featuring
works by emerging artists, a shop
selling design objects and a café.

Fish, Imanol Ossa

3 Siesta
MAP K2 ■ C/Ferlandina 18
■ Open 11am–2pm & 5–8:30pm Mon–
Fri (to 2pm Sat) ■ siestaweb.com

Part boutique, part art gallery, Siesta
sells unique ceramics, jewellery and
glass art. It also hosts exhibitions.

4 MACBA Store Laie
MAP K2 ■ Plaça dels Àngels 1
■ Open Fri–Sun ■ www.macba.cat/es/
visita/tienda-libreria

This museum bookshop has a range
of designer gifts, including stationery,
homeware, toys and games as well
as books on art.

5 Grey Street
MAP D4 ■ C/Peu de la Creu 25
■ Open 11am–3pm & 4–9pm Mon–Sat
■ www.greystreetbarcelona.com

This lovingly curated shop sells
mostly locally made gifts and crafts,
from stationery to jewellery and bags.

6 La Capella
MAP K3 ■ C/Hospital 56
■ Opening times vary, check
website ■ lacapella.barcelona/ca

This Gothic chapel at the Antic
Hospital de la Santa Creu (see p89)
is now a contemporary art gallery
(see p70) run by the city and
dedicated to emerging artists.

7 Imanol Ossa
MAP D4 & K2 ■ C/Peu de
la Creu 24 ■ www.imanolossa.com

Original lamps, jewellery, and
mobiles are made from all kinds
of upcycled treasures at this studio,
run by a young designer. Call for
opening hours.

8 La Xina A.R.T.
MAP J4 ■ C/Hort de
la Bomba 6 ■ Open 5:30–
8:30pm Thu–Sat ■ www.
laxinaart.org

The latest contemporary art features
at this innovative gallery started by
four local artists in the late 1990s.

9 NuOvum
MAP L2 ■ C/Pintor Fortuny 30
■ Open 11am–8:30pm Mon–Sat
■ nuovum.com

Unusual designs – from jewellery to
paintings to lamps – are sold here.

The quaint lamps of NuOvum

10 Room Service
MAP E4 ■ C/dels Àngels
16 ■ Open Sep–Jul: 11am–2pm &
4:30–7pm Mon–Fri ■ www.room
sd.com

This commercial gallery is dedicated
to cutting-edge design, principally
for the home. International creators
are represented, along with up-and-
coming local talent.

Vintage and Second-Hand Shops

1 Flamingos
MAP D4 & K2 ■ C/de
Ferlandina 20 ■ 93 182 43 87
■ Open 11am–9pm Mon–Sat
This fabulous vintage store,
also selling old posters and
bric-a-brac, operates on a
weight system: you pay per
kilo, depending on the clothing
category you choose.

2 Holala Ibiza
MAP L1 ■ C/Tallers 73
■ 933 02 05 93 ■ Open 11am–
9pm Mon–Sat
Rummage for an outfit at this
three-floor vintage store, with
everything from original silk
kimonos to army pants and
colourful 1950s bathing suits.

A vintage furniture store in Barri Gotic

3 Fusta'm
MAP K1 ■ C/Joaquim Costa
62 ■ 639 527 076 ■ Open 10am–
2pm & 4–8pm Mon–Fri
Discover second-hand furniture,
lighting and decorative objects
from around the world in the
style of the 1950s, 60s and 70s,
all of them completely restored
at the store's own workshop.

4 Revólver Records
MAP L2 ■ C/Tallers 11 ■ 93 412
73 58 ■ Open 10am–9pm Mon–Sat
The speciality here is classic rock,
and the wall art fittingly depicts The
Rolling Stones and Jimi Hendrix. One
floor houses CDs, the other vinyl.

5 Wilde Sunglasses Store
MAP K2 ■ C/Joaquin Costa 2
This dimly-lit boudoiresque boutique
is lined with vintage-style sunglasses,
that range from aviator shades to
pairs of cat's-eye specs.

6 Holala Plaza
MAP L1 ■ Pl Castella 2 ■ 933 02
05 93 ■ Open 11am–9pm Mon–Sat
This huge shop in the heart of the
Raval sells second-hand clothes,
furniture and bric-a-brac.

7 La Principal Retro & Co
MAP K1 ■ C/Valldonzella 52
■ 60 726 57 57 ■ Open noon–2:30pm
& 4:30–9:30pm Mon–Sat
Set in a charming old dairy, this chic
boutique has a lovely range of vintage
clothing for men and women.

8 Soul BCN
MAP L1 ■ C/Tallers 15 ■ 93 481
32 94 ■ Open 11am–8:30pm Mon–Sat
A vintage-style shop, Soul BCN sells
1950s frocks, cat's-eye sunglasses,
flirty Bardot tops and much more.

9 Discos Tesla
MAP L2 ■ C/Tallers 3 ■ 664 095
091 ■ Open 9:30am–9:30pm Mon–Sat
This record and CD store focuses on
alternative music from decades past.
Visitors can hum a few lines of a song
and the owner will track it down.

10 Boomerang
MAP D4 ■ C/Peu de la
Creu 16 bis ■ 647 63 26 94 ■ Open
Sep–Jul: noon–2:30pm & 5–8pm
Mon–Sat
Furniture and home decor from the
1950s to 1970s is sold in this funky
showroom. Smaller pieces include
light fittings, lamps and ceramics
mostly from Italy and Germany.

See map on p86

Bars

Bar Almirall, founded in 1860

1 Bar Almirall
MAP K2 ▪ C/Joaquin Costa 33 ▪ Opening times vary ▪ www.casa almirall.com

Founded in 1860, the city's oldest bar retains many original fittings and has eclectic music and strong cocktails.

2 El Jardí
MAP K3 ▪ C/Hospital 56 ▪ 93 681 92 34 ▪ Open 5–11pm daily

Escape the crowds in this peaceful outdoor café-bar *(see p60)*, overlooking a garden. Go for the *vermut (see p65)* and some olives.

3 Bar Resolis
MAP K3 ▪ C/Riera Baixa 22 ▪ Open 7pm–12:30am daily (to 1am Fri & Sat)

Formerly an old-fashioned bar, this is now an appealing boho-chic tavern with a small terrace. Cocktails and wine accompany delicious tapas.

4 Marsella
MAP K4 ▪ C/Sant Pau 65 ▪ Open 10pm–2:30am daily

This-dimly lit Modernista bar serves up cocktails and absinthe to regulars and first-timers.

5 Ultramarinos
MAP E5 ▪ Las Ramblas 31 ▪ Open noon–3am daily ▪ www. ultramarinosbarcelona.com

Once a cinema, this space is now a drinking and dining destination. It serves creative share plates. Try the tuna *tataki* and the potent cocktails.

6 Betty Ford's
MAP K1 ▪ C/Joaquin Costa 56 ▪ 93 304 13 68 ▪ Open 7pm–2:30am daily

Named after the Hollywood set's favourite rehab and detox centre, this cocktail bar has a 1950s vibe.

7 Bar Kasparo
MAP L2 ▪ Pl Vicenç Martorell 4 ▪ Open Tue–Sat ▪ www.kasparo.es

During the day, this charming bar *(see p60)* is a favourite with families, but come dusk it's a fabulous place to chill out over a glass of wine.

8 Boadas Cocktail Bar
MAP L2 ▪ C/Tallers 1 ▪ Open noon–2am Mon–Sat ▪ www. boadascocktails.com

Founded in 1933, Boadas continues to mix the best martinis in town.

9 Bar Palosanto
MAP K4 ▪ Rambla de Raval 26 ▪ Open 6–11:30pm Mon, Thu–Sun

A colourful café-bar with a few outdoor tables, this is a cosy spot for drinks, tapas and light meals.

10 Bar Muy Buenas
MAP D4 ▪ C/del Carme 63 ▪ Opening times vary ▪ www.muy buenas.cat ▪ €

A Modernista-era bar, Muy Buenas serves spirits and wine made in Catalonia along with plates of local cheese and premium chacuterie.

Modernista decor at Muy Buenas

Places to Eat

1 Caravelle
MAP E4 ■ C/Pintor Fortuny 31
■ 93 317 98 92 ■ Closed Sun–Wed D
■ €

This spot near the MACBA museum has become a favourite for weekend brunch and long coffee breaks. The menu changes regularly but is likely to include delicious huevos rancheros and vegetarian options.

2 Can Lluís
MAP J3 ■ C/de la Cera 49
■ 93 441 11 87 ■ Closed Sun ■ €€

Run by three generations, this restaurant has been preparing its family recipes since 1929. The food is simple and delicious, and the fixed-price lunch menu is a good bargain.

3 La Esquina
MAP E3 ■ C/Bergara 2 ■ www.laesquinabarcelona.com ■ €

A spacious café, La Esquina serves delicious all-day brunch and light lunch fare such as pulled pork tacos and Caeser salad.

4 Teresa Carles
MAP L1 ■ C/Jovellanos 2
■ 93 317 18 29 ■ teresacarles.com ■ €

Come here for imaginative vegetarian fare, such as crêpes with artichokes and brie. It's the flagship of a small chain of healthy food restaurants.

5 Biocenter
MAP L2 ■ C/Pintor Fortuny 25
■ 93 301 45 83 ■ Opening times vary
■ www.restaurantebiocenter.es ■ €

At this vegetarian restaurant, dishes are prepared with organic produce. There's an array of dishes to choose from, especially on Tuesdays when all the specials are vegan.

6 A Tu Bola
MAP D4 ■ C/de Hospital 78
■ 93 315 32 44 ■ Closed Tue ■ €

A local favourite, A Tu Bola is well known for its fish, meat and vegetable balls served between bread with a range of dips and sauces.

PRICE CATEGORIES

For a three-course meal for one with half a bottle of wine (or equivalent meal), including taxes and extra charges.

....

€ under €35   €€ €35–50   €€€ over €50

7 Bacaro
MAP L3 ■ C/Jerusalén 6
■ Closed Sun ■ 672 17 60 68 ■ www.bacarobarcelona.com ■ €€

Tucked behind the Boqueria market, this convivial little Italian restaurant-bar serves modern Venetian cuisine.

The bar at Marmalade

8 Marmalade
MAP J2 ■ C/Riera Alta 4–6
■ 93 442 39 66 ■ Closed Mon–Thu L
■ www.marmaladebarcelona.com ■ €

A loft-style bar serving cocktails, snacks and meals in the evenings, plus a great brunch on weekends.

9 Els Ocellets
MAP D4 ■ Ronda Sant Pau 55 ■ Closed Sun D, Mon, late Jul–late Aug ■ €

Traditional cuisine with a creative touch in elegant surroundings. Good value fixed-price menus.

10 L'Havana
MAP K2 ■ C/Lleó 1 ■ 93 302 21 06 ■ Closed Sun D, Mon, 4 weeks in Jul–Aug ■ €€

This eatery serves superb Catalan cuisine. Try the fresh fish of the day or classic Catalan dishes such as pig's trotters.

See map on p86

ᴛᴏᴘ10 Montjuïc

Named the "Jewish Mountain" after an important Jewish cemetery that existed here in the Middle Ages, this sizable park was first landscaped for the 1929 International Exhibition, when the Palau Nacional and the Mies van der Rohe Pavilion were also built. However, the area soon fell into general disuse, becoming synonymous with decline. With the grim shadow left by the castle, which for years acted as a slaughterhouse for Franco's firing squads, it is little short of miraculous that Montjuïc is now one of the city's biggest draws. As the site for the 1992 Olympics, it was transformed into a beautiful green oasis, with fabulous museums and sports facilities all connected by a network of outdoor escalators and interlaced with quiet, shady gardens.

Statue, Castell de Montjuïc

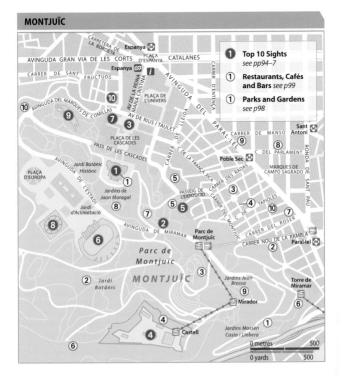

MONTJUÏC

1 **Top 10 Sights** see pp94–7

① **Restaurants, Cafés and Bars** see p99

① **Parks and Gardens** see p98

1 Palau Nacional and Museu Nacional d'Art de Catalunya

The Palau Nacional is home to the Museu Nacional d'Art de Catalunya (see pp20–21), which exhibits Catalonia's historic art collections. Boasting one of Europe's finest displays of Romanesque art, the museum includes a series of 12th-century frescoes, rescued from Catalan Pyrenean churches and painstakingly reassembled in a series of galleries.

2 Fundació Joan Miró

One of Catalonia's most acclaimed painters and sculptors, Joan Miró (1893–1983) donated many of the 11,000 works held by the museum. Housed in a stark white building designed by his friend, architect Josep Lluís Sert, this (see pp28–9) is the world's most complete collection of Miró's work.

3 Font Màgica

MAP B4 ■ Pl Carles Buigas 1 (off Av Reina Maria Cristina) ■ Shows: Apr, May & Oct: 9pm & 9:30pm Thu–Sat; Jun–Sep: 9:30pm & 10pm Wed–Sun; Nov–Mar: 8pm & 8:30pm Thu–Sat; no shows Jan & Feb

Below the cascades and fountains that decend from the Palau Nacional is the Magic Fountain (see p70), designed by Carles Buigas for the International Exhibition of 1929. 3As darkness falls, countless jets of water are choreographed in a mesmerizing sound and light show. When the

Font Màgica's soaring jets of water

water meets in a single jet it can soar to 15 m (50 ft). The extravagant finale is often accompanied by a recording of Freddie Mercury and soprano Montserrat Caballé singing the anthem *Barcelona* as the water fades from pink to green and back to white. The Four Columns behind the fountain represent the Catalan flag and are a symbol of the Catalanism movement.

4 Castell de Montjuïc

MAP B6 ■ Carretera de Montjuïc 66 ■ Open 10am–6pm daily (to 8pm Apr–Oct) ■ Adm ■ ajunta ment.barcelona.cat/castelldemontjuic

Dominating Montjuïc's hill, this gloomy castle was once a prison and torture centre for political prisoners. At the end of the Spanish Civil War, 4,000 Catalan nationalists and republicans were shot in the nearby Fossar de la Pedrera. After such a tragic history, the castle is entering a happier phase: it has been developed into an international peace centre. Visitors can still climb the fort's sturdy bastions for superb views of the port below.

Castell de Montjuïc

The atmospheric Teatre Grec

5 Teatre Grec
MAP C4 ■ Pg Santa Madrona ■ Open for visits 10am–dusk daily ■ Adm for shows ■ www.barcelona.cat/grec

This beautiful amphitheatre *(see p54)* was inspired by the Classical ideas of what was known as *Noucentisme*. This late 19th-century Catalan architectural movement was a reaction to the overly-decorative nature of *Modernisme*. With its leafy green backdrop and beautiful gardens, there are few places more enchanting than this to watch *Swan Lake* or listen to some jazz. The open-air theatre is used for shows during the summertime Grec Festival *(see p73)*, when it also becomes home to a luxurious outdoor restaurant.

6 Estadi Olímpic
MAP B5 ■ Av de l'Estadi 60 ■ Museum: open 10am–6pm Tue–Sat, 10am–2:30pm Sun ■ Adm for museum ■ www.estadiolimpic.cat

The stadium was first built for the 1936 Workers' Olympics, which were cancelled with the outbreak of the Spanish Civil War *(see pp38–9)*. The original Neo-Classical façade is still in place, but the stadium was rebuilt for the 1992 Olympic Games *(see p39)*. The interactive Museu Olímpic i de l'Esport nearby is dedicated to all aspects of sport. You can also view the stadium from the upper levels.

7 Pavelló Mies van der Rohe
MAP B4 ■ Av Francesc Ferrer i Guàrdia 7 ■ Open 10am–8pm daily ■ Adm (free for under 16s) ■ miesbcn.com

You might wonder exactly what this box-like pavilion of stone, marble, onyx and glass is doing in the middle of Montjuïc's monumental architecture. This architectural gem was Germany's contribution to the 1929 International Exhibition. Built by Ludwig Mies van der Rohe (1886–1969), the Rationalist pavilion was soon demolished, but reconstructed in 1986. Inside, the sculpture *Morning* by Georg Kolbe (1877–1947) is reflected in a small lake.

8 Palau Sant Jordi
MAP A4 ■ Pg Olímpic 5–7 ■ Open 10am–6pm Sat & Sun ■ www.palausantjordi.cat

The biggest star of all the Olympic facilities is this steel-and-glass indoor stadium (closed to the public) and multipurpose installation designed by Japanese architect Arata Isozaki. Holding around 17,000 people, the stadium is the home of the city's basketball team. The esplanade – a surreal forest of concrete and metal pillars – was designed by Aiko Isozaki, Arata's wife. Further down the hill are the indoor and outdoor Bernat Picornell Olympic pools, both of which are open to the public.

Palau Sant Jordi

9 Poble Espanyol
MAP A3 ■ Av Francesc Ferrer i Guàrdia ■ Open 9am–8pm Mon, 9am–midnight Tue–Thu & Sun, 9am–3am Fri, 9am–4pm Sat ■ Adm ■ www.poble-espanyol.com

This Spanish *poble* (village) features famous buildings and streets from around Spain recreated in full-scale. Poble Espanyol has become a centre for arts and crafts, including an impressive glass-blowers' workshop, and is one of the city's most popular attractions. There are many shops selling local crafts and also plenty of restaurants and cafés.

Traditional alleys of Poble Espanyol

10 CaixaForum
MAP B3 ■ Av Francesc Ferrer i Guàrdia 6–8 ■ Open 10am–8pm daily ■ Adm ■ caixaforum.es

The Fundació La Caixa's impressive collection of contemporary art is housed in a former textile factory built in 1911 by Catalan Modernista architect Puig i Cadafalch. Restored and opened as a gallery in 2002, it assembles almost 800 works by Spanish and foreign artists, shown in rotation along with temporary international exhibitions. The roof terrace offers great views of the city.

A DAY IN MONTJUÏC

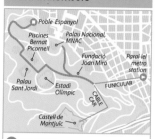

▶ MORNING

To get to the **Fundació Joan Miró** (see pp28–9) before the crowds and with energy to spare, hop on the funicular from Paral·lel metro station. It is a short walk from the funicular to the museum, where you'll need an hour and a half to absorb the impressive collection of Miró paintings, sketches and sculptures. When you've had your fill of contemporary art, refuel with a *cafè amb llet* (see p65) on the restaurant terrace before backtracking along Av de Miramar and jumping on the cable car up to **Castell de Montjuïc** (see p95). Wander the castle gardens and look out over the city and the bustling docks. Return to Av de Miramar by cable car and pop back in to the Miró Foundation for a simple lunch at the café (note there are quite a few eating options on Montjuïc). Then follow signs for MNAC in the **Palau Nacional** (see p95).

AFTERNOON

After lunch, spend time admiring the extraordinary Romanesque art collection at **MNAC** (see pp20–21). When you exit, turn right and follow the signs to the Olympic complex. The **Estadi Olímpic** is worth a look, but the silver-domed **Palau Sant Jordi** steals the limelight. Spend the late afternoon cooling down with a dip in the fantastic open-air pool at nearby Bernat Picornell. From here it is a short stroll to the **Poble Espanyol,** where you can settle in at a terrace bar in Plaça Major.

See map on p94 ←

Parks and Gardens

1 Jardins Mossèn Costa i Llobera
MAP C5

These are among Europe's most important cactus and succulent gardens. They are particularly impressive as the sun sets, when surreal shapes and shadows emerge.

2 Jardí Botànic
MAP A5 ▪ Open Apr–Sep: 10am–8pm daily; Oct–Mar: 10am–5pm daily ▪ Adm (free first Sun of month, every Sun after 3pm) ▪ museuciencies.cat

Barcelona's botanical gardens are found among the stadiums used in the Olympics of 1992. Dating from 1999, they boast hundreds of examples of typical Mediterranean flora. Don't miss the charming Jardí Botànic Històric nearby *(see p71)*.

3 Jardins Mossèn Cinto Verdaguer
MAP C5

The best time to visit these wonderfully elegant gardens is during spring, when the plants are in blossom and the colours and scents are in full force.

4 Jardins del Castell
MAP B5

Cannons dotted among the rose bushes and pathways along the walls of a flower-filled moat are the highlights of these gardens which ring the castle.

5 Jardins del Teatre Grec
MAP C4

Reminiscent of the Hanging Gardens of Babylon, this gracious oasis surrounding the Greek amphitheatre is officially known as La Rosadela.

6 Jardins de Miramar
MAP C5

Opposite the Miramar, these gardens are scattered with stairways leading to enchanting leafy groves with vistas across the city and the port area.

7 Jardins Laribal
MAP B4

This multilevel park hides a small Modernista house by architect Puig i Cadafalch and the Font del Gat, a drinking fountain which has inspired many local songs.

8 Jardins de Joan Maragall
MAP B4 ▪ Open 10am–3pm Sat & Sun

An avenue lined with sculptures by Frederic Marès and Ernest Maragall is the main delight in the Jardins de Joan Maragall, which also has the last of the city's *ginjoler* trees.

A sculpture at Joan Brossa gardens

9 Jardins de Joan Brossa
MAP C5

The variety of grasses and trees alone make Joan Brossa gardens truly fascinating. A cross between city gardens and a woodland park, these gardens come into their own in spring, but are popular all year- thanks to the musical instruments, climbing frames and a flying fox.

10 El Mirador del Llobregat
MAP A3

A viewing area with small gardens nearby, this is the only place in the city where you can see the plains of the Llobregat stretching below.

Restaurants, Cafés and Bars

PRICE CATEGORIES

For a three-course meal for one with half a bottle of wine (or equivalent meal), including taxes and extra charges.

€ under €35   €€ €35–50   €€€ over €50

1 Pizza del Sortidor
MAP C4 ▪ C/Blasco de Garay 46 ▪ 93 173 04 90 ▪ Closed Sun D, Mon, Tue–Fri L ▪ No credit cards ▪ €

A local favourite, this restaurant offers excellent wood-fired pizzas, beer and great barrelled wine.

2 Seco
MAP C5 ▪ Pg Montjuïc 74 ▪ 93 329 63 74 ▪ Closed Mon & D daily ▪ €

A café with a summer terrace, Seco serves the local cuisine as well as delicious cakes and snacks.

3 El Sortidor
MAP C4 ▪ Pl del Sortidor 5 ▪ 63 634 26 11 ▪ Closed Mon ▪ €

Boasting original stained-glass doors and tiled floors from 1908, El Sortidor serves meals in a romantic setting.

4 La Tomaquera
MAP C4 ▪ C/Margarit 58 ▪ 675 902 389 ▪ Closed Sun D, Mon, Aug & Easter week ▪ €

Gorge on delicious Catalan home food at bargain prices at this restaurant. The snails served here are considered the best in town.

5 El Lliure
MAP B4 ▪ Pg Santa Madrona 40-46 ▪ Closed Sun & Mon–Fri D (except on days with performances) ▪ €

The Lliure theatre has a café with an adjoining restaurant and terrace area. Ideal for having a meal before a show.

6 La Caseta del Migdia
MAP B6 ▪ Mirador del Migdia ▪ Closed Apr–Sep: Mon & Tue; Oct–Mar: Mon–Fri ▪ €

Leave the city behind and head for this lofty outdoor bar *(see p60)* at

The stylish La Caseta del Migdia

the top of Montjuïc, where you can enjoy ice-cold drinks, a welcome breeze and amazing views.

7 La Federica
MAP D4 ▪ C/de Salvà 3 ▪ 93 600 59 01 ▪ Closed Sun & Mon ▪ €

This vintage-style bar serves brunch as well as tasty and imaginative tapas to go with its good range of cocktails.

8 Bar Calders
MAP C4 ▪ C/Parlament 25 ▪ 93 329 93 49 ▪ Closed Mon–Fri L ▪ €

This sought-after terrace spot *(see p61)* is ideal for relaxing over a *vermut (see p65)* or an expertly mixed gin and tonic.

9 Tickets Bar
MAP C4 ▪ Av Paral·lel 164 ▪ 93 292 42 52 ▪ Closed Tue–Fri L, Sun, Mon, 3 weeks in Aug, Christmas & New Year ▪ €€

Prepare to be blown away by the incredible tapas at this Michelin-starred restaurant *(see p63)*. Be sure to reserve ahead.

10 Quimet & Quimet
MAP C4 ▪ C/Poeta Cabanyes 25 ▪ 93 442 31 42 ▪ Closed Sat, Sun & three weeks in Aug ▪ €

This tiny bodega has standing room only, but serves delicious tapas and wonderful wines.

See map on p94

🔟 The Seafront

The azure waters of the Mediterranean are only ever a few metro stops away. The city's beaches were once hidden behind an industrial wasteland, but things changed radically in preparation for the 1992 Olympics. The plan was to create a city *oberta al mar* (open to the

Statue, Parc de la Ciutadella

sea); the result is phenomenal. Sandy beaches and shady palm trees now stretch from Barceloneta to the yacht-filled Port Olímpic and beyond. Behind it is Poblenou, a once humble neighbourhood that has been transformed and is now a hub for tech companies and design studios. Just inland, the leafy expanse of the Parc de la Ciutadella, with its fountain and boating lake, is the perfect green retreat.

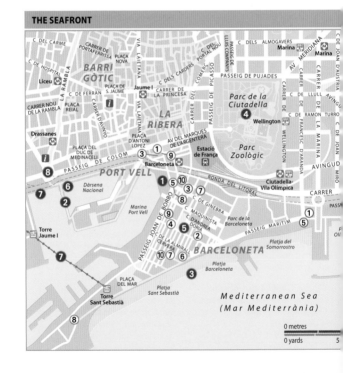

THE SEAFRONT

1 Museu d'Història de Catalunya

MAP N6 ▪ Pl Pau Vila 3 ▪ Open 10am–7pm Tue–Sat (to 8pm Wed), 10am–2:30pm Sun ▪ Adm; free first Sun of the month ▪ www.mhcat.cat

Housed in the Palau de Mar, a renovated portside warehouse, this museum *(see p53)* offers a broad, interactive exploration of Catalonia's history since prehistoric times. Kids especially will have a ball with the engaging exhibits, such as a Civil War-era bunker and a recreated Catalan bar from the 1960s with an ancient *futbolín* (table football) game.

2 Rambla de Mar

MAP E5 ▪ Moll d'Espanya ▪ Maremagnum: open 10am–10pm daily

Saunter along the Rambla de Mar, a floating wooden pier that leads to the flashy Maremagnum

The floating Rambla de Mar pier

mall. It is open every day of the year, which makes it particularly popular with shoppers on Sundays.

3 Beaches

MAP E6

If a splash in the Mediterranean interests you, head down to the end of La Rambla, wander along the palm tree-lined Moll de la Fusta, and down the restaurant-packed Passeig Joan de Borbó where the sea beckons. More than 7 km (4.3 miles) of blue-flag beaches stretch north from Barceloneta to Port Olímpic and beyond. The seawater quality can vary, depending on the tides. Facilities are top-notch, including showers, deck chairs, lifeguards and beach volleyball courts. The beachfront boardwalk is the perfect spot for a stroll. Look out for Rebecca Horn's beautiful sculpture, *L'Estel Ferit* (The Wounded Star), a local landmark.

4 Parc de la Ciutadella

MAP R4 ▪ Pg Pujades ▪ Open 10am–10:30pm daily; zoo timings vary ▪ Zoo: adm

Colourful parrots take flight from the top of palm trees and orange groves dotted around this famous park. A perfect picnic spot, the city's largest central green space *(see p48)* is particularly popular on Sunday after-noons when people gather to play instruments, relax, head out onto the boating lake for a punt, or visit the museum and the zoo. The north-eastern corner of the park features a magnificent fountain – a cascading waterfall topped by a chariot rider flanked by griffins caught mid-roar.

Top 10 Sights
see pp100–103

Restaurants and Cafés see p105

Bars and Tapas Bars see p104

Old buildings of Barceloneta

5 Barceloneta
MAP F5

A portside warren of narrow streets, small squares and ancient bars, this traditional neighbourhood of *pescadors* (fishermen) and *mariners* (sailors) seems worlds apart from the megamalls and disco lights of nearby Port Olímpic. A refreshing foray through this tight-knit community yields a glimpse into the Barcelona of 150 years ago. Older couples still pull chairs out onto the street to gossip and watch the world go by, and small seafood restaurants serve a *menú del dia* of whatever is fresh off the boat. Running the length of Barceloneta's western edge is the Passeig Joan de Borbó, which is lined with restaurants serving *mariscs* (shellfish) and paellas.

6 Pailebot Santa Eulàlia
MAP L6 ■ Moll de la Fusta
■ Opening times vary, check website
■ Adm ■ www.mmb.cat

Bobbing in the water at the Moll de la Fusta (Timber Quay) is this restored three-mast schooner, originally christened *Carmen Flores*. It first set sail from Spain in 1918. On journeys to Cuba, the ship used to transport textiles and salt, returning with tobacco, coffee, cereals and wood. In 1997, the Museu Marítim *(see p87)* bought and restored the ship as part of a project to create a collection of seaworthy historical Catalan vessels.

7 Boat and Cable-Car Trips
MAP E5/6 ■ Telefèric: from Torre San Sebastià ■ Las Golondrinas: Portal de la Pau ■ Approximately every 30 mins from 11:15am ■ https://lasgolondrinas.com ■ Orsom: Portal de la Pau; https://barcelona-orsom.com ■ For timings call 93 441 05 37 ■ barcelona-orsom.com

Observe all the activity at Barcelona's bustling port area from a different perspective, either from the air or the sea. The *Transbordador Aeri* cable cars offer sweeping bird's-eye views of Barcelona and its coast, while the old-fashioned Las Golondrinas "swallow boats" and the Orsom Catamaran make regular sightseeing trips around the harbour, the beaches and the port area.

8 Monument a Colom
MAP E5

This 60-m- (197-ft-) high column was built between 1882 and 1888 for Barcelona's Universal Exhibition and commemorates Christopher Columbus's first voyage to the Americas – it was in Barcelona that Columbus met Ferdinand and Isabel on his return. Columbus himself stands on top of the column *(see p16)*, pointing out to sea, supposedly towards the New World but actually towards Italy. A lift (closed due to COVID-19) swooshes up the column to a viewing

platform located just below
Columbus's feet, which
offers fabulous 360° views.

9 Poblenou and Palo Alto Design Complex

MAP H5 ■ www.poblenouurbandis
trict.com/en ■ www.paloalto.barcelona

The increasingly fashionable Poblenou
district has become a hub for startups
and tech companies. A burgeoning
number of trendy cafés and shops
have opened, bold contemporary
buildings are sprouting up and the
old industrial warehouses are being
restored and repurposed. One
contains BD Design, the city's most
prestigious design showroom, while
the Palo Alto complex houses the
studios of big-name designers.

10 Museu de Ciències Naturals

Pl Leonardo da Vinci 4–5, Parc del
Fórum ■ 93 256 60 02 ■ Open 10am–
8pm Tue–Sat ■ Adm; free first Sun
of the month, every Sun after 3pm
■ museuciencies.cat

The main site of the Museu de
Ciències Naturals occupies a raised
triangular building constructed by
Herzog & de Meuron for Barcelona's
Forum 2004 event. This is a great,
family-friendly place, with an appealing mix of contemporary exhibits and
old-fashioned cabinets full of stuffed
animals. The main exhibition is a
"biography of the earth", with interactive audiovisual displays about
"the origins of the world. There is a
special area for the under-7s to learn
about science, plus a library and
café. The Jardí Botànic (see p98)
is also part of the Museu de
Ciències Naturals.

**Museu de Ciències
Naturals**

▶ MORNING

Begin your port *passeig* (stroll)
with a visit to the **Museu Marítim**
(see p87), where you can sense
Barcelona's status as one of
the most active ports in the
Mediterranean. From here, head
towards the Monument a Colom
and stroll along the Moll de la
Fusta to admire the **Pailebot
Santa Eulàlia**, which has been
meticulously restored by the
museum. Take a stroll down
the **Rambla de Mar** (see p101),
an undulating wooden drawbridge
that leads to the **Maremagnum**
(see p67) shopping mall. At the
start of the pier, take a boat
ride on the Orsom Catamaran,
where you can grab a drink
and a snack. Soak up the
sunshine and the port skyline
while sprawled out on a net just
inches above the water. Back
on land, stroll down the Moll
d'Espanya and turn towards the
traditional fisherman's quarter
of **Barceloneta**, an atmospheric
pocket of narrow streets and
timeworn bars. Get a real taste
of old-style Barcelona at the
boisterous tapas place, **El Vaso
de Oro** (C/Balboa 6). Head to the
bar and savour tasty seafood.

AFTERNOON

Head to Passeig Joan de Borbó
and the beach. Douse yourself
in the Med, then siesta in the
afternoon sun. Pick yourself
up with sangria at the beachside **Salamanca** *xiringuito* (at
the end of Pg Joan de Borbó),
where you can watch the waves
lap the shore as the sun dips
below the horizon.

See map on pp100–101

Bars and Tapas Bars

The opulent poolside club Arola

① Arola
MAP G5 ■ Hotel Arts, C/Marina 19–21 ■ www.hotelartsbarcelona.com/en/arola

A, summer-only poolside bar at the Hotel Arts, the Arola has huge white beds covered with silk cushions, DJ sessions, and a range of cocktails.

② Xiringuito Escribà
Av Litoral 62, Platja de Bogatell ■ www.restaurantsescriba.com

A beach bar right on the sand, this spot offers breakfast, tapas, light meals, cocktails and more.

③ Bar Jai Ca
MAP F5 ■ C/Ginebra 13 ■ www.barjaica.com

This is a relaxed neighbourhood favourite. Delicious tapas and good wine are on offer.

④ Mar Bella beach bars
Platja Nova Mar Bella ■ Closed winters

Head to one of the *xiringuitos* (beach bars) found on Barcelona's hippest beach and enjoy the DJ sessions.

⑤ Eclipse
MAP F6 ■ W Hotel, Pl de la Rosa dels Vents 1 ■ www.eclipse-barcelona.com

The spectacular bar on the 26th floor of the W Hotel (commonly known as the Hotel Vela) offers lovely views of the city. Smart dress code.

⑥ Bus Terraza
Parc del Fòrum, Avda del Litoral 488 ■ Opening hours vary ■ www.busterraza.com

There are regular DJ sessions and live jazz concerts at this converted double-decker bus *(see p61)*.

⑦ Segons Mercat
MAP F5 & Q6 ■ C/Balboa 16 ■ 93 310 78 80 ■ Closed Sat, to 1pm Sun

Tuck into tasty tapas from grilled cuttlefish to *patates braves* at this stylish, modern spot, which also serves more substantial rice and seafood dishes.

⑧ La Bombeta
MAP F6 ■ C/Maquinista 33 ■ 93 319 94 45 ■ Closed Wed

This popular, traditional Catalan bar offers a wonderful glimpse of life in Barcelona before the tourists arrived. The house speciality is the *bombas*, deep-fried balls of mashed potatoes served with a spicy tomato sauce. Be prepared to wait for a table.

⑨ Can Ganassa
MAP F6 ■ Pl de la Barceloneta 4–6 ■ 93 252 84 49 ■ Closed Mon

An old-style, family-run tapas bar that has been serving fresh seafood tapas to locals for decades.

⑩ El Vaso de Oro
MAP F5 ■ C/Balboa 6 ■ 933 19 30 98

A traditional bar, El Vaso de Oro has served ice-cold beer and fresh tapas for more than half a century. Grab a stool at the long, narrow counter early; it gets packed very quickly.

Restaurants and Cafés

PRICE CATEGORIES

For a three-course meal for one with half a bottle of wine (or equivalent meal), including taxes and extra charges.

€ under €35 €€ €35–50 €€€ over €50

1 Set Portes
MAP N5 ▪ Pg Isabel II 14
▪ 93 319 30 33 ▪ €€

Founded in 1836, this legendary city institution serves some of the finest Catalan cuisine in the city, including a variety of paellas.

2 El Filferro
MAP F6 ▪ C/Sant Carles 29
▪ 600 83 66 74 ▪ Open 10–1am
Tue–Sun ▪ €

This charming café *(see p64)*, with tables set on the square, is perfect for coffee and cake, a delicious light lunch of Mediterranean specialities or a *vermut* on a summer evening.

3 Green Spot
MAP P5 ▪ C/Reina Cristina 12
▪ 93 802 55 65 ▪ €€

A spacious restaurant with sleek, minimalist design, Green Spot serves some of the best vegan and vegetarian food in the city.

4 Somorrostro
MAP F6 ▪ C/Sant Carles 11
▪ 93 225 00 10 ▪ Open 1pm–midnight daily ▪ €

Sample the superb Catalan dishes prepared with fresh ingredients at this chic restaurant. The menu here changes daily, and the decor generates a relaxed, welcoming vibe.

5 Brunch & Cake By The Sea
MAP F5 ▪ Pg Joan de Borbó 5 ▪ 93 138 35 72 ▪ Open 10am–7pm daily ▪ €

Furnished with a rustic decor, this bright café features an extensive brunch menu of classics such as eggs Benedict. Find vegan and gluten-free options as well as great cakes.

6 Salamanca
MAP F6 ▪ C/Almirall Cervera 34
▪ 93 221 50 33 ▪ €€

This may feel like a tourist trap at first, but the food is top notch. There are plenty of meat dishes on offer.

7 La Roseta
MAP F6 ▪ C/Meer 37 ▪ 673 81 69 76 ▪ Open 8:30am–7pm daily ▪ €

This cosy little place offers delicious homemade cakes, including a legendary cheesecake, as well as great coffee and sandwiches.

8 El Gallito
Passeig del Mare Nostrum 19
▪ 933 12 35 85 ▪ €€

This stylish spot serves a range of delicacies, including Mediterranean rice seafood dishes.

9 Oaxaca
MAP F5 ▪ Pla de Palau 20
▪ 93 018 06 59 ▪ Open 1pm–midnight daily ▪ €€

This is one of the best Mexican restaurants in the city, offering authentic and creative dishes such as *Sopa Azteca con tortillas* (soup) or quesadillas with spider crab.

10 La Mar Salada
MAP E6 ▪ Pg de Joan de Borbó 58
▪ 93 221 21 27 ▪ Open Wed–Mon ▪ €€

Light and bright, this restaurant near the sea serves modern fare with an emphasis on seafood, such as monkfish served with wild mushrooms and artichokes, and paella. The weekday set lunch menu is great value.

Tàrtar de sorell at La Mar Salada

See map on pp100–101

TOP10 Eixample

If the old town is the heart of Barcelona and green Tibidabo and Montjuïc its lungs, the Eixample is its nervous system – its economic and commercial core. The area took shape in 1860, when the city was allowed to expand beyond the medieval walls. Based on plans by Catalan engineer Ildefons Cerdà, the Eixample is laid out on a grid. Construction continued into the 20th century at a time when the elite was patronizing the most daring architects. *Modernisme* was flourishing and the area became home to the best of Barcelona's Modernista architecture, with its elegant façades and

Rooftop, La Pedrera

balconies. Today, enchanting cafés, funky design shops, gourmet restaurants and hip bars draw the professional crowd, which has adopted the neighbourhood as its own.

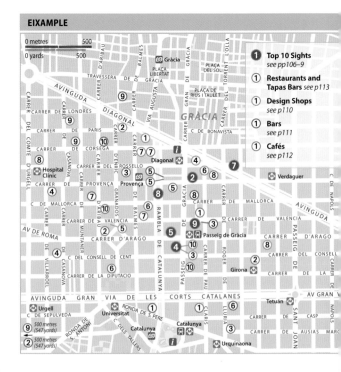

EIXAMPLE

1	**Top 10 Sights** see pp106–9
1	**Restaurants and Tapas Bars** see p113
1	**Design Shops** see p110
1	**Bars** see p111
1	**Cafés** see p112

1 Sagrada Família
Gaudí's wizardry culminated in this enchanting, wild, unconventional church (see pp12–15), which dominates the city skyline.

2 La Pedrera
A daring, surreal fantasyland, and Gaudí's most remarkable civic work (see pp26–7).

3 Sant Pau Recinte Modernista
MAP H1 ■ C/Sant Antoni Maria Claret 167 ■ 93 553 78 11 ■ Open 10am–5pm Tue–Sat, 10am–2:30pm Sun ■ Adm; guided tours in English 11am daily ■ www.santpaubarcelona.org

Founded in 1401, the Hospital de la Santa Creu i de Sant Pau (see pp44–5) was a fully-functioning hospital until 2009, when all medical activities were moved to a new building and the UNESCO World Heritage Site exquisitely restored and opened

Sant Pau Recinte Modernista

to the public as a cultural centre. The Art Nouveau site, created by Domènech i Montaner between 1902 and 1930, is a tribute to *Modernisme* – and Domènech's answer to Gaudí's Sagrada Família. There are eight pavilions, which recall the history of Catalonia using murals, mosaics and sculptures, and other buildings, all linked by underground tunnels. The buildings are interlaced by gardens and courtyards. The site is part of the Ruta del Modernisme (see p137).

4 Mansana de la Discòrdia
MAP E2 ■ Pg de Gràcia 35–45

At the heart of the city's *Quadrat d'Or* (Golden Square) lies this stunning row of houses. The "block of discord" is so named because of the dramatic contrast between its three flagship buildings. Built between 1900 and 1907 by the three Modernista greats, rival architects Gaudí, Domènech i Montaner and Puig i Cadafalch, the houses were commissioned by competing bourgeois families. Domènech is represented by the ornate Casa Lleó Morera (see p45), Puig by the Gothic-inspired Casa Amatller (see p45), and Gaudí by the whimsical Casa Batlló (see p45). Among them, the Casa Amatller and Casa Batlló can be toured. The houses at Nos. 37 and 39 add to the splendour of the block. At No. 39 is the Museu del Perfum (see p43).

ILDEFONS CERDÀ

Ildefons Cerdà's design for the new city, comprising a uniform grid of square blocks, received backing in 1859. Reflecting Cerdà's utopian socialist ideals, each block was to have a garden-like courtyard surrounded by uniform flats. Real estate vultures soon intervened, though, and the courtyards were converted into warehouses and factories. Today these green spaces are gradually being reinstated.

The Els Encants market space

6 Els Encants

MAP H3 ■ Av Meridiana 69 ■ 92 246 30 30 ■ Open 9am–8pm Mon, Wed, Fri, Sat ■ encantsbarcelona.com

For almost a hundred years, the Els Encants market *(see p68)* was a rambling, chaotic jumble of street stalls. In 2014 it got a striking new home and now its stalls are arranged in a gentle upward spiral under a mirrored, angled canopy designed to keep off the sun. As well as antiques, bric-a-brac and plain old junk, you'll find textiles, household goods, records and vintage clothes here.

7 Casa Terrades – "Casa de les Punxes"

MAP F2 ■ Av Diagonal 416 ■ Guided tours 9am–8pm daily (last entrance by 6pm) ■ Adm ■ casadelespunxes.com

This Gothic-style castle with four towers was designed by Modernista architect Josep Puig i Cadafalch and finished in 1905 for the Terrades sisters. It has always housed private homes. From the outside you can admire the forged ironwork on the balconies, the carved reliefs and the colourful stained-glass windows. The ceramic panels mounted on the façade represent the patriotic symbols of Catalonia.

Cloud and Chair, **Fundació Tàpies**

5 Fundació Tàpies

MAP E2 ■ C/Aragó 255 ■ 93 487 03 15 ■ Open 10am–7pm Tue–Thu & Sat (to 3pm Sun) ■ Adm (free for under 16s) ■ fundaciotapies.org

Paintings and sculptures by Antoni Tàpies (1923–2012), Catalonia's foremost artist, are housed in this early Modernista building *(see pp32–3)*. For a glimpse of what awaits inside, look up – crowning the museum is the artist's eye-catching wire sculpture *Cloud and Chair* (1990). The collection of over 300 pieces covers Tàpies' whole range of work, including abstract pieces such as *Grey Ochre on Brown* (1962). Temporary exhibitions are also held here, with past shows by Mario Herz and Hans Hacke.

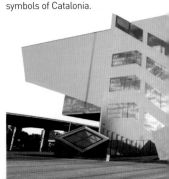

8 Rambla de Catalunya
MAP E2

This elegant extension of the better-known Rambla is a more upmarket version. Lined with trees that form a leafy green tunnel in summer, it boasts scores of pretty façades and shops, including the Modernista Farmàcia Bolos (No. 77). The avenue (see pp66–7) teems with terrace bars and cafés.

9 Museu Egipci
MAP E2 ▪ C/València 284 ▪ 93 488 01 88 ▪ Open 11am– 3pm & 4–7pm Mon–Sat ▪ Adm ▪ www.museuegipci.com

Spain's most important Egyptology museum houses more than 350 exhibits from over 3,000 years of Ancient Egyptian history. Exhibits include terracotta figures, human and animal mummies, and a bust of the goddess Sekhmet (700–300 BC).

10 Museu del Disseny de Barcelona
MAP H3 ▪ Pl de les Glòries Catalanes 37–38 ▪ 93 256 68 00 ▪ Open 10am– 2pm & 3–8pm Tue–Sun ▪ ajuntament. barcelona.cat/museudeldisseny

A monolithic hulk hosts this museum showcasing architecure, fashion, product and graphic design. The glass-and-zinc-clad building is a design statement in its own right. It also houses two leading independent, non-profit associations promoting design and architecture, the Foment de les Arts i del Disseny (FAD) and Barcelona Centre de Disseny (BCD).

Disseny Museum

THE MODERNISTA ROUTE

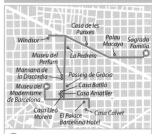

▶ **MORNING**

Visit the **Museu del Modernisme de Barcelona** (C/Balmes 48, www. mmbcn.cat) for an introduction to Catalan Art Nouveau via a series of temporary exhibitions, then stroll around the gardens of the university. Head east along Gran Via past the **El Palace Barcelona Hotel** (see p142) and turn right down C/Bruc and right again onto C/Casp for a glimpse of Gaudí's **Casa Calvet** (see p113). Walk two blocks west to the majestic Pg de Gràcia; then go right again three blocks to the **Mansana de la Discòrdia** (see p107) and explore **Casa Lleó Morera, Casa Amatller** or **Casa Batlló** – or all three (see p45) if you have the time. Sniff around the **Museu del Perfum** and **Regia** perfume shop (see p110) before continuing north to marvel at Gaudí's **La Pedrera** (see pp26–7). Take a lunch break at **Windsor** (see p113). Their set menu is an enjoyable way to experience Catalan haute cuisine.

AFTERNOON

After lunch, return to Pg de Gràcia then turn right along Av Diagonal, taking in the fairy-tale **Casa de les Punxes** (see p45) at No. 416. Continue on Diagonal, turning left at Pg Sant Joan to see the exhibition on Modernism in the Palau Macaya at No. 108. Then stroll along C/Mallorca to the **Sagrada Família** (see pp12– 15). Here you can take in the Nativity Façade and rest weary legs in the Plaça de Gaudí before climbing the bell towers for a breathtaking view of the city.

See map on pp106–7 ←

Design Shops

A dazzling display at Pilma

1 Pilma
MAP E1 ■ Av Diagonal 403
■ Closed Sun ■ www.pilma.com

This shop sells modern furniture and interior accessories by big names, as well as cutting-edge creations by a range of Catalan designers.

2 DomésticoShop
MAP D1 ■ C/ Diagonal 419
■ Closed Sun ■ www.domestico shop.com

A household name in the interior design world, this split-level shop has furniture, domestic knick-knacks and a cute café.

3 Regia
MAP E2 ■ Pg de Gràcia 39
■ Closed Sun ■ www.regia.es

The biggest perfume shop in the city has over 1,000 scents to choose from, including all the leading brands, and smaller makers. The space also plays host to the Museu del Perfum (see p43).

4 Dos i Una
MAP E2 ■ C/Roselló 275
■ 932 17 70 32

This designer gift shop with a steel-tiled floor and psychedelic colour scheme sells "made in Barcelona" items and souvenirs.

5 Odd Kiosk
MAP D2 ■ C/València 222

Barcelona's first LGBT+ news kiosk is slick and is packed with style magazines, fanzines and cards.

6 Nanimarquina
MAP F2 ■ Rosselló 256
■ Closed Sun & Mon
■ nanimarquina.com

Exquisite handmade carpets and textiles are sold in this artful shop.

7 Azul Tierra
MAP E2 ■ C/Córsega 276–282
■ Closed Sun & Mon ■ azultierra.es

A huge, warehouse-style space with exquisite furniture as well as lighting and all kinds of decorative objects ranging from mirrors to candles.

8 Àmbit
MAP F2 ■ C/Aragó 338
■ 93 459 24 20

This huge showroom has a wide range of furniture from top designers, plus a selection of kilims, carpets, cushions, mirrors and other decorative objects.

The chic and cosy Nordik Think

9 Nordik Think
MAP D1 ■ C/Casanova 214
■ Closed Sun ■ es.nordicthink.com/showroom

This beautiful showroom for Scandinavian design displays elegant and minimalist furnishings, lighting, decorative objects and much more by top designers from northern Europe.

10 Bagués Joieria
MAP E2 ■ Pg de Gràcia 41
■ Closed Sun ■ www.bagues-masriera.com

Every piece at this jewellery shop is handmade using traditional methods.

Bars

1 Milano
MAP E3 ▪ Ronda Universitat 35
▪ 93 112 71 50 ▪ Opening times vary

Sip on your cocktails while lounging on the red-velvet sofas at Milano. There are periodic live jazz performances as well.

2 Xixbar
MAP C4 ▪ C/Rocafort 19 ▪ 93 416 13 99 ▪ Opening times vary

A reputed bar that prepares gin and tonics with the city's best spirits sold in the shop next door.

3 Les Gens Que J'aime
MAP E2 ▪ C/Valencia 286 ▪ 93 215 68 79 ▪ Open 6pm–1am Mon–Thu & Sun, 7pm–1am Fri–Sat

This is an ideal place to have a drink and enjoy lounge music after exploring the area around Passeig de Gràcia and Rambla Catalunya.

4 Slow Bar
MAP D1 ▪ C/París 186 ▪ 93 368 14 55 ▪ Open 7pm–5am Mon–Fri, 6pm–6am Sat

This red-hued bar also has a club and live music venue. It offers a range of cocktails which you can sample.

5 Bar Marfil
MAP E2 ▪ Rambla de Catalunya 104 ▪ 93 550 06 06 ▪ Open 8am–midnight daily

Located inside Hotel Murmuri, this is a trendy bar on a fancy shopping street. Sink into a plush faux-Baroque armchair and sip a cocktail.

6 Cotton House Hotel Terrace
MAP F3 ▪ Gran Via de les Corts Catalans 670 ▪ 93 450 50 45 ▪ Open 7am–midnight daily

A jungle of plants, elegant wicker furnishings and fabulous cocktails make this chic hotel terrace bar *(see p61)* the perfect place for a drink.

7 Ideal
MAP D2 ▪ C/Aribau 89 ▪ 93 453 10 28 ▪ Open noon–2:30am daily

Opened by legendary barman José María Gotarda in 1931, this place offers more than 80 kinds of whisky.

8 Jardin del Alma
MAP E2 ▪ C/Mallorca 271 ▪ 93 216 44 78 ▪ Open 4–8pm daily

An enchanting secret garden awaits at this chic hotel *(see p61)*. Sink into a plush sofa and enjoy a glass of wine and some tapas.

9 Ajoblanco
MAP E1 ▪ C/Tuset 20 ▪ 93 667 87 66 ▪ Opening times vary

This swish eatery is a hotspot for cocktails and wines in the evening. There's live music on Wednesdays and fun DJs on the weekends.

10 Dry Martini
MAP D2 ▪ C/Aribau 162 ▪ 93 217 50 72 ▪ Opening times vary

A classic and elegant venue where extraordinarily talented bartenders are ready to prepare your favourite cocktail. Jazz sounds play unobtrusively in the background.

Bar area at Dry Martini

See map on pp106–7

Cafés

Gallery café Galeria Cosmo is decorated with artworks

1 Laie Llibreria Cafè
MAP E3 ■ C/Pau Claris 85
■ 93 318 17 39 ■ Closed Sun

A cultural meeting place with a lively atmosphere, airy terrace and one of the best bookshops in town *(see p64)*. There's an excellent set lunch.

2 Cafè del Centre
MAP F3 ■ C/Girona 69
■ 93 488 11 01 ■ Closed Sun

Said to be the oldest café in the Eixample area, with dark wooden interiors that have not changed for a century, this is an unpretentious spot for a quiet coffee.

3 Casa Alfonso
MAP F3 ■ C/Roger de Llúria 6
■ 93 301 97 83 ■ Closed Sun

This classy café has been in business since 1929. It offers arguably the best *pernil* (serrano ham) in the city.

4 Oma Bistro
MAP D3 ■ C/Consell de
Cent 227 ■ 93 348 70 49

A welcoming, loft-style space with colourful, mismatched furnishings, Oma Bistro is a local favourite. It is known for its superb brunch.

5 Pastelerias Mauri
MAP E2 ■ Rambla Catalunya
102 ■ 93 215 10 20 ■ Closed Sun D

One of the best pastry shops in town ever since its opening in 1929. Enjoy a hot drink with an elaborate dessert in Modernista surroundings.

6 Galeria Cosmo
MAP E2 ■ C/Enric Granados 3
■ 93 105 79 92

This art gallery café, located on a semi-pedestrianized street, offers sandwiches, cakes and tapas.

7 Baluard
MAP F2 ■ Praktik Bakery
Hotel, C/Provença ■ 93 269 48 18
■ Closed Sun D

Located inside the lobby of a Scandinavian-style urban hotel, this café-bakery offers gourmet salads, sandwiches and pastries.

8 Velódromo
MAP D1 ■ C/Muntaner 213
■ 93 430 60 22

This historic bar with original 1930s furnishings was reopened by celebrity chef Carles Abellan. The menu features versions of Catalan classics.

9 Manso's Café
MAP C4 ■ C/Manso 1 ■ 93 348
63 46

Enjoy fabulous homemade cakes, great coffee (with a choice of milks), delicious soups and quiches at this café. Dine on the little terrace or in the cosy interior.

10 Granja Petitbo
MAP D2 ■ C/Mallorca 194
■ www.granjapetitbo.com

Sink into a sofa and tuck into light meals at this café. Plenty of vegan and vegetarian options are available.

Restaurants and Tapas Bars

PRICE CATEGORIES

For a three-course meal for one with half a bottle of wine (or equivalent meal), including taxes and extra charges.

€ under €35 ▪ €€ €35–50 ▪ €€€ over €50

1 Joséphine
MAP E2 ▪ C/Pau Claris 147 ▪ 93 853 55 40 ▪ Closed Sat & Sun ▪ €

Coffee and snacks are served all day at this French colonial café. There's also an evening menu.

2 Cinc Sentits
MAP D2 ▪ C/Aribau 58 ▪ 93 323 94 90 ▪ Closed Mon–Wed ▪ €€€

Indulge the five senses (*cinc sentits* in Catalan) at this stylish restaurant where the chef's contemporary interpretations of classic Catalan cuisine have won it a Michelin star.

3 Igueldo
MAP E2 ▪ C/Rosselló 186 ▪ 93 452 25 55 ▪ Closed Sun ▪ €€

Updated Basque cuisine is served in elegant surroundings here (see p62). There's a tapas counter too.

4 Disfrutar
MAP D2 ▪ Carrer de Villarroel, 163 ▪ 93 348 68 96 ▪ Closed Sun & Mon ▪ €€

Located in front of Ninot market, Disfrutar (see p63) lets you feast on avant-garde dishes that offer a complete gastronomic experience.

5 El Principal del Eixample
MAP E2 ▪ C/Provença 286–288 ▪ Closed Sun D ▪ €€

Excellent Mediterranean dishes are served here on the terrace garden. The set lunch menu is good value.

6 Cervecería Catalana
MAP E2 ▪ C/Mallorca 236 ▪ 93 216 03 68 ▪ €

Some of the best tapas in town served with a variety of beers, close to the Rambla de Catalunya.

7 Windsor
MAP E1 ▪ C/Còrsega 286 ▪ 93 237 75 88 ▪ Closed 3 weeks in Aug ▪ €€€

Catalan *haute cuisine* is served (see p62) in elegant surroundings with chandeliers and red upholstered furniture. There's also a garden for alfresco dining.

8 La Taverna del Clínic
MAP D2 ▪ C/Rosselló 155 ▪ 93 410 42 21 ▪ Closed Sun ▪ €€

This bar (see p62) looks ordinary, but its excellent, contemporary tapas is among the best in the city.

9 Paco Meralgo
MAP D1 ▪ C/Muntaner 171 ▪ 93 430 90 27 ▪ €

This bright, stylish tapas bar has a gourmet menu based on recipes from around the country.

10 Moments
MAP E3 ▪ Pg de Gràcia 38–40 ▪ 93 151 87 81 ▪ Closed Tue–Thu L & Sun ▪ €€€

Set in the ultra-luxurious Mandarin Oriental (see p145), Moments has been awarded two Michelin stars for its sublime renditions of Catalan classics, from langoustine tartare to scallops with artichokes. A la carte and tasting menus offered.

Moments at the Mandarin Oriental

See map on pp106–7

TOP 10 Gràcia, Tibidabo and Zona Alta

The hilly Zona Alta covers several neighbourhoods, from the moneyed Pedralbes and Tibidabo to bohemian Gràcia. The area offers stunning views and regal attractions, but what sets it apart are its 15 parks – the best are Collserola, spread like green baize over Tibidabo mountain, and Gaudí's Park Güell. Cosmopolitan Gràcia's political tradition and gypsy community have long drawn artists and writers to its labyrinthine streets, and its squares are now home to lively bars and stores.

Torre de Collserola

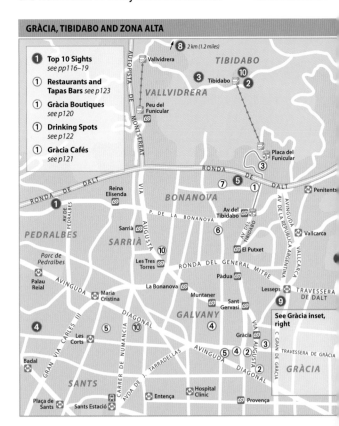

GRÀCIA, TIBIDABO AND ZONA ALTA

1. **Top 10 Sights** see pp116–19
1. **Restaurants and Tapas Bars** see p123
1. **Gràcia Boutiques** see p120
1. **Drinking Spots** see p122
1. **Gràcia Cafés** see p121

8 2 km (1.2 miles)

Vallvidrera — TIBIDABO
3 Tibidabo 10
VALLVIDRERA
Peu del Funicular

Plaça del Funicular
3
RONDA DE DALT
Reina Elisenda
7 5 1 Penitents
BONANOVA
Av del Tibidabo
P. DE LA BONANOVA
Sarrià 6 Vallcarca
PEDRALBES SARRIÀ El Putxet
Parc de Pedralbes Les Tres Torres
RONDA DEL GENERAL MITRE
Palau Reial Pàdua
Maria Cristina La Bonanova Lesseps TRAVESSERA
Muntaner Sant DE DALT
Gervasi
4 GALVANY
Les Corts 4 See Gràcia inset, right
Gràcia TRAVESSERA DE GRÀCIA
Badal AVINGUDA 5 4 2
DIAGONAL GRÀCIA
SANTS Hospital Clínic
Plaça de Sants Sants Estació Entença Provença

Previous pages The surreal façade of the Teatre-Museu Dalí, Figueres

1 Monestir de Pedralbes

MAP A1 ▪ C/Baixada del Monestir 9 ▪ Open Apr–Sep: 10am–5pm Tue–Fri (to 7pm Sat, to 8pm Sun); Oct–Mar: 10am–2pm Tue–Fri (to 5pm Sat & Sun) ▪ Adm; free first Sun of the month, every Sun 3–8pm) ▪ monestirpedralbes. barcelona

Named after the Latin *petras albas*, which means "white stones", this outstandingly beautiful Gothic monastery *(see p40)* was founded by Queen Elisenda de Montcada de Piños in 1327 with the support of her husband James II of Aragón. Her alabaster tomb lies in the wall between the church and the impressive three-storey Gothic cloister. The furnished kitchens, cells, infirmary

The Gothic Monestir de Pedralbes

and refectory, which are all well preserved, provide an interesting glimpse into medieval life.

2 Parc d'Atraccions del Tibidabo

MAP B1 ▪ Pl de Tibidabo ▪ Opening times vary, check website ▪ Adm ▪ www.tibidabo.cat

Take the funicular up to the top of Tibidabo's 517-m (1,695-ft) mountain to visit this traditional amusement park, which opened in 1908 *(see p52)*. There are a couple of white-knuckle rides, but the real attractions are the old-fashioned ones, including a beautifully-preserved carousel and a Ferris wheel. There's also the Museu dels Autòmates *(see p43)*, with automatons, mechanical models and a scale model of the park.

3 Torre de Collserola

MAP B1 ▪ Parc de Collserola ▪ Opening times vary, check website ▪ Adm ▪ www.torrede collserola.com

This slender telecommunications tower was designed by British architect Sir Norman Foster. The needle-like upper structure rests on a concrete pillar, anchored by 12 huge steel cables. Rising to a height of 288 m (945 ft), the top is reached by a glass-fronted lift. On a clear day, you can see Montserrat and the Pyrenees.

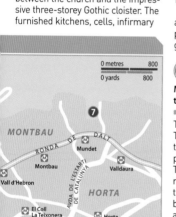

The grand Camp Nou, FC Barcelona's home stadium

Barça Stadium Tour & Museum

MAP A2 ■ Entrance 9 Stadium, Av Arístides Maillol ■ Opening times vary, check website; advance booking recommended ■ Adm ■ www.fc barcelona.com

The Museu del FC Barcelona (see p42), Barcelona's most visited museum, is a must for the fans. Numerous displays of football memorabilia show all you need to know about the club. Work donated by some of Catalonia's top artists is also on display. Admission includes access to Barça's 100,000-seater stadium, Camp Nou, a monument to the city's love affair with the game.

CosmoCaixa Museu de la Ciència

MAP B1 ■ C/Isaac Newton 26 ■ 93 212 60 50 ■ Open 10am–8pm daily ■ Adm (free for under 16s) ■ https://cosmocaixa.es

Barcelona's science museum is a thoroughly stimulating and interactive affair. It occupies a glass-and-steel building, with six of its nine storeys set underground. Displays include a wide range of historic objects, flora and fauna. One of its most important pieces is a recreated section of flooded Amazon rainforest, including fish, reptiles, mammals, birds and plants. A tour through Earth's geological history explains processes such as erosion and sedimentation. There are also innovative temporary exhibitions on environmental issues (see p43).

Park Güell

A UNESCO World Heritage Site, this heady brew of architectural wizardry (see pp22–3) includes trencadís tiling, fairy-tale pavilions, Gothic archways and the columned Sala Hipóstila (originally designed as a market hall). In true Gaudí style, playfulness and symbolism pervade every aspect of the park. The Casa-Museu Gaudí, where Gaudí lived for 20 years, is dedicated to his life.

Parc del Laberint d'Horta

MAP C1 ■ C/German Desvalls ■ Open 10am–dusk daily ■ Adm; free Wed, Sun

In 1802, the Marquès d'Alfarràs hosted a huge party in these wonderful Neo-Classical gardens in honor of Charles IV. Designed by Italian architect Domenico Bagutti, they feature pavilions, a lake, a waterfall, canals and a cypress-tree hedge maze. The gardens are closed in November.

GRÀCIA

Until the late 19th century, Gràcia was a fiercely proud independent city. Despite locals' protests, it became part of Barcelona proper in 1898, but has maintained a sense of separatism and has been a hotbed of political activity. It is now home to a booming cottage industry nurtured by a growing band of artisans. Do not miss the barri's annual fiesta (see p72) in the second week of August.

8 Parc de Collserola

MAP B1 ■ Info point:
C/Església 92 ■ 93 280 35 52
■ www.parcnaturalcollserola.cat

Beyond the peaks of Tibidabo mountain, this 6,500-ha (16,000-acre) natural park of wild forest and winding paths is an oasis of calm. It is great for hiking and biking, with signposted paths and nature trails.

9 Casa Vicens

Carrer de les Carolines 20
■ Open 10am–8pm daily (last entry 1 hr before closing) ■ Adm ■ www.casavicens.org

Gaudí's first major commission, this former private home (see p45) is situated on a quiet residential street. It was once surrounded by orchards and fields, a fact the architect has referenced on the façade; a patchwork of tiles decorated with marigolds. Inside, rooms are replete with florid marquetry, arabesque detailing and nature-inspired ambiances.

10 Temple Expiatori del Sagrat Cor

The Neo-Gothic Temple of the Sacred Heart (see p40) was built by Enric Sagnier between 1902 and 1911. It has a dramatic sculpture of Jesus, and an elaborate door. Take the elevator up the main tower, or climb up to the outside terrace for great views.

Temple Expiatori del Sagrat Cor

EXPLORING THE HEIGHTS

▶ MORNING

Taking the northern route of the Bus Turístic is the easiest way to negotiate the vast northern area of Barcelona; it also gives discounts on entrance to major sights en route. Start off at **Plaça de Catalunya** (see p46) – tickets can be bought on board – and sit on the top deck for a good view of the Modernista magic along Pg de Gràcia. Make the whimsical **Park Güell** your first stop and spend the morning ambling around Gaudí's other-worldly park. Get back on the bus and continue north to the southern end of Av Tibidabo. Walk about 500 m (1,600 ft) up Av Tibidabo and stop off for a leisurely lunch in the garden of the palatial **El Asador d'Aranda** (see p123).

AFTERNOON

After you've had your fill of fine Castilian cuisine, stroll up Av Tibidabo to Plaça Doctor Andreu, where you can hop on the funicular train to go higher still to Plaça de Tibidabo. Pop into the **Parc d'Atraccions** (see p117) for a ride on the dodgems or the Ferris wheel. Then head over to the landmark **Torre de Collserola** (see p117), where a glass elevator whisks you up to an observation deck for spectacular views. Return to Pl Doctor Andreu on the funicular and treat yourself to a *granissat* (see p65) in one of the terrace bars. Catch the number 196 bus down the Av Tibidabo, then take Bus Turístic back to the city centre.

See map on pp116–17 ←

Gràcia Boutiques

Contemporary fashion at Boo

1 Boo
C/Bonavista 2 ■ 93 368 14 58
■ Open 11am–8:30pm Mon–Sat

An elegantly decorated space, Boo offers contemporary clothing and accessories with a vintage feel. International labels like Saint James, Norse Projects and tailored shirts by Tuk Tuk are available. There's also a selection of books and perfumes.

2 Lydia Delgado
C/Séneca 28 ■ 93 218 16 30
■ Open 10:30am–8:30pm Mon–Sat

This well-established Catalan designer creates clothing for women inspired by the 1950s and 1960s. Touches of embroidery, patchwork and other details enliven the fabrics.

3 José Rivero
C/Astúries 43 ■ 93 237 33 88 ■ Open 11am–2pm & 5–9pm Mon–Sat

José provides his own original in-house creations for men and women; he also sells accessories, including handbags, crafted by young, local designers.

4 Berta Sumpsi
MAP F1 ■ C/Verdi 98 ■ 676 870 122 ■ Open 11am–8pm Mon–Sat

This little space doubles as a workshop and showroom. There is an extraordinary range of simple as well as sculptural jewellery displayed in minimal surroundings.

5 Érase Una Vez
C/Goya 7 ■ 697 805 409
■ Open 10:30am–2pm & 4:30–8pm Mon–Fri, 11am–2pm Sat

Literally translating to "once upon a time", this tiny shop creates unique wedding gowns. It also stocks some of the most exclusive designers.

6 The Vos Shop
C/ Verdi 24 ■ 93 311 21 14
■ Open 11am–9pm Mon–Sat

The vibe of Gràcia is captured in this boutique that stocks creations of young, local designers. Collections range from bright overalls to graphic t-shirts for men and women.

7 Rock 01 Baby
C/Bonavista 16 ■ 93 368 89 80 ■ Open 10:30am–8:30pm Mon–Fri (from 11am Sat)

Dress your baby in the latest fashions from this little shop, which has funky slogan T-shirts, Babygros and mini Ugg boots as well.

8 Mushi Mushi
C/Bonavista 12 ■ 93 292 29 74
■ Open 11am–3pm & 4:30–8:30pm Mon–Sat

From hard-to-find small labels to the best international collections, Mushi Mushi stocks a selection of women's fashion and accessories.

9 El Piano
C/Verdi 20 bis ■ 93 415 51 76
■ Open 11am–9pm Mon–Sat

El Piano sells elegant and stylish womenswear with a retro flair made by Catalan designer Tina García. It also stocks clothes by other independent designers.

10 Botó and Co
C/Bonavista 3 ■ 93 676 22 71
■ Open 10am–9pm Mon–Sat

This is the third and newest of the Botó and Co boutiques in Barcelona, selling high-quality women's fashion, including Current/Elliot jeans, Humanoid sweaters, and more.

Gràcia Cafés

1 Cafè del Sol
Pl del Sol 16 ▪ 93 237 14 48

This café-bar is a cut above the others in the lively, bohemian Plaça del Sol. The atmosphere buzzes, the conversation inspires and the excellent coffee keeps on coming.

2 Cafè Salambó
C/Torrijos 51 ▪ 93 218 69 66

Scrumptious sandwiches and a tasty range of salads are the draw at this beautiful bar-cum-café. There are pool tables upstairs.

3 Bar Quimet
MAP E1 ▪ C/Vic 23 ▪ 93 218 41 89

An authentic, old-fashioned bar with marble-topped tables and big wooden barrels, this is a great spot for an aperitif. Try the *vermut* (vermouth) and a selection of olives and *boquerones* (fresh anchovies).

4 La Cafetera
Pl de la Virreina 2 ▪ 93 667 79 38

Of all the cafés on Plaça de la Virreina, La Cafetera, with its outdoor terrace and tiny patio full of potted plants, is perhaps one of the nicest options for a quiet and leisurely morning coffee and a sandwich or pastry.

5 Suís & Bowls
Travessera de Gràcia 151 ▪ 93 415 3698

This is a colourful café that serves healthy meals and fresh salads. Additionally, fresh juices, cakes and pastries are also on offer.

6 Mama's Café
MAP F1 ▪ C/Torrijos 26 ▪ 93 210 00 50 ▪ Closed Tue

A pretty minimalist café with a small patio at the back. Organic sandwiches, salads and homemade cakes are served all day, as well as fresh fruit juices and cocktails.

7 Onna Coffee
MAP E1 ▪ C/Santa Teresa 1 ▪ 93 269 48 70

This tiny coffee bar attracts the hipster set of Gràcia with its house-roasted coffee beans. You will also find a range of homemade cakes as well as healthy sandwiches to choose from.

8 Cafè del Teatre
C/Torrijos 41 ▪ 93 416 06 51

This is a great place to find a young, friendly crowd and good conversation. The only connection with the theatre, however, seems to be the velvet curtains on the sign over the door of this scruffy yet popular café.

9 La Nena
MAP F1 ▪ C/Ramón y Cajal 36 ▪ 93 285 14 76

This café is popular with parents of young children, thanks to the room with tables and games for children. Their range of home-made cakes, juices and hot drinks make this a neighbourhood favourite.

10 Sabio Infante
C/Torrent de l'Olla 39 ▪ 93 720 46 36 ▪ Closed Mon

Homemade cakes and great coffee are the draw at this colourful café, which is decorated with all sorts of weird and wonderful kitsch finds.

Alfresco dining at La Cafetera

See map on pp116–17 ←

Drinking Spots

The bar area at Bobby Gin

1 Bobby Gin
MAP E1 ■ C/Francisco Giner 47
■ www.bobbygin.com

This cocktail bar stocks some 60 premium gins – floral, citric, spiced and vintage. Their slogan, "Respect the gin", comes courtesy of the eponymous bartender.

2 Las Vermudas
MAP F1 ■ C/Robíe 32 ■ Closed Mon ■ www.lasvermudas.com/es/embajada-de-gracia

Vermut (vermouth) shows no signs of losing popularity, and Las Vermudas features a fantastic selection of it. Enjoy a glass out on the terrace, or at one of the live concerts.

3 Mirablau
Pl Dr Andreu ■ Closed Thu
■ www.mirablaubcn.com

A slightly older, well-heeled set who adhere to the smart dress code come to this bar for a combination of cocktails and views of the city.

4 Gimlet
C/Santaló 46 ■ Closed Sun
■ www.drymartiniorg.com

Opened in 1982 by Javier de las Muelas, a well-known name on the international cocktail scene, Gimlet is a classic bar with contemporary flair, where you can enjoy premium drinks in elegant surroundings.

5 Luz de Gas
MAP D1 ■ C/Muntaner 246
■ Closed Sun–Tue ■ www.luzdegas.com

A major player since the mid-1990s, this former theatre retains plenty of its retro charm with red velvet drapes and chandeliers. It now features live bands and DJs.

6 The Hideout Bar
C/Alzina 2

Tucked away behind the Plaça de la Virreina, this friendly spot is furnished with quirky vintage finds. It has a cosy atmosphere and a pretty terrace – ideal for relaxing.

7 Torre Rosa
C/Francesc Tàrrega 22
■ Closed L daily ■ www.torrerosa.com

This neighbourhood favourite *(see p61)* is ideal for escaping the summer heat, with tables scattered under a cluster of palm trees. There is a wide range of cocktails on offer.

8 La Cervesera Artesana
MAP F1 ■ C/Sant Agustí 14

A friendly microbrewery, this spot serves a good range of imported beers in addition to their own excellent brews. The Iberian Pale Ale, a mellow amber beer, is certainly worth a try.

9 Elephanta
Torrent d'en Vidalet, 37
■ www.elephanta.cat

Specializing in choicest flavoured gins, Elephanta also offers perfectly mixed cocktails, served in a cheerful, intimate space. The bar doubles as a mellow cafe during early evenings.

10 Bikini
Av Diagonal 547 ■ Closed Mon & Tue ■ Adm ■ www.bikinibcn.com

Open from midnight, this huge venue has three spaces, offering dance and Latin music and a cocktail lounge. Regular live music includes some of the best acts in Europe.

Restaurants and Tapas Bars

PRICE CATEGORIES

For a three-course meal for one with half a bottle of wine (or equivalent meal), including taxes and extra charges.

€ under €35 €€ €35–50 €€€ over €50

① El Asador d'Aranda
Av Tibidabo 31 ▪ 93 417 01 15 ▪ Closed Sun D (except Jun–Oct) ▪ €€

Set in the magnificent Modernista Casa Roviralta, this restaurant *(see p62)* is a magnet for businesspeople. Order the delicious lamb roasted in an oak-burning oven and dine in the beautiful garden.

② Hofmann
C/La Granada del Penedès 14–16 ▪ 93 218 71 65 ▪ Closed Sat L, Sun, Easter Week, Aug, Christmas ▪ €€€

Established by the late chef Mey Hofmann, this Michelin-starred place serves exceptional Catalan cuisine. Save room for the desserts.

③ Abissínia
C/Torrent de les Flors 55 ▪ 93 213 07 85 ▪ Closed Tue ▪ €

Traditional Ethiopian stews are served with *injera* bread here. This is a good restaurant for vegetarians.

④ Il Giardinetto
MAP E1 ▪ C/La Granada del Penedès 28 ▪ 93 218 75 36 ▪ Closed Tue ▪ €€

This eatery features whimsical, garden-themed decor and serves classic Mediterranean dishes with a twist such as spaghetti alla Sofia Loren (pasta served with anchovy and parsley sauce).

⑤ Fragments Café
Pl de la Concòrdia 12 ▪ 93 419 96 13 ▪ Closed Mon ▪ €

Plaça de la Concòrdia, in the Les Corts neighbourhood, retains a small-town appeal. Gourmet tapas and cocktails are served in the lovely garden *(see p61)* at the back.

⑥ Bonanova
C/Sant Gervasi de Cassoles 103 ▪ 93 417 10 33 ▪ Closed Sun D, Mon ▪ €€

Away from the tourist routes, Bonanova has been serving fresh, seasonal fare cooked in a simple and traditional way since 1964.

⑦ La Balsa
C/Infanta Isabel 4 ▪ 93 211 50 48 ▪ Closed Sun D, Mon, Easter, Aug L ▪ €€

With two garden terraces, La Balsa is a beautiful spot in the Bonanova area, serving fine Basque, Catalan and Mediterranean dishes.

⑧ Pappa e Citti
MAP F1 ▪ C/Encarnación 38 ▪ 687 657 111 ▪ Closed Sun ▪ €

A cozy restaurant, this place offers wonderful Sardinian dishes. Try the platter of breads, cheeses, cured meats or the stews or pastas.

⑨ Botafumeiro
C/Gran de Gràcia 81 ▪ 93 218 42 30 ▪ €€€

The fish tanks at this seafood place teem with crabs and lobsters destined for dinner plates. Try the *pulpo Gallego* (Galician octopus). Be sure to book ahead.

⑩ Acontraluz
C/Milanesat 19 ▪ 93 203 06 58 ▪ Closed Sun D ▪ €€

This restaurant has a charming terrace and a retractable roof for alfresco dining. The modern Catalan menu includes a range of tapas.

Acontraluz restaurant

See map on pp116–17

🔟 Beyond Barcelona

Teatre-Museu Dalí

Steeped in tradition, with its own language and pride in its identity, Catalonia is rich in both cultural heritage and physical beauty. It is not hyperbole to say that Catalonia has everything. The coastline has beautiful sandy beaches, intimate rocky coves and clear waters, while to the north are the 3,000-m (9,840-ft) Pyrenean peaks. These natural treasures are complemented by fabulous churches and monasteries in stunning mountain settings. The cuisine is rewarding, while the local *cava* holds its own against its French champagne counterparts.

BEYOND BARCELONA

1 Montserrat

Tourist Information: Pl de la Creu; 93 877 77 01 ▪ www. montserratvisita.com

The dramatic Montserrat mountain, with its remote Benedictine monastery (dating from 1025), is a religious symbol and a place of pilgrimage for the Catalan people. The basilica houses a statue of the patron saint of Catalonia, La Moreneta, also known as the "Black Virgin" *(see p41)*. Some legends date the statue to AD 50, but research suggests it was carved in the 12th century. The monastery was largely destroyed in 1811, during the War of Independence, and rebuilt some 30 years later.

The monastery at Montserrat

Montserrat – Catalan for "jagged mountain" – forms part of a ridge that rises suddenly from the plains. Take the funicular up to the peaks, where paths run alongside spectacular gorges to numerous hermitages.

2 Teatre-Museu Dalí, Figueres

Teatre-Museu Dalí: Pl Gala-Salvador Dalí, Figueres: 97 267 75 00; opening times vary ▪ Casa-Museu Salvador Dalí: Portlligat, Cadaqués: 97 225 10 15; opening times vary ▪ Adm ▪ www.salvador-dali.org

Salvador Dalí was born in the town of Figueres in 1904. Paying tribute to the artist is the fantastic Teatre-Museu Dalí, which is filled with his eccentric works. Housed in a former theatre, the country's second-most-visited museum (after the Prado in Madrid) provides a unique insight into the artist's extraordinary creations, from *La Cesta de Pan* (1926) to *El Torero Alucinógeno* (1970). A 30-minute drive away, close to the beach town of Cadaqués, the Dalí connection continues. Here, you can visit the Casa-Museu Salvador Dalí, which served as the artist's summer home for nearly 60 years until his death in 1989. These two sights are the main attractions of the 'Dalí triangle'. The third sight that completes this so-called triangle is the Gala Dalí Castle House-Museum located in Púbol, which was his gift to his wife, Gala.

1 Top 10 Sights *see pp124–7*

1 Places to Eat *see p131*

1 Outdoor Activities *see p130*

1 National Parks and Nature Reserves *see p129*

1 Churches and Monasteries *see p128*

③ Costa Brava

The Costa Brava is a beautiful stretch of Mediterranean coastline, which runs from Blanes (about 60 km (37 miles) north of Barcelona) all the way to the French border. There are a few big resorts, including Lloret de Mar and Roses, but many of the towns and resorts here, such as Calella de Palfrugell and Tamariu, have remained refreshingly low-key. Cultural highlights include the medieval citadel that crowns Tossa de Mar, and the Thyssen Museum in Sant Feliu de Guíxols. The area also has some excellent seafront hiking paths, the Camins de Ronda.

④ Alt Penedès

Tourist Information: C/Hermengild Ciascar 2, Vilafranca del Penedès; 93 818 12 54 ▪ Contact the tourist office for details on all winery visits in the region ▪ turismevilafranca.com

Catalonia's most famous wine region is the *cava*-producing area of the Penedès. The *cava* brands of Cordoníu and Freixenet have become household names worldwide. Many of the area's wineries and bodegas are open to the public. Cordoníu's is one of the most spectacular, housed in a Modernista building designed by Puig i Cadafalch, with a phenomenal 26 km (16 miles) of cellars on five floors.

⑤ Begur and around

Tourist Information: Av Onze de Setembre 5; 97 262 45 20 ▪ visitbegur.cat

The elegant hilltop town of Begur, with its ruined 14th-century castle, looks down over pristine wetlands and some of the prettiest coves on the Costa Brava. The town's population quadruples in summer as visitors make this their base for exploring nearby beaches and small, isolated coves. Many of the area's beaches stage jazz concerts during the summer. This is perhaps the best stretch of coastline in Catalonia.

Ruins of Tarragona's Roman wall

⑥ Tarragona

Tourist Information: C/Major 39; 97 725 07 95 ▪ www.tarragona turisme.cat

Now a huge industrial port, Tarragona was once the capital of Roman Catalonia, and the city's main attractions are from this era. Archaeological treasures include an impressive amphitheatre and well-preserved Roman walls that lead past the Museu Nacional Arqueològic and the Torre de Pilatos, where Christians were supposedly imprisoned before being thrown to the lions. The Catedral de Santa Tecla *(see p128)* is also in Tarragona.

⑦ Girona

Tourist Information: Rambla de la Llibertat 1; 972 01 00 01 ▪ www.girona.cat/turisme

Girona is a beautiful town surrounded by lush green hills. Hidden away in the old town, the atmospheric Jewish quarter, known as El Call, is one of Europe's best-preserved medieval enclaves. Visiting Girona's cathedral *(see p128)* is a must.

Statue, El Call

(8) Empúries

C/Puig i Cadafalch s/n,
Empúries ■ 97 277 02 08 ■ Open
10am–5pm (Jun–Sep: to 8pm, Oct–
mid-Nov & mid-Feb–May: to 6pm)
■ Adm; free last Tue of month Oct–
Jun ■ www.macempuries.cat

After Tarragona, Empúries is
Catalonia's second most important
Roman site. Located by the sea, it is
more than 40 ha (99 acres) of land
scattered with Greek and Roman
ruins, the highlights of which are the
remains of a market street, various
temples and a Roman amphitheatre.
It's an ideal spot for those looking to
mix a bit of history with a dip in the sea.

(9) PortAventura World

Av Pere Molas, Vila-seca,
Tarragona ■ 97 712 90 57 ■ For
opening times see website ■ Adm
■ www.portaventuraworld.com

This theme park is divided into six
areas, including the Far West and
Polynesia, and has some of Europe's
biggest rollercoasters, as well as
a thrilling Ferrari Land.

(10) Costa Daurada and Sitges

Tourist Information: Pl Eduard
Maristany 2, Sitges; 93 894 42 51
■ www.visitsitges.com

With its sandy beaches and shallow
waters, the Costa Daurada is a prime
attraction. Torredembarra is a family
resort, but the crown jewel is Sitges,
the summer home to Barcelona's
chic crowd, and a popular destination
for LGBT+ travellers. Restaurants
and bars line Sitges's main boulevard, the Passeig Marítim, while
Modernista architecture is scattered
among the 1970s blocks.

Sitges, as seen from the beach

A SCENIC DRIVE

Port de la Selva
Cap de Creus
Monestis de Sant
Pere de Rodes
Selva del Mar
Cadaqués
AP7
C260
N-II

From Barcelona 85 km (53 miles)

▶ **MORNING**

This drive should take about
5 hours for the round trip. From
Barcelona take the AP7 motorway
until exit 4, then take the C260
to **Cadaqués**. Just before dropping down to the town, stop at
the viewpoint and take in the
azure coastline and the whitewashed houses of this former
fishing village. Once in Cadaqués,
now one of Catalonia's trendiest
beach towns, wander the charming boutique-filled streets. After
a splash in the sea and a coffee
at one of the chic terrace cafés,
take the road leaving Port Lligat
and head for the lighthouse in
Cap de Creus (see p129). Drive
through the desolately beautiful
landscape of this rocky headland
before doubling back and heading
off to Port de la Selva. The road
twists and winds interminably,
but the picture-perfect scenery
will leave you speechless.

AFTERNOON

Enjoy a seafood lunch at Ca
l'Herminda (C/Illa 7), in the small,
mountain-enclosed Port de la
Selva. Then drive to the neighbouring village of Selva del Mar,
with its tiny river, for a post-
prandial coffee on the terrace
of the Bar Stop (C/Port de la Selva
1), before continuing up to the
Monestir de Sant Pere de Rodes
(see p128). You'll be tempted to
stop frequently on the way up
to take in the views. Don't, because
the best is to be had from the
monastery itself – a sweeping
vista of the whole area. There are
plenty of well-signposted walks
around the mountain top, and it
is worth sticking around to see
the sun set slowly over the bay.

See map on pp124–5 ←

Churches and Monasteries

1 Monestir de Montserrat
Montserrat ■ 93 877 77 01
■ Adm (museums) ■ www.abadia
montserrat.cat

Catalonia's holiest place and its
most visited monastery (see p125)
boasts beautiful Romanesque art
and a statue of the "Black Virgin".

2 Monestir de Poblet
Off N240, 10 km W of
Montblanc ■ Adm ■ www.poblet.cat

This beautiful working monastery
contains the Gothic Capella de Sant
Jordi, a Romanesque church, and
the Porta Daurada, a doorway that
was gilded for Felipe II's visit in 1564.

3 Monestir de Ripoll
Ripoll ■ 97 270 42 03
■ Adm ■ www.monestirderipoll.cat

The west portal of this monastery
(AD 879) has reputedly the finest
Romanesque carvings in Spain.
Of the original buildings, only the
doorway and cloister remain.

4 Monestir de Santes Creus
Santes Creus, 25 km NW of
Montblanc ■ 97 763 83 29 ■ Closed
Mon ■ Adm ■ www.mhcat.cat

The cloister here (1150) is notable
for the beautifully sculpted capitals
by English artist Reinard Funoll.

5 Sant Joan de les Abadesses
Sant Joan de les Abadesses ■ 97
272 05 99 ■ Adm ■ www.santjoan
delesabadesses.cat

This monastery, established in the
9th century, boasts a magnificent
Romanesque sculpture representing
the Descent from the Cross.

6 Sant Climent i Santa Maria de Taüll
138 km N of Lleida ■ 97 369 67
15 ■ www.centreromanic.com

These two Romanesque churches,
dating from 1123, are perfect
examples of those that pepper
the Pyrenees. The frescoes are
reproductions of the originals,
now housed in Barcelona's
MNAC (see pp20–21).

7 Catedral de La Seu d'Urgell
La Seu d'Urgell ■ 97 335 32 42 ■ Adm
■ www.laseumedieval.com/en

Dating from around 1040, this
cathedral is one of the most
elegant in Catalonia.

8 Catedral de Girona
Plaça de la Catedral s/n, Girona
■ 97 242 71 89 ■ www.catedralde
girona.cat ■ Adm; Mass free

This cathedral possesses the widest
Gothic nave in Europe, after the
basilica in the Vatican.

9 Catedral de Santa Tecla
Old Town, Tarragona ■ Adm;
Mass free ■ Guided tours ■ www.
tarragonaturisme.cat

At 104 m (340 ft) long, Tarragona's
cathedral is the largest in the region.
Its architecture is a mixture of Gothic
and Romanesque.

10 Monestir de Sant Pere de Rodes
22 km E of Figueres ■ Closed Mon
■ Adm ■ patrimoni.gencat.cat/en/
monuments

Perched on a hilltop, this ancient
UNESCO World Heritage Site offers
breathtaking views over Cap de
Creus and Port de la Selva.

Monestir de Sant Pere de Rodes

National Parks and Nature Reserves

1 Parc Nacional d'Aigüestortes i Estany de Sant Maurici

148 km N of Lleida ▪ parcsnaturals. gencat.cat/en/aiguestortes

The magnificent peaks of Catalonia's only national park are accessible from the village of Espot. You'll discover beautiful waterfalls, lakes and glacial tarns 2,000 m (6,560 ft) up.

2 Delta de l'Ebre

28 km SE of Tortosa ▪ parcsnaturals.gencat.cat/ ca/delta-ebre

A patchwork of paddy fields, the wide expanse of the River Ebre is a nature reserve for migratory birds and has many bird-watching stations.

3 Parc Natural de la Zona Volcànica de la Garrotxa

40 km NW of Girona ▪ parcs naturals.gencat.cat/ca/garrotxa

La Garrotxa last erupted 10,000 years ago. The largest crater is the Santa Margalida, 500 m (1,640 ft) wide. It is best to visit in spring.

Purple heron, Delta de l'Ebre

4 Cap de Creus

36 km E of Figueres ▪ parcs naturals.gencat.cat/ca/cap-creus

The Pyrenees mountains form Catalonia's most easterly point offering great views of the coastline.

5 Parc Natural del Cadí-Moixeró

20 km E of La Seu d'Urgell ▪ parcs naturals.gencat.cat/ca/cad

Covered in a carpet of conifers and oaks, this mountain range has lush vegetation. Several of the peaks here are over 2,000 m (6,560 ft) high.

6 Parc Natural del Montseny

48 km NW of Barcelona ▪ parcs naturals.gencat.cat/ca

Catalonia's most accessible natural park, these woodland hills are suitable for walkers and mountain bikers, with a vast network of trails. Take the popular climb up Turó de l'Home, the highest peak.

7 Massís de Pedraforca

64 km N of Manresa ▪ parcs naturals.gencat.cat/ca/ pedraforca

A nature reserve surrounds this outcrop of mountains, a favourite of rock climbers.

8 Serra de l'Albera

15 km N of Figueres ▪ parcsnaturals.gencat. cat/ca/albera

The Albera Massif is home to ancient dolmens, Romanesque sanctuaries and one of the last colonies of the Mediterranean tortoise.

9 Parc Natural dels Aiguamolls de l'Empordà

15 km E of Figueres ▪ parcsnaturals. gencat.cat/ca

This nature reserve hides a number of birdwatching towers. Those in the Laguna de Vilalt and La Bassa de Gall Mari allow the observation of herons, moorhens and other bird species nesting in spring.

10 Parc Natural de Sant Llorenç del Munt

12 km E of Manresa ▪ parcs.diba.cat/ web/santllorenc

Close to Barcelona, this park is home to large numbers of wild boar. Visit the Romanesque monastery at Cerro de la Mola, which is now a restaurant.

See map on pp124–5

Outdoor Activities

Rafting on La Noguera Pallaresa

1 Rafting and Kayaking
Noguera Aventura: Lleida; 97 329 01 76; www.noguera ventura.com

One of Europe's best rivers for whitewater sports is La Noguera Pallaresa in the Pyrenees. Late spring is the best time to go, as the mountain snow begins to thaw.

2 Scuba Diving
Aquàtica: L'Estartit; 97 275 06 56; www.aquatica-sub.com

The Reserva Natural de les Illes Medes has thousands of species of fish and red coral reefs. Glass-bottom boats cater to non-divers.

3 Water Sports and Sailing
Club de Mar Sitges: Pg Marítim, Sitges; 93 894 09 05; clubmar sitges.com

Good sailing can be found in Sitges, along with yachts for rent and classes for novices. Canoeing and windsurfing are also available.

4 Skiing
La Molina: 25 km S of Puigcerdà; 97 289 20 31; www.lamolina.cat ▪ Baqueira-Beret: 97 363 90 00; www.baqueira.es

La Molina is the most accessible Pyrenean ski-resort from Barcelona, but Baqueira-Beret is where the jet-set goes. Both offer all levels of skiing (including off-piste) from December onwards.

5 Golf
Santa Cristina d'Aro: 97 283 70 55 ▪ Platja d'Aro: 97 281 67 27

The Costa Brava is one of Europe's top golf destinations; the best courses are around Platja d'Aro.

6 Horse Riding
Hípica Can Tramp: Ctra Cànoves; 93 871 16 08; www. hipicacantramp.es

Montseny Natural Park (see p129) is ideal for horse riding, with a number of stables.

7 Ballooning
Vol de Coloms: 97 268 02 55, 689 47 18 72; www.voldecoloms.cat

A balloon journey over the volcanic area of La Garrotxa is an unbeatable way to get a bird's-eye view of the beautiful Catalonian landscape.

8 Boat Trips
Dofi Jet Boats: Blanes; 97 235 20 21; Boats every hour daily from Blanes and Lloret de Mar (twice daily from Calella); closed Oct–Mar; www. dofijetboats.com

Take a cruise from Calella and Blanes along the Costa Brava, stopping at the old town and medieval castle of Tossa de Mar.

9 Activities at the Canal Olímpic
Canal Olímpic: Av Canal Olímpic, Castelldefels; 93 636 28 96; www. canalolimpic.cat

Used for rowing competitions in the 1992 Olympics, the huge Canal Olímpic is now a leisure complex offering a host of activities.

10 Foraging for Mushrooms
Diputació de Barcelona: www. diba.cat

From late September to late October, Catalans flock to the hills in search of the highly-prized *rovelló* mushrooms. Some are poisonous, so amateurs should make sure they get a guide through the Diputació de Barcelona.

Places to Eat

PRICE CATEGORIES

For a three-course meal for one with half a bottle of wine (or equivalent meal), including taxes and extra charges.

€ under €35 €€ €35–50 €€€ over €50

1 Tragamar

Platja de Canadell s/n, Calella de Palafrugell ▪ 97 261 43 36 ▪ Closed Tue ▪ €€€

Book ahead for a table on the terrace or by one of the bay windows at this beachside restaurant, and enjoy stellar seafood dishes such as tuna carpaccio or lobster paella.

2 Les Cols

Mas les Cols, Ctra de la Canya s/n, Olot ▪ 97 226 92 09 ▪ Closed Sun D, Mon & Tue ▪ www.lescols. com ▪ €€€

Two-Michelin-starred Les Cols prepares contemporary Spanish cuisine with local seasonal produce in a stunning modern setting.

3 La Torre del Remei

Camí del Remei 3, Bolvir, Cerdanya ▪ 97 214 01 82 ▪ €€

A Modernista palace provides an elegant setting for wonderfully presented Catalan food.

4 Cal Ticus

C/Raval 19, Sant Sadurní d'Anoia ▪ 93 818 41 60 ▪ Closed Sun, Mon & Tue–Thu D ▪ €

This modern restaurant serves traditional cuisine using seasonal products from nearby suppliers. A good selection of Penedès wines are on the list and for sale in their shop.

5 Fonda Europa

C/Anselm Clavé 1, Granollers ▪ 93 870 03 12 ▪ €€

Established in 1771, Fonda Europa was the first in a line of successful Catalan restaurants. Dishes include pig's trotters and a Catalan stockpot with meat and vegetables.

6 Lasal de Varador

Pg Marítim 1, Mataró ▪ 93 114 05 80 ▪ Closed Dec–Feb ▪ €€

This beachfront restaurant serves tasty paellas, seafood and a range of other dishes, using organic and sustainably sourced ingredients.

7 Els Pescadors

Muelle Pesquero s/n, Arenys de Mar ▪ 937 92 3304 ▪ Closed Sun D ▪ €

Set inside the local *llotja* (wholesale fish market), this eatery serves fresh seafood. There are a few tables outside on the port overlooking the boats. Book ahead on the weekends.

8 Toc Al Mar

Pl d'Aiguablava, Begur ▪ 972 11 32 32 ▪ Closed Dec–Feb

Located on a beach in Costa Brava, Toc Al Mar has tables on the sands. On offer is freshly grilled seafood, such as lobster, Palamós prawns, paella, black rice with squid ink and delicacies from the Mediterranean.

9 El Celler de Can Roca

C/Can Sunyer 48, Girona ▪ 97 222 21 57 ▪ Closed Sun, Mon, Tue L ▪ www. cellercanroca.com ▪ €€€

The Roca brothers' exciting Catalan cuisine is complemented by great wines. The restaurant has three Michelin stars and an 11-month waiting list. It is best to reserve ahead.

Prawn dish at El Celler

10 Cal Ton

C/Casal 8, Vilafranca del Penedès ▪ 93 890 37 41 ▪ Closed Mon, Tue D, Sun D, Easter, 3 weeks Aug ▪ €€

Contemporary cuisine in the heart of Catalonia's biggest wine region. Order the *menu degustació*.

See map on pp124–5

Streetsmart

Looking down on the two entrance
pavilions at Park Güell

Getting Around	**134**
Practical Information	**138**
Places to Stay	**142**
General Index	**150**
Acknowledgments	**156**
Phrase Book	**158**

Getting Around

Arriving by Air

Most flights arrive at **Barcelona El Prat Josep Tarradellas**, located 12 km (7.5 miles) south-west of the city centre. The airport has two terminals, linked by a shuttle bus. Local train services run every 30 minutes to the city centre, (about 25 mins), while metro Line 9 Sud links Zona Universitària station (Line 3) on the western side of the city (about 30 mins). There is also an express airport bus service, **Aerobús** (20–30 mins). Taxi ranks are located at both terminals (€25–35 into central Barcelona), as well as a number of car rental companies.

European budget airlines fly to Barcelona all year round. There are regular internal flights to local airports: Sabadell Airport, 20 km (12 miles) north of Barcelona, Lleida–Alguaire Airport, Reus Airport in Tarragona, Girona–Costa Brava Airport and Andorra–La Seu d'Urgell Airport.

Iberia offers a shuttle service between Madrid and Barcelona, with several flights a day, and also links to many other domestic destinations, as do **Vueling** and **Air Europa**. There are direct flights on national and low-cost airlines from the UK and most major European cities. Some low-cost and charter airlines also fly to Girona and Reus, both about 100 km (62 miles) away.

There are direct flights from New York, Miami and Atlanta, and flights from Australia and New Zealand via Dubai and other stopovers.

International Train Travel

Spain's rail services are operated by state-run **Renfe** (Red Nacional de Ferrocarriles Españoles). Buy your ticket on their website well ahead of travel, particularly for the peak summer season.

There are several routes to Spain from France. Trains from London, Brussels, Amsterdam, Geneva, Zürich and Milan reach Barcelona via Cerbère, on the French border with Catalonia. Direct, high-speed luxury TALGO (Tren Articulado Ligero Goicoechea Oriol) trains, operated by Renfe, go to Barcelona from Paris, Milan, Geneva and Zürich. International trains arrive at Barcelona's Sants mainline station.

Sants offers a number of facilities, including lockers, ATMs and bureaux de change,

Domestic Train Travel

The fastest intercity services are the TALGO and AVE (operated by Renfe), which link Madrid with Barcelona in three hours. AVE routes link Barcelona with Seville and Málaga in five and a half hours. The *largo recorrido* (long-distance) trains are cheap but so slow that you usually

need to travel overnight. *Regionales y cercanías* (regional and local services) are frequent and cheap. Overnight trains are offered by Estrella (a basic service) to Madrid, and by Trenhotel (more sophisticated) to A Coruña and Vigo, in Galicia.

Long-Distance Bus Travel

Often the cheapest way to reach and travel around Spain is by coach.

Spain has no national coach company; private regional companies operate routes around the country. The largest is **Alsa**, with routes and services covering most of Spain. Tickets and information are available at all main coach stations and on company websites.

Buses from towns and cities in Spain arrive at Estació del Nord and Sants. Several companies run day trips or longer tours around Catalonia. **Turisme de Catalunya** has details of trips.

Public Transport

Most towns and cities in Catalonia only offer a bus service, but the larger cities operate multiple public transport systems, including trams. Barcelona, **Girona**, **Tarragona** and **Lleida** all have cheap and efficient bus services. Barcelona also has a well-run metro system. For up-todate information about public transport, as well as ticket advice, check out municipal websites.

TMB (Transports Metropolitans de Barcelona) runs the extensive public transport network in Barcelona and the suburbs. TMB has a useful interactive website, as well as an app. Both provide travel information, route finders, maps and schedules. Metro maps are also available at stations, while bus maps are available at the bigger tourist offices.

Tickets

A range of tickets and money-saving travel cards are available to tourists. Some cover train, bus and metro. Combined tickets allow you to hop from metro to FGC to bus lines without having to pay again. The senzill ticket, for a single journey, is €2.40 and can be used on metro, bus and FGC; the T-Casual is €10.20, can be shared and is the most useful for tourists, allowing ten trips on metro, bus and FGC (these can be combined with a time limit of an hour and a half); T-Dia and T-Mes are for unlimited daily and monthly travel respectively; the T-50/30 is for 50 journeys in 30 days on metro, bus and FGC.

For tourists, there are two-, three-, four- and five-day Hola Barcelona travel cards available (€15.20, €22.20, €28.80 and €35.40 if bought online through TMB) – these offer unlimited journeys on the metro, FGC and bus. Hola Barcelona cards also include the metro supplement for trips to and from the airport.

Metro

There are 12 underground metro lines in Barcelona, run by TMB. Lines are identified by number and colour. Platform signs distinguish between trains and their direction by displaying the last station on the line. In the street, look for a sign bearing a red "M" on a white diamond background. The metro is usually the quickest way to get around the city, especially as all multijourney tickets are valid for the metro and FGC lines (in Zone 1), as well as on the bus and local Renfe services. A Renfe or FGC sign at a metro station indicates that it has a Renfe or FGC connection. Metro trains run from 5am to midnight from Monday to Thursday, to midnight on Sunday and weekday public holidays, from 5am to 2am on Friday and the day before a public holiday, and all night on Saturdays.

The L9 metro line connects the city with the airport, and it stops at terminals 1 and 2, but is only really useful if you are headed to the north or west of the city. An airport supplement is charged on this route, and you will not be able to use the T-10 or other standard transport passes. However, the Hola Barcelona pass includes the airport supplement and is accepted on this route.

Trams

Barcelona has two comprehensive tram networks, Trambaix (T1, T2, T3) and Trambesòs (T4, T5, T6), which run between 4:55am and 12:30am daily (each line has slightly different hours). They are operated by **TRAM** (check website for routes and schedules). Trams are a cheap and efficient way to travel, and are often more accessible than other modes of public transport for those with limited mobility or travelling with pushchairs.

DIRECTORY

ARRIVING BY AIR

Aerobús
w aerobusbcn.com

Air Europa
w aireuropa.com

Barcelona El Prat Josep Tarradellas
w aena.es

Iberia
w iberia.com

Vueling
w vueling.com

INTERNATIONAL TRAIN TRAVEL

Renfe
w renfe.com

LONG-DISTANCE BUS TRAVEL

Alsa
w alsa.es

Turisme de Catalunya
w catalunyaturisme.cat

PUBLIC TRANSPORT

Girona
w girona.cat

Lleida
w atmlleida.cat

Tarragona
w tarragonaturisme.cat

TMB
w tmb.cat

TRAMS

TRAM
w tram.cat

Bus

Buses are the most common mode of public transport in Catalonia, but timetables can be erratic. Many services do not run after 10pm, but there are some night buses in the cities.

In Barcelona the main city buses are white and red. Bus numbers beginning with H (for horizontal) run from one side of the city to another and those beginning with V (vertical) run top to bottom; D is diagonal. The Nitbus service runs nightly from around 10:30pm to 5am. Bus maps are available from the main tourist office in Plaça de Catalunya and on the TMB (Transports Metropolitans de Barcelona; see p135) website and app.

The privately owned **Aerobús** runs between Plaça de Catalunya and El Prat airport. Public transport passes are not valid on the Aerobús.

Local Trains

Renfe's network of local trains, *cercanías*, is useful for longer distances within Barcelona, particularly between the main train stations: Sants and Estació de França. They are also useful for short hops to Sitges or the northern coastal towns. Maps are displayed at stations, or are available on the Renfe website (see p135) and app. Trains run 5:30am to 11:30pm daily, but hours vary from line to line. **Ferrocarrils de la Generalitat de Catalunya (FGC)** is a network of suburban trains run by the Catalan Government in and around Barcelona. They are useful for trips to Tibidabo, Pedralbes and the Collserola neighbourhoods.

Taxis

Barcelona's taxis are yellow and black, displaying a green light when free. All taxis are metered and show a minimum fee at the start of a journey. Generally speaking, the journey starts with a flat fee and then increases depending on the distance travelled. Rates increase between 8pm and 8am, and there is a €2.10 surcharge from midnight to 6am Friday to Sunday and on public holidays. Surcharges usually apply for going to and from the airport, the port and major train stations. You can flag taxis in the street, or call **Radio Taxis**, **Taxi Ecològic**, **Barna Taxi**, or **Taxi Class** to order one. **Taxi Amic** has cars adapted for people with a disability, though these need to be booked a day ahead.

Driving

If you drive to Spain in your own car, you must carry the vehicle's registration document, a valid insurance certificate, a passport or a national identity card and your driving licence at all times. You must also display a sticker on the back of the car showing its country of registration.

Spain has two types of motorway: *autopistas*, (toll roads) and *autovías* (toll-free). You can establish whether a motorway is toll-free by the letters that prefix the number of the road: A = free motorway, AP = toll motorway.

Carreteras nacionales, Spain's main roads, have black-and-white signs and are designated by the letter N (Nacional) plus a number. *Carreteras comarcales*, secondary roads, have a number preceded by the letter C.

Driving in Barcelona is not recommended. The narrow roads and one-way systems are tricky and parking can be difficult. The city has a pay-and-display system from 9am to 2pm and 4pm to 8pm Monday to Friday and all day Saturday. You can park in blue spaces for about €2–3 per hour. Tickets are valid for two hours but can be renewed. Green spaces are reserved for residents but can be used, if available, at a higher rate and are free at off-peak hours. At underground car parks, *lliure* means there is space, *complet* means full. Most are attended, but in automatic ones, you pay before returning to your car. Do not park where the pavement edge is yellow or where there is a private exit (*gual*). Blue and red signs saying "1–15" or "16–30" mean that you cannot park in the areas indicated on those dates of the month.

Driving to Barcelona

Many people drive to Catalonia via France. The most direct routes across the Pyrenees are the motorways through

Hendaye in the west and La Jonquera in the east. Port Bou is on a coastal route, while other routes snake over the top, entering Catalonia via the Val d'Aran, Andorra and Puigcerdà in the Cerdanya. From the UK, car ferries run from Plymouth to Santander and from Portsmouth to Santander and Bilbao.

Car Rental

The most popular car-rental companies are **Avis**, **Europcar** and **Hertz**. All have offices at airports, major train stations and in the larger cities.

Rules of the Road

Most traffic regulations and warnings to motorists are represented on signs by easily recognized symbols. To turn left at a busy junction or across oncoming traffic, you may have to turn right first and cross a main road, often by way of traffic lights, a bridge or underpass. If you are accidentally going in the wrong direction on a motorway or a main road with a solid white line, turn round at a sign for a *cambio de sentido*. At crossings, give way to the right unless a sign indicates otherwise.

Cycling

Barcelona has a growing network of cycle lanes that provide access to all the major sights of the city. There are a number of cycle-hire shops, including **Budget Bikes**, **Rabbit Bike** and **Un Cotxe Menys**. Maps are available at these shops. Keep to cycle paths in the city centre, as cycling on roads can be unsafe.

Bicing, the municipal government-run free service, can be used with a Bicing card and supplies maps of the city's cycle lanes. Though this system is currently open to residents only, commercial operators offer rentals to visitors from around €10 for two hours to €60 for a week.

Many bike rental places also conduct cycling tours of the city. **Bike Tours Barcelona** has several themed tours, including a Modernista cycling tour and a beach tour, while **Steel Donkey** focuses on the quirky side of Barcelona. You can also explore the streets on a vintage-style Ural motorcycle and sidecar with **Bright Side Tours**.

Walking

Most areas are best seen on foot, especially the old town and Gràcia, where a leisurely stroll is the only way to soak up the architectural and cultural riches. The seafront, from Port Vell to Port Olímpic, is also great for walking.

Try one of the excellent themed walking tours offered by the Barcelona Turisme office *(see p141)*. Their website offers an overview of the available tours, plus a discount if you buy them online.

Fans of Modernista architecture can book onto Barcelona Turisme's Modernista walking tour, which visits the main sites in the Eixample area, or pick up the free **Ruta del Modernisme** map at the tourist office.

(see p141)

DIRECTORY

BUS

Aerobús
W aerobusbcn.com

LOCAL TRAINS

Ferrocarrils de la Generalitat de Catalunya (FGC)
W fgc.cat

TAXIS

Barna Taxi
W barnataxi.com

Radio Taxis
W radiotaxibarcelona.info

Taxi Amic
W taxi-amic-adaptat.com

Taxi Class
W taxiclassrent.com

Taxi Ecològic
W taxiecologic.com

CAR RENTAL

Avis
W avis.com

Europcar
W europcar.com

Hertz
W hertz-europe.com

CYCLING

Bicing
W bicing.barcelona

Budget Bikes
W budgetbikes.eu

Bike Tours Barcelona
W biketoursbarcelona.com

Bright Side Tours
W brightsidetours.com

Rabbit Bike
W rabbitbike.es

Steel Donkey
W steeldonkeybiketours.com

Un Cotxe Menys
W biketoursbarcelona.com

WALKING

Ruta del Modernisme
W rutadelmodernisme.com

Practical Information

Passports and Visas

For entry requirements, including visas, consult your nearest Spanish embassy or check the Spanish government's **Exteriores** and **Spain Travel Health** websites.

EU nationals may visit for an unlimited period, registering with local authorities after three months. Citizens of the US, Canada, the UK, New Zealand and Australia can visit Spain for up to 90 days without a visa. For those arriving from other countries, check with your local Spanish embassy or on the Spanish government's Exteriores website.

Government Advice

Now more than ever, it is important to consult both your and the Spanish government's advice before travelling. The **UK Foreign and Commonwealth Office**, the **US Department of State**, the **Australian Department of Foreign Affairs and Trade** and the Spanish government's Exteriores website offer the latest information on security, health and local regulations.

Customs Information

You can find information on the laws relating to goods and currency taken in or out of Spain on the **Turespaña** (Spain's national tourist board) website.

For EU citizens there are no limits on most goods carried in or out of Spain,

as long as they are only for personal use. Exceptions include weapons, some types of food and plants, and endangered species. Limits vary if travelling outside the EU, so always check restrictions before travelling. Non-EU residents can claim back VAT on EU purchases (see p141).

Insurance

We recommend that you take out a comprehensive insurance policy covering theft, loss of belongings, medical care, cancellations and delays, and read the small print carefully.

EU citizens are eligible for free emergency medical care in Spain provided they have a valid **EHIC** (European Health Insurance Card).

Health

Spain has a world-class healthcare system. Emergency medical care in Spain is free for all EU citizens. If you have an EHIC card, be sure to present this as soon as possible. You may have to pay after treatment and reclaim the money later.

For other visitors, payment of medical expenses is the patient's responsibility. It is therefore important to arrange comprehensive medical insurance before travelling.

No vaccinations are necessary for Spain. Carry with you any prescriptions for medications that you take. Tap water is safe to drink unless stated otherwise.

For minor ailments, go to a *farmàcia* (pharmacy), identified by a red or green cross. When closed, they will post a sign giving the location of the nearest *farmàcia de guàrdia* that will be open. Pharmacies that are open 24 hours include the **Farmàcia Clapés** on La Rambla.

Smoking, Alcohol and Drugs

Smoking is banned in enclosed public spaces and is a fineable offence, although you can still smoke on the terraces of bars and restaurants.

Spain has a relaxed attitude towards alcohol consumption, but it is frowned upon to be openly drunk. In cities it is common to drink on the street outside the bar of purchase.

Most recreational drugs are illegal, and possession of even a very small quantity can lead to an extremely hefty fine. Amounts that suggest an intent to supply drugs to other people can lead to custodial sentences. Cannabis clubs can supply the drug to members, but it remains illegal to smoke it in public spaces.

ID

By law you must carry identification with you at all times in Spain. A photocopy of your passport should suffice. If stopped by the police, you may be asked to report to a police station with the original document.

Personal Security

Barcelona is a relatively safe city, although petty crimes such as pickpocketing and bag-snatching remain problematic. Usual safety precautions apply. Take particular care at markets, tourist sights and stations, and wear bags and cameras across your body, not on your shoulder. Be especially careful of pickpockets when getting on or off a crowded train or metro. Avoid walking alone in poorly lit areas.

To report a crime, go to the nearest *comissaria*. Although you may see police from other forces, contact is usually with the Mossos d'Esquadra, who wear navy blue uniforms.

Contact your embassy if you have your passport stolen, or in the event of a serious crime or accident.

The ambulance, police and fire brigade can be reached on the Europe-wide **emergency** number 112. There are also dedicated lines for the **Policía Nacional** (the national police force), the **Guàrdia Urbana** (the municipal police force), the **Mossos d'Esquadra** (the Catalonian police force) as well as for calling an **ambulance**.

As a rule, Catalans are very accepting of all people, regardless of their race, gender or sexuality. Homosexuality was legalized in 1979 and in 2007, Spain recognized the right to legally change your gender. If you do feel unsafe, the **Safe Space Alliance** pinpoints your nearest place of refuge.

Travellers with Specific Requirements

Spain's **COCEMFE** (Confederación Española de Personas con Discapacidad Física y Orgánica) and **Accessible Spain** provide useful information, while companies, such as **Tourism For All**, offer specialist tours for those with reduced mobility, sight and hearing.

Spain's public transport system generally caters for all passengers, with wheelchairs, adapted toilets, and reserved car parking available at airports and stations. Trains and some buses accommodate wheelchair-bound passengers. Metro maps in Braille are available from **ONCE** (Organización Nacional de Ciegos).

DIRECTORY

PASSPORTS AND VISAS

Exteriores
w exteriores.gob.es

Spain Travel Health
w spth.gob.es

GOVERNMENT ADVICE

Australian Department of Foreign Affairs and Trade
w smartraveller.gov.au

UK Foreign and Commonwealth Office
w gov.uk/foreign-travel-advice

US Department of State
w travel.state.gov

CUSTOMS INFORMATION

Turespaña
w spain.info

INSURANCE

EHIC
w gov.uk/european-health-insurance-card

HEALTH

Farmàcia Clapés
MAP L3 ■ La Rambla 98
w farmaciaclapes.com

PERSONAL SECURITY

Ambulance
C 061

Emergency
C 112

Guàrdia Urbana
C 092

Mossos d'Esquadra
C 112

Policía Nacional
C 091

Safe Space Alliance
w safespacealliance.com

TRAVELLERS WITH SPECIFIC REQUIREMENTS

Accessible Spaine
w accessiblespaintravel.com

COCEMFE
w cocemfe.es

ONCE
w once.es

Tourism For All
w tourismforall.org.uk

Time Zone

Spain operates on Central European Time (CET), which is one hour ahead of Greenwich Mean Time (GMT) and six hours ahead of US Eastern Standard Time (EST). The clock moves forward one hour during daylight savings time, from the last Sunday in March until the last Sunday in November.

Money

Spain uses the euro (€). Most urban establishments accept major credit, debit and prepaid currency cards. Contactless payments are common in Barcelona, but it's a good idea to carry cash for smaller items. ATMs are widely available, although many charge for cash withdrawals. Tipping is not expected for hotel housekeeping, but porters will expect €1–2 per bag. Rounding up the fare to the nearest euro is expected by taxi drivers and it is usual to tip waiters 5–10 per cent.

Electrical Appliances

Spain uses plugs with two round pins and an electrical voltage and frequency of 230V/50Hz. North American devices will need adaptors and voltage converters.

Mobile Phones and Wi-Fi

Free Wi-Fi is reasonably common, particularly in libraries, large public spaces, restaurants and bars. Some places, such as airports and hotels, may charge for using their Wi-Fi. The city council provides free Wi-Fi around Barcelona. Use the **WiFi Map** website and app to find free Wi-Fi hotspots near you.

Visitors travelling to Spain with EU tariffs can use their devices abroad without being affected by roaming charges. Users will be charged the same rates for data, calls and texts as at home.

Postal Services

Main branches of Spain's **Correos** post offices are usually open 8:30am–8:30pm Monday to Friday and 9:30am–1pm on Saturdays. Suburban and village branches open 9am–2pm during the week and 9:30am–1pm Saturday. Mailboxes are painted bright yellow.

Weather

The climate is typically Mediterranean, with cool winters and warm summers. July can be hot and humid, with temperatures reaching 35° C (95° F). January and February are the two coldest months, although temperatures rarely drop below 10° C (50° F).

Opening Hours

Many shops and some museums and public buildings may close for the siesta, roughly between 1pm and 5pm. Larger shops and department stores don't close at lunchtime and are usually open until 9 or 10pm.

Many museums, public buildings and monuments are closed on Monday.

Opening hours for museums and galleries vary and may change with the season. It is best to check their websites before you visit.

On Sundays, churches and cathedrals will generally not permit visitors during Mass.

Most museums, public buildings and many shops close early or for the day on public holidays: New Year's Day, Epiphany (6 Jan), Good Friday, Easter Sunday, Feast of Sant Jordi (23 Apr), Labour Day (1 May), Feast of Sant Joan (24 Jun), Ascension Day (15 Aug), Catalan Day (11 Sep), Hispanic Day (12 Oct), All Saints' Day (1 Nov), Constitution Day (6 Dec), Immaculate Conception (8 Dec), Christmas Day (25 Dec), and the Feast of St Stephen (26 Dec).

COVID-19 The pandemic continues to affect Barcelona. Some museums, tourist attractions and hospitality venues are operating on reduced or temporary opening hours, and require visitors to make advance bookings for a specific date and time. Always check ahead before visiting.

Visitor Information

Multilingual staff give out free maps and information at the **Barcelona Turisme** main tourist information office at Plaça de Catalunya. They also have a useful accommodation booking service and bureau de change.

There are additional Barcelona Turisme offices at the airport, La Rambla, Estació de Sants and Plaça de Sant Jaume, and booths at Estació del Nord, Plaça Espanya and other key tourist spots.

In summer red-jacketed tourist information officers roam the busiest areas giving out maps and advice. Barcelona Turisme's excellent website provides information, sells tickets and lets you book accommodation. It also has useful apps, including a general guide to the city, as well as specific guides to Medieval Barcelona, Roman Barcelona and Gaudí's Barcelona.

Barcelona offers the **Barcelona Card**, a visitor's pass or discount card for exhibitions, events and museum entry, plus participating restaurants. This is not free, so consider carefully how many of the offers you are likely to take advantage of before purchasing a card.

The **Culture Institute** in the Palau de la Virreina offers information on cultural and arts events and a ticket-purchase service. The **Barcelona City Council's** website and the **Turisme de Catalunya** office as well as website are also good sources of information.

Useful apps include Moovit and Citymapper for route planning and transport information.

Local Customs

Regional pride is strong throughout Spain. Be wary of referring to Catalans as "Spanish", as this can sometimes cause offence.

A famous Spanish tradition is the siesta which sees many shops closing between 1pm and 5pm. This is not always observed by large stores or in very touristy areas.

It is wise to ensure that you are dressed modestly when you are visiting religious buildings, with knees and shoulders covered.

Language

The two official languages of Catalonia are *castellano* (Castilian Spanish) and Catalan. Almost every Catalan can speak Castilian Spanish, but most consider Catalan their first language. As a visitor, it is perfectly acceptable to speak Castilian wherever you are. English is widely spoken in the cities and other tourist spots, but not always in rural areas.

Taxes and Refunds

IVA (VAT) is normally 21 per cent, but with lower rates for certain goods and services, such as hotels and restaurants. Under certain conditions, non-EU citizens can claim a rebate of these taxes. Retailers can give you a form to fill out, which you can then present to a customs officer with your receipts as you leave. If the shop offers DIVA, you can fill that form out instead and validate it automatically at selfservice machines found in the airport.

Accommodation

Catalonia offers a range of accommodation, including government-run hotels called paradors. A useful list of accommodation can be found on the **Turespaña** website. Try to book your accommodation well in advance if you plan to visit in the peak season (July and August). Rates are also higher during major fiestas. Most hotels quote prices without including tax (IVA), which is 10 per cent. In Barcelona, visitors must pay a nightly tax that varies from 75¢ to €2.50 depending on the number of stars of the hotel. There is a seven-day maximum.

DIRECTORY

MOBILE PHONES AND WI-FI

WiFi Map
w wifimap.io

POSTAL SERVICES

Correos
w correos.es

VISITOR INFORMATION

Barcelona Card
w barcelonacard.org

Barcelona City Council
w barcelona.cat

Barcelona Turisme
MAP M1 ■ Pl de Catalunya 17
w barcelonaturisme.com

Catalunya Turisme
w catalunyaturisme.cat

Culture Institute
MAP L3 ■ La Rambla 99
📞 93 316 10 00

Turisme de Catalunya
MAP E2 ■ Palau Robert, Pg de Gràcia 107
w catalunya.com

ACCOMMODATION

Turespaña
w spain.info

Places to Stay

PRICE CATEGORIES

For a standard double room per night (with breakfast if included), including taxes and extra charges.

€ under €120   €€ €120–240   €€€ over €240

Luxury Hotels

Granados 83

MAP E2 ■ C/Enric Granados 83 ■ 93 492 96 70 ■ www.hotel granados83.com ■ €€
Rooms at this designer hotel are decorated with African zebrawood, chocolate brown leather and original pieces of Hindu and Buddhist art. Suites have private terraces that overlook a plunge pool. There is a restaurant, and a pretty rooftop pool with a fashionable bar.

ABaC Restaurant and Hotel

MAP B1 ■ Av Tibidabo 1 ■ 93 319 66 00 ■ www. abacbarcelona.com ■ €€€
This boutique hotel, set in a listed building, boasts luxury amenities perfectly suited for the smaller number of guests. The 17 gorgeous rooms are stylishly decorated in a contemporary, minimal style. There is a wellness spa with a hammam and Jacuzzi, plus a small garden. It also has one of the city's finest restaurants, ABaC, which earned its chef Jordi Cruz three Michelin stars.

Alma Barcelona

MAP E2 ■ C/Mallorca 271 ■ 93 216 44 90 ■ www.almahotels. com/barcelona ■ €€€
This hotel exudes elegance and is renowned for its excellent service.

Several original 19th-century details have been preserved, but the rooms are chic and minimalist. The glorious garden *(see p61)* and the stylish roof terrace are ideal for relaxing after a day's sightseeing.

Almanac Hotel

MAP E3 ■ Gran Via de les Corts Catalanes 619 ■ 93 018 70 00 ■ www.almanac hotels.com ■ €€€
A plush luxury hotel kitted out by top local designer Jaime Beriestain, who took an Art Deco ethos to fashionable heights with velvety textiles, fine noble wood and brass fittings. Here, smooth elegance is complemented by premium service. The rooftop sundeck and pool are as spectacular as one would expect for the price, the silver service breakfast is unmatched, and each room has an enclosed balcony where guests can snuggle up on a day bed.

Casa Camper

MAP L2 ■ C/Elisabets 11 ■ 93 342 62 80 ■ www. casacamper.com ■ €€€
A converted 19th-century mansion, this hotel is filled with innovative yet comfortable design touches. It has stylish rooms, a roof terrace, an extraordinary vertical garden and a free 24-hour bar. The Dos Palillos

restaurant is run by Albert Raurich, former chef at El Bulli. Well-deserving of its Michelin star, it specializes in creative, tapas-style Asian dishes.

El Palace Barcelona Hotel

MAP F3 ■ Gran Via de les Corts Catalanes 668 ■ 93 510 11 30 ■ www. hotelpalacebarcelona. com ■ €€€
With its 1919 Neo-Classical façade, grand public areas and excellent service, this hotel is synonymous with tradition and style. The Caelis restaurant, with one Michelin star, exudes 19th-century elegance and offers an innovative gourmet menu created by chef Romain Fornell.

Grand Hotel Central

MAP E4 ■ Via Laietana 30 ■ 93 295 79 00 ■ www. grandhotelcentral.com ■ €€€
Large, elegant hotel located close to the Barri Gòtic and El Born. It has accommodating staff, a fitness centre and an elegant restaurant serving excellent Mediterranean cuisine. But the real highlight is the hotel's stunning rooftop infinity pool, which provides spectacular views of the city.

Hotel Arts Barcelona

MAP G5 ■ C/Marina 19–21 ■ 93 221 10 00 ■ www.hotelarts barcelona.com ■ €€€
The *ne plus ultra* of the city's five-star hotels, this hotel is located a

few steps from the sea, with large rooms and top-notch places to dine. Enoteca, run by Catalan chef Paco Pérez (of the Costa Brava's Miramar restaurant), offers imaginative Mediterranean cuisine and boasts two Michelin stars. The outdoor pool on the first floor has fantastic views.

Majestic Hotel and Spa
MAP E2 ■ Pg de Gràcia 68 ■ 93 488 17 17 ■ https://majestichotelgroup.com ■ €€€
Faultless service and stately decor are the hallmarks of this aptly named hotel. Exit through the reassuringly heavy brass-and-glass doors and you'll find yourself just a few steps from the Modernista gems of Eixample. The rooftop plunge pool has great views of the Barcelona cityscape and Gaudí's incredible masterpiece, the Sagrada Família.

W Barcelona
MAP E5 ■ Pl de la Rosa dels Vents 1 ■ 93 295 28 00 ■ www.w-barcelona.cat ■ €€€
Popularly known as the Hotel Vela ("Sail Hotel"), thanks to its nautically billowing form and location right next to the water, this lavishly appointed five-star option enjoys unparalleled sea views. With its massive floor-to-ceiling windows it is not hard to imagine you are at sea. The hotel has all the usual luxury extras, from a stunning outdoor pool and 7,500-sq-ft (700-sq-m) spa to six designer bars and restaurants.

Historic Hotels

Hotel Duquesa de Cardona
MAP M6 ■ Pg Colón 12 ■ 93 268 90 90 ■ www.hduquesadecardona.com ■ €€
The 16th-century home of the noble Cardona family used to host the royal court on its visits to the city. Now a stylish hotel, it combines the original structure with avant-garde decor and modern facilities. The rooftop terrace has a plunge pool and great views over the Port Vell area.

Hotel España
MAP L4 ■ C/Sant Pau 9 ■ 93 550 00 00 ■ www.hotelespanya.com ■ €€
This little gem of Catalan *Modernisme* is set in an 1850 building renovated in 1903 by Modernista architect Lluís Domènech i Montaner, artist Ramón Casas and sculptor Eusebi Arnau, who carved the splendid alabaster fireplace. There is a rooftop pool and solarium, and the Fonda España restaurant is run by Michelin-starred chef Martín Berasategui.

Praktik Rambla
MAP E3 ■ Rambla de Catalunya 27 ■ 93 343 66 90 ■ www.hotelpraktikrambla.com ■ €€
The centrally located budget hotel is set in a Modernista mansion. It combines traditional and avant-garde decor. The original tiling and carved woodwork from the 20th century make a striking contrast with the contemporary furnishings. The hotel has an outdoor terrace and also provides free Wi-Fi. Book in advance as there are only a few rooms.

Casa Fuster
MAP E1 ■ Pg de Gràcia 132 ■ 93 255 30 00 ■ www.hotelcasafuster.com ■ €€€
Originally designed by Domènech i Montaner, whose works have been declared World Heritage Sites by the UNESCO. This hotel is one of the city's most prestigious and luxurious. The Modernista details have been retained, but elegantly fused with 21st-century amenities.

Gran Hotel La Florida
MAP B1 ■ Ctra Vallvidrera al Tibidabo 83–93 ■ 93 259 30 00 ■ www.hotelfloridabarcelona.com ■ €€€
Set in a Modernista villa high up in the hills in Tibidabo, this luxurious hotel has maintained its legendary views over the city since 1924, when it was built for Dr. Andreu, pharmaceutical entrepreneur and philanthropist. Its guests have included Ernest Hemingway, Princess Fabiola and the prince of Belgium. In 2001 it was meticulously and beautifully restored to its former glory.

Hotel 1898
MAP L2 ■ La Rambla 109 ■ 93 552 95 52 ■ www.hotel1898.com ■ €€€
This chic hotel has retained some of the building's original fittings, such as the 20th-century revolving door, and added modern amenities, such as a swimming pool, a fitness centre and spa, and a good restaurant.

Hotel Claris

MAP E2 ▪ C/Pau Claris 150 ▪ 93 487 62 62 ▪ www.hotelclaris.com ▪ €€€

This 19th-century palace was once home to the Counts of Vedruna. It has a small collection of Pre-Columbian art, some objects from which also decorate the suites. Guests can relax at the Mayan spa and cool off in the rooftop plunge pool.

Hotel Neri

MAP M3 ▪ C/Sant Sever 5 ▪ 93 304 06 55 ▪ www.hotelneri.com ▪ €€€

This 17th-century former palace at the heart of the Barri Gòtic offers an exclusive combination of history, the avant-garde and glamour. There is a library, a solarium and a roof terrace with views to the cathedral.

Mercer Hotel

MAP N4 ▪ C/Lledó 7 ▪ 93 310 74 80 ▪ www.mercerbarcelona.com ▪ €€€

This boutique hotel in the old part of town has 28 large, comfortable rooms and the decor has a cutting-edge, designer feel to it. You can take in the amazing views of the city from the swimming pool on the roof terrace. There is also a cocktail bar and restaurant.

Monument

MAP E2 ▪ Pg de Gràcia 75 ▪ 93 548 20 00 ▪ www.monumenthotel.com ▪ €€€

An old neo-Gothic palace right on the posh Passeig de Gràcia has been converted to a luxury hotel with an arty feel, including some bold contemporary design pieces. Guests can choose the street-facing rooms or the rear ones, which look out onto a typical Eixample courtyard.

Central Stays

chic&basic Born

MAP P4 ▪ C/Princesa 50 ▪ 93 295 46 52 ▪ www.chicandbasic.com ▪ €€

This 19th-century town house is a big hit with fashionistas. Rooms are minimalist with contemporary glass and steel bathrooms and colourful LED lights. Bike hire and activities such as stand-up paddle board are on offer, and there's a common area where you can mingle with other guests.

Hotel Banys Orientals

MAP N4 ▪ C/Argenteria 37 ▪ 93 268 84 60 ▪ www.hotelbanysorientals.com ▪ €€

Behind the traditional frontage lies a modern, cosy hotel. Plusher suites are available in a separate building. The hotel's Senyor Parellada restaurant serves excellent Catalan cuisine, including speciality *bacalao* (cod) and *butifarra* (sausage). The cathedral, Museu Picasso and Barceloneta beach are close by.

Hotel Colón

MAP N3 ▪ Av de la Catedral 7 ▪ 93 301 14 04 ▪ hotelcolonbarcelona.es ▪ €€

A handsome, family-owned Barri Gòtic hotel, the Colón has traditional decor with mirrors and oil paintings throughout. The magnificent views of the cathedral and Plaça de la Seu are stunning.

Hotel guests have included Sartre, Arata Isozaki and Joan Miró, who made this place his home in the 1960 and 70s.

Hotel Constanza

MAP F3 ▪ C/Bruc 33 ▪ 93 270 19 10 ▪ www.hotelconstanza.com ▪ €€

This elegant mid-sized hotel is near Eixample's main sights. Some of the stylish rooms come with terraces. The adjoining Bruc 33 restaurant serves homemade tapas and Mediterranean specialities.

Hotel Jazz

MAP L1 ▪ C/Pelai 3 ▪ 93 552 96 96 ▪ www.hoteljazz.com ▪ €€

The modern Hotel Jazz may not be the most characterful option, but it is centrally located and has several amenities, including a small rooftop pool. It is great value for money, and the friendly staff are always on hand to offer help and advice.

Hotel Soho Barcelona

MAP D3 ▪ Gran Vía Corts Catalanes 543 ▪ 93 552 96 10 ▪ www.hotelsohobarcelona.com ▪ €€

Top Spanish architect Alfredo Arribas designed this stylish, contemporary hotel. Located in the heart of Eixample, it's perfect for shopping, sightseeing and enjoying the nightlife. The rooftop pool has magnificent views.

Park Hotel

MAP F5 ▪ Av Marquès de l'Argentera 11 ▪ 93 319 60 00 ▪ www.parkhotelbarcelona.com ▪ €€

A 1950s design classic with a gorgeous wrap-around staircase, the Park Hotel was redone by the original architect's son. Rooms are small but comfortably furnished, and some have balconies. It is located near the fashionable Born clubs and boutiques.

Room Mate Emma

MAP E2 ▪ C/Rosselló 205 ▪ 93 238 56 06 ▪ roommatehotels.com/en/emma ▪ €€

A great option if you're looking for style on a budget, the Room Mate Emma offers compact but gorgeously designed bedrooms in the very centre of the city. There's no restaurant, but the staff can give recommendations.

Mandarin Oriental Barcelona

MAP E3 ▪ Pg de Gràcia 38–40 ▪ 93 151 88 88 ▪ www.mandarinoriental.es/barcelona/passeig-de-gracia/luxury-hotel ▪ €€€

This ultra-luxurious hotel boasts rooms overlooking either the iconic Passeig de Gràcia or the gorgeous interior gardens. It has a spa and a roof terrace with a splash pool. The gourmet restaurant, Moments, which serves exquisite Catalan cuisine and boasts two Michelin stars, is run by renowned chef Carme Ruscalleda of Sant Pau fame *(see p131)* – who has seven Michelin stars to her name – and her son Raül Balam.

Pullman Barcelona Skipper

MAP G6 ▪ Av Litoral 10 ▪ 93 221 65 65 ▪ www.pullman-barcelona-skipper.com ▪ €€€

Overlooking the sea close to the beach, the Pullman is the perfect spot for a summer city break. Ideal

for business travellers, it has all the facilities guests would expect of a five-star hotel. Weekend bargains are often available.

Mid-Range Hotels

Circa 1905

MAP E2 ▪ C/Provença 286 ▪ 93 505 69 60 ▪ www.circa1905.com ▪ €€

This is one of a new breed of boutique B&Bs, and has just nine rooms (one with a private terrace) in a charming Modernista mansion. Furnished with a tasteful mix of antique and contemporary pieces, it has an elegant lounge where you can leaf through the books and enjoy a drink. Long-term rates available.

H10 Art Gallery

MAP E2 ▪ C/Enric Granados 62 ▪ 932 14 20 30 ▪ www.h10hotels.com ▪ €€

Colourful, contemporary and very chic, H10 Art Gallery has a beautiful interior patio and a rooftop terrace with a plunge pool. Rooms are bright and minimalist, and each floor draws inspiration from a different artist, from Miró to Lichtenstein. It's on one of Barcelona's prettiest streets, and has its own restaurant and café-bar.

Hotel Barcelona Catedral

MAP M3 ▪ C/Capellans 4 ▪ 93 304 22 55 ▪ www.barcelonacatedral.com ▪ €€

Enjoy phenomenal views over the Barri Gòtic from the roof terrace at this modern hotel, which also boasts a rooftop plunge pool and a small

fitness room. The guest rooms are spacious and bright, the service excellent, and the off-season prices a bargain. The hotel offers free bike hire, and conducts complimentary walking tours through the quarter on Wednesdays and Sundays.

Hotel Casa Luz

MAP E3 ▪ Ronda de Universitat 1 ▪ 93 002 25 05 ▪ https://hotel casaluz.com ▪ €€

Set in an elegant 19th-century building, this boutique hotel offers exquisite rooms, some with a private terrace. There is also a beautiful rooftop bar with scenic views over the skyline.

Hotel Ciutat Vella

MAP L1 ▪ C/Tallers 66 ▪ 934 81 37 99 ▪ www.hotelciutatvella.com ▪ €€

Offering modern rooms decorated in warm colours, this great value option is located just a 5-minute walk from La Rambla. Some rooms have small terraces, and there is a plunge pool and sun deck on the roof.

Hotel Granvía

MAP F3 ▪ Gran Vía de les Corts Catalanes 642 ▪ 93 318 19 00 ▪ www.hotel granvia.com ▪ €€

Totally refurbished in 2013, this opulent late 19th-century mansion, built for a Barcelona philanthropist, has a domed stained-glass entrance, a fairy-tale staircase and lavish stucco ceilings. The rooms have understated modern decor, and there is a charming hidden patio garden at the back.

For a key to hotel price categories see p142

Musik Boutique Hotel

MAP P3 ■ C/Sant Pere Més Baix 62 ■ 93 222 55 44 ■ www.musik boutiquehotel.com ■ €€

Close to the magnificent Palau de la Música, this small and welcoming hotel has a contemporary, interior façade an 18th-century façade. The largest of the rooms have private terraces.

Primero Primera

MAP B1 ■ C/Doctor Carulla 25–29 ■ 93 417 56 00 ■ www.primero primera.com ■ €€

This plush hotel in the upmarket Sant Gervasi area combines vintage chic with contemporary sophistication. There's a cosy lounge with an open fire and leather armchairs and a romantic little garden with a small pool and sun loungers.

Villa Emilia

MAP C3 ■ C/Calàbria 115 ■ 93 252 52 85 ■ www. hotelvillaemilia.com ■ €€

Slightly off the beaten track, but close to the hip Sant Antoni neighbourhood, which is packed with bars and boutiques, this friendly hotel offers stylish rooms and a roof terrace for barbecues in summer and cocktails under heaters in winter. The lobby bar has regular jazz concerts.

Violeta Boutique

MAP F3 & N1 ■ C/Caspe 38 ■ 93 302 81 58 ■ violet aboutique.com ■ €€

Each of the spacious rooms at this lovely guesthouse has been individually decorated, and guests can sit out on a pretty balcony with a drink or the newspaper. They also offer a small apartment which has its own kitchen and terrace.

Budget Hotels

chic&basic Zoo

MAP Q4 ■ Pg Picasso 22 ■ 93 295 46 52 ■ www. chicandbasic.com ■ €

Part of the chic&basic chain, this small hotel is located in a historic building in the heart of the Born district, opposite Parc de la Ciutadella. The largest rooms have balconies facing the park.

El Jardí

MAP M3 ■ Pl Sant Josep Oriol 1 ■ 93 301 59 00 ■ www.eljardi-barcelona. com ■ €

In the snug heart of the Barri Gòtic, this hostel has simple, spotless en suite rooms done up in light wood and cool colours. The bright breakfast room has balconies overlooking the square.

Hostal Goya

MAP N1 ■ C/Pau Claris 74 ■ 93 302 25 65 ■ www.hostalgoya. com ■ €

This well-run hostel was established in 1952. The rooms are bright and modern, with some designer touches. Most have en suite bathrooms, but only some have air conditioning.

Hostal Oliva

MAP E3 ■ Pg de Gràcia 32 ■ 93 488 01 62 ■ www. hostaloliva.com ■ €

From the the individually wrapped soaps to the lovely vintage elevator, this cheerful, family-run hostel is one of the city's best. The beautiful Modernista building has airy rooms, some with en suite bathrooms.

Market

MAP D3 ■ Comte Borrell 68 ■ 93 325 12 05 ■ www. hotelmarketbarcelona. com ■ €

Close to the Modernista Sant Antoni market, the rooms in this stylish hotel have an oriental feel, with glossy lacquered wood and a red, white and black colour scheme. Book well in advance.

Motel One Barcelona–Ciutadella

MAP Q3 ■ Passeig de Pujades 11–13 ■ 93 626 19 00 ■ €

Offering glorious views of the Ciutadella Park, this hotel is perfect for those on a budget. The rooms, some with balconies, are decorated in teal and aqua, and the roof terrace is a dreamy spot to relax.

Praktik Vinoteca

MAP E3 ■ C/Balmes 51 ■ 93 454 50 28 ■ www. hotelpraktikvinoteca.com ■ €

Ideal if you're looking for style on a budget, this wine-themed boutique hotel in Eixample has small but well-designed rooms. You can enjoy a wide range of local wines – over 900 or so on display – in the elegant and inviting lobby bar, and there's also a miniature terrace backed by plants.

Sol y k

MAP M5 ■ C/Cervantes 2 ■ 93 318 81 48 ■ hostal-sol-y-k.hotelbcn-barcelona.com/en ■ €

A budget option in the heart of the Barri Gòtic.

A handful of individually decorated rooms with mosaic headboards and original art set the Sol y k apart from other guest-houses. Some rooms have en suites.

Hotel Acta Mimic

MAP K5 ■ C/Arc del Teatre 58 ■ 93 329 94 50 ■ www. hotel-mimic.com ■ €€
Close to La Rambla, this hotel is set in a building that once housed a theatre. The rooms are well-lit and airy, with large windows and sleek, modern decor. Guests can relax on the sunbeds arranged on the roof terrace, which doubles as a solarium with a view over the old town and the port.

Hotel Brummell

MAP 5C ■ C/Nou de la Rambla 174 ■ 93 125 86 22 ■ www.hotel brummell.com ■ €€
A stylish little charmer in lively Poble Sec, this hotel has a rooftop sun deck and plunge pool to go with the contemporarily styled rooms. Complimentary yoga classes, a sauna and a courtyard filled with plants make it the perfect city oasis.

Campsites and Aparthotels

Aparthotel Atenea

C/Joan Güell 207–211 ■ 93 490 66 40 ■ www. aparthotelatenea. com ■ €
Designed with business travellers in mind, this top-notch aparthotel is sited near the business and financial district around upper Diagonal. Rooms are spacious and well equipped, and there

are several conference rooms and a 24-hour laundry service.

Aparthotel Bertran

C/de Bertran 150 ■ 93 212 75 50 ■ www. bertran-hotel.com ■ €
This accommodation has generous studios and apartments (many with balconies), a rooftop swimming pool, a small gym and 24-hour laundry service. Breakfast is served in your apartment.

Cala Llevadó

Ctra GI-682 km 18.9, Tossa de Mar ■ 97 234 03 14 ■ Closed Oct–Easter ■ calallevado.com ■ €
A well-kept, eco-friendly campsite on the Costa Brava near the beautiful beach town of Tamariu. It is just 200 m (656 ft) from the beach and within walking distance of the town for bars, restaurants and grocery shops. The campsite has a picturesque location by the sea, with palm-shaded pitches for tents. Great for families.

Camping Barcelona

Ctra N-II, km 650, 8 km (5 miles) E of Mataró ■ 93 790 47 20 ■ Closed Nov–Mar ■ www.camping barcelona.com ■ €
Located 28 km (17 miles) north of Barcelona, this is set next to a small beach. Bungalows are available to rent as are pitches.

Camping Globo Rojo

Ctra N-II km 660, 9, Canet de Mar ■ 93 794 11 43 ■ Closed Oct–Mar ■ www. globo-rojo.com ■ €
Close to the beaches of Canet de Mar, Globo Rojo offers pitches, mobile homes, bungalows and other accommodation

units. There is a pool, tennis court and football pitch. Great for kids. Direct bus and train to Barcelona.

Camping Masnou Barcelona

C/Camil Fabra 33 (N-II, km 663), El Masnou ■ 93 555 15 03 ■ www. campingmasnou barcelona.com ■ €
Family-owned campsite located 11 km (7 miles) north of Barcelona and close to the El Masnou train station, which is a 20-minute journey from the city. The site faces the sea and has a small beach close by. They offer shaded pitches as well as rooms. Facilities include a pool, a supermarket and a terrace bar with Wi-Fi.

Camping Roca Grossa

Ctra N-II km 665, Calella ■ 93 769 12 97 ■ Closed Oct–Mar ■ www.roca grossa.com ■ €
Positioned between the mountains and the sea, this modern, family-oriented campsite has good installations and access to the nearby beach. It has a large swimming pool, a restaurant and bar and is only 1 km (0.6 mile) from the lively resort of Calella. Both pitches and bungalows are available.

Camping Sitges

Ctra Comarcal C-246a, km 38, Sitges ■ 93 894 10 80 ■ Closed mid-Oct–mid-March ■ www. campingsitges.com ■ €
This is a small, well-kept campsite with a swimming pool, playground and a supermarket. It is located 2 km (1 mile) south of Sitges, and close to its renowned beaches.

For a key to hotel price categories see p142

Sant Jordi Sagrada Família

MAP E2 ▪ C/Freser 5 ▪ 93 446 05 17 ▪ www. santjordihostels.com ▪ €
The Sant Jordi group's most comfortable accommodation in Barcelona, this features a skateboard theme, complete with a mini-ramp. Guests can choose from rooms, dorms as well as private apartments for their stay.

Citadines

MAP L2 ▪ La Rambla 122 ▪ 93 270 11 11 ▪ www. citadines.com ▪ €€
If you're smitten with the city, try an aparthotel for a longer stay. This one on La Rambla has well-appointed studios and small apartments with a kitchenette, iron and CD stereo. The rooftop terrace has beach chairs and showers and is just the spot to unwind.

Suites Avenue

MAP E2 ▪ Pg de Gràcia 83 ▪ 93 272 37 16 ▪ www. suitesavenue.com ▪ €€€
These apartments set on Barcelona's grandest avenue, are housed in a striking building with a rippling façade. The chic, minimalist design is complemented by artworks and numerous antiquities. The amenities include a spa area and a stunning terrace with a plunge pool.

Hostels

Be Dream Hostel Barcelona

Av Alfonso XIII 28b, Badalona ▪ 93 399 14 20 ▪ www.behostels.com/ dream ▪ €
A 20-minute metro ride from the city centre, but close to the beaches, this hostel is well priced, with rooms and dorms sleeping between 2 and 12 guests. Kitchen as well as laundry facilities are included.

Fabrizzio's Petit

MAP F3 ▪ C/Bruc 65, 2–2 ▪ 93 215 40 59 ▪ www. fabrizzios.com ▪ €
Choose from either simple rooms or dorms at this friendly hostel, which also has a terrace, a kitchen and a lounge. The staff arrange all sorts of activities, including communal dinners, walking tours and other events.

Feetup Garden House Hostel

C/ d'Hedilla 58 ▪ 93 427 24 79 ▪ feetuphostels. com ▪ €
This friendly hostel is located on the outskirts of the city, near Gaudí's beautiful Park Güell. It's only a 15-minute metro ride into the centre of town. There is a lovely garden and roof terrace, and a relaxed vibe.

INOUT Hostel

C/Major del Rectoret 2, Vallvidrera ▪ 93 280 09 85 ▪ www.inouthostel.com ▪ €
Located at a 12-minute train ride from the city centre in the forest-filled enclave Vallvidrera, INOUT Hostel is an admirable, enterprise that provides employment to people who are differently-abled. Nearly 90 per cent of their work force consists of people with specific needs. Rooms accommodate four to ten people. There are sports facilities as well as a pool here.

Itaca Hostel

MAP N3 ▪ C/Ripoll 21 ▪ 93 301 97 51 ▪ www. itacahostel.com ▪ €
Located in the heart of the Barri Gòtic Quarter, this hostel has space for 30 guests in double rooms, dorms (for up to 6 people) and apartments. Bedding and lockers are included in the price and there is Wi-Fi available in the main building.

Kabul Hostel

MAP L4 ▪ Pl Reial 17 ▪ 93 318 51 90 ▪ www. kabul.es ▪ €
Kabul is a favourite with young backpackers, so it's often full. Dorm rooms, all with air conditioning and some with balconies, sleep 4–20 people. There's a gorgeous roof terrace with hammocks. Other services include free Internet access, lockers, a laundry, and a small café open during the day.

Mambo Tango

MAP C4 ▪ C/Poeta Cabanyes 23 ▪ 93 442 51 64 ▪ hostelmambo tango.com ▪ €
Former travellers Toto and Marino are behind this warm and welcoming hostel. It has dorms for four, six, eight and nine people, breakfast and sheet-hire are included in the price, and extras include complimentary hot drinks and fruit. Party animals are actively discouraged, so you can count on getting a good night's sleep during your stay.

Primavera Hostel

MAP F2 ▪ C/Mallorca 330 ▪ 93 175 21 51 ▪ www. primavera-hostel.com ▪ €
Full of charming details, including the original

vaulted ceilings and tiled floors, this hostel offers private and dorm rooms. You can cook in the kitchen and chill out with fellow travellers in the lounge.

Pars Tailor's Hostel

MAP D3 ▪ C/Sepulveda 146 ▪ 93 250 56 84 ▪ pars hostels.com ▪ €€
A mother-and-daughter team run this charming hostel, which features vintage interiors designed to evoke a Parisian tailor's in the 1930s. The well-equipped air-conditioned dorms have lockers. There is a terrace, lounge and many free activities.

Beyond Barcelona

Ca l'Aliu

C/Roca 6, Peratallada, 12 km (7.5 miles) NW of Palafrugell ▪ 97 263 40 61 ▪ www.calaliu.com ▪ €
In the tiny medieval town of Peratallada stands this restored 18th-century *casa rural*. The cosy, comfortable rooms have antique furniture and are all en suite.

Hostal Sa Tuna

Pg de Ancora 6, Platja Sa Tuna, 5 km N of Begur ▪ 97 262 21 98 ▪ Closed Nov–Mar ▪ www.hostal satuna.com ▪ €€
Take in the sea views from your terrace at this stylish, five-room boutique hotel overlooking bays on the Costa Brava. The elegant on-site restaurant serves seafood and other local dishes.

Hotel Aigua Blava

Platja de Fornells, Begur ▪ 97 262 20 58 ▪ Closed mid-Oct–late Mar ▪ www. hotelaiguablava.com ▪ €€
This coastal institution, perched atop rugged cliffs overlooking the sea, is run by the fourth generation of the same family. Many of the rooms – each individually decorated – have splendid views of the Mediterranean. There's a large outdoor pool and breakfast is included in the price. Apartments are also available.

Hotel Aiguaclara

C/Sant Miquel 2, Begur ▪ 97 262 29 05 ▪ www. hotelaiguaclarabegur.com ▪ €€
A charming hotel set in a whitewashed 1866 colonial villa in the centre of town, it was built by a Begur "indiano" – a local nickname for those who made their fortunes in Cuba in the early 19th century. The beautiful rooms are a mix of contemporary furnishings and original features. The wonderful restaurant and outstanding service make this the ideal place for a romantic break.

Hotel Blau Mar

C/Farena 36, Llafranc ▪ 97 261 00 55 ▪ www. hllafranch.com ▪ €€
Set in a pretty seaside village, Blau Mar has traditionally decorated rooms (most with terraces), lovely gardens and a pool with sea-views. There are several clifftop walks and coves to explore nearby.

Hotel Can Barrina

Ctra de Palautordera al Montseny, km 12, 670, Montseny ▪ 93 847 30 65 ▪ canbarrina.com/en ▪ €€
Built in the 18th century, this farmhouse set in the hills of Montseny, is now an excellent restaurant which also has a handful of comfortable, rustic rooms. The charming setting, extensive gardens and an outdoor pool make it the perfect place to relax.

Hotel Històric

C/Belmirall 4a, Girona ▪ 97 222 35 83 ▪ www. hotelhistoric.com ▪ €€
Located in the heart of the old quarter, this is a good base for exploring Girona. Guests have the option of choosing either the rooms or the self-catering apartments.

Parador de Tortosa

Castillo de la Zuda, Tortosa ▪ 97 744 44 50 ▪ www.parador.es ▪ €€
Looming over the town of Tortosa is the ancient Arab Castillo de la Zuda, within which this *parador* is housed. The decor is suitably old-world, with dark-wood furniture and antique features. The view of the countryside and mountains is superb.

Val de Neu

C/Perimetrau s/n ▪ 97 363 50 00 ▪ Closed May–Sep ▪ www.hotelbaqueira valdeneu.com ▪ €€
A sumptuous ski hotel in the chic resort of Baqueria Beret, Val de Neu is located right next to the slopes. Among the five-star amenities are a spa, a pool and an array of restaurants.

El Castell de la Ciutat

Crta N-260, km 229, La Seu d'Urgell ▪ 97 335 00 00 ▪ www.hotelelcastell. com ▪ €€€
Located right next to a 16th-century castle, this hotel offers refined luxury in the heart of the Pyrenees. There are a couple of restaurants, a spa, gardens, pools, and wonderful views of the mountains.

For a key to hotel price categories see p142

General Index

Page numbers in **bold**
refer to Top 10 highlights.

A

Accommodation
  booking 141
  see also Hotels
Air, Arriving by 134, 135
Alcohol 138
Alfarràs, Marquès d' 118
Alt Penedès 126
Ambulances 139
Amusement parks
  Parc d'Atraccions del
    Tibidabo 52, 117, 119
  PortAventura World
    127
Angelico, Fra 20
Antic Hospital de la Santa
  Creu 89
Antoni de Padua, Sant 41
Aparthotels 147–8
L'Aquàrium de Barcelona
  53
Aranu, Eusebi 32
Architecture
  Modernista buildings
    15, 32–3, 44–5, 109
  Arlequi (Picasso) 31
Arnau, Eusebi 45
Arranz Bravo, Eduardo
  34
Art Nouveau 44–5, 107
Arts Santa Mònica 17
L'Auditori 54
Autoretrat amb perruca
  (Picasso) 30
Avinguda Diagonal 67
Avinguda Paral·lel 88

B

Bacon, Francis 26
Bagutti, Domenico 118
Ballooning 130
Bank holidays 140
Barça Stadium Tour &
  Museum 118
Barcelona Cathedral 6, 10,
  18–19, 40, 58, 77
Barcelona History Museum
  (MUHBA) 22
Barceloneta 102, 103
Barri Gòtic and La Ribera
  5, 76–85
  cafés and light eats 84
  cocktail and
    conversation   spots 83
  map 76–7

Barri Gòtic and La Ribera
  (cont.)
  remains of Roman
    Barcino 81
  restaurants and tapas
    bars 85
  shops 82
Bars 60–61
  Barri Gòtic and La
    Ribera 85
  Gràcia, Tibidabo and
    Zona Alta 122
  Montjuïc 99
  El Ravel 92
  The Seafront 104
Basílica de la Puríssima
  Concepció 51
Beaches
  Barcelona for free 70
  Castelldefels 49
  children's attractions 53
  city beaches 49, 101
  El Masnou 49
  photo spots 59
  Premià de Mar 49
Beethoven, Ludwig van
  33
Begur 126
Benedict XVI, Pope 14
Berenguer de Montagut
  78–9
Beyond Barcelona 124–31
  accommodation 149
  churches and
    monasteries 128
  map 124–5
  national parks and
    nature reserves 129
  outdoor activities 130
  restaurants 131
Blay, Miquel 44
Boats
  boat trips 53, 102, 130
  Museu Marítim 43, 52,
    87, 103
  Pailebot *Santa Eulàlia*
    102, 103
  sailing 130
Book Market 68
Borgonya, Joan de 18
El Born 67, 78
Botero, Fernando 71
Bruno Quadras Building 17
Budget travel
  Barcelona for free
    70–71
  hotels 146–7
Buigas, Carles 95

Bunkers del Carmel
  50–51, 59
Bus travel 136, 137
  long-distance 134, 135

C

Caballé, Montserrat 16,
  95
Cable cars 53, 102
Cadaqués 125, 127
Cafés 64–5
  Barri Gòtic and La
    Ribera 84
  drinks 65
  Eixample 112
  Gràcia, Tibidabo and
    Zona Alta 121
  Montjuïc 99
CaixaForum 97
Calder, Alexander
  Font de Mercuri 28
El Call 79
Cambó, Francesc 20
Campsites–8
Can Framis 43
Canal Olímpic 130
Cap de Barcelona
  (Lichtenstein) 43
Cap de Creus 127, 129
La Capella 70
Capella MACBA 35
Capella de San Cristòfol
  80
Capella de Sant Jordi
  41
Capella de Sant Miquel
  40
Capella de Santa Àgata
  41
Carnivals 72
Car rental 137
Carrer del Bisbe 80
Carrer del Correu Vell
  80
Carrer Girona 66
Carrer Montcada 80
Carrer Pelai 67
Carrer Petritxol 80
Carrer Portaferrissa 67
Carrer Regomir 80
Carrer Riera Baixa 88
Carrer de Santa Llúcia
  80
Carrer Tallers 88
Carretera de les Aigües 71
Casa Amatller 45, 107
Casa Batlló 15, 45
Casa Calvet 15, 109

Casa Lleó Morera 45
Casa Milà see La Pedrera
Casa-Museu Gaudí 23
Casa de les Punxes 45, 108, 109
Casa Terrades 45, 108, 109
Casa Vicens 15, 119
Casas, Ramon
  Ramon Casas and Pere Romeu on a Tandem 21
Castell de Montjuïc 58, 95, 97
Castelldefels 49
Castells (human castles) 72
Catalan Peasant by Moonlight (Miró) 28
Cathedrals
  Barcelona Cathedral 6, 10, **18–19**, 40, 77
  Catedral de Girona 128
  Catedral de La Seu d'Urgell 128
  Catedral de Santa Tecla (Tarragona) 128
  see also Churches
Cavalcada de Reis 73
Cavall banyegat (Picasso) 31
Centre de Cultura Contemporània (CCCB) 7, 11, **34–5**, 36–7, 42, 87, 89
Centre d'Interpretació del Call 43
Cerdà, Ildefons 39, 108
Chagall, Marc 26
Chapels see Churches and chapels
Charlemagne 38
Children's attractions 52–3
Christmas 73
Churches and chapels 40–41
  Basílica de la Puríssima Concepció 51
  Capella de Sant Jordi 41
  Capella de Sant Miquel 40
  Capella de Santa Àgata 41
  Església de Betlem 17, 41
  Església al Monestir de Pedralbes 40
  Església de Sant Just i Sant Pastor 80
  Església de Sant Pau del Camp 40, 89
  Església de Sant Pere de les Puelles 40

Churches and chapels (cont.)
  Església de Santa Anna 80
  Església de Santa Maria 78–9
  Església de Santa Maria del Mar 40
  Església de Santa Maria del Pi 41
  Sagrada Família 5, 6, 8–9, 10, **12–14**, 44, 107, 109
  Sant Climent i Santa Maria de Taüll 128
  Sant Joan de les Abadesses 128
  Temple Expiatori del Sagrat Cor 40, 119
  see also Cathedrals
Ciència i Caritat (Picasso) 30
Cinema see Films
Civil War 38–9
Clavé, Josep Anselm 33
Clubs
  Barri Gòtic and La Ribera 83
  Eixample 111
Coin Market 68
Colegio Teresiano 15
Columbus, Christopher
  Monument a Colom 16, 102–3
Companys, Lluís 39
Convent de Sant Agustí 51
CosmoCaixa Museu de la Ciència 43, 118
Costa Brava 126
Costa Daurada 127
COVID-19 140
Credit cards 140
Crime 139
Cristòfol, Sant 41
Currency 140
Customs information 138
Cycling 137
  tours 137

D

Dalí, Salvador 26
  Teatre-Museu Dalí (Figueres) 125
Dalmau, Lluís
  The Madonna of the Councillors 20
Delta de l'Ebre 129
Design shops
  Eixample 110
  El Ravel 90
El Dia de Sant Jordi 72

Discount card 141
Disseny museum 109
Diving 130
Domènech i Montaner, Lluís
  Casa Lleó Morera 45, 107
  Palau de la Música Catalana 32, 44, 54
  Sant Pau Art Recinte Modernista 107
Drinks, in cafés 65
Driving 136–7
Drugs 138

E

Eixample 106–13
  bars 111
  cafés 112
  design shops 110
  map 106–7
  Modernista architecture 5, 44
  restaurants and tapas bars 113
Electrical appliances 140
Elena, Santa 41
Elisenda, Queen 40, 117
Emergency services 139
Empúries 127
Els Encants 68, 108
Entertainment 54–5
Església de Betlem 17, 41
Església al Monestir de Pedralbes 40
Església de Sant Just i Sant Pastor 80
Església de Sant Pau del Camp 40, 89
Església de Sant Pere de les Puelles 40
Església de Santa Anna 80
Església de Santa Maria 78–9
Església de Santa Maria del Mar 40
Església de Santa Maria del Pi 41
L'Espera (Margot) (Picasso) 30
Estadi Olímpic 96, 97
L'Estel Matinal (Miró) 28
Eulàlia, Santa 18, 41

F

Ferdinand the Catholic 39
Festa Major de Gràcia 72
Festes 70
Festes de la Mercè 73

Festivals and events 72–3
  film 55
Figueres
  Teatre-Museu Dalí 125
Films
  Filmoteca 88–9
  Versión Original cinemas
    55
Finca Güell 15
Fira Artesana 68
Fira de Filatelia i
  Numismàtica 69
Fira de Santa Llúcia 68
Fire services 139
El Foll (Picasso) 30
Font de Canaletes 16
Font de Mercuri (Calder) 28
Font Màgica 7, 58, 70, 95
Food and drink
  café drinks 65
  tapas 63
  see also Cafés; Restaurants;
    Tapas bars
Football 42
  Barça Stadium Tour &
    Museum 118
Foraging for mushrooms
  130
Foster, Norman 117
Fountains
  Font de Canaletes 16
  Font Màgica 7, 58, 70,
    95
Franco, Francisco 39
Free Barcelona 70–71
Fundació Joan Miró 6, 7,
  11, **28–9**, 42, 95, 97
Fundació Tàpies 42, 44,
  108
Funfair
  Parc d'Atraccions del
    Tibidabo 52, 117,
    119
  PortAventura World
    127

G

Galleries and design shops
  El Ravel 90
  see also Museums and
    galleries
Gardens see Parks and
  gardens
Gaudí, Antoni 15, 39
  Casa Batlló 45, 107
  Casa Calvet 109
  Casa-Museu Gaudí 23
  furniture 21
  Casa Vicens 119
  Güell Pavilions 50
  Palau Güell 45, 87, 89

Gaudí, Antoni (cont.)
  Park Güell 10, **22–3**, 118,
    58, 119
  La Pedrera 11, **26–7**, 44,
    107, 109
  Plaça Reial 46
  Sagrada Família 5, 6, 10,
    12–14, 44, 107
  tomb 13, 14
Gaudí Exhibition Centre 19
Gehry, Frank 43, 71
Girona 126, 128
Golf 130
Government Advice 138
Gràcia, Tibidabo and Zona
  Alta 116–23
  bars 122
  boutiques 120
  cafés 121
  map 116–17
  restaurants and tapas
    bars 123
  shops 67
Gran Teatre del Liceu 16,
  54
Güell, Eusebi 22, 23,
  50, 87
Güell Pavilions 50
Guifre II, Count of
  Barcelona 40
Guifré the Hairy 39

H

Harlem Jazz Club 54
Health 138, 139
Herzog & de Meuron 103
History 38–9
Home amb boina (Picasso)
  30
Home assegut (Picasso)
  31
*Home i Dona Davant un
  Munt d'Excrement* (Miró)
  28
Horse riding 130
Hostels 148–9
Hotels 142–7
  beyond Barcelona 149
  booking 141
  budget hotels 146–7
  central hotels 144–5
  historical hotels 143–4
  luxury hotels 142–3
  mid-priced hotels 145–6
Huguet, Jaume 41

I

ID 138
Insurance 138, 139
Isozaki, Aiko 96
Isozaki, Arata 96

J

James II, King of Aragon
  117
Jardí Botànic 98
Jardí Botànic Històric
  71
Jardins d'Austri 22
Jardins des Castell 98
Jardins de Joan Brossa
  98
Jardins de Joan Maragall
  98
Jardins Laribal 7, 98
Jardins de Miramar 7,
  98
Jardins Mossèn Cinto
  Verdaguer 98
Jardins Mossèn Costa i
  Llobera 98
Jardins del Palau de
  Pedralbes 48–9
Jardins de la Rambla de
  Sants 50
Jardins del Teatre Grec
  98
Jaume I the Conqueror
  39
Jazz 54, 55, 73
JazzSí Club 55
Joan, Sant 41
Jordi, Sant 41
Jujol, Josep Maria 22

K

Kayaking 130
Kolbe, Georg 96

L

Language 141
Léger, Fernand 29
Lichtenstein, Roy 43, 71
Llúcia, Santa 41
Llull, Ramon 39
Local customs 141

M

Macià, Francesc 39
Madonna and Child
  (Rubens) 30
*The Madonna of the
  Councillors* (Dalmau)
  20
Magritte, René 29
Mansana de la Discòrdia
  107, 109
Maps
  Barcelona's highlights
    10–11
  Barri Gòtic and La
    Ribera 76–7
  beyond Barcelona 124–5

Maps (cont.)
   children's attractions
      53
   Eixample 106–7
   exploring Barcelona 6–7
   Gràcia, Tibidabo and
      Zona Alta 116–17
   markets 69
   Modernista buildings
      44
   Montjuïc 94
   off the beaten track 51
   outdoor bars
      60–61
   parks and beaches 49
   public squares 47
   La Rambla 17
   El Ravel 86, 89
   Roman Barcelona 79
   The Seafront 100–101
   shopping areas 66
Maremagnum 67
Marès, Frédéric
   Museu Frederic Marès
      43, 78
Mariscal, Javier 71
Markets 68–9
   Els Encants 68, 108
   Fira Artesana 68
   Fira de Filatelia i
      Numismàtica 69
   Fira de Santa Llúcia 68
   Mercat dels Antiquaris
      69
   Mercat del Art de la
      Plaça de Sant Josep
      69
   Mercat de Barceloneta
      69
   Mercat de La Boqueria 6,
      16, 68
   Mercat de la Llibertat
      50
   Mercat de Sant Antoni
      68
   Mercat de Santa
      Caterina 69
Martorell, Bernat 19
El Masnou 49
Massis de Pedraforca 129
Meier, Richard 34
Las Meninas series
   (Picasso) 31
Mercat dels Antiquaris
   69
Mercat del Art de la Plaça
   de Sant Josep 69
Mercat de Barceloneta
   69
Mercat de La Boqueria
   6, 16, 68

Mercat de les Flors 55
Mercat de la Llibertat 50
Mercat de Sant Antoni 68
Mercat de Santa Caterina
   69
Mercury, Freddie 95
Metro 135
Mies van der Rohe, Ludwig
   96
Millet, Lluís 33
The Minuet (Tiepolo) 20
El Mirador del Llobregat
   98
Miró, Joan 71
   Fundació Joan Miró 6, 7,
      11, **28–9**, 42, 95, 97
   Miró Mosaic 17
   Park Güell 22
   Parc de Joan Miró 49
Mobile phones 140
Modernista architecture
   15, 32–3, 44–5, 109
El Molino 54
Monasteries 128
Monestir de Montserrat
   128
Monestir de Pedralbes 117
Monestir de Poblet 128
Monestir de Ripoll 128
Monestir de Sant Pere de
   Rodes 127, 128
Monestir de Santes Creus
   128
Money 140
Montjuïc 5, 94–9
   cable cars 53
   map 94
   parks and gardens 98
   restaurants, cafés and
      bars 99
Montserrat 125
Monument a Colom 16,
   102–3
Museums and galleries
   42–3
   Barça Stadium Tour &
      Museum 118
   budget travel 70
   opening hours 140
   Arts Santa Mònica 17
   Barcelona History
      Museum (MUHBA)
      22
   CaixaForum 97
   La Capella 70
   Casa-Museu Gaudí 23
   Casa Vicens 119
   Centre de Cultura
      Contemporània (CCCB)
      7, 11, **34–5**, 36–7, 42,
      87, 89

Museums and galleries
   (cont.)
   Centre d'Interpretació
      del Call 43
   CosmoCaixa Museu de
      la Ciència 43, 118
   Espai Gaudí 26
   Fundació Joan Miró
      6, 7, 11, **28–9**, 42,
      95, 97
   Fundació Tàpies 42, 44,
      108
   Gaudí Exhibition Centre
      19
   Museu d'Art
      Contemporani
      (MACBA) 7, 11, **34–5**,
      36–7, 42, 59, 87, 89
   Museu dels Autòmates
      43
   Museu de Cera 43
   Museu de Ciències
      Naturals 103
   Museu del Disseny 43,
      109
   Museu Egipci 109
   Museu de Cultures del
      Món 43, 79
   Museu del FC Barcelona
      42
   Museu Frederic Marès
      43, 78
   Museu d'Història de
      Barcelona (MUHBA)
      42, 78, 79
   Museu d'Història de
      Catalunya 53, 58, 101
   Museu Marítim 43, 52,
      87, 103
   Museu del Modernisme
      de Barcelona 109
   Museu Nacional d'Art de
      Catalunya (MNAC) 7,
      10, 20–21, 42, 95, 97
   Museu del Perfum
      43, 109
   Museu Picasso 6, 11,
      30–31, 42, 77
   Museu de la Xocolata
      43
Sagrada Família 13
Teatre-Museu Dalí
   (Figueres) 125
Mushroom foraging 130
Music
   festivals 73
   music venues 54–5
   Música als Parcs 70
   Palau de la Música
      Catalana 6, 7, 11, **32–3**,
      44, 54, 77

N

La Nana (Picasso) 30
National parks 129
Nature reserves 129

O

Olympic Games (1992) 39, 96
Open House Barcelona 71
Opening hours 140
Orfeó Català 33
Outdoor activities, beyond Barcelona 130

P

Pailebot Santa Eulàlia 102, 103
Palau Güell 15, 45, 87, 89
Palau Macaya 109
Palau de la Música Catalana 11, **32–3**, 54, 77
  exploring Barcelona 6, 7
  Modernista architecture 44
Palau Nacional 95, 97
Palau Sant Jordi 96, 97
Palau de la Virreina 17
Palo Alto Design Complex 103
Parc d'Atraccions del Tibidabo 52, 59, 117, 119
Parc de Cervantes 48, 51
Parc de ltCiutadella 48
Parc de Collserola 119
Parc de l'Espanya Industrial 49
Park Güell 5, 6, 10, 15, **22–3**, 48, 58, 118, 119
Parc de Joan Miró 49
Parc de l'Oreneta 52
Parc del Laberint d'Horta 5, 48, 50, 52–3, 118
Parc Nacional d'Aigüestortes i Estany de Sant Maurici 129
Parc Natural dels Aiguamolls de l'Empordà 129
Parc Natural del Cadí-Moixeró 129
Parc Natural del Montseny 129
Parc Natural de Sant Llorenç del Munt 129
Parc Natural de la Zona Volcànica de la Garrotxa 129

Parks and gardens 48–9
  Jardí Botànic 98
  Jardí Botànic Històric 71
  Jardins d'Austri 22
  Jardins des Castell 98
  Jardins de Joan Brossa 98
  Jardins de Joan Maragall 98
  Jardins Laribal 7, 98
  Jardins de Miramar 7, 98
  Jardins Mossèn Cinto Verdaguer 98
  Jardins Mossèn Costa i Llobera 98
  Jardins del Palau de Pedralbes 48–9
  Jardins de la Rambla de Sants 98
  Jardins del Teatre Grec 98
  El Mirador del Llobregat 98
  Música als Parcs 70
  Parc de Cervantes 48, 51
  Parc de la Ciutadella 48
  Parc de Collserola 119
  Parc de l'Espanya Industrial 49
  Park Güell 5, 6, 10, 15, **22–3**, 48, 118, 119
  Parc de Joan Miró 49
  Parc del Laberint d'Horta 5, 48, 50, 52–3, 118
Passeig de Gràcia 6, 27, 66
Passports 138, 139
El Pati de les Dones/CCCB 35
Pati Llimona 79
Pavelló Mies van der Rohe 96
La Pedrera 11, 15, **26–7**, 107, 109
  exploring Barcelona 6
  Modernista architecture 44
Peix (Gehry) 43
Peña Ganchegui, Luis 49
Performing arts and music venues 54–5
Personal security 139
Pharmacies 138, 139
Photo Spots 58–9
Picasso, Pablo
  Museu Picasso 6, 11, **30–31**, 42, 77
  Woman with Hat and Fur Collar 21
Plaça de Catalunya 46, 66
Plaça Comercial 47
Plaça Joan Coromines 35

Plaça Osca 51
Plaça del Pi 47
Plaça de Ramon Berenguer el Gran 79, 80
Plaça del Rei 46
Plaça Reial 46, 78
Plaça de Sant Felip Neri 58, 80
Plaça de Sant Jaume 46, 77, 79
Plaça de Sant Josep Oriol 47
Plaça de Santa Maria 47
Plaça del Sol 47
Plaça de la Vila de Madrid 47, 79
Plaça de la Vita de Gràcia 47
Poble Espanyol 97
Police 139
PortAventura World 127
Port de la Selva 127
Portal de l'Àngel 67
Postal services 140, 141
Premià de Mar 49
Public transport 134–5
  tickets 135
Puig i Cadafalch, Josep 126
  CaixaForum 97
  Casa Amatller 45, 107
  Casa de les Punxes (Casa Terrades) 45, 108, 109
Pujol, Jordi 39

R

Rafting 130
Rail travel 134, 135, 136, 137
La Rambla 10, **16–17**
  children's attractions 53
  exploring Barcelona 6
Rambla de Catalunya 66–7, 109
Rambla de Mar 101, 103
La Rambla del Raval 7, 88, 89
Ramon Berenguer IV, Count of Barcelona 39
Ramon Casas and Pere Romeu on a Tandem (Casas) 21
El Ravel 86–93
  bars 92
  map 86, 89
  places to eat 93
  shops 90–91
Razzmatazz 55

El Refugi 50
Restaurants 62–3
    Barri Gòtic and La
        Ribera 85
    beyond Barcena 131
    budget travel 71
    Eixample 113
    Gràcia, Tibidabo and
        Zona Alta 123
    Montjuïc 99
    El Ravel
    The Seafront 105
    see also Food and drink
La Revetlla de Sant Joan
    72
La Ribera see Barri Gòtic
    and La Ribera
Rita, Santa 41
Roig, Bartomeu 87
Rothko, Mark 29
Rubens, Peter Paul
    Madonna and Child 20
Rules of the road 137

S

Safety
    government advice
        138, 139
    personal security 139
Sagnier, Enric 119
Sagrada Família 5, 8–9, 10,
    12–14, 107, 109
    exploring Barcelona 6
    key dates 14
    Modernista architecture
        44
Sailing 130
Saints 41
Sala Apolo 55
Sant Climent i Santa Maria
    de Taüll 128
Sant Joan de les
    Abadesses 128
Sant Pau Recinte
    Modernista 44–5,
    107
Santa Eulàlia, Pailebot 102,
    103
Scuba diving 130
The Seafront 100–105
    bars and
        104
    map 100–101
    restaurants and cafés
        bars 104
Second-hand shops
    El Ravel 91
Selva del Mar 127
Sèrie Barcelona (Miró)
    28
Serra de l'Albera 129

Sert, Josep Lluís 29,
    95
Shopping 66–7
    Barri Gòtic and La
        Ribera 82
    budget travel 71
    Eixample
    Gràcia, Tibidabo and
        Zona Alta
    opening hours 140
    El Ravel 90–91
    Sitges
        Carnival 72
Skiing 130
Smoking 138
Sports 130
Squares 46–7
Street art 71
Student residences
    148–9
Subirachs, Josep Maria
    12, 14
A Sudden Awakening
    (Tàpies) 35

T

Tapas 63
Tapas bars
    Barri Gòtic and La
        Ribera 85
    Eixample 113
    Gràcia, Tibidabo and
        Zona Alta 123
    The Seafront 104
Tàpies, Antoni
    Fundació Tàpies 42, 44,
        108
    A Sudden Awakening
        35
Tapis de la Fundació (Miró)
    28–9
Tarragona 126, 128
Taxes 141
Taxis 136, 137
Teatre Grec 54, 96, 98
Teatre-Museu Dalí
    (Figueres) 125
Telephone services, 140
Temple d'August 79
Temple Expiatori del
    Sagrat Cor 40, 119
Theatres
    budget travel 71
    festivals 73
    Gran Teatre del Liceu
        16, 54
Theme parks
    PortAventura World
        127
Thyssen-Bornemisza
    Collection 20

Tibidabo see Gràcia,
    Tibidabo and Zona Alta
Tiepolo, Giovanni Battista
    20
Time zone 140
Torre Bellesguard 15
Torre de Collserola 117,
    119
Traditions, folk 72–3
Train travel 134, 135,
    136, 137
Tram travel 135
Travel
    budget travel 71
    getting around 134–7
    government advice
        138, 139
Travel insurance 138
Travellers with specific
    requirements 139

U

UNESCO World Heritage
    Sites
    Park Güell 10, 15, **22–3**,
        48, 58, 118, 119
    Sant Pau Recinte
        Modernista 44–5, 107

V

Vaccinations 138
Velázquez, Diego de
    31
Versión Original cinemas
    55
Villar, Francesc del 14
Vintage and second-hand
    shops
    El Ravel 91
Virgin Mercé 41
Virgin of Montserrat 41
Visas 138, 139
Visitor information
    140–141

W

Walking 137
    tours 137
Warhol, Andy 29
Watersports 130
Weather 140
Wi-Fi 140, 141
Wildlife 129
Wine
    Alt Penedès 126
    Woman with Hat and Fur
        Collar (Picasso) 21

Z

Zona Alta see Gràcia,
    Tibidabo and Zona Alta

Acknowledgments

The Authors

Travel writer, reporter and editor AnneLise Sorensen is half-Catalan and has lived and worked in Barcelona. She has penned her way across four continents, contributing to guidebooks, magazines and newspapers.

Ryan Chandler is a writer and journalist who has been working in Barcelona for over ten years. He previously worked as Barcelona correspondent for the Spanish magazine *The Broadsheet*.

Additional contributor
Mary-Ann Gallagher

Publishing Director Georgina Dee

Publisher Vivien Antwi

Design Director Phil Ormerod

Editorial Ankita Awasthi-Tröger, Michelle Crane, Rachel Fox, Fíodhna Ní Ghríofa, Freddie Marriage, Scarlett O'Hara, Sally Schafer, Jackie Staddon, Christine Stroyan

Cover Design Maxine Pedliham, Vinita Venugopal

Design Tessa Bindloss

Picture Research Phoebe Lowndes, Susie Peachey, Ellen Root, Oran Tarjan

Cartography Subhashree Bharti, Tom Coulson, Martin Darlison, Simonetta Giori, Suresh Kumar, Casper Morris

DTP Jason Little, George Nimmo, Azeem Siddiqui

Production Linda Dare

Factchecker Paula Canal

Proofreader Kate Berens

Indexer Hilary Bird

Illustrator Chris Orr & Associates, Lee Redmond

First edition created by Departure Lounge, London

Revisions Avanika, Parnika Bagla, Kate Berens, Marta Bescos, Laura O'Brien, Aishwarya Gosain, Bharti Karakoti, Nayan Keshan, Sumita Khatwani, Shikha Kulkarni, Suresh Kumar, Arushi Mathur, Alison McGill, Meghna, George Nimmo, Bandana Paul, Adrian Potts, Vagisha Pushp, Rohit Rojal, Ankita Sharma, Lucy Sienkowska, Mark Silas, Rituraj Singh, Beverly Smart, Hollie Teague, Priyanka Thakur, Stuti Tiwari, Vinita Venugopal, Richa Verma, Penny Walker, Suzanne Wales, Åsa Westerlund, Tanveer Zaidi.

Commissioned Photography Max Alexander, Departure Lounge/Ella Milroy, Departure Lounge/ Paul Young, Joan Farre, Heidi Grassley, Alex Robinson, Rough Guides/Ian Aitken, Rough Guides/ Chris Christoforou, Rough Guides/Tim Kavenagh.

Picture Credits

The publisher would like to thank the following for their kind permission to reproduce their photographs:

Key: a-above; b-below/bottom; c-centre; f-far; l-left; r-right; t-top

123RF.com: dudlajov 59tr; Lucian Milasan 7cr; Luciano Mortula 7tr; Tagstock Japan 14ca.

4Corners: SIME/Pietro Canali 24–5.

Acontaluz: Acontaluz 123br.

Alamy Images: /Alfred Abad 108cl, /Mike Finn-Kelcey 130tl; Manfred Gottschalk 16–17cr;

Hemis 85cl; Hemis /Patrice Hauser 110tl; John Henshall 27tl; LOOK Die Bildagentur der Fotografen GmbH/Juergen Richter 43tr; Stefano Politi Markovina 68bl; Giuseppe Masci 55tr; Hercules Milas 26-7c; Radharc Images 16br; Sam Bloomberg-Rissman 69b; Marek Stepan 91tr; Gregory Wrona 78cb.

Alamy Stock Photo: agefotostock / Christian Goupi 4crb; Image Professionals GmbH / Küppers, Andrea 60tl; Image Professionals GmbH / Langlotz, Tim 99tr; Stefano Politi Markovina 54c, 58tr; Cisco Pelay 79cl; Emily Riddell 81bl; Marc Soler 121bl; Topseee 100tr; travelstock44.de / Juergen Held 60b; travelpix 59b; Andrew Wilson 47bl.

Hotel Arts Barcelona: David Monfil 104tl.

AWL Images: Marco Bottigelli 1, Sabine Lubenow 2tl, 8–9; Stefano Politi Markovina 114–5.

Bar Almirall: Bar Almirall 92tl.

Bar del Pla: Bar del Pla 84br.

Bar Muy Buenas: 92b

Bobby Gin: Pau Esculies 122tl.

Boo: 120tl.

Bridgeman Images: Museu d'Art Contemporani de Barcelona © ADAGP, Paris and DACS, London 2015. Homea, 1974 Eduardo Arranz Bravo (b.1941) 34dr; Museu Picasso, Barcelona © Succession Picasso/ DACS, London 2015 Harlequin, 1917, Pablo Picasso (1881–1973) 31tl, Seated Man, 1917, Pablo Picasso (1881–1973) 31tr; Menu from 'Els Quatre Gats', 1899, Pablo Picasso (1881–1973) 30cb; Las Meninas, No.30, 1957, Pablo Picasso (1881–1973) 30-31c.

Bus Terraza: 61br.

Corbis: Ken Welsh 39tr; Gavin Jackson 35cb; Heritage Images 15tl; JAI/Stefano Politi Markovina 73cla; Jean-Pierre Lescourret 34bl; René Mattes 41tr; Charlie Pérez 54tl; Sylvain Sonnet 18–19c; Wally McNamee 39bl.

Dorling Kindersley: Museu d'Art Contemporani, Barcelona © Foundation Antoni Tapies, Barcelona/ VEGAP, Madrid and DACS, London 2015 Deconstructed bed (1992–3) 35tl; Courtesy of the Palau de la Musica Catalana 33tl.

Dreamstime.com: Igor Abramovych 98cr; Alexvaneekelen 80tl; Steve Allen 45br, 87br, 95tr; Danilo Ascione 48tr; Christian Bertrand 55cl, 73tr; Daniel Sanchez Blasco 87tl; Byelikova 124tl; Catalby 3tr, Charles03 50tl; Juan Bautista Cofreces 64bl; Demerzel21 96tl; Dennis Dolkens 119bl; Dimbar76 4b; Dinozzaver 44b; Edufoto 6cla; Ego450 23tl; Elxeneize 16bl, 116tr; Emotionart 10cla; Alexandre Fagundes De Fagundes 41clb; Fazon1 10bl, Fotoember 26cb; Gelia 125tr; Iakov Filimonov 43clb, 52clb, 72br, 72tl; Christian Horz 68cra; Jackf 50cb, 51b, 70br, 107tr, 126tr, 126–7b; Javarman 4cr, 32cl; Jiawangkun 106tl; Karsol 12cr, 17cr; Pavel Kavalenkau 71tr; Kemaltaner 4t; Kyolshin 14bl; Lanaufoto 129c; Lavendertime 18cl; Lisja 11tl, Loflo69 128br; Mark52 32–3c, Carlos Soler Martinez 68tl; Alberto Masnovo 42t, Masterlu 15b; Matteocozzi 40ca; Anamaria Mejia 2tr, 36-7; Lucian Milasan 96b; Miluxian 22br; Miskolin 118t; Mkoudis 11crb; Luciano Mortula 45tl; Juan Mayano 40bl, 46t, 48b, 102–3b; Nito100 70tl, 108tr; Andrey Omelyanchuk 56–7, 88bl; Irina Paley 67tl; Patßßxs4all.nl 22cla; Pathastings 63tr; Photoaliona 28-9c; Marek Poplawski 71cl, 102tl; Rquemades 4cl; Sanguer 49tr; Santirf 108–9b; Victor Zastol'skiy 97cl; Elena Solodovnikova 117tr; Ron Sumners 65tr;

Tanaonte 66b; Thecriss 26br; Toniflap 48c, 76tl; Typhoonski 77tr; Vichie81 12bl; Vitalyedush 4clb, 95b; Dmitry Volkov 89bl; Yuri4u80 22–3c; Yuryz 27bl.

El Celler de Can Roca: Joan Pujol-Creus 131cb.

Escriba: Escriba 82ca.

Galeria Cosmo: Galeria Cosmo 112t.

Getty Images: Culture Club 38c; Popperfoto 39cla; Sylvain Sonnet 10tr.

Granja Dulcinea: Granja Dulcinea 65clb.

Imanol Ossa: 90c.

iStockphoto.com: MasterLu 5tr, 132–133; kanuman 3tl, 74–5; thehague 4cla.

Fundacio Joan Miro: © Successió Miró / ADAGP, Paris and DACS London 2015 11cra, Catalan Peasant by Moonlight 28bc, Tapis de la Fundacio 28cl, Sculpture on the Terrace Garden at Fundacio Joan Miro in Barcelona 29tc.

L'Arca: 82br.

La Manual Alpargatera: 81tc.

La Mar Salada: 105br.

Bar Lobo: Olga Planas 64tr.

Moments/Mandarin Oriental Hotel Group: George Apostolidis 113br.

Marmalade : Duda Bussolin 93cra.

Dry Martini: Javier de las Muelas 111br.

Metro: 60c.

Milk Bar & Bistro: Duda Bussolin 83cl.

Museu d'Art Contemporani de Barcelona (MACBA): Rafael Vargas 11bl, 34–35c.

Nordik Think: 110cr.

NuOvum: 90crb.

Polaroids: Meg Diaz 83tr.

Photo Scala, Florence: © Succession Picasso/DACS, London 2015 Painting of Margot, or Waiting, 1901 Pablo Picasso 11c.

SuperStock: DeAgostini Painting of Our Lady of Councilors 1445, by Lluis Dalmau 10br; Fine Art Images The Virgin of Humility (Madonna dell' Umilita) Angelico, Fra Giovanni, da Fiesole (ca. 1400–1455) 20bl; Hemis.fr 33br; Iberfoto /National Art Museum of Catalonia /Painting of The Minuet. 1756. Bequest of Francesc Camb by TIEPOLO, Giovanni Domenico (1727–1804) 20cr, /Ramon Casas and Pere Romeu on a Tandem. 1897. by CASAS i CARBO, Ramn (1866–1932) 21tl, /Ducat with the image of Philip V (1703). Coin 21cra; JTB Photo 32br; Joan Miro Foundation, Barcelona © Successió Miró/ADAGP, Paris and DACS London 2015. Sculpture gallery display 29cr; Picasso Museum, Barcelona © Succession Picasso/DACS, London 2015 Dwarf Dancer (Nana) (Danseuse Naine (La Nana)) 1901 Pablo Picasso (1881–1973 /Spanish) 30cl.

La Taverna del Clinic: 62t.

Windsor: 62br.

Cover
Front and spine: **AWL Images:** Marco Bottigelli. Back: **AWL Images:** Marco Bottigelli b; **Dreamstime.com:** Boule13 tr, Iakov Filimonov crb, Javarman tl, Vitalyedush cla.

Pull out map cover
Alamy Stock Photo: Marco Bottigelli.

All other images are: © Dorling Kindersley. For further information see www.dkimages.com.

Penguin Random House

Printed and bound in China
First edition 2002
First published in Great Britian by
Dorling Kindersley Limited
DK, One Embassy Gardens, 8 Viaduct Gardens, London, SW11 7BW, UK
The authorised representative in the EEA is Dorling Kindersley Verlag GmbH. Arnulfstr. 124, 80636 Munich, Germany

Published in the United States by DK Publishing, 1745 Broadway, 20th Floor, New York, NY 10019, USA

Copyright © 2002, 2021 Dorling Kindersley Limited

A Penguin Random House Company

22 23 24 10 9 8

Reprinted with revisions 2004, 2005, 2006, 2007, 2008, 2009, 2010, 2011, 2012, 2013, 2014, 2016 (twice), 2017, 2018, 2019, 2020, 2021

All rights reserved.

The publishers cannot accept responsibility for any consequences arising from the use of this book, nor for any material on third party websites, and cannot guarantee that any website address in this book will be a suitable source of travel information.

A CIP catalogue record is available from the British Library.

A catalogue record for this book is available from the Library of Congress.

ISSN 1479-344X
ISBN 978-0-2415-0974-6

As a guide to abbreviations in visitor information:
Adm = admission charge; **D** = dinner; **L** = lunch.

MIX
Paper from responsible sources
FSC
www.fsc.org
FSC™ C018179

This book was made with Forest Stewardship Council ™ certified paper – one small step in DK's commitment to a sustainable future.
For more information go to
www.dk.com/our-green-pledge

English-Catalan Phrase Book

In an Emergency

Help!	Auxili!	ow-gzee-lee
Stop!	Pareu!	pah-reh-oo
Call a doctor!	Telefoneu un metge!	teh-leh-fon-eh-oo oon meh-djuh
Call an ambulance!	Telefoneu una ambulància!	teh-leh-fon-eh-oo oo-nah ahm-boo-lahn-see-ah
Call the police!	Telefoneu la policia	teh-leh-fon-eh-oo lah poh-lee-see-ah
Call the fire brigade!	Telefoneu els bombers!	teh-leh-fon-eh-oo uhlz bom-behs
Where is the nearest telephone?	On és el telèfon més proper?	on-ehs uhl tuh-leh fon mehs proo-peh
Where is the nearest hospital?	On és l'hospital més proper?	on-ehs looss-pee-tahl mehs proo-peh

Communication Essentials

Yes	Sí	see
No	No	noh
Please	Si us plau	sees plah-oo
Thank you	Gràcies	grah-see-uhs
Excuse me	Perdoni	puhr-thoh-nee
Hello	Hola	oh-lah
Goodbye	Adéu	ah-they-oo
Good night	Bona nit	bo-nah neet
Morning	El matí	uhl muh-tee
Afternoon	La tarda	lah tahr-thuh
Evening	El vespre	uhl vehs-pruh
Yesterday	Ahir	ah-ee
Today	Avui	uh-voo-ee
Tomorrow	Demà	duh-mah
Here	Aquí	uh-kee
There	Allà	uh-lyah
What?	Què?	keh
When?	Quan?	kwahn
Why?	Per què?	puhr keh
Where?	On?	ohn

Useful Phrases

How are you?	Com està?	kom uhs-tah
Very well, thank you.	Molt bé, gràcies.	mol beh grah-see-uhs
Pleased to meet you.	Molt de gust.	mol duh goost
See you soon.	Fins aviat.	feenz uhv-yat
Where is/are .?	On és/són?	ohn ehs/sohn
How far is it to?	Quants metres/ kilòmetres hi ha d'aquí a ...?	kwahnz meh-truhs/kee-loh-muh-truhs yah dah-kee uh
Which way to ...?	Per on es va a ...?	puhr on uhs bah ah
Do you speak English?	Parla anglès?	par-luh an-glehs
I don't understand	No l'entenc.	noh luhn-teng
Could you speak more slowly, please?	Pot parlar més a poc a poc, si us plau?	pot par-lah mehs pok uh pok sees plah-oo
I'm sorry.	Ho sento.	oo sehn-too

Useful Words

big	gran	gran
small	petit	puh-teet
hot	calent	kah-len
cold	fred	fred
good	bo	boh
bad	dolent	doo-len
enough	bastant	bahs-tan
well	bé	beh
open	obert	oo-behr
closed	tancat	tan-kat
left	esquerra	uhs-kehr-ruh
right	dreta	dreh-tuh
straight on	recte	rehk-tuh
near	a prop	uh prop
far	lluny	lyoonyuh
up/over	a dalt	uh dahl
down/under	a baix	uh bah-eeshh
early	aviat	uhv-yat
late	tard	tahrt
entrance	entrada	uhn-trah-thuh
exit	sortida	soor-tee-thuh
toilet	lavabos/ serveis	luh-vah-boos sehr-beh-ees
more	més	mess
less	menys	menyees

Shopping

How much does this cost?	Quant costa això?	kwahn kost ehs-shoh
I would like …	M'agradaria …	muh-grah-thuh-ree-ah
Do you have?	Tenen?	tehn-un
I'm just looking, thank you	Només estic mirant, gràcies.	noo-mess ehs-teek mee-rahn grah-see-uhs
Do you take credit cards?	Accepten targes de crèdit?	ak-sehp-tuhn tahr-zhuhs duh kreh-deet
What time do you open?	A quina hora obren?	ah keen-uh oh-ruh oh-bruhn
What time do you close?	A quina hora tanquen?	ah keen-uh oh-ruh tan-kuhn
This one.	Aquest	ah-ket
That one.	Aquell	ah-kehl
That's fine.	Està bé.	uhs-tah beh
expensive	car	kahr
cheap	bé de preu/ barat	beh thuh preh-oo/bah-rat
size (clothes)	talla/mida	tah-lyah/mee-thuh
size (shoes)	número	noo-mehr-oo
white	blanc	blang
black	negre	neh-gruh
red	vermell	vuhr-mel
yellow	groc	grok
green	verd	behrt
blue	blau	blah-oo
antique store	antiquari/ botiga d'antiguitats	an-tee-kwah-ree/boo-tee-gah/dan-tee-ghee-tats
bakery	el forn	uhl forn
bank	el banc	uhl bang

book store	**la llibreria**	*lah lyee-bruh-ree-ah*
butcher's	**la carnisseria**	*lah kahr-nee-suh-ree-uh*
pastry shop	**la pastisseria**	*lah pahs-tee-suh-ree-uh*
chemist's	**la farmàcia**	*lah fuhr-mah-see-ah*
fishmonger's	**la peixateria**	*lah peh-shuh-tuh-ree-uh*
greengrocer's	**la fruiteria**	*lah froo-ee-tuh-ree-uh*
grocer's	**la botiga de queviures**	*lah boo-tee-guh duh keh-vee-oo-ruhs*
hairdresser's	**la perruqueria**	*lah peh-roo-kuh-ree-uh*
market	**el mercat**	*uhl muhr-kat*
newsagent's	**el quiosc de premsa**	*uhl kee-ohsk duh prem-suh*
post office	**l'oficina de correus**	*loo-fee-see-nuh duh koo-reh-oos*
shoe store	**la sabateria**	*lah sah-bah-tuh-ree-uh*
supermarket	**el supermercat**	*uhl soo-puhr-muhr-kat*
travel agency	**l'agència de viatges**	*la-jen-see-uh duh vee-ad-juhs*

Sightseeing

art gallery	**la galeria d' art**	*lah gah-luh-ree-yuh dart*
cathedral	**la catedral**	*lah kuh-tuh-thrahl*
church	**l'església**	*luhz-gleh-zee-uh*
garden	**el jardí**	*uhl zhahr-dee*
library	**la biblioteca**	*lah bee-blee-oo-teh-kuh*
museum	**el museu**	*uhl moo-seh-oo*
tourist information office	**l'oficina de turisme**	*loo-fee-see-nuh thuh too-reez-muh*
town hall	**l'ajuntament**	*luh-djoon-tuh-men*
closed for holiday	**tancat per vacances**	*tan-kat puhr bah-kan-suhs*
bus station	**l'estació d'autobusos**	*luhs-tah-see-oh dow-toh-boo-zoos*
railway station	**l'estació de tren**	*luhs-tah-see-oh thuh tren*

Staying in a Hotel

Do you have a vacant room?	**¿Tenen una habitació lliure?**	*teh-nuhn oo-nuh ah-bee-tuh-see-oh lyuh-ruh*
double room with double bed	**habitació doble amb llit de matrimoni**	*ah-bee-tuh-see-oh doh-bluh am lyeet duh mah-tree-moh-nee*
twin room	**habitació amb dos llits/ amb llits individuals**	*ah-bee-tuh-see-oh am dohs lyeets/am lyeets in-thee-vee-thoo-ahls*
single room	**habitació individual**	*ah-bee-tuh-see-oh een-dee-vee-thoo-ahl*
room with	**habitació**	*ah-bee-tuh-see-oh*
a bath	**amb bany**	*am bahnyuh*
shower	**dutxa**	*doo-chuh*
porter	**el grum**	*uhl groom*
key	**la clau**	*lah klah-oo*
I have a reservation	**Tinc una habitació reservada**	*ting oo-nuh ah-bee-tuh-see-oh reh-sehr-vah-thah*

Eating Out

Have you got a table for…?	**Tenen taula per…?**	*teh-nuhn tow-luh puhr*
I would like to reserve a table.	**Voldria reservar una taula.**	*vool-dree-uh reh-sehr-vahr oo-nuh tow-luh*
The bill please	**El compte, si us plau.**	*uhl kohm-tuh sees plah-oo*
I am a vegetarian	**Sóc vegetarià/ vegetariana**	*sok buh-zhuh-tuh-ree-ah/buh-zhuh-tuh-ree-ah-nah*
waitress	**cambrera**	*kam-breh-ruh*
waiter	**cambrer**	*kam-breh*
menu	**la carta**	*lah kahr-tuh*
fixed-price menu	**menú del migdia**	*muh-noo thuhl meech-dee-uh*
wine list	**la carta de vins**	*ah kahr-tuh thuh veens*
glass of water	**un got d'aigua**	*oon got dah-ee-gwah*
glass of wine	**una copa de vi**	*oo-nuh ko-pah thuh vee*
bottle	**una ampolla**	*oo-nuh am-pol-yuh*
knife	**un ganivet**	*oon gun-ee-veht*
fork	**una forquilla**	*oo-nuh foor-keel-yuh*
spoon	**una cullera**	*oo-nuh kool-yeh-ruh*
breakfast	**l'esmorzar**	*les-moor-sah*
lunch	**el dinar**	*uhl dee-nah*
dinner	**el sopar**	*uhl soo-pah*
main course	**el primer plat**	*uhl pree-meh plat*
starters	**els entrants**	*uhlz ehn-tranz*
dish of the day	**el plat del dia**	*uhl plat duhl dee-uh*
coffee	**el cafè**	*uhl kah-feh*
rare	**poc fet**	*pok fet*
medium	**al punt**	*ahl poon*
well done	**molt fet**	*mol fet*

Menu Decoder

l'aigua mineral	*lah-ee-gwuh mee-nuh-rahl*	mineral water
sense gas/ amb gas	*sen-zuh gas/ am gas*	still sparkling
al forn	*ahl forn*	baked
l'all	*lahlyuh*	garlic
l'arròs	*lahr-roz*	rice
les botifarres	*lahs boo-tee-fah-rahs*	sausages

la carn	*lah karn*	meat
la ceba	*lah seh-buh*	onion
la cervesa	*lah-sehr-ve-sah*	beer
l'embotit	*lum-boo-teet*	cold meat
el filet	*uhl fee-let*	sirloin
el formatge	*uhl for-mah-djuh*	cheese
fregit	*freh-zheet*	fried
la fruita	*lah froo-ee-tah*	fruit
els fruits secs	*uhlz froo-eets seks*	nuts
les gambes	*lahs gam-bus*	prawns
el gelat	*uhl djuh-lat*	ice cream
la llagosta	*lah lyah-gos-tah*	lobster
la llet	*lah lyet*	milk
la llimona	*lah lyee-moh-nah*	lemon
la llimonada	*lah lyee-moh-nah-tuh*	lemonade
la mantega	*lah mahn-teh-gah*	butter
el marisc	*uhl muh-reesk*	seafood
la menestra	*lah muh-nehs-truh*	vegetable stew
l'oli	*loll-ee*	oil
les olives	*luhs oo-lee-vuhs*	olives
l'ou	*loh-oo*	egg
el pa	*uhl pah*	bread
el pastís	*uhl pahs-tees*	pie/cake
les patates	*lahs pah-tah-tuhs*	potatoes
el pebre	*uhl peh-bruh*	pepper
el peix	*uhl pehsh*	fish
el pernil salat serrà	*uhl puhr-neel suh-lat sehr-rah*	cured ham
el plàtan	*uhl plah-tun*	banana
el pollastre	*uhl poo-lyah-struh*	chicken
la poma	*la poh-mah*	apple
el porc	*uhl pohr*	pork
les postres	*lahs pohs-truhs*	dessert
rostit	*rohs-teet*	roast
la sal	*lah sahl*	salt
la salsa	*lah sahl-suh*	sauce
les salsitxes	*lahs sahl-see-chuhs*	sausages
sec	*sehk*	dry
la sopa	*lah soh-puh*	soup
el sucre	*uhl-soo-kruh*	sugar
la taronja	*lah tuh-rohn-djuh*	orange
el te	*uhl teh*	tea
les torrades	*lahs too-rah-thuhs*	toast
la vedella	*lah veh-theh-lyuh*	beef
el vi blanc	*uhl bee blang*	white wine
el vi negre	*uhl bee neh-gruh*	red wine
el vi rosat	*uhl bee roo-zaht*	rosé wine
el vinagre	*uhl bee-nah-gruh*	vinegar
el xai/el be	*uhl shahee/uhl beh*	lamb
la xocolata	*lah shoo-koo-lah-tuh*	chocolate
el xoriç	*uhl shoo-rees*	red sausage

Numbers

0	zero	*seh-roo*
1	un (masc)	*oon*
	una (fem)	*oon-uh*
2	dos (masc)	*dohs*
	dues (fem)	*doo-uhs*
3	tres	*trehs*
4	quatre	*kwa-truh*
5	cinc	*seeng*
6	sis	*sees*
7	set	*set*
8	vuit	*voo-eet*
9	nou	*noh-oo*
10	deu	*deh-oo*
11	onze	*on-zuh*
12	dotze	*doh-dzuh*
13	tretze	*treh-dzuh*
14	catorze	*kah-tohr-dzuh*
15	quinze	*keen-zuh*
16	setze	*set-zuh*
17	disset	*dee-set*
18	divuit	*dee-voo-eet*
19	dinou	*dee-noh-oo*
20	vint	*been*
21	vint-i-un	*been-tee-oon*
22	vint-i-dos	*been-tee-dohs*
30	trenta	*tren-tah*
31	trenta-un	*tren-tah oon*
40	quaranta	*kwuh-ran-tah*
50	cinquanta	*seen-kwahn-tah*
60	seixanta	*seh-ee-shan-tah*
70	setanta	*seh-tan-tah*
80	vuitanta	*voo-ee-tan-tah*
90	noranta	*noh-ran-tah*
100	cent	*sen*
101	cent un	*sent oon*
102	cent dos	*sen dohs*
200	dos-sens	*dohs-sens*
	dues-centes (fem)	*doo-uhs sen-tuhs*
300	tres-cents	*trehs-senz*
400	quatre-cents	*kwah-truh-senz*
500	cinc-cents	*seeng-senz*
600	sis-cents	*sees-senz*
700	set-cents	*set-senz*
800	vuit-cents	*voo-eet-senz*
900	nou-cents	*noh-oo-cenz*
1,000	mil	*meel*
1,001	mil un	*meel oon*

Time

one minute	un minut	*oon mee-noot*
one hour	una hora	*oo-nuh oh-ruh*
half an hour	mitja hora	*mee-juh oh-ruh*
Monday	dilluns	*dee-lyoonz*
Tuesday	dimarts	*dee-marts*
Wednesday	dimecres	*dee-meh-kruhs*
Thursday	dijous	*dee-zhoh-oos*
Friday	divendres	*dee-ven-druhs*
Saturday	dissabte	*dee-sab-tuh*
Sunday	diumenge	*dee-oo-men-juh*

A noise woke Hiram. He thought it was a howl.

Crack!

Michael snapped awake. "What the hell was that, Pap?"

"Who's there?" Hiram called.

He heard footsteps, and a sound that might be laughter. A high-pitched giggle.

"Jesus Christ, Pap." Michael sprang to his side. "It sounds like it might be people out there."

"Hello out there!" Hiram called.

There was no answer. He reached into the gunny sack, under his extra clothes he used for a pillow, and came out with his revolver.

He heard laughter again, high-pitched, a cackle, from something that might or might not be human.

Hiram felt a shiver trace cold fingers down his spine. "Let's get to the truck." With no visible moon, the sky was pitch black. That cackle again, staccato, high, and then crashing into a giggle. An image of a dead girl, leering with black teeth, filled his vision. In one hand, the dead child held an equally dead cat by the tail. The other gripped a cottonwood stick spear. That was Callista, with a maniacal gleam in her eye. Was it his imagination? A hallucination?

He heard the sound of running footsteps. "Into the truck, now!" he barked.

BAEN BOOKS by D.J. BUTLER

The Cunning Man Series
(with Aaron Michael Ritchey)
The Cunning Man
The Jupiter Knife (forthcoming)

The Witchy War Series
Witchy Eye
Witchy Winter
Witchy Kingdom
Serpent Daughter

Tales of Indrajit and Fix
In the Palace of Shadow and Joy

To purchase any of these titles in e-book form,
please go to www.baen.com.

The Cunning Man

D.J. Butler
Aaron Michael Ritchey

Copyright © 2019 by D.J. Butler and Aaron Michael Ritchey

A Baen Books Original

Baen Publishing Enterprises
P.O. Box 1403
Riverdale, NY 10471
www.baen.com

ISBN: 978-1-9821-2495-3

Cover art by Dan dos Santos

First printing, November 2019
First mass market printing, October 2020

Distributed by Simon & Schuster
1230 Avenue of the Americas
New York, NY 10020

Library of Congress Control Number: 2019029051

Pages by Joy Freeman (www.pagesbyjoy.com)
Printed in the United States of America
10 9 8 7 6 5 4 3 2 1

*This book is dedicated
to our wives,
Emily and Laura.*

We would like to thank Tan Smyth for her sensitive early read and comments, and Jason Huntzinger for helping us envision Helper in the 1930s.

Many thanks also to this book's *two* editors, Toni Weisskopf and Tony Daniel. Thanks also to J.R. Dunn, for busting us on a few anachronisms.

And again, we are grateful to and for our wives.

"*Magus* is a Persian word primitively, whereby is exprest such a one as is altogether conversant in things divine; and as *Plato* affirmeth, the art of Magick is the art of worshipping God."

—*Henry Cornelius Agrippa, His Fourth Book of Occult Philosophy*, "Preface to the Unprejudiced Reader," Robert Turner, 1655

"And it came to pass that there were sorceries, and witchcrafts, and magics; and the power of the evil one was wrought upon all the face of the land."

—*The Book of Mormon*, Mormon 2:19

Chapter One

"I'VE HEARD DISTURBING THINGS ABOUT YOU." BISHOP Smith was the youngest of the three men who made up the Presiding Bishopric, and his Van Dyke beard certainly made him the jauntiest. It jutted forward like a knife.

Hiram Woolley felt his heart lurch like a toad in his chest.

Bishop Wells, sitting in a chair beside Bishop Smith, had a face round as a pie and a cream-colored complexion. Behind round spectacle lenses, his eyes smiled, though the line of his mouth was flat. Smith and Wells were the counselors, number two and number three respectively; the Presiding Bishop himself, Bishop Cannon, wasn't with them.

They had heard Hiram was a magician.

Smith and Wells both wore slacks and waistcoats, their jackets slung over the backs of chairs; Hiram was in his overalls, with his faded olive-green wool coat and his hat on his knee. The Bishops wore polished black shoes, and Hiram had dirty Redwing Harvesters.

1

"Oh?" he said.

"About you and your grandmother."

"Hettie," Hiram said. "God rest her soul."

"She was a witch."

"No," Hiram said immediately.

Bishop Smith leaned forward, nostrils flaring. "And *you* have magical powers."

Hiram ran the fingers of one hand through his thinning hair. He wanted to stand, put his fedora back on, and leave, but he owed respect to Bishop Smith. To the office at least, if not to the man. "No, I don't."

"Jedediah Banks said you caught a thief. Found out who it was using balls of clay that dissolved in a dishpan." Bishop Smith smirked.

Hiram said nothing.

"And Beulah Wiseman said you dowsed her a new well when her old one dried up."

"Hiram wouldn't be the only dowser in Utah." John Wells spoke in mild English tones. He and Hiram had met at a barn-raising in Butlerville, several years earlier. Hiram had taught John how to drive a straight nail, in the process of which he'd seen a protective lamen, an amulet written on paper, around Wells's neck. He'd driven Wells home that night, and Wells had told him of his experience as a child in Nottinghamshire, being healed of an abscess in his foot by a cunning woman named Granny Jenkins.

"There's more than one adulterer, too." Smith squinted at Hiram. "Well?"

Hiram could repeat the simple truth that he didn't have magical powers, but that would make the final admission worse. "I helped Beulah. And Jedediah, too. And the thief, for that matter. Got him to return Jedediah's mule and ask forgiveness."

Smith steepled his fingers before him. "And do you believe God gave you magical abilities?"

Hiram carefully controlled his breath to avoid sighing. "Yes," he said. "And no."

"You're being evasive." Smith frowned. "Do you know James Anderson? In American Fork?"

"At the People's State Bank," Hiram murmured. Jim Anderson was his loan officer.

"James Anderson is a faithful brother." Smith's frown twisted slowly into a smile.

"He is." Hiram's heart was thumping.

"I don't think Brother Anderson would want to have anything to do with witches."

Like any farmer, Hiram was sometimes late in his payments, and his personal relationship with his bankers was the only thing that got him the days—and sometimes weeks or months—of grace he needed to stay afloat.

"I'm not trying to be evasive," Hiram said. "Look, you're a healthy man with two legs, you walked into this room. Did God give you the power to walk?"

Smith looked suspicious. "This is irrelevant."

Wells smiled slightly. "Let's hear him out, David."

Hiram continued. "Without God, you wouldn't walk. You wouldn't have legs, the earth you stand on wouldn't exist and wouldn't be spinning around to generate gravity—anyway, that's what Michael says makes gravity. You can walk because of God, but that doesn't mean you have a special power of walking. You're just an ordinary man, doing an ordinary thing—walking—in the world as God made it. In the same way, you could say that God gave you the power to read, or swim, or drive a car."

"I'm not a witch." Smith's voice was cold.

"Neither was Grandma Hettie." Hiram avoided making eye contact with John Wells, feeling he might implicate his friend. "And neither am I. A witch is someone who hurts others, but I help people. That's what Brother Banks and Sister Wiseman both told you about me."

"So you would call yourself what, then?" Was that a hint of triumph in Smith's eyes? "A wizard? A charmer?"

It was a trap. Those words were both associated with condemnation in the Bible.

Hiram shrugged. "If people ask, I tell them I farm sugar beets. Which is the truth."

"I would hate to have to drive home past the bank, Brother Woolley," Smith said. "On the way here I stopped to talk with Brother Anderson, and he told me you're late on your payments as we speak."

The egg-shaped, red-flecked green stone Hiram always carried in his pocket—his bloodstone, or heliotropius—lay inert. So Bishop Smith was telling the truth.

"I'll catch up on payments. Harvest should be good this year."

"I hope you catch up in time."

What could Hiram say that was safe? "Grandma Hettie said that the things she did made her a 'cunning woman.' I suppose that makes me a 'cunning man,' though that's not a term you hear so much anymore."

"A wizard."

Hiram shook his head. "Just someone who knows

how things work. And who uses his knowledge for good."

"And this knowledge ... these things you do ... you're convinced they work?"

Hiram nodded. "Ask Beulah and Jedediah. In the mouth of two witnesses."

"Do they *always* work?" Smith smirked. "Or do they only *sometimes* work?"

"Well," Hiram said, "sometimes a man who knows perfectly well how to walk trips over his own feet anyway, or steps into a puddle, or isn't looking where he's going, so he walks into a wall, or someone else kicks his feet out from under him. You wouldn't say his walking only works some of the time. And some things depend on faith, or a pure heart—mine, or the person I'm helping—so yes, sometimes my lore fails."

"And does your lore include the use of ... sacred things?"

The hair on the back of Hiram's neck stood up. This was a dangerous question. Certain sacred names or gestures were very effective against illnesses or wicked spirits, especially if repeated multiple times. He shrugged slowly. "If making the sign of the cross over a sick person, or singing a psalm to an excited mule, helps a person in need, then yes, I do it."

"Is this *nineteen* thirty-five ... or *eighteen* thirty-five?" Bishop Smith leaned back in his chair and looked at Bishop Wells. "You really want to send this man to the Kimball Mine as our representative?"

"To say 'representative' is a bit much." Wells smiled softly. "We need someone to take food to the miners, and Hiram is ready to go. And he does this sort of thing for me often. I trust him."

"The food's loaded on the back of my Double-A," Hiram said. "Three different Lehi congregations pitched in. But I can unload it. I'm not the only man in town with a truck."

Bishop Smith looked at the two other men through slitted eyes. "Take the food to the men of Kimball Mine, Brother Woolley," he said. "And then come back home. Don't do anything else, and don't imagine we won't hear if you do. Even in godforsaken Helper, there are those who will tell us what happens."

Smith stood with a dancer's grace—back erect, heels snapping sharply together—and left. The door fell shut behind him and Hiram heard the clicking of his heels on the wooden floor of the halls.

Hiram Woolley and John Wells stood more slowly, then shook hands.

"Maybe I should stop trying," Hiram suggested. "Keep to myself. Farm beets."

"*Can* you?" Wells asked, the dark eyes in his cheese-like face glittering.

Hiram grunted.

"Listen," Wells added as they walked together to the exit. "The Kimball family, they followed . . . older ways."

"Heber Kimball saw signs in the heavens, back about eighteen thirty-five." Hiram nodded. "Or . . . do you mean polygamy?"

"Both," Wells said. "Teancum was a polygamist like his father."

"Are you saying . . . there's something more than a closed mine happening here?"

Hiram had been acting as unofficial assistant to John Wells since nearly the day they'd met. Sometimes, John called on Hiram because of Hiram's farming skills, or because he owned a truck. Other times, he needed Hiram because Hiram was a cunning man.

"I don't know for sure," Wells said. "Teancum Kimball was said to have had prophetic gifts, and at least one of his children is mad. Keep your eyes open, and stay out of trouble."

Hiram grunted again and nodded. Could he stay out of trouble? He had to . . . for himself and for Michael.

They left the building, and Wells turned right, walking toward his dusty white Terraplane parked under a black walnut tree. Hiram turned left, and found his adopted son Michael waiting beside their Ford Model AA pickup truck, strumming on his Sears, Roebuck guitar.

Michael's birth parents had been Navajo, so the two looked nothing alike; Michael was stocky, with a solid chest and a dark complexion, where Hiram was thin, rangy, and naturally pale. Hiram tended to introduce him as my son, Michael, not including any surname in order to avoid the thorny question whether Michael's last name was *Woolley* or *Yazzie*.

Michael ended the blues song he'd been yodeling and put the guitar away.

Hiram checked the apple crates and brown sacks of groceries in the back of the truck, piled so high the Double-A looked like one of the gypsy family vehicles he'd seen in France. He found them all secure, tightly roped to iron rings along with Hiram's shovel, water cans, spare gas can, camping gear, and toolbox.

Michael drifted over.

"You could have come inside," Hiram said.

Michael snorted. "I'd feel like a hypocrite, Pap. What did they want to do, tell you who to give the food to?"

"I already know that. There's a mine foreman. Name of Sorenson." Hiram climbed into the shotgun seat and Michael got behind the wheel. Michael drove because Hiram had fainting spells. Only occasionally, but often enough that he preferred Michael to drive.

"Anything else they want to talk about?" Michael asked.

Hiram tried to avoid lying directly to his son. "They had the idea that I've been carrying on Grandma Hettie's craft. Her special skills."

Michael started the truck. "You mean *magic?*"

The sudden note of disdain in Michael's voice stabbed Hiram in the belly.

"Yeah," he said, as the truck rolled from the church parking lot and turned south. "Crazy, I know."

Chapter Two

DRIVING DOWN FROM LEHI FELT GOOD. HIRAM liked the road, the blue skies, and the mountain ledges dotted with sagebrush, gambol oak and pine, and tall yellow grass. Snow sat in nooks of orange stone, hiding from the sun and the nearly-warm breeze. He also liked the engine smell of the Double-A. The dirt road was graded, but scarred by plenty of washboard ruts. The government had been paving all the highways until the stock market had jumped off a cliff, dragging the rest of the economy with it.

They were descending through Price Canyon toward Helper when Michael asked, "So, how long do you plan to keep running these errands for Bishop Wells?"

Ye have the poor always with you, Hiram thought. "You hear back from any of those colleges?"

"No," Michael admitted. "I wrote to a few more. Mahonri helped."

Hiram had known Mahonri Young all of his life. They'd played on Sundays in the marshes around the mouth of the Jordan, slipping out of the white-slat chapel on any pretext whatsoever. They had whiled away many days racing off into the mountains to swim, fish, and memorize the stars. Mahonri was still his best friend and, other than Michael, the smartest man Hiram had ever met. Smart enough he'd gotten schooling. Then he'd gotten a job working at Brigham Young High School, in the library.

Hiram gripped his son's shoulder with pride. He would have tousled Michael's hair, once, but Michael was too big for that. "You decide what you want to do with a degree? You can't say 'spaceman,' there are no spacemen. No Flash . . . Flash . . ."

"Flash Gordon."

"Right. No Flash Gordons."

"There'll be spacemen soon enough, Pap."

"Hoping to meet a blue-skinned beauty of Venus?"

Michael's grin collapsed. "Well, Jenny Lindow turned me down for the Mutual Improvement Association dance. That makes three girls in a row."

"Jenny's a nice girl," Hiram said.

Michael nodded. "And she turned me down, anyway."

"You know, I was never very handy with the girls."

"Yeah, Pap," Michael said. "But you're white."

"You're my son," Hiram said. Maybe that was why Jenny had said no. Maybe her parents didn't want her going to the dance with the cunning man's son.

Michael nodded. "I grew up with you and Mamma and Grandma Hettie. I went to church, I worked the farm, I learned my ABCs. But I'm not like you, Pap. Not . . . *quite.*"

Hiram's heart ached. He saw his son's world diverging from his as fast as Flash Gordon's rocket. "A spaceman, then?"

Michael grinned again. "Probably a scientist first. Geologist, maybe. Or entomologist. Or . . . there are just too many choices."

Hiram clapped a hand gently on his son's shoulder. "You'll find your place in this world, Michael."

"So will you, Pap."

Hiram chuckled.

Rounding a corner, Michael hit the brakes. A heavily rusted Model T lay stopped across the road, blocking it. Three men in overalls, thick gray sweaters, and boots clustered around the open hood. Black streaks marked their sweaters, and where undershirts peeped out, they were gray, rather than white.

The Double-A threw up dust as it stopped. One of the men removed a hat and fanned away the cloud, revealing a hairline rising steeply from a widow's peak. He settled the hat over his face; he kept his dark heavy-lidded eyes on Hiram and Michael.

The other two men huddled over the engine, faces hidden.

On Hiram's right rose a steep hill, thick with pines. To the left a slope fell into the ice-choked Price River.

"Well, I'm having no luck finding a girlfriend." Michael laughed. "But I'm having a better day than those poor shmoes. Let me guess. We're going to help them?"

Widow's Peak lifted a hand, keeping his hat over this face. He had dark eyes, dark hair, and skin that looked tan despite the winter. A Greek or a Turk, maybe? Hiram had known both in the war.

Hiram touched the pocket of his overalls. His blood-stone clicked softly against his clasp knife.

"Pap?" Michael asked. "Are we going to help them?"

Hiram reached up and tilted the rearview mirror so he could see behind them. Another dark-haired man, this one in work pants and a gray-stained sheepskin coat buttoned all the way up and covering his face below his nose, came ambling out of a stand of pine trees, about a hundred feet away.

Had he been relieving himself? Or was this the lookout, and the extra muscle?

"Maybe," he murmured.

"Jeez, Pap, what's going on?"

Hiram opened the door and stepped out. "Did your car break down?" he called.

He pressed the bloodstone against his thigh.

"Yes, yes, the car, she is broke," the man said.

The bloodstone pinched his leg.

The Greek was lying.

"One second," Hiram said.

The Greek nodded. The fourth man stood stock still, watching.

"Michael," Hiram said in a low voice, "I'm going to move their car. When it's clear, you're going to drive past them. I'll jump in the back. If you see trouble, and I can't get to you, drive on to Helper and get the police."

Michael lowered his voice. "You mean . . . these guys are bandits?"

"These guys are hungry."

Michael gripped the steering wheel. "What is this, cowboy times?"

"Just watch for an opening. Then give her the gas, son." Hiram slapped the roof and got down. He didn't reach into the glove box to grab the Colt M1917—Hiram's other great reminder of his friend from the war, Yas Yazzie.

Hiram walked up to them, smiling widely. "Bad luck with your car." His breath came quicker, and a thick sweat oozed down his sides, cold against his skin. With the first two fingers of his left hand he tapped his breastbone, drawing comfort from the metallic feel of the round iron chi-rho talisman that bumped against his skin. It was the very same amulet Grandma Hettie had given him the day his mother had disappeared. It was a disk of pure cast iron, forged at the new moon and well-fumigated with the Spirits of Mars before ever being worn. Its front and back faces were identical, bearing the chi-rho symbol, the great icon of Christ's victory, in the center, and around the outer rim at the clock positions of midnight, three, six, and nine, the four Latin words IN HOC SIGNO VINCES. The amulet protected the bearer against his enemies.

He hoped these men weren't his enemies.

Widow's Peak nodded. His eyes were fixed on Hiram. Hiram smelled liquor.

"Can I help you move her so me and my son can get by?" he asked. "We're on our way to the Kimball mine."

Something flashed in the Greek's eyes. He grunted and reached into his pocket. "She no move."

The bloodstone pinched Hiram again.

Hiram saw a smudge of white wood—ax handles hidden in the engine, within reach of the two men standing there.

Hiram's heart filled his ears. He fixed his eye on the Greek. "Your car isn't broken, and you're thinking about robbing us. I won't let that happen, but I guess you might have families. I can give you some bread and canned vegetables."

"Maybe . . . maybe that's okay." Widow's Peak looked uncertainly at his companions.

The two men spun. Red bandanas covered their face. They pulled out the ax handles and barked words Hiram couldn't understand at their friend.

Widow's Peak dropped his hat, revealing a mustache like a Fuller brush. From out of his pocket he pulled a gray sock sagging with something heavy in its end.

A bag of groceries wasn't going to resolve this conflict.

Hiram charged Widow's Peak, raising a fist. The Greek flinched, and Hiram plucked the sap out of his hand.

Behind him, the Double-A growled. What if the fourth man on the road attacked Michael, rather than Hiram?

Hiram spun the sap over his head like a sling and released it into the face of one of the ax-handle men. It struck him in the forehead and he dropped.

The second man darted forward, raising his ax handle over his head.

Hiram showed him his right fist, and then hammered the man's face with his left. His knuckles crashed right into the red bandana, and sent the attacker staggering away.

Hiram didn't dare look back. He hurled himself on the seat of the Model T, pushed the clutch down with his left, and shifted the car into neutral with his right.

The Model T didn't move. Hiram glanced at the hand brake to the left and under the steering wheel. It was set.

Hands grabbed Hiram's left arm. He threw himself right and kicked backward like a mule. He saw his Harvesters connect with the nose over the Fuller brush, and then blood sprayed onto the Model T's window. Widow's Peak fell.

The fourth man charged the car.

Hiram released the brake and the Model T lurched forward.

A sharp scream cut through the air.

Michael pulled the Double-A past the Model T on the right side, as the rusted car rolled toward the river.

Hiram squeezed out of the car. He stepped over Widow's Peak, who lay hollering in the road and clutching his leg. The men with bandanas were standing up, and the fourth man was yelling urgently at them.

Hiram jumped onto the running boards of the Double-A. He slammed a hand onto the roof. "Go, son!"

The men stopped chasing Hiram, and jumped into the Model T to stop it from rolling downhill into the river.

Michael gave the truck gas and they sped away.

When they were around a corner and out of sight, Hiram plunked himself back down on the seat. He let out a long breath.

Michael drove with his mouth open. Sweat dripped off his nose. "Those guys, they would have robbed us. How did you know? What the hell, Pap?"

Hiram closed his eyes, feeling light-headed. "Nice work, not running them over."

"You surprised me as much as you surprised those guys." Michael laughed. "What were you saying to that guy before you took his sock away?"

Hiram gave his son a weary grin. "I offered them a bag of groceries. Maybe I should have offered two?"

Michael laughed in spite of himself. "I think they

wanted the whole truck. Where did you learn to fight like that?"

Hiram sighed. He needed a long cool drink from the water jug in the back. Should he tell the police there were bandits in the canyon? But they might be the very men he had come here to help. At least he should tell someone about the injured fellow.

The man *he* had injured.

Hiram said a silent prayer for the hungry men who had attacked him.

Michael finally had to answer his own question. "Yeah, the Great War. Punching out the Hun."

Chapter Three

THE TRUCK CLIMBED UP SPRING CANYON, THE LONG valley above Helper that was home to many coal mines. The interior of the Double-A quickly became stifling, and stayed hot even when Hiram cracked a window. Hiram fished a green bandana from the bib pocket of his overalls and mopped at the sweat on his forehead. There wasn't enough room in the cab of the truck to shrug out of his coat.

Hiram was intensely thirsty.

The road turned right in a broad loop around a stand of pine and the canyon opened. Three smaller canyons continued like splayed fingers, the yellow rock like skin and the junipers cloaked with snow like skinned knuckles. On the left side of the road a two-story white clapboard building hove into view. The two-foot tall wooden sign running the length of the building, above a deep porch and three rocking chairs, read DOLLARS.

"Hey, Pap, in these errands we do," Michael said,

"maybe we could arrange to go somewhere exciting. Like, I don't know, Denver. Or California."

"I'm not sure I'd call them errands," Hiram objected.

"Would you call them...*quests?*" Michael asked. "We deliver groceries, we try to help people find jobs, we settle family disputes. Or anyway, *you* do those things. I'm more of a servant, really."

"We're both servants," Hiram said. "It's a ministry. We're trying to help people in need."

"I, for one," Michael said, "need a drink."

"I could use a Coke, myself." Hiram generally drank water, but at the moment, a cold Coca-Cola sounded inviting. This was a fasting day—Hiram tried to fast one day a week—but he drank when he fasted. A man had to, when his living included physical labor.

Michael stroked his chin. "If you were driving this truck, I guess you could pull over and get a dope, if you wanted."

Hiram kept his gaze mild, but didn't back away from Michael's challenging eyes.

Michael looked away first. "Coke. You know I just mean a Coke."

Hiram nodded. "I was thinking *you* might like a Coke, too."

"It's like you're a magician, reading my mind." Michael grinned and eased over into a gravel drive beside the store.

Hiram cringed at his son's words.

"Keep your boots on." He climbed out of the truck, shutting the door and smiling in through the window.

Was that a train whistle he heard, or the sound of distant music from one of the town's bars or bordellos?

But no, he was too far away to hear either. It had to be the wind.

"It's February, Pap. It's freezing, and I'm driving the Double-A. Am I really going to take off my shoes?"

"It's just an expression," Hiram said.

"No one says it but you." Michael grinned. Even wide open, his eyes seemed to be all dark brown iris. Like his father's.

Wide open, like Yas Yazzie's eyes had been in the moment he died, in Europe's frozen mud, thousands of miles from his red-rock home.

"Old-fashioned, I guess." Hiram loped toward the store with his long, bone-rattling strides.

"Don't I know it!"

Stepping up onto the porch, Hiram sneaked a hand into his right pocket to touch the cool heliotropius.

The other objects in the same pocket were his clasp knife and his Zippo lighter. He didn't smoke, but many others did. A quick offer of a light could soften a heart.

He stopped, hand on the doorknob. Hanging in the window, on the other side of glass, were bunches of herbs. They hung stem-up and leaf-down, and many men would have simply walked past them, oblivious.

Hiram knew the herbs, and he knew their uses. Peppermint and bay.

You could cook with bay, and peppermint made a lovely tea. But both had a further use: they warded off hexes.

The lead holding the shop's windowpanes in place was twisted into irregular patterns. No, a single irregular pattern, repeating in each window. What was the meaning of the pattern? The planets, as well as angels and demons, each had a unique written sign. The signs were like the drawn equivalent of secret names.

This kind of lore was beyond Hiram, though. It was book-lore, and his lore had mostly come to him by word of mouth.

He turned back to see Michael, head lolling back against the seat, eyes closed.

Hiram shook his head, chasing away baseless fears. He touched the Saturn ring on the ring finger of his left hand. He'd never worn a wedding band while Elmina was alive, but shortly after her death, he'd put the Saturn ring on. He'd never taken it off since.

The night before, Hiram had dreamed of driving slowly on a desert road and calling Michael's name, to no response. But not all dreams were prophetic. Hiram hadn't bothered to consult the little dream dictionary in the bottom of his toolbox.

And in the case of a truly dire emergency, Michael knew Hiram's revolver was in the glove box, loaded with five rounds, one empty chamber for safety. There were six more bullets in a full moon clip beside the Colt.

Hiram opened the shop door.

He heard the chainsaw-like sound of two large dogs growling. Two black beasts leaned in his direction, snarling and yipping. Hiram recognized them as Rottweilers—he'd seen them in Germany.

"Down, boys!" called a voice.

The dogs retreated and Hiram entered.

A second sign hung over the counter inside. It read: *Scrip from all Spring Canyon mines accepted at eighty percent of face value, credit extended only to those who don't need it*. The short counter held a cash register, a book of accounts, and a dog-eared copy of the Sears, Roebuck catalog. Three walls of the room, floor to ceiling, were covered with deep wooden shelves, groaning under the panoply of goods a miner's family could use to make a life, from Clabber Girl baking soda and White King soap to bolts of cloth and carpentry tools. Washboards and metal basins hung between the windows, and shovels leaned into the corners of the room. The shop floor was occupied by mannequins in Sunday frocks, iceboxes, and a washing machine with a very large drum.

The Rottweilers slunk behind the counter, growls subsiding.

A man in a white shirt and red suspenders stood at the register. His hair was white and so bristle-thick that Hiram thought he could count the hairs on the man's head from across the room. It shot straight up like a rooster's comb, without the glisten of pomade.

"Hallo!" the old man bellowed. "Welcome!"

Hiram nodded, squeezing the heliotropius and forcing himself not to touch the chi-rho talisman. "German?"

The old man laughed merrily. "How did you know? I didn't slip and say *velcome*, did I?"

Hiram shrugged. "I knew a few Germans."

"My name is Gus. Gus Dollar. And yes, I'm German. Or at least I was . . . in another life." The old man pointed at Hiram's coat. "You were a Doughboy?"

Hiram nodded.

With an explosion of laughter, two small children rushed into the storeroom from an open door in back. They were tow-headed balls of mercury, skittering back and forth across the planks, giggling at each change of direction.

Would Hiram and Elmina have had children such

as these, had she not carried such a fatal darkness within her?

Stepping out of the way of the tumbling children, Hiram bumped a shelf and knocked a poppet off it. He caught the poppet in his large, callused hands and carefully placed it back into position, sitting on a shelf beside cans of Gibson and Maxwell House ground coffee.

Next to the coffee, and not next to other toys.

He looked at the poppet again, smiling blandly. It was made of orange wax and nearly featureless. It wore tiny overalls cut from calico, and tucked within the overalls and also wedged into the poppet's wax was a buffalo nickel. It was a new coin, with the bison on one side and the Indian head on the other.

It was a hex, an old shopkeeper's charm for drawing customers into any business. Grandma Hettie had pointed out similar poppets in a tack and saddle shop in Santaquin and a greengrocer in Provo.

Hiram bit back a laugh. It hadn't been the heat inside the truck's cab that had made him want to come inside and buy two Cokes, it had been this poppet. The idea was a tad disturbing, despite the fact that the charm was fundamentally harmless.

He turned to look again at Gus Dollar. The old man chased the two children in one final circle around the room. He looked sixty, but he moved with the agility of a much younger man. Something was not quite right with his eyes.

His left eye, Hiram realized. It didn't move, it was fixed forward.

A false eye? An injury?

But for all that he had a bad eye and was old, Gus

Dollar's shop and his charm and the two children racing around him struck a deep bass note of envy in the bottom of Hiram Woolley's soul.

Gus chased the children out and met Hiram at the counter again. "Forgive me."

Hiram forced himself to smile. "Children. Nothing to forgive."

"You don't look like a miner," Gus said. "Or a doctor, or a deputy sheriff."

"Is that who usually visits Spring Canyon and the mines?"

Gus nodded. "Undertaker, once in a while. Peddlers. And I heard some of the miners talk about a union man, which I didn't believe until I saw it with my own...*eye*." He rolled his good eye in a circle, the inert one staying fixed on Hiram.

"Is that glass?"

Gus leaned forward, gripped the eyeball in question with the fingers of one hand, and popped it from its socket. Setting it on the countertop, he rolled it toward Hiram.

Hiram caught the eye. The sphere lay warm in his hand, staring up at him. It might have been a large marble. He handed it back to Gus. "Might want to wash that off."

The shopkeeper laughed, his eye socket now a sunken pit with mostly-closed eyelids hanging loosely over it. He tucked the glass eye into a breast pocket. "Old injury. Now, what can I do for you?"

"Two dopes." Hiram instantly regretted the word. "Cokes, I mean. From the icebox, if you have any."

"Cold day outside, though. You sure you wouldn't rather have a hot coffee?"

Hiram in fact would have preferred a hot coffee. Black, and if sweetened, then with a little beet syrup. The way Grandma Hettie had always taken it, and the way Hiram had grown up taking it, with bacon, eggs, and fried potatoes, before going out to work the farm. Food that filled your stomach, food you could work on.

But he'd promised John Wells he would give up coffee, and Hiram Woolley kept his promises. Wells had made it clear that Bishop Cannon felt strongly about the matter, and that as the bishop's second counsellor, Wells would sustain the man.

"Two Cokes, please." Hiram hesitated. The herbs, the strange windows, the poppet, all made him wonder if he should reveal himself to Gus Dollar.

Or had Gus already guessed?

"I've heard men say," Gus said slowly, his accent becoming more German with each word, "that drinking Coca-Cola, instead of coffee and wine, helps a man keep a chaste and sober mind."

"Hmm," Hiram murmured.

"Or on the other hand," Gus said, "you could just be one of these Mormons."

Hiram smiled. "Maybe both things could be true."

"Maybe." Gus chuckled. "So, what are you doing, driving up to the coal mines, dressed like a farmer in those overalls, and your old soldier's coat over the top?"

"I'm looking for the Kimball Mine. I didn't see a sign."

"Left fork," Gus said. "But that doesn't answer my question."

"I'm buying two Cokes. And I *am* a farmer."

Gus retrieved two bottles from the icebox in the rear corner of the store. "Your business."

The shopkeeper's nonchalance embarrassed Hiram. Was he being rude because he envied the man? "I'm delivering food. To a man named William Sorenson. Food for the miners out of work."

"That's every miner at the Kimball Mine. Caring for the widows and the fatherless, eh? Pure religion and undefiled?" Gus set the Cokes on the counter. "Five cents. *Bill* Sorenson. The mine foreman. His real name is actually *Vilhelm*, but he insists on being called Bill."

"Shouldn't that be ten cents?" Hiram gestured at the price, clearly spelled out on the bright red door of the icebox. "Vilhelm Sorenson...is he a Swede, then?"

"A Dane. If you personally plan to drink both these bottles, the price is ten cents." Gus Dollar smiled. "But if one of them is for the young man sitting in that truck outside, then I'll accept a nickel."

Hiram wanted to refuse the gift, insist on paying the full dime, but he didn't. It would be an act of foolish pride to refuse another man the opportunity to do a kindness.

"And if I get a Snickers, too?"

"Then a dime in total."

Hiram tendered a dull coin and took the Cokes and the candy, putting the cream-paper-wrapped square into his pocket. He wouldn't eat it today, but Michael might need it later on. "Why would you... what would make you say that thing you said, about a chaste and sober mind?"

"You look like a man acquainted with fasting," Gus said with a faint smile.

Hiram smiled back. "President Roosevelt might say we've all become better acquainted with fasting in recent years."

Gus nodded. "White man and an Indian traveling together. Maybe he's your teacher. Your master in the mysterious arts."

"He's my son." Hiram felt his brow furrowing, against his will. "He was a baby when his mother died from the Spanish flu. I knew his father in the Great War, so I adopted him."

"I'm joking." The word sounded very German, like *choking.* "I saw the way you looked at my charm."

Involuntarily, Hiram shot a glance at the poppet and blushed. "My grandmother raised me. She... read the almanac. Understood the true meanings of the Psalms."

"A *hexe.* A cunning woman. Knew the properties of stones?"

Hiram nodded.

"Had a library of strange books?" Gus pressed.

Hiram rushed to change the subject. "The miners need food." He gestured at the sign over the counter. "You could give them credit."

"I do," Gus said. "Despite what I wrote on the sign. But I've given just about all I can give now. A storekeeper who offers everyone credit starves to death. Or his children starve."

"The mine will be open soon." Hiram said it hopefully, willing it to be true.

Gus Dollar nodded. "The mine will be open soon. And if not, soon enough the men will take to the rails. The good thing about being so close to Helper is that there's always a train to catch."

"And if the men go hoboing, what happens to the families?"

Gus shrugged. "The good men send money back.

But you can't ride the blinds with a small child, or a pregnant woman."

"Bad time to be looking for work."

"Bad time." Gus nodded. "And what food are you bringing the miners, then?"

"Ham," Hiram said. "Flour. Tinned vegetables."

Gus reached across the counter to clap Hiram's shoulder. "You'll do alright, cunning man. You'll do alright."

Hiram wasn't so sure.

Chapter Four

HIRAM AND MICHAEL CONTINUED UP THE LEFT fork of Spring Canyon, the Double-A rattling on every stone. A sharp turn to the right brought them to a steep hill. Michael tried to take it in third gear and the engine protested.

"You'll want to drop into second gear, son."

"Just have to go faster is all," Michael insisted.

Michael might damage the truck. Or worse, spill the pile of groceries strapped to the Double-A's bed. Hiram kept those worries to himself. "You're driving."

Michael stomped on the accelerator pedal and the engine cycled faster.

Hiram's thoughts lingered on Gus Dollar and his store, the wax poppet, the herbs in the windows, the curious lead shapes. Hiram was uncomfortable that the man was so open about his hexing, and yet he was... content. His business thrived and his family prospered.

The cab of the Double-A again grew chill, and Hiram shrugged down into his green overcoat as far as he could. No Model A or Double-A left Henry Ford's factory with a heater, but there was a jobber you could install after the fact. Hiram kept meaning to get one, but it seemed just as easy to keep an extra coat and gloves in the truck.

Hiram glanced behind him to check that the crates of beets and groceries were okay, given the steepness and roughness of the road. Michael had done a good job roping them down to the wooden slats of the truck; knots were one of the things he'd mastered before dropping out of the Boy Scouts.

The engine sputtered and they lost speed, a little short of the top. Michael set his sweating Coke bottle between his legs to shift back into second. "You were right. Fortunately, you're the kind of father not much given to rubbing my nose in my mistakes."

"And you're the kind of son who always holds his tongue."

Michael laughed out loud. "Bullseye, Pap."

Hiram smiled.

"Once again, you've taken me to the middle of nowhere." Michael shook his head and grimaced. "I'm fairly certain that there are families in San Francisco that could use groceries. Los Angeles is also probably low on sugar beets."

"What about Tooele?" Hiram grinned.

"We've already been there," Michael said. "That was the time you were out all night, messing with the well on that one guy's farm."

"Abramović's ranch." Hiram had lied to Michael about the reason why he hadn't slept that night. The farm had been plagued by the spirit of Mr. Abramović's mother, who had been cruel in life and vengeful in death. Hiram had eased her transition with a charm, but he had a scar on his back from her cold fingernails.

He hated lying to Michael. Guilt filled his pockets like stones.

They turned another corner and Hiram got his first look at the Kimball mining camp.

"Stop for a second, son." To the right was the camp itself, a city of irregular, leaning buildings. Hiram saw single-room houses and larger dormitories, all of their roofs and many of their walls tacked against the weather with tar paper. There were also tents and other larger buildings: a school maybe, or the company store, a church, a union hall. At the very top, pressed into the crack of a narrow stone-walled side canyon, was the mine entrance itself, surrounded by a handful of more solidly-built yellow stone buildings. Two tracks of rails led from the opening to the right and a long wooden structure with a metal chute, crouching above the canyon atop a skeletal tower of thick timbers like a giant mountain lion, ready to pounce; the tipple was where the coal would be sorted and dumped into big trucks to be driven down the canyon to the train.

Electric wire jostled up the canyon on low poles, but it only seemed to connect to the larger buildings. Outhouses sprang up among the houses like weeds in a neglected furrow. Cars—mostly Model Ts, battered, dirty, and rusting—squatted in front of the many of the houses on a track that was more a stream of mud than a road.

If the food on the back of Hiram's truck had to feed all those people, it would be gone in forty-eight hours.

A gaggle of red-faced children ran past, waving carved sticks at each other. They were stick-thin and dirty, their coats too thin for winter. "Bang, bang, bang!" one group shouted.

"Bang, bang! You're dead, Butch!" the others yelled.

"Nobody kills Butch Cassidy! Ain't you heard? He's still alive and living in Urgentina!"

The gang and pursuing posse both skidded through dirty snow and dropped out of sight down the hill.

The north-facing side of the canyon had far more plant life; below the camp were clusters of willows and cottonwoods, leafless and gray along the creek. Across the water and the road, the south-facing canyon cliffs collected big boulders and few plants. The Kimball house perched there, a shadowy red against the washed-out red rock cliffs like a vulture fresh from its feast. The house didn't even flirt with trees, a lawn, or a garden. Someone had hammered the wood together in front of a dusty driveway, painted it red, and called it good. Telephone lines reached from the eaves to the rocks and wooden posts jammed into the rocks above.

That would have been the work of Teancum Kimball, the man who opened the mine some thirty-odd years ago. Teancum was gone now, and his children owned the mine.

"Know why those rocks are red, Pap?" Michael asked.

Hiram didn't respond. The bishops had also said that Teancum had been a polygamist. How did a man with three wives end up building a house without a single tree or a garden?

"It's the iron in rocks," Michael said. "Hematite is a common mineral, an iron oxide, found in Utah. It comes from the Greek word 'haema' which means blood. Blood rocks."

Blood rocks. In his pocket, Hiram carried a blood-stone.

He stepped out of the truck, feeling slightly ill.

"Are you listening to what I'm saying, Pap?"

"Yes." Hiram stepped to the front of the truck and leaned on the hood. That red house surrounded by the blood rocks had dark windows the color of pitch.

Hiram's ears started ringing. He blinked, trying to resist a sudden dizziness. A sweet smell with a hint of spice, like onions, garlic, and maybe horseradish, filled his nose. He was on the edge of falling into the smell, and the ringing grew harsher in his ears. Or was it the loud, sharp whistle that wasn't the wind, wasn't a train, might not even be anything outside of his own senses. His vision narrowed.

Hiram blinked. The cold bit his cheeks.

"Rupert and Giles," he murmured. "Rupert and Giles..." He couldn't remember the charm to stop fainting spells.

He couldn't catch a breath. The ringing in his ears got louder, only it wasn't a ringing, it was a buzzing. A fly a quarter-inch long, black as ink, hummed slowly through past Hiram's face and then landed on his neck. He whipped his hand back to smack it.

And missed.

Suddenly, the phantom odor dissipated. Hiram's knees buckled, but he caught himself, and his hearing returned to normal.

"Pap, are you okay?" Michael was leaning out of the truck.

Hiram squeezed his eyes shut. "Yes."

He got back into the passenger seat, Michael squeaked the gears into first, and they trundled off.

Michael knocked Hiram's thigh with the Coke bottle. "Were you having a spell, Pap?"

"Not quite. Almost."

Michael sighed. "Jesus Christ, you're lucky I'm here."

Hiram took a deep breath. "I *am* lucky. No need to cuss."

"I tried saying cripes, and you objected to *that*, too."

"Yes, well. I'm not crazy about that word."

"'Cripes'? It doesn't mean anything."

"It means the same thing as the curse word you're pretending not to say."

Michael snorted; that might be as close to an acknowledgement as Hiram would get. "I might sing some blues while you unload."

Michael was trying to get his goat. "That jazz music is dangerous." Hiram grinned to lighten the mood. Jazz music didn't really bother him, though some jazz *musicians* did.

"Pap, I'm seventeen years old. I'm in my prime. I'm *supposed* to be rowdy, and engaged in all manner of unwise behavior."

"Not your prime," Hiram said. "You're just starting out."

"Mahonri says you're giving me good guidance, and that you're just trying to save me heartache later. That does nothing to soothe me, I can tell you."

"Mahonri Young is a smart man," Hiram muttered. "It's why he works in a library. Slow down, son, to save on the dust."

"The dust is behind us. What do you care?"

"Butch Cassidy's behind us, too."

They reached the camp. Men sat on rough wooden stools beside a long leaning building. It must be a boarding house, but it looked more like a poorly-built chicken coop. Coal dust blackened both the men and the buildings.

On the opposite side of the track, a row of houses leaned against each other to remain standing.

An orange streak—a cat—flashed across the road. Michael slammed on the brakes and the Double-A bounced to a halt. The tabby sped under the steps leading up into a little shack, leaning hard to the right.

Michael exhaled and pushed himself back from the wheel. The car seat springs squeaked. "Well, that was a close one."

Five kids ran across the road, following the cat. They all looked to be under ten, wearing patched clothes and shoes that were too big or held together with twine. The oldest was a girl in a formless dress that might once have been white but was now a sooty gray. The dress's lace looked like a spiderweb torn apart by a rainstorm. She carried a long cottonwood stick, the end sharpened to a point.

The other children followed the girl. She yelled something in a foreign tongue; the children fanned out. A pair of young greasy-faced boys crouched on either side of the house's steps. The girl calmly carried her spear forward.

Hiram clambered out of the truck. "Hey, girl, easy there. Let's not hurt the cat."

She glared to him, shouted something he didn't understand, and waved her spear. Then she pointed at the steps.

The cat yowled and hissed.

"You don't want to torture that animal," Hiram said. One of littlest children in the group wiped at his mouth. He might be five years old, and the whites of his eyes were bright pink. He was stick-thin.

They all were.

The door swung open and a lean woman emerged, muscular arms busting out of a gray dress with dull red flowers printed on it. Her thick black hair was held back in a red bandana. Gray cotton long john pants peeped out below her dress, and her feet were bare. She glanced at Hiram and the truck behind him, and then shouted to her children.

Her shouts didn't make the cat any calmer.

"Mister," the woman said, "what is it you want?" She had furious brown eyes and her mouth slanted downward to the left.

Hiram swept off his hat and smoothed down the sparse hairs on his head. "I'm Hiram Woolley. I just don't want anyone to hurt that cat."

The woman's frowned jammed further down her face, slanting like her home. "What business is it of yours? Are you the sheriff?"

"No," Hiram said. "I have groceries. I'm taking it to Bill Sorenson, but . . . I'll happily give you some now."

The girl with the spear went on a run of foreign jabber, pointing at Hiram, at the cat, and then at the woman.

The woman must be her mother; they had the same eyes.

She squinted at Hiram for a long time.

"Medea Markopoulos," she finally said. "My warrior daughter is Callista. Most of these others are my children, too. Park. We'll take the food."

The daughter wouldn't stop talking. Medea plucked the spear out of Callista's hand and used it to shoo her sons away from the steps.

The cat skedaddled.

Hiram went back to his truck and walked with Michael as he parked it in a scraggly patch of weeds. Hiram lifted an apple box of food, as did Michael. They followed Medea into her house.

Without her spear, Callista folded her arms across her chest, glaring at Hiram. With dark eyes and dark hair, and the look of defiance in her face, she reminded Hiram of how Michael had looked, six or seven years earlier.

Around the time, say, that Elmina had died.

Callista's brothers stood with her, but their eyes went to the tins of beans, the long green stalks of root vegetables, and the sacks of flour. The little one drooled down his chin.

Inside, the only light came from a single window in the back of the room. A man lay on a stuffed mattress on the corner of the floor; pillows and blankets were stacked under him, propping his head up. His eyes were closed and his leg was wrapped in bandages. Two other mattresses leaned against the walls.

A stove in the opposite corner radiated heat. Shelves made of long slats of wood nailed into one wall held dishes, eating utensils, pots, pans, and other necessaries. A table and a cluster of chairs were pushed against the wall between the door and the stove.

Hiram set the food down and took off his hat again. Michael set down a sack with more food in it; Hiram smiled at his son. The woman backed up against the homemade cabinetry. Leaning against the shelves were an ancient rifle and a curved sword.

The man on the bed coughed.

"Pap," Michael said, "it's the . . . guy . . ."

Hiram recognized the man's widow's peak and Fuller brush moustache. The man's thigh turned at an unnatural angle.

Medea moved to stand beside Widow's Peak. "My Basil. He hurt his leg."

"Yeah." Hiram's heart was heavy. "Basil needs to see a doctor. If his leg heals like that, he'll be lame for life."

Medea's eyes flashed pride and anger. "This is none of your business."

Hiram nodded slowly. "Have a good day, ma'am."

"Nice meeting you," Michael mumbled.

Medea nodded once.

They returned to the truck. The kids poured into the house. Those beans weren't going to last long against those hungry mouths. Callista stood last in the open doorway, watching them.

Michael drove them away. Hiram sat with his hand covering his mouth. A heavy feeling hung in his stomach.

"And they can't pay for a doctor, right?" Michael said. "Because the mine is closed?"

Hiram nodded. "Maybe the mine won't stay closed. And at least they're eating today."

"Gee, that's just great," Michael said. "Until the food runs out. We have to get that mine back open. Or . . . something. This isn't right."

"Even though they tried to rob us?"

"They were hungry, Pap. You said it yourself. And did you see those kids? They weren't just playing with that cat, Pap. They were going to eat it."

Hiram looked out the window and they drove on through the camp.

Men in denim stared at them. Children played.

But no chickens, no goats, no pigs.

Hiram lifted two fingers in a greeting at a knot of men.

They spat on the ground.

"This place is making me feel lucky to be a farmer." Michael licked the mouth of the now-empty Coke bottle.

"You're not a farmer. You're a future geologist."

"Or spaceman."

"Turn left there," Hiram said, and they left the main track. He was looking for the biggest houses in the camp itself, trying to find Vilhelm Sorenson.

They trundled down a slope, across the bridge, and up the other side. Laundry, streaked and mottled gray with soot, flapped on lines around the hastily-made single room clapboard houses. The houses had tar-paper roofs and siding but very few had windows. They did, however, have gardens, limp and yellow with weeds and winter. As the track became narrow and Michael's driving slowed, Hiram could smell the wafting reek of the outhouses.

They made a turn, following the road as it twisted up through houses that seemed abandoned. Michael and Hiram fell silent. Even the Double-A seemed to putter a bit more quietly.

Three men walked up the road, blocking it. Michael was forced to stop. All of the men wore dusty overalls and long-sleeved shirts. The fedoras on their heads were black with coal-soot. Each of the newcomers had a shock of blond hair on his head; one wore a red waistcoat and had a thick goiter on his neck. They were solid working men, driving their heels into the mud of the road at each step. In their hands they held ax handles.

Everyone in this camp seemed prepared to fight.

Hiram stepped out of the truck, kept the door open, and tried to stay calm. "I'm looking for Vilhelm Sorenson."

The three men stopped and glowered. Two of them turned to their comrade Goiter, likely the one who spoke the best English. "*Ja*," he said, "up the hill. *Einundfünfzig*. One and fifty."

Hiram nodded. "Thank you . . . *danke*."

"You a friend of Sorenson's?" the German asked.

"I try to be everyone's friend. I brought food for the camp." He gave them a final nod and retreated to the truck.

He slid in and Michael got the truck going again. The boy muttered under his breath, chanting through the steps of starting the vehicle. They took another turn, drove past a school and a company store. Worried women in dresses talked, ragged children played, and lean men sat in groups. Hiram saw Serbs, Croats, more Greeks, more Germans, and a few Orientals.

The house numbered 51 had a pig-shaped piece of wood nailed to the door.

Chapter Five

A HUGE MAN BURST FROM THE HOUSE. HE TROMPED heavily, stooped, left shoulder lowered, swatting at unseen enemies with a rolled-up newspaper in one fist. His thin hair showed a forehead like a limestone cliff; the tangle of eyebrows rose as high as a full inch and his smashed nose dangled slightly sideways. "Hey, dere, mister. You want to see me? If you're from de railroad, you turn around, or else I bloody your nose."

"We got everyone's attention," Michael said. "Perhaps you should run for local office, Pap."

Hiram eased out of the truck and raised his hands. "I'm looking for Vilhelm Sorenson."

"And who sent you?" The giant's left hand was missing its last two fingers.

"I have groceries for the camp," Hiram said. "It's got some beets on account I'm a beet farmer, in from Lehi." He must be nervous; he felt his grammar slipping. "But some bishops in Utah Valley let me into their storehouses, so I have other groceries, too. Ham.

Flour. Beans. About two days' worth, maybe." The camp was bigger than Hiram had expected.

"Bishops? Catholic bishops?"

"Mormon bishops," Hiram said.

The man-cliff lowered the newspaper. "I'm Sorenson. I'm de foreman here. And you are what, Mr. Mormon? A do-gooder?"

Hiram knew that he stood in the least Mormon part of the State of Utah, and *do-gooder* sounded a lot like *meddler* and maybe *hypocrite*.

"I'm a man with a truck full of food," Hiram said. "Do you want to help pass it out? Or shall I just leave it at your door?"

The Dane lumped his way forward to the edge of the porch. "A Mormon beet-farmer, on my doorstep. *Gud*, what a world."

Even stooped, the Dane stood eye to eye with Hiram. Hiram smelled pomade in the giant's hair and smoke on his clothes.

Sorenson softened further. "Maybe you should come inside. We can talk a bit. I'll tell de men to come for de food. We'll take it. Gratefully. Your boy can park de truck dere." He waved to men across the track, then pointed to a space in front of the house.

"That's Michael, my son," Hiram said.

Michael flicked some fingers at the Dane, then clutched and shifted. He eased the Double-A into the offered spot.

"I hear the mine is closed." Hiram said, and immediately regretted it. His words would only make him sound like a meddler.

"You a friend of de Kimballs?" Sorenson smacked the newspaper into his left hand.

Hiram repeated what he'd said to the men. "Never met them, but I'd like to think I'm everyone's friend. Do-gooder, remember?"

Sorenson smiled, revealing a big cracked front tooth, blackened where it wasn't yellow. "*Ja*, funny guy. I like guys dat make me laugh. Like Charlie Chaplin, he's always funny."

"Michael's the funny one." Hiram motioned for Michael to join them and he followed Sorenson inside. Despite his limp, the Dane moved with a quick step.

Hiram gave the pig-shaped design nailed to the door a long look.

Sorenson noticed. "De Germans, dey think de pig and de numbers bring luck. Something about de three kings. We need de luck now, dat's for sure, and my wife believes."

Memories of Elmina's smile and the way she looked at him while he washed the dishes flooded over Hiram, wiping the smile from his face. Bitter, gut-punching echoes of her final screams, as she lay dying of some hidden sickness on their marriage bed, followed. Six years. Had six years passed, since her death and the Crash?

He took off his hat and finger-combed his hair.

The house had three rooms: a parlor; a bedroom on the left, bed just visible through the cracked door; and a kitchen on the right. Needlepoint images of boys and girls playing hung on the parlor walls and a little side table was covered with a lacy doily. Heat radiated into the parlor from a cast-iron wood-burning stove in the kitchen. A hissing kerosene lamp hung from a hook. The camp had electricity, and the Sorensons didn't seem poor. Did Bill Sorenson prefer not to have electricity in his home?

Hiram and Michael followed Sorenson into the kitchen. Below the kitchen counter, which was little more than a shelf fixed to the wall, stood a wooden keg. On the counter lay a bowl of yellowing milk and a crust of white bread. Sorenson drew out two chairs from a small table. Both Michael and Hiram sat.

Hiram motioned to the bowl and the crust of bread. "Is that for Robin Goodfellow?"

Sorenson raised an eyebrow, a feat of strength that would have crushed a lesser man. "What? De wife again. But we are not here to talk about bogeymen and spirits. We have problems. You bring food? Fine. But dat won't fix us for long. De men need jobs, or dey need to leave. Maybe I tell you, and you tell de bishop, and he talks to Ammon Kimball. And we fix dis for good."

Sorenson gripped his newspaper roll with both hands. "You want beer, boy? Or are you Mormon, too?"

"Officially, I suppose I am," Michael said. "Really, I'm unaffiliated. However, I'm not one to touch intoxicating liquors."

"Water would be fine," Hiram said. "And I agree with you. It's not good for men to be idle. Food only solves the problem for a couple of days."

Sorenson rose and went to a bucket next to the stove. "Ammon runs de mine. No, he doesn't run anything, he sits over dere in de big red house, scratching his boils. De mine is closed while de Kimballs claw each udder's eyes out. Teancum disappeared two years now, him and his new wife. My wife says he is dead. I say he had wife number four, who was younger dan his daughters, what man wouldn't want to run away with her? But she dreamed he was dead, but den she dreamed about de ghosts of de eastern seam. Dreams." He snorted.

Hiram listened closely. Without meaning to, he found himself fingering his Saturn ring. "Is that what Robin Goodfellow does? Does he bring your wife dreams?"

"*Gud* help me if I know. I thought he killed mice." Sorenson took the bucket and poured water into three tin cups. "My men always talk of de haunts, too. Some of de men say dey heard whispers in de eastern seam, and of course, dere are shadows and laughing. It sounds like a bad movie, no? Not a funny movie, with Charlie Chaplin. And den dere are stories of strange animal things running around on top of de mesa. If dat weren't bad enough, robbers are on de roads. Nothing is good. Nowhere is safe."

Hiram thought of Basil and Medea Markopoulos and their hungry children.

Sorenson splashed the bucket down on the counter. "Robbers are real enough. Ghosts? I think not. Before de mine closed, I had to pay Chinamen extra to go down dere. We got it done. I always get de work done, when dere is work."

Hiram closed his eyes. A haunted mine was probably just overactive imaginations, gossip, idleness, and liquor.

But if not . . . Wells had told him to keep his eyes open.

"If the mine is closed, what are the men still doing here?" Michael asked. "I'd have figured they'd take off for greener pastures."

"What green pastures?" Sorenson stood with his arms crossed. "Farmers come up from de fields to mine in de winter. Dey wait. Might as well wait here, radder dan wait at home in dead fields. Dey're okay, dey gotta go plant soon, anyway. But de real miners? Dey're in deep to de company store. We pay rent here, and dat works as long as we're getting paid. But when we don't get paid, we still owe rent. We owe, and we can't leave, not until we're paid off. No paychecks, dough. And every week, more rent."

Hiram sighed.

Michael jumped from his seat. "Come on! How is that fair?"

Sorenson laughed. "Boy, maybe somebody promised you life will be fair. Instead ... rich men drink cream and eat beef, arguing with each other, while we get poorer."

"It's *Michael*, not *boy*." If Michael's mind was sharp, his tongue was sharper. "But ... at some point, you have to cut loose and take off, and try to find work somewhere else. It's not like the Kimballs could come after you."

The big Dane turned to Hiram and rumbled out more laughter. "Oh, your boy is quite a talker."

"Always has been," Hiram admitted. Maybe he should have taught Michael to curb his tongue more, but he'd never had the heart for that fight. Especially after Hettie and Elmina had died.

Sorenson nodded. "My boy, Anders, he says we should go to de lawyers. He works in de big city now, over in Price. All my udder children moved off. Michael, my friend, we live in bad times, and dere is little work. Udder mines are busy, and dey have problems of deir own. You get a reputation as a trouble-starter, or a debt-dodger, you won't find anyone to hire you." He turned to Hiram. "You don't talk much. Not de funny guy I thought. But now you see, a few groceries won't do a thing. Can you fix dis, do-gooder?"

Could Hiram fix it? Was the mine closed because some people thought it was haunted? Maybe he could consecrate the mine, or perform an exorcism. Or if it was a matter of setting the men's minds at ease, maybe he could invite a Catholic priest in to do it. How did the Chinese do exorcisms? "My son's the funny one."

"True," Michael said.

"Funny don't open de mine."

Hiram let out a long breath. "You said the Kimballs are fighting. What are they fighting about?"

Sorenson rose and tried to pace the kitchen, but it was too small a space. He wound up leaning against the back wall. "Dat's not so simple. Ammon is an okay joe. He's a mean boss, but dat's okay, I understand dat a mean boss gets de work done."

"Hold on there, old-timer," Michael said. "All the names are running together for me. So Ammon is Teancum's son. Is he the oldest?"

"No, Eliza, de sister, she's de oldest. She was born when Teancum ran cattle here, before de mine. The Kimballs are Mormon, and dey used to have all de wives around here. First wife, first child, Eliza. But old Teancum liked 'em young." He raised his eyebrows at Hiram.

"I only had the one wife," Hiram said. "Don't know what I'd do with two."

He tried not to think about the dark day when he'd learned two things at the same time. One, that the reason he saw his father so rarely was that Abner Woolley was a polygamist, and spent most of his time with other wives and children. And two, via a letter postmarked from Phoenix, that Abner was leaving for Mexico and wouldn't come back.

That day, Hiram had staggered to the edge of Grandma Hettie's farm and stared southward across the lake until well after midnight.

He shook off the memory.

Sorenson laughed some more. "Agreed. Second wife, and out came Ammon. One child per wife, or one living child, anyway. Lots of babies born dead. Dat's how it goes, sometimes. Third wife died giving birth to Samuel, but by dat time, Teancum's wives weren't so happy. So dey all leave, and Eliza, she leaves too. Ammon and Samuel stay, but only for a time. Samuel was always de strange one, an artist. Soft in de head. He leaves too and it's just Teancum and Ammon."

"How long ago was that?" Michael asked.

"During de Great War," Sorenson said. "Dat's what? Seventeen years now?"

Hiram felt the years. He felt the war, too. That was where he'd met Michael's father, in the trenches of Verdun.

"And Teancum got a fourth wife?" he asked.

"She was pregnant when dey ran off." Sorenson nodded. "Two years ago, it was. And Ammon took over when Teancum went." Sorenson drew a thumb across his throat and made a quacking sound. "We work through de change, no problem. Den Samuel comes back, and he says Ammon is doing everything wrong. Den Eliza comes back, and she fights, too. For what? I don't know. Ammon comes to me and he says de mine must close. He gets de Germans on his side, some of de Croats, de Serbs, and den Samuel gets de Greeks, de Chinamen, de Japs, to go for him, and everything stops."

Hiram furrowed his brow and squinted. "There's still coal in the mine?"

"*Ja*. But Ammon says we got to dig in one place, and Samuel says he wants a new shaft entirely, and each of dem got a gang. So we don't dig nowhere. We stopped and can't start again until de family decides what to do, since dey all own it togedder. Your bishop wants to fix things, maybe he can get de family to stop fighting."

"Or at least get two of them to agree," Hiram said.

"And every damned day, you owe the company more rent." Michael shook his head.

"That's not much better than *cripes*," Hiram murmured.

"Yes, cursing is fitting in dis case," Sorenson shot back. "You know what I think?"

Hiram said nothing.

"Tell us," Michael said.

"I think it is de railroad, again, damn railroad, and I curse when I say it, you hear me?" He smacked the rolled-up newspaper into his palm. "Dere's a man, Naaman Rettig, and he works in de Hotel Utah. Denver and Rio Grande Western, de D and RGW. He comes into town, and maybe he talks to Eliza, since she is in de hotel as well. Pah! She has de big house across de way, and she spends de money de miners should be getting to live in a hotel. Eliza and de Rettig railroad man, maybe dey talk. And maybe I'm out of a job."

"How's that?" Michael asked.

"I don't have such a good history with de railroad," Sorenson replied.

Hiram sighed, trying to find a handhold on the problem. Where to start?

"That doesn't make sense," Michael insisted. "Spring Canyon is useless to the railroad. It doesn't go anywhere, so there's no point running tracks up here."

"Papa Charlie Chaplin, what do you say to dat?" Sorenson asked.

Hiram leaned forward, elbows on his knees. "If the railroad had the mine, they'd get the coal at cost."

"And damn de miners." Sorenson slapped the newspaper against the wall. "You think our debt is unfair now? Wait until de Denver and Rio Grande Western railroad comes. Dey will pay us pennies. Dere's a woman, McGill maybe, and she says de boys gotta form a local of her union. She says we can make it fair, and she tries to help, but what can a woman do?"

"Vote, for one thing," Michael said. "Finally."

The door to the Sorenson house was thrown open and filled by the three large blond men. "Bill, ve make you stay here," Goiter said. "Zere's a meetink, and you aren't invited."

Sorenson sprang to his feet. "You mean, something's happening, and you been sent to keep me out of it. Who did dat? Wagner, wasn't it?"

With the foreman looming over them, the three men with ax handles looked embarrassed and small. They said nothing.

"You idiots!" Sorenson lurched through Michael and Hiram, spilling them off their chairs. The Germans raised their weapons, surprise evident in their faces, and the foreman battered them back with his rolled-newspaper club, then disappeared out the door.

Hiram stumbled for the door, the cowed Germans scattering at his approach. "Stay here, Michael. Don't leave the house."

Michael was speechless, for once, but he wasn't any more obedient than usual, and bounced right into Hiram's wake.

Hiram broke out of the house and went to the truck. The groceries were gone. He snatched the Colt from the glove box, praying he wouldn't have to use it.

With Michael following at his heels, Hiram headed toward the mine.

Chapter Six

MARY MCGILL FOUND HERSELF TROTTING, SWEPT along with the crowd of German miners. The sky overhead was a pale blue, devoid of clouds. The mob surrounding her stank of the anger and sweat of working men. It was a familiar smell.

The tipple sat unused, no trucks under the scored chute, and the conveyor belts inside silent. No cars carrying coal emerged from the mine entrance.

"You've got to save your outrage for the main event," she said.

Hermann Wagner was a paunchy German with a perfect cube of a head, its symmetry only barely disturbed by tiny, constantly-blinking eyes and crumpled ears. The ears weren't even opposite each other— Wagner looked as if he'd bobbed for apples in a bin full of cauliflower, and come up with two florets stuck to random sides of his squared-off noggin.

He had no official title, but by popular deference Wagner was the Head German of the Kimball Mine.

"I can give it to those Greek bastards all night and still have enough for Sam Kimball." Wagner chuckled. "What did you call it, Gil? A body shoot for young Sam."

"Body *shot*," Mary said. "But Sam isn't the main event. It's *all* the Kimballs. You need the mine open, you need better prices for the coal you pull out, you need no interest on advances at the company store and for your rent, you need the child labor law actually *enforced*—"

"Hold on," Wagner said. "My Klaus is a good boy. He don't mind the work."

Mary sighed, lengthening her stride to keep up. McClatchy hadn't wanted her to come out to the mining camps around Helper, but when he'd enumerated the list of reasons why, it had consisted mostly of physical dangers to which his fading sense of chivalry didn't want Mary McGill exposed: bandits, the remoteness of doctors, bad roads, restless Indians, rockslides, and rattlesnakes. He'd never suggested she might encounter miners too eager to side with the mine owners for their own good.

"If you made enough for your own work," she said, "Klaus wouldn't have to sort rocks out of the mine carts and carry messages up and down the mine. He could go to school. Maybe become a doctor. Doesn't that sound good?"

"*Ja*," Wagner agreed. "*Ja*, Gil, okay. But first we got to get the mine open, and that means digging out the east seam like Mr. Ammon says. None of this stupid new shaft nonsense like Sam wants. That guy gets a body shoot, him and all his Greek friends."

Mary bit her tongue.

They passed through two tarpaper shanties and into

the open space below the mouth of Kimball Mine. The mine buildings, mortared sheds of the yellow and orange stone poking through the juniper all around Kimball Canyon, lined an avenue that tumbled down from the gaping mine-mouth and then opened into a rough and muddy plaza. Behind a coal shed, and stretching away on two earth shelves that had been created by splitting a long slope in two with a retaining wall of railroad ties, stood the tarpaper shacks and the rickety boarding houses in which the miners lived. The Kimball Mine was the shaft, Kimball was the name of the shantytown in which the miners lived, the Kimball Corporation held the deeds, and Kimball was the name of the family that owned it all. The red Kimball house brooded on the north side of the canyon, across the road and the seasonal Kimball Creek.

Ammon Kimball stood in the lane leading up to the mine. He was a heavy man, all shoulders, whose hanging head and perpetual frown made him look like an angry bull. He wore plain blue jeans and a navy work coat, and he shifted from foot to foot as if he were in discomfort. His eyes were sunk deep in dark pits, like all his family's were.

The two plaster strips on his neck were probably covering shaving cuts, but they nevertheless made Mary feel abruptly self-conscious about the fact that the entire left side of her face was marked with a large red blotch. An angel's kiss, her mother had called it. *Damn, but that must have been one enormous and excitable angel*, her father had said while drunk.

She forced herself not to touch her own face.

Ammon stood glowering at a crowd of Greek miners. Mary recognized Dimitrios Kalakis with his

single enormous eyebrow and the waves of eastern
cologne he favored; that stuff smelled like cloves and
oranges on the verge of going bad. With him stood
club-footed Stavros Alafouzos and a third man Mary
didn't immediately recognize; he was small, but he
had well-muscled arms crossed over his chest, and a
red bandana covering his face.

"Go home," Ammon growled. "Unless you're prepared to dig the east seam."

"Or stand aside and let Germans do the work!"
Hermann Wagner thumped a fist to his sternum, then
stepped to Ammon Kimball's side.

Ammon snorted.

That was when Mary noticed the gun.

There was nothing unusual about firearms in Kimball. Even in good times, many of the men hunted deer,
rabbits, and elk to supplement the canned peaches and
biscuit flour they bought from the company store. But
the Kimball Corporation was strict about firearms anywhere near the mine. In addition to the obvious risk
of shooting other employees, any kind of spark might
ignite the coal dust and the coal in the mine. The miners were forbidden to smoke within a hundred yards of
the mineshaft, for the same reason.

So the fact that Paul Schneider—Mary thought of
him as "Stinky," despite the delicate carpentry work
he did, because the man apparently never bathed and
lived on a diet of the strongest available cheese—
carried a rifle over his shoulder was not strange. The
fact that he had the rifle within a dozen steps of the
mine shaft opening was odd, and would have ordinarily
gotten him docked pay, if not fired.

But if Ammon noticed the rifle, he said nothing.

"Strong Germans, my feet!" Dimitrios Kalakis trilled. Despite his heavy features and the single eyebrow like a black caterpillar slung ear to ear across his face, he had the high-pitched, trilling voice of a nervous woman. "If you want to dig, the only thing to do is to get a Greek, always! Have you heard of Herakles? One of his greatest feats was rescuing the three thousand cattle of King Augeas, who were trapped in their byre, how do you say it? Their cattle shed. And how did Herakles do it? He *dug!* He dug a hole so vast that in one day all three thousand cows could walk through it! And Herakles, was he a German?"

"If he had been German," Hermann Wagner bellowed, "he would have done it in six hours!"

Dimitrios waved his fist. "He was a Greek!"

"Stand aside and let us work!" Wagner shouted.

Mary kept her eye on Stinky. The man shifted from foot to foot and licked his lips.

"You do not decide what work gets done in this mine!" Dimitrios shrieked.

"No!" Ammon roared. "But *I* do!"

The door of the shed behind Dimitrios slid open, revealing Samuel Kimball, flanked by two more Greeks. Samuel looked like a lighter version of Ammon; they were the same height and had the same eyes, but the younger brother might have had fifty percent of Ammon's weight removed from each limb. Where Ammon glowered and stared into each step he took, Samuel stood as if perpetually recoiling, his long, pale, stained fingers fluttering over his chest.

Black feathers protruded from the neck and sleeves of his shirt. Had he pasted them there, or had Samuel Kimball been sleeping in a literal crows' nest?

"Samuel!" Ammon snarled. "Get off my land!"

"No, brother!" Samuel's sudden arm movements looked like the flapping of a bird's wings. "I'm a Kimball and I will have my say! And you know as well as I do that the east seam is petering out. Not to mention the things, Ammon, the things we've seen down there in the deep, in the dark, down, down, down below. It's a poisoned place. We need to sink a new shaft. You *know* it to be true! *You know!*"

Mary wanted to slap him.

"I know no such thing," Ammon growled back at his brother.

"You know it." Samuel stroked his own nose. "*You* know it the same way that *I* know it."

"Nonsense," Ammon snarled.

"He must have told you." Samuel stared with large eyes magnified by his glasses.

"Gil," a German miner at her elbow whispered, pointing. "Look!"

The crusty old foreman, Bill Sorenson, charged to the edge of the ring, just a few steps to Mary's right. Behind Sorenson came someone new. He was tall and lanky, and he would have been handsome if he'd had a little more meat on his bones. It was hard to tell with the fedora he wore, but Mary guessed he was in his forties. He wore a faded Army coat over blue overalls, and his hands were in his pockets. Behind him came a tall young man—slightly taller than the fellow with the fedora, and with a solid chest—whose complexion and features suggested he was some kind of Indian. Navajo, maybe? The kid wore a sneer, and looked around at the entire mining camp as if he couldn't believe his surroundings.

"You've been smoking that horseshit again!" Ammon's faced was turning red and the muscles in his neck stood out like the straining lines of a ship running before a strong wind. "No wonder the money ran out!"

"The money ran out because of you, you, all because of you, and your pig head! Your big, pig head!" Samuel crowed. "I know you know! It's time to sink a new shaft!"

"Everybody calm down dere! Right now!" Bill Sorenson bellowed.

Hiram surveyed the two groups of miners. The Germans clustered around the larger of the Kimball brothers, Ammon. With them was a woman who was strikingly free of the black coal dust that stained all the miners' clothing. Hiram didn't know what to call her outfit, but she had a kind of navy-blue woolen suit coat with a matching skirt that dropped to below her calves—he tried not to look too long at her legs—and a wool coat over the top. She looked like she belonged in a city.

Plumes of white breath rose from all present. The place smelled of rough men, lathered up for a fight.

What had gone wrong between the two brothers?

Why did Samuel seem to believe that he and Ammon shared a secret?

A flicker of black caught Hiram's eye, standing out in this grim world in which almost everything was coated with a thin layer of gray. Downhill from the mine entrance, a woman stood beside the passenger's seat of a Model T on the camp's main track. The woman's dress was as black as the paint job of the car; her eyes were sunk in two dark pits below her brow and her face was angry.

Hiram turned back to the fighting men.

"I'm going to mine the east seam," Ammon growled. "Hermann Wagner and his men will mine it for me, ghosts be damned. Dimitrios, if you and your men don't want to get paid anymore, you can clear out." The older Kimball shifted as he talked, an expression of discomfort and irascibility on his face. Caused by the boils Sorenson had mentioned? "Just pay your bills before you leave."

A German with a cube for a head folded his arms across his chest and nodded. Hermann Wagner, presumably.

"Not ghosts be damned!" shouted one of the Greeks in the crowd. "I have seen them!"

There was a round of nodding among the men, and not only on the Greek side of the mob.

"We have families!" This came from one of the Greeks, a lean man whose face was covered by a red bandana. Maybe the bandana filtered out the coal dust from the air to protect his lungs.

"If you go down into that mine," Samuel Kimball said to the Germans, "you'll be trespassing. I'll have you shot as you come up." He waved an arm, and black feathers drifted to the ground.

"I'll do the shooting personally," a Greek with a single thick eyebrow over his entire face and a woman's voice said. Was the smell of wassail coming from him? "Greeks are wonderful shots. Do you know the story of story of the great hunter Orion?"

"You wouldn't dare, Dimitrios!" Wagner told him.

"It would give me joy!" the Greek answered. Beside him, a Greek miner paced back and forth with a traipsing, curious gait; some kind of club foot.

"No one will do dat!" Bill Sorenson bellowed, hurling himself into the ring. "No one will go into de mine without my direction. Anyone who does will answer to me."

"And if I fire you, Sorenson?" Ammon Kimball shouted.

Bill Sorenson laughed. "If you fire me, den you will have to deal with all dese pigheaded sons of bitches on your own."

Ammon and Samuel both glared, Samuel stroking his own temples.

And then Hiram realized who the woman in black must be. He turned just in time to see her getting into the Model T. An unseen chauffeur then drove her away, and as the car turned Hiram saw the word TAXI painted on the side of the Model T in bright yellow.

Eliza Kimball.

"I can replace you, Bill," Ammon growled.

As if that was a signal, Hermann Wagner reached into his pockets and stepped forward. When he pulled his hands from his pants, he held a short length of iron bar in each fist. The bars were too short to swing as clubs, but by holding the iron in his hand, he was weighting his punches.

With a nod to Samuel Kimball, Dimitrios stepped forward, too. He drew a sock from his coat pocket and gave it a swing to test its heft. Hiram heard the jingle of coins in what had become a makeshift sap.

The Greek and the German advanced on each other.

Michael bounced at Hiram's side, antsy.

Sorenson laughed and got between the miners. "You know what de word 'chickenshit' means, boys?" He shoved both sleeves up over his elbows and swatted the air with his newspaper.

Hiram hung back, not sure what to do. Michael stood close to him. Again, a motion drew Hiram's eyes away from the unfolding fight. In the same dirt lane barely vacated by the Model T taxi, a Ford Model B with HELPER CITY POLICE painted on the side threw open its doors and disgorged two men in blue uniforms. One was a tall, scowling colored man, and the other was a pink-faced gasping white man weighed down by a thick ring of belly fat. The white man staggered with the fingers of one hand splayed open, crawling his way through the air as if by main force, and the fingers of the other clenched tight into a fist.

Hermann let out a yell. "Ammon!" His side echoed him.

The others, led by Dimitrios, responded with a battle cry of "Samuel!"

Sorenson shoved Hermann back, raising his newspaper in warning. Dimitrios took that opportunity to whirl the sap around to strike at the Dane. Hiram leaped forward; he spun the Greek about and knocked the weapon out of his hands.

Dimitrios snarled and grabbed at Hiram's throat. Hiram feinted back, drawing the man in, then punched the miner in his breadbasket, knocking the wind out of him.

By that time, Hermann had dodged his foreman to go after an Oriental miner. The German's fists were still loaded with the iron bars. His punches could prove deadly, and the very last thing Kimball Mine needed was a murder.

So when Hermann charged forward, Hiram kicked his legs out from under him.

"No!" the woman in blue shouted. "Don't shoot!"

Hiram whirled. One of the Germans had stepped forward and was now pointing a bolt-action rifle at Samuel Kimball. The woman had grabbed the rifle with both hands and struggled to get control of it.

Time seemed to slow down and accelerate at the same moment.

Hiram threw himself toward the woman.

"The gun, Pap!"

Hiram touched his left hand to his protective amulet and grabbed for the rifle. The chi-rho amulet protected Hiram from enemies. Were these miners his enemies?

They were if they shot at him.

With one hand only, Hiram was at a disadvantage in the three-sided struggle. He succeeded in jerking the barrel away from Samuel Kimball's direction. Hiram ended up in front of the rifle.

Bang!

The shot was loud in Hiram's ears. He smelled the powder and felt the shock of the gun discharging. Something stung his left arm and he lost his grip. Stepping forward, he balled his right hand into a fist and coldcocked the shooter with one punch to the jaw.

As the man collapsed to the ground, Hiram smelled the stink of sour milk.

The woman was left holding the rifle.

The gunshot had stopped the fight. Germans, Greeks, and others drew back as Sorenson stormed about, swinging his newspaper to keep both sides apart.

One of the cops bellowed, "Stop right there! This is the police!"

"Quite the haymaker," the woman said.

Hiram shrugged. "I didn't have much choice."

"My name's Mary." She worked the lever to eject

the shell and then pointed the rifle at the mud. "Some people call me Gil."

"Hiram."

"You're under arrest!" the white policeman blustered.

Dimitrios and Hermann glared at each other, surrounded by their countrymen. Sorenson spat on the ground. "You two started dis. I won't forget it."

Hiram expected to see the policemen taking away the Greek and German leaders. He was shocked when, instead, the colored man grabbed him and roughly twisted him to one side, looking at his arm. "This fella's been shot."

The sting. "I must have just been grazed," Hiram said. "I barely noticed it."

"You're under arrest," the white policeman said again. He grabbed Mary, dragging her down toward the Model B.

"She didn't shoot me," Hiram said.

The colored policeman squinted at Hiram.

"No?" the white policeman said. "Then she can explain it to us in the station. She's trouble, this one. Organizing labor to try to force honest businessmen out of business."

"That's nonsense!" Mary cried. The Germans looked embarrassed, but none of them moved to intervene. "I just want them to pay a fair wage and to stop sending children down into the mines!"

"Explain it at the station!" the policeman said again.

Hiram touched his arm where it stung and found blood on his fingertips. "Officer, she's telling the truth."

The pudgy white policeman turned to Hiram. "You wouldn't happen to be Hiram Woolley, would you?"

Hiram nearly snorted in surprise. "I am."

The officer pushed Mary over to the colored policeman and the pair marched toward the Model B. She
didn't fight.

The white policeman reached into his pocket and
took out a card. "Naaman Rettig, from the D and
RGW, is looking to talk to you. He heard you might
be arriving today. Lucky I found you, huh?"

Hiram took the card; it was white, with raised gold
lettering. "Look, officer, I'll let this man know you
gave me his card, but about this woman, she didn't
do anything wrong."

The fat cop harrumphed. "She's done plenty wrong."
He turned and followed his comrade down the hill.

"I'll come to the station!" Hiram called to Mary
as she was pushed into the back seat of the police
car. "I promise!"

Chapter Seven

THE MINERS WERE DISPERSING, BILL SORENSON chasing them away. Ammon and Samuel stood staring at each other across foot-churned mud.

Hiram wanted to follow Gil...Mary...the arrested union organizer, but he was afraid that if he left, Ammon Kimball would grab his brother and snap him in two.

"Pap," Michael said. "The gun."

"It's only a flesh wound," Hiram murmured. "There's hydrogen peroxide in the car." He probed the wound with his fingers again, and was pleased; the blood flow had virtually stopped.

That was his heliotropius at work. The dark green stone with blood-red streaks prevented him from being deceived and also stanched the flow of blood. It was also said to drive out poison and bring rain.

Also fame, which made Hiram reluctant to carry it. He didn't want fame.

He slipped Naaman Rettig's card into his pocket.

The railroad man might be able to do something about Mary McGill.

"You've corrupted Dimitrios Kalakis, I see." Ammon Kimball glowered at his brother.

"No more than you've corrupted Hermann Wagner. I bet you promised him Bill Sorenson's job!" Samuel's face flushed bright red, sweat dripped from his round eyeglasses, and spittle speckled his lips.

"You never cared about the mine," Ammon growled. "Father's disappearance wasn't enough to bring you back, so what did it? Is it money? You've run out of money again and you've come home to beg, only you're too proud to ask for anything, so you've talked poor old Dimitrios into helping you try to steal my inheritance?"

Samuel let out a yowl. "The mine belongs to all of us! And so do, so did, so will, Father's other things. His other things!"

Ammon's eyes narrowed. "It was you. You were the thief!"

Hiram stepped forward, putting himself between the two brothers. They ignored him. He closed his fist around the bloodstone and concentrated. Which brother was lying?

"Pap." Michael's voice was soft, but insistent.

Samuel's flushed face darkened further. "I have taken nothing, nothing, nothing that didn't belong to me." His mouth worked soundlessly for a moment. "What I was given, I have returned! You know, Ammon, you know, but you hate me. You hate me and it's blinded you!"

Ammon laughed, a single bark like a dog losing interest. "Go back to your paint squirts, and get the hell off Kimball Corporation land. Before one of the monsters you're so anxious to believe in gets hold of you!"

The bloodstone lay inert throughout the conversation.

The older Kimball stomped away, shouldering past Hiram and heading down the hill and across the canyon toward his house. Samuel stared after Ammon, the round glasses unable to hide the rapid fluttering of his eyelashes. Then the younger brother moved, with less certainty, feet dragging in the mud-crusted snow, and seemed to fade into the landscape in a cloud of his own frozen breath as he moved down the canyon.

"Pap," Michael said, "you should have shot that guy with the rifle. This is the whole reason to have a gun, so you can shoot someone who's threatening you."

"There were too many innocents standing around," Hiram said. "And that's not the reason I carry the pistol."

Michael looked skeptical. "Well, you don't carry it to let me target shoot."

"I carry the revolver so I can shoot someone who's threatening *you*," Hiram said.

"Thanks for that, I guess." Michael frowned, hands on hips. "You want to go down to the jail to try to rescue that lady unionist, aren't you?"

"Don't you?"

They turned and headed down to the Double-A.

"Yeah. Only the difference is, I want to do it because it's the right thing to do, and you want to do it because you made a promise."

"Keeping promises is not a terrible thing, Michael." One of the large promises Hiram had kept in his life was his vow to Yas Yazzie to take care of Yas's son.

Michael. He'd promised it in Yas's dying moments, as he'd accepted Yas's revolver, and, at Yas's insistence, scratched his own initials next to his friend's on the barrel—an *H.W.* next to a *Y.Y.* Yas's wife Betty, Michael's mother, had died of the Spanish flux shortly after Michael's birth.

Michael had never known his birth parents. He'd lost Grandma Hettie while he was quite young, and then his adopted mother. The boy had grown up surrounded by tragedy. Maybe that was why Hiram had never been hard on Michael. Maybe that also explained the young man's tendency to lash out.

"I'll drive," Michael said. "You're so righteous, the truck might wither at your very touch."

As they descended to town, the late afternoon sun gave a blue cast to the snow frosting the hills around Kimball Canyon. Beneath the blue-white caps, the canyon walls tumbled down in yellow and orange scree, split by horizontal shelves of stone.

Michael explained how the forces of erosions cut the canyon through the layers of rock, wind and rain, ice and sunshine. He pointed out that south and west, the layers were cracked into multiple thin slices. On the north and east, the stone remained in larger blocks, rounded divots scooped out of the stone.

For Michael, it was all the action of wind and rain on the stone.

To Hiram, the divots made the stone appear as if dozens of skulls lurked just behind the façade of the rock and were straining to push through. The land felt haunted. He remembered how he'd almost succumbed to one of his spells when he'd gazed into the dark windows of the Kimball family home.

What had gone wrong in the Kimball family?

And should Hiram do anything about it? He had delivered the groceries; his job was done.

Or was his work truly done, if he left the mine unopened? Did that make him like a doctor who only dispensed morphine to relieve the pain, and didn't try to treat the underlying disease? If he only gave the men food, but left them idle and without means to feed themselves in the future, he had only delayed the pain and violence that must result.

And there were Medea and her children. He had personally run over Medea's husband. Could he really leave while that family was in such dire straits?

And if the problem at the root of all this trouble was a haunted mine, could Bill Sorenson or Ammon Kimball or any of the others really do anything? Or would it take someone with the wisdom and lore of a cunning man?

Hiram sighed. In any case, he had to get Mary out of jail. Surely when he made a formal statement that she hadn't shot him, she'd be released.

Though that might mean he'd have to implicate the German fellow as the shooter. He didn't relish that idea. But surely he could say the shooting had been an accident.

There was some truth in that.

Kimball Canyon opened into the larger Spring Canyon at the site of Dollar's.

"I kind of want to stop and get a Coke, Pap."

Hiram, too, felt hot and thirsty. He thought of Gus Dollar's wax poppet, though, and wanted to push on. "Let's wait until we get down into town."

He looked at Dollar's as they drove past. Three

cars were parked beside the clapboard building. The other canyons opening at this crossroads into Spring held other mines; this was the coal center of the state, and, together with the railroad, that made the area the industrial heart of Utah. Gus Dollar made his living selling things the company stores didn't provide, and he drew traffic in by a charm. He must talk to many miners, and miners' wives and children.

Could Gus tell Hiram what had happened to the Kimballs?

But the thought of talking too much with Gus made Hiram uneasy. He examined his heart to find the cause. Was it that he disliked another man knowing that Hiram knew hexes and charms, or that his father had had other wives? That surely was a part of it. Hiram was private by nature. Grandma Hettie had taught him to be even more discreet than he was already naturally inclined to be; a person who worked charms was often misunderstood, and easily accused of being a witch.

What else, though?

Hiram laughed out loud. Michael stared at him, swerved slightly, but managed to stay on the road.

"What's so funny?" his son asked.

"Mankind," Hiram answered. "The Fall. Me."

Envy. Wasn't that it? Envy, pure and simple. Gus was wealthy and successful and by every indication better at hexing than Hiram. Their very first encounter has consisted of Gus besting Hiram with a charm, drawing Hiram into his store to sell him Cokes.

And then, as if to rub in his superiority, the man had given him one of the Cokes for free.

But no, that hadn't been Gus's purpose. He'd given Michael a free drink out of generosity.

Though . . . could a free bottle of chilled Coca-Cola be a vehicle for a hex? Was it possible that Gus Dollar had given Hiram the second Coke for free as a way to bewitch Michael?

Hiram laughed out loud again.

Envy.

"You're weird, Pap," Michael said. "I'm not saying I don't love you. But you're an odd one."

Hiram took the revolver from his coat pocket and put it back in the glove box, along with the loaded full moon.

Spring Canyon was broad and green. Junipers and lodgepole pines climbed up the canyon walls, and the gambol oak and cottonwoods clustering along the banks of the water flowing down the canyon's center—Spring Creek, probably?—would add further green, come spring. The canyon twisted gently this way and that, revealing small herds of cattle sheltering in each new bend and drinking at man-made pools. The canyon opened for the final time sinking down toward the Price River.

Michael continued his geology lesson. "And this decline is known as a high alluvial fan. The creek grew wider and dumped more sediment out as it slowed down."

"And I wanted you to stay in school. It seems you got schooling."

"Libraries are fun, teachers aren't, and I can talk to girls at church, which might be the only good reason to go."

The road wound down the fan, past a row of small bungalows and then a wooden sign that read *Helper*.

"That's us," Michael said. "Professional helpers. Only we don't get paid. So volunteers, I guess."

"The town got its name from the railroads," Hiram told him.

"The Helper Railroad?" Michael frowned. "I thought it was something longer, the DGGWR, or something."

"The D and RGW. Denver and Rio Grande Western. No, a helper locomotive is an extra engine car they attach to a train when it needs additional push to get it uphill. West of here, the railroad goes uphill steeply."

"Back along Highway 89," Michael said. "The way we came."

"Right. So they have to attach a helper locomotive here. Or more than one helper, sometimes. And they called the railroad station where they did that *Helper*, and then that became the name of the town."

"Surely," Michael said, "such prosaically minded town fathers must soon rename the town Brothel. Or Prostituteville, that sounds very scenic. Or maybe they could use the French word for a prostitute. Is that something you learned in the war, by any chance?"

"Michael," Hiram said.

"I'm just going by what you told me. Far more brothels than Lehi, you said."

"Well, that isn't hard." Hiram took the card out of his pocket and examined it. The front of the card had both Price, Utah, and Denver, Colorado addresses. On the back, scrawled in tight, almost illegible penmanship, were the words: Hotel Utah. "Anyway, we can ask this Naaman Rettig what he thinks the name of the town should be. We talk to him first, because maybe he can help us get the union lady out of jail."

"And then drive home?" Michael asked.

Hiram didn't respond.

The road followed Spring Creek until it joined the Price River. Crossing the river on a bridge made of railroad ties, the Double-A was struck by a sudden fierce breeze, blowing from the north.

Michael laughed.

"You think it's funny we might get pushed into the river?" Hiram asked.

"No, I think it's funny because it's like Salt Lake City is huffing and puffing down the canyon, trying to blow Prostituteville right out of the state. Wait, is it *Putain*?"

"Helper." The Double-A left the bridge and bumped down onto dirt again. "Stop the truck for a moment."

Michael dutifully braked.

Ahead of them and stretching away to their right was Helper. It was a town organized in parallel strips. Immediately to their right, along the river, was a tangle of bare trees and brush. Beside that stretched a field of desert grass, beaten brown by the winter. Across a gravel road stood the backs of the brick buildings of Helper's Main Street. From this side, Hiram saw iron fire escapes, back doors, loading docks, and private parking spaces. Beyond Main Street and slightly uphill of it ran the railroad tracks. A train puffed westward now, its second and third "helper" engines pushing right behind the first and a line of coal cars stretching out behind. On the far side of the tracks, on a gentle slope rising up and away from town, stood several streets of brick, adobe, and wooden bungalows. He smelled the coal smoke and cinders along with the dry winter grasses and the river. Above it all and to Hiram's left rose a stark white and yellow cliff, hundreds of feet tall. Without a doubt, Michael would know the geology of the cliff.

When Michael had quit school, Hiram had been uneasy; some of Michael's teachers had looked relieved, liberated from the boy's constant challenging. But Michael had attacked book after book on his own, most of the volumes provided by Mahonri Young. Mahonri had assured Hiram that Michael could get into a good college by taking written entrance exams, and Hiram had relaxed.

Somewhat.

Michael tapped the wheel and flashed Hiram a smile. "You don't want to drive onto Main Street and see the brothels. And you don't want to talk about them, so now you're trying to distract me with trains."

"I wish you didn't know what a brothel was," Hiram said.

"I'm seventeen, Pap, not seven."

"When I was seventeen, I had no idea there were brothels in the world." Hiram sighed and then pointed along the river to a pair of tall cottonwoods surrounded by a clump of scrub oak. "Let's just park it here, so we can be a little more discreet."

Michael parked the car. "Maybe we can sleep in this thicket too, Pap."

"Only if we have to."

The wind buffeted them again as they crossed the weeds. Passing between a stone wall and a gravel parking lot, they entered an alleyway. The sun dropped below the hills behind them, and the way abruptly transitioned from shade to near darkness. Ahead, on Main Street, Hiram saw passing automobiles and the harsh red and yellow glows that suggested neon lights.

Lehi didn't have neon lights. Hiram braced himself for what he knew was coming.

Gravel crunched beneath Hiram's and Michael's Redwing Harvesters—they wore boots that were identical, though Michael's were slightly larger.

"What do you think they charge at these brothels?" Michael asked.

"You and I are not going to find out."

"That's not the right answer."

Hiram shook his head. "Yes, it is."

"No, you should be saying *ooh-la-la*. Did they teach you nothing in Paris?"

They exited the alley onto the main street of Helper. Main Street was full of neon lights: Hiram saw two, no three, movie theaters, and a bowling alley, and restaurants of various kinds. There were bars, and sidewalks full of people laughing and drifting from one entertainment to the next, but it wasn't the full-blown bacchanalia he had feared.

"That one." Hiram pointed at a signboard that read *Hotel Utah*. The words were spelled out in a cross, centering on the shared letter *T*, and that struck him as a good omen. It made the sign of the cross, and also it reminded him of the *Sator Arepo* charm, the Abracadabra pyramid, and other written charms, in which words intersected in meaningful combinations.

"I'm following you, Pap."

Hiram stepped toward the hotel. First Naaman Rettig, then Mary McGill.

Chapter Eight

THE STREETS GREW MORE CROWDED. A CHATTERING herd of men spilling from one of the town's movie theaters jostled Hiram and Michael at the door of the hotel. The letters on the movie marquee spelled out *The Mystery of Edwin Drood.*

Hiram and Michael struggled past the filmgoers and into a warm, dark foyer.

But . . . could this be the Hotel Utah? It was a crowded space, the wallpaper fraying, the carpet underfoot unevenly worn into tangled ruts. The front desk was slapped next to the bar and somewhere in the building, frying fat emitted greasy smoke.

A man with a handlebar mustache walked, elbows locked with a cool-eyed, gigantic woman, her arms as big as Hiram's thighs. Her caramel-colored dress tented off her in a wash of thick perfume. The man wore a turquoise and silver bolo tie, a bright orange waistcoat, and tightly-cut trousers the color of a ripe lime over cowboy boots polished to a dull red shine.

His snapping, roosterlike strut suggested that he was dressed to impress.

The couple moved toward a back hallway.

A man with two older women on his arms started up the steps to Hiram's right. The women wore black lace gowns with plunging necklines and their lips were bright red.

"Pap," Michael said. "Pap?"

Hiram's mind was elsewhere.

He remembered a town called Rouen, a couple hours' drive from the sea and on the Seine. He was thinking of a red lamp he'd seen, casting a rosy glow on dozens of women in silky lingerie.

Brits, Aussies, and Yankees were lined up fifty feet deep to get in, every man filthy from the trenches and most looking forward to a bath and a shave as a prelude to the other services on offer. Hiram and his friend Yas Yazzie stood in the back of the crowd, unable to look each other in the eye.

Yas was a big Navajo, broad-shouldered, with dark eyes and jet-black hair. His skin was a smooth brown and when he smiled, his face glowed. But Yas wasn't smiling then, in Rouen, when some British lieutenant went careening by on a bicycle in a cloud of gin. He wasn't smiling a few minutes later, when one of the women admitting the soldiers at the front of the line let her lacy robe slip open.

Hiram wasn't smiling, either. He felt ill and embarrassed. He wanted a bath, but he figured he'd get the bath and then bow out from any other kind of encounter. He had a wife at home, as did Yas, but then, many of the boys in their unit were married.

Charlie Casey insisted that being at war, five thousand miles from home, gave them all a free pass with the ladies. And besides, the women were French. It wasn't like they were sleeping with American girls.

And back home, who would ever know?

Those arguments seemed hollow from the start, but especially when Hiram found himself looking at a half-naked French girl, walking along the line of Doughboys to encourage them. Hiram had made a promise to Elmina Shepherd to be true when they'd wed, a promise for all time and all eternity. Yas had done something similar.

"Yas," Hiram said, "we're not over here for this."

The two men weren't exactly in the business of soldiering either, at least not in the normal sense of the word. Both of their wives had wondered why they'd signed up at all. Neither man had been drafted . . . again, at least not in the normal sense of the word. They were as much as ten years older than the other fellows in the platoon. Older than most of the guys in the regiment.

Older, and wiser.

Yas nodded. "I'm only sad you said it before I did. Maybe we can find a bath somewhere less crowded."

It took them six hours. They found a bathtub on the second story of a wrecked hotel, half the walls gone and the roof open to the sky. They built a fire of shattered hotel furniture under a soup pot from the hotel's kitchen and shuttled pans from hand to hand until they could fill the tub with water that very nearly passed for hot. They took turns getting clean while looking up at a clear night sky.

✧   ✧   ✧

Seventeen years later, Hiram stood in the crowded lobby with Yas's son, Michael, now *his* son. Hiram wasn't sure he'd grow to be as tall or wide as Yas, but he had the hands and feet for it. And he was sprouting like a weed, a bit taller than Hiram and not done growing yet.

What could Hiram tell the boy? That it wasn't what Michael imagined? That he regretted bringing his son along to Helper? Not to look?

"Remember that every woman deserves respect," he found himself saying.

He expected a sarcastic response, but Michael only nodded.

Hiram led his son to the front desk. The clerk was a stick-bug of a man, thin and slow-moving, with an Adam's apple that looked as if it had come from a foundry. A mustache overflowed his upper lip.

"Can you ring a suite for me?" Hiram asked. "I'm here to see Naaman Rettig."

The insect man grinned and a gold tooth winked from his smile. "Wrong hotel, Captain. But if you and your Indian pal want some fun, this is the best place in town."

Michael raised his hands. "Aw, Pap, am I your Indian pal? Though I'm thinking this doesn't seem like that much fun, after all." He walked away, through clouds of perfume, and Hiram followed him to the sidewalk.

The Hotel Utah was one door down. The crowd emerging from the theater had made Hiram miss his door. That same crowd was now packed into the hotel's bar to drink, voices raised to the pitch and volume of a stampede.

In front of the hotel stood parked a row of cars. Most of them could have belonged to miners or railroad engineers or local farmers, but one stood out: it was a bright red Chrysler Phaeton, the carriage of a rich man, with its whitewall tires and its leather ragtop. The Phaeton was polished to a shine that hurt to look at, and it was deliberately parked straddling two spaces, as if to keep lesser cars away.

This lobby had brown and gold wallpaper down to a wainscoting of polished wood. Cigar smoke residue oozed from the wood, and a berrylike hint of old wine made Hiram feel that merely to inhale was to risk intoxication. Underfoot was thick red carpet that swarmed with golden bees and hives; out of respect, Hiram avoided stepping on the gold thread. When he asked about Naaman Rettig, the clerk, an older man in a gray suit, rang the railroad man's room.

"Go right on up," the clerk said.

Hiram wondered why Rettig wanted to see him. And where had he got Hiram's name? Had Hiram's heliotropius finally betrayed him to fame?

He and Michael started up the stairs, climbing through the tobacco smoke from the bar and the watery electric lights.

Michael was chuckling. "That was hilarious. My first brothel and I go there with my straight-as-a-shovel Mormon father. Quite the rip-snorting place, but none of those gals were ginchy enough for me."

Hiram didn't want to ask what "ginchy" was.

"It's fine, Pap," Michael said. "I'm not going to become a sex maniac or a boozer."

Hiram sighed.

They walked up four flights of stairs and down a red-carpeted, golden wallpapered hallway to a door. The bees and their hives were banished from this floor, with nothing to replace them and break up the oxblood of the carpet.

A man without a neck stood at the door, arms crossed over his chest. Instead of tall, nature had made him wide, so wide that Hiram doubted he could walk through the door without turning sideways first. The sides of his heads were shaved, while the rest of his thick black hair was greased forward. He wore slacks, wingtip shoes polished to a mirrorlike shine, and a black sweater. And he didn't look happy.

"I'm Hiram Woolley. I'm here to talk with—"

The big man pushed open the double-doors.

The first room of the hotel suite had been transformed into an office. A corkboard covered one wall, next to the door to the bathroom, and push pins, papers, and all manner of receipts were transfixed there. On the other wall, beside the bedroom door, was a map of the region, more pushpins, and some string.

A desk dominated the space in front of the wide windows letting in the multicolored light of Main Street. Stacks of paper clipped or stapled together littered the top of the desk, along with more maps and several coffee mugs, their bottoms stained dark.

A slightly short middle-aged man rose from the desk. His thick shock of hair was so blond it was almost white. Pale hair also burst out of the collar of his shirt above his cravat.

Hiram removed his hat and held it in his hands.

Rettig's desk job had widened him a bit, but his shoulders and arms had the muscles of a fit man. He wore a frock coat and waistcoat. He pulled on soft gray kid leather gloves.

Before those gloves went on, however, Hiram saw

the twisted pink skin left by burns, severely disfiguring scars, marking the man's hands and wrists.

Rettig squinted at them with light green eyes far too small for his face. He slapped a hand down on his desk. "Welcome, welcome, Mr. Woolley. I just have to find my cheaters."

Michael moved forward to the desk and lifted handled glasses, a lorgnette, so Rettig could reach them. He put them to his face, which made his eyes look even tinier. "Much better," the railroad man said. "But Lord, where are my manners?"

He walked to the front of the desk, forcing Michael backward. Hiram stepped forward to shake Rettig's hand. "Naaman Julius Rettig, that is my full Christian name, and remember, it's *Naaman*, but I *won't* take 'nay' for an answer. I'm glad Chief Fox found you so quickly."

"I'm Hiram Woolley, but you know that." And *how* did the railroad man know it? "And this is my son, Michael."

Holding his glasses on his nose, Rettig shook Michael's hand. "Yes, yes, the Navajo son." Rettig dropped Michael's hand abruptly. "Now, Mr. Woolley, I appreciate your accepting my invitation. For we have business to discuss, not only the business of my railroad, but the business of humanity. I believe I'm quoting Dickens."

They all sat, Rettig behind the desk, Hiram and Michael in chairs, a bit too close to the ground. The chairs were so short, their legs must have been sawed. Rettig sat tall, and they had to look up at him; his desk sat on a low platform.

"Your office is impressive," Hiram said. Then he guessed: "Is that your Chrysler parked out front?"

"It's even swankier on the inside." Rettig smiled. "Do you like it?"

Hiram shrugged. "My truck suits me."

Naaman dropped his glasses to his desk to squint furiously at them. "I got a telegram from your Bishop Smith, who is very concerned about the Kimball mine situation."

That was how Rettig knew. "He asked you to help me?"

Naaman Rettig laughed. "Oh, in a manner of speaking. He said you were bringing food to Kimball Mine. The Kimballs are known to him. It's a prominent name among your people, and he worried about them. As he should. He said you were bringing food, and asked if my trains would carry more food down to the Kimballs, from Utah Valley."

Hiram wanted to feel relieved, but something warned him he shouldn't. "That's good to hear."

"What is a 'presiding bishop'?" Rettig asked. "Is Bishop Smith the head of your church?"

"There are three men in the presiding bishopric," Hiram said. "They don't run the church. They run the physical side, the secular things. Such as the buildings. And now they're trying to figure out how to deal with the Crash. I help them. Bishop Smith is . . . he's the second man of the three."

"Very good. As for the use of my trains, of course, I had to tell him no." Naaman Rettig nodded and smiled. "I'm the trustee of the railroad's investment here, and I can't go squandering that investment on some mine. Not unless, of course, the railroad owned the mine. I'm glad you're here, Mr. Woolley."

"You don't have to call him Mr. Woolley, sir," Michael

put in. "*Hiram* is fine. And thank you for being such a good steward of your shareholders' money."

"Easy, son," Hiram said.

Rettig licked his lips and blinked, obviously caught off guard. "Yes, I am a good steward. Now, let's talk about the Kimball Mine, the Kimball Corporation, how much do you know about the Kimballs?"

Michael answered as if rattling off a list of facts out of a book. "It was a ranch, back before the railroad. Teancum did well with the mine, until all the wives and most of the kids left, or died, and he was left all alone with Ammon. Teancum disappeared a couple years back, maybe with his new fourth wife. With old Teancum gone, Samuel and Eliza came home. The kids fight over how to run the mine, and it's shut down. And we brought them beets. We're beet farmers when we're not serving the good people of the State of Utah."

Rettig plucked up the lorgnette and looked through it at Hiram. "Beets?"

"We brought more than beets," Hiram said. "These being hard times, it wouldn't be right for us not help out."

"I can respect that." Rettig put his glasses back on the desk. "Here's more of the story for you to consider. Teancum Kimball was a rancher in 1881, when the D and RGW first made Mr. Kimball an offer on his land. Kimball proved there was coal in the hills, and our railroad needs coal. Kimball refused. Actually, the story goes, he had an old blunderbuss that he waved around, saying he'd rather be damned than sell his ranch. I wasn't there myself, you understand, but the incident made such an impression on the director at the time that he recorded it in the company's minute books. And Teancum never did sell. Instead, he started mining the land himself. Eighteen ninety-one, that's when Teancum Kimball opened his mine."

Michael sat straight up and cocked his head to one side. "Sir, thank you so much for the history lesson. I had no idea 1891 was so fascinating. What happened in 1892?"

Rettig let a scowl cross his face, but only for a moment. "Nineteen oh-three was the year of the great mine riots. Men were killed. Again, the D and RGW offered to help Teancum with his troubles. Again, he refused to sell. And that was the same year his wives ran off, all except for one, Samuel's mother. Samuel came the next year, but alas, Teancum's remaining wife died. If anything, that hardened him."

"You know an awful lot about the wives of Teancum Kimball," Hiram observed.

"Kimball is a prominent name here in Helper, too." Rettig paused. "Some say Ammon himself had been in love with the young woman, Samuel's mother, that sweet young sister wife. And when Samuel sprang into the world, Ammon swore to hate him forever. A family drama, Biblical."

"Biblical?" Michael asked. "Do you mean there was a plague of frogs next? Or did the Price River turn to blood?"

Rettig frowned at Michael. "Others believe it was Teancum who turned Ammon's heart against his little brother because he was weak, a fancy boy, who didn't want to dirty his hands with anything but paint. Regardless, no one around here was surprised when Samuel left."

"Let's cut to current events, Mr. Rettig," Michael said. "Two years ago, Teancum and his new wife disappeared—"

"God rest their souls," Rettig cut him off and directed his tiny-eyed gaze at Hiram. "Though a man that age taking a girl scarcely into her twenties to wife is perhaps not looking for rest. Again, the D and RGW made an offer. Ammon refused. No firearms were involved, thankfully, and that brings us here, today. You want to help the men of the Kimball Mine, do you not, Mr. Woolley?"

"*Hiram* is fine. And I do want to help. That's why Michael and I are here."

Rettig squinted through his lorgnette and found a manila envelope. "This is our thirteenth offer to purchase the Kimball Mine. My predecessor's failure to convince Ammon Kimball to sell might be one reason he lost the confidence of the board, and then his job."

Hiram's heart felt heavy. "How can I help, Mr. Rettig?"

"I'm hoping you might take them the offer."

Michael laughed out loud.

"Why me?" Hiram didn't relish the thought of getting between the feuding brothers.

"You and the Kimballs share a faith. I hope that you'll be able to talk with Ammon and Samuel, get them to bury their differences."

Hiram ran his fingers through his hair.

"As the Lord is my witness," Naaman Rettig said, "my motives are pure. I'm only in town three more days, because, believe it or not, I have much larger issues to deal with on the Denver end. A faulty survey means one of our lines is in danger of falling into the river. The chaos in Helper can be easily ended. Instead of a family torn asunder by feud, the mine should be owned by a solid business with a clear-eyed Board of Directors, with the united purpose of giving the men of Kimball steady jobs with good pay."

"I think that calls for a God bless America, sir." Michael sat tall, with his shoulders back.

Rettig scowled. "Don't mistake me; the railroad wants to profit. But the railroad's profit requires it to have coal, and obtaining coal requires the work of miners, so the D and RGW's desire for profit will lead it inexorably and directly to re-opening the mine. And in the meantime, yes, I would bring food down from Utah Valley for the men and their families. So yes, my boy, God bless America. Now, I'm a busy man, Hiram. Will you take my offer to the Kimballs?"

"Mr. Rettig," Hiram said, "I heard from Sorenson, the foreman at the mine, that Eliza Kimball was staying at this hotel. Perhaps she might be a better messenger."

Rettig shook his head. "She refuses to see me."

Hiram surrendered. "I'll try."

"Don't fret, Mr. Rettig," Michael said. "We Mormons have secret handshakes. We'll get them to sign."

Rettig burst into laughter. "Your son has a quick wit, Hiram. I believe he's been funning me, and none too gently. I thank you for agreeing to help."

Hiram wasn't sure if it was the right move, showing up on the Kimballs' doorstep with the railroad's man's offer. But maybe even an offer they rejected could unite the Kimballs. Maybe Ammon and Samuel could come together against a common enemy.

And Eliza?

"I'll do this as a favor to you, Mr. Rettig," Hiram said, "but I'm going to ask for something in return. There's a woman in jail here in town, Mary McGill. I was wondering if you could do something to help her out. She's innocent."

Rettig lifted his lorgnette back up to his eyes. "Hiram, I truly am sorry. But that is between her and the local authorities. I have no power."

Hiram found he had nothing to say, so he took his leave with Michael in tow.

Chapter Nine

HIRAM AND MICHAEL LEFT THE HOTEL. THE CHILL air drove their hands into their pockets, where Hiram felt Rettig's envelope.

The police station was a solid cube of heavy brick, like a bank with all the grandeur stripped away. Its windows were sealed with black iron bars and its blinds were drawn, but the doors were open. Light spilled out onto the sidewalk, splashing into yellow puddles in the blue of the early evening. Two police cars were parked in front. A train chugged by the distance in a rush of engines. A long whistle blew. The scent of the coal burning and the hot metal of the wheels on the tracks were brought to Hiram by the breeze.

A woman laughed raucously from inside a nearby saloon.

"*Ooh-la-la,*" Michael said.

"You know why I don't ground you when you make comments like that?" Hiram said.

"Because I'm seventeen years old, practically a man,

and soon hopefully going off to college to become a physicist?"

"Because you're funny. I like that in a fellow."

"Also, who would drive the truck?"

"I would drive it myself. I know how, believe it or not. And my license is just as valid as yours."

"But you would fall asleep and crash."

"Only once in a while. It might still be worth it."

"I guess I'll keep being funny, then."

"*Ooh-la-la*," Hiram said.

"Now you're getting the hang of it."

Hiram walked up the steps and through the open door, and Michael followed. Inside, a wide waiting room with hardwood floors was dominated by a single desk. On the desk rested a logbook and a pen. Benches for waiting lined three walls. Closed doors at the back of the reception room, and wooden stairs leading up, hinted at other spaces.

Through a large window of pebbled glass set in a door, Hiram saw and faintly heard two policemen interviewing someone. The third person sounded drunk and belligerent.

The colored policeman sat at the desk, watching Hiram and Michael. His head was shaved bare beneath his uniform cap. His eyes were set wide in his face, and his ears were large, and maybe just a tiny bit pointed. His expression was emotionless; did that reflect cruelty? Fatigue?

"My name is Hiram Woolley," Hiram said.

"I remember you," the policeman said.

"I'm not from here," Hiram began.

"I know who you are. A Mormon farmer come down from Salt Lake with food for the miners. You and your boy here. You drive that Ford Double-A. Only *he* drives it, not you. Maybe your eyesight is bad? But you don't wear glasses."

"I have occasional fainting spells." Hiram shot Michael a glance before his son could say anything. "*Very* occasional." Who had the policeman been talking to? Naaman Rettig? "I'm sorry, you have me at a disadvantage."

"You mean you don't know my name." The policeman blinked slowly, as if it were a conscious act. "I'm Sergeant G. Washington Dixon, but most people call me Shanks."

"Because you're tall?"

"On account of my long legs."

"Sergeant Shanks," Hiram began again, "the woman you have in custody, Mary McGill, didn't shoot me."

"That's what you said up at the mine. What I can't figure out is, this is the least Mormon town in this whole state. Those miners you brung food to ain't Mormons, they're Orthodox and Catholic and Lutheran. At least their wives are, since most of the men are just godless sons of bitches slugging out their lives underground to add a little *oomph* to the locomotives of the D and RGW. What are you doing here?"

"They're God's children, regardless," Hiram said. That was true, but then he felt compelled to tell a little additional truth. "Also, the Kimballs are Mormon."

Michael shook his head. "They're not just Mormon, they're *really* Mormon."

Sergeant Shanks raised his eyebrows. "What, you mean like, really righteous?"

Michael shook his head. "They're from one of the old families. I bet you wouldn't know the name Heber Kimball, but you've heard of Brigham Young."

"My schooling was limited, but I ain't *completely* ignorant."

"Heber Kimball was his best buddy," Michael said. "And Ammon and the rest of them haven't yet fallen so far from the tree that the boys in Salt Lake have forgotten them. You know, they're part of that whole old polygamy upper-class set."

That was more truth than Hiram would have liked to share. Michael wasn't wrong, but the fact that Hiram might be down here to help the scions of an old Salt Lake clan, as much as the miners and their families, made Hiram slightly uncomfortable. "But the point is, Mary McGill didn't shoot anyone. She was trying to get the rifle away from one of the miners. When I stepped in to help, I got shot accidentally."

"You might draw a lesson from that." Sergeant Shanks stared at Hiram and sucked a tooth. "One of the Germans, wasn't it? What was he going to do, shoot little Sammy Kimball?"

Hiram sighed. "Maybe."

Sergeant Shanks nodded. "I tell you what I *do* like, though. I like that you brought food for the miners, and not just for Ammon Kimball. Anyways, I ain't gonna let her out. We got her held on disturbing the peace, and regardless of what happens with the shooting, she's been stirring up the miners, so it's a fair charge."

"Stirring up the miners, heavens to Betsy!" Michael feigned shock. "What did she ask for, decent wages? No more seven-year-old kids sorting coal from rocks with their bare hands?"

Hiram frowned at Michael. The boy was going to get them both into trouble one day.

Michael ignored his signal.

Sergeant Shanks laughed. "Yeah, well, the state legislature don't share your views. Throw in vagrancy, she might be looking at a few months in Sugar House. But I expect it'd be alright if you wanted to talk to her a bit."

"Can Michael stay here with you?" Hiram asked.

Michael went to protest. Hiram put up a hand.

Shanks laughed some more. "Sure, I like your mouthy boy. I was a mouthy young man, myself."

"Our Father, who art in heaven, hallowed be thy name; thy kingdom come; thy will be done on earth as it is in heaven." Mary McGill clutched the first bead of her rosary between her thumb and the knuckle of her forefinger.

The cell was a standalone cage of iron strips, each strip an inch and a half wide and painted white. The strips ran horizontally and vertically, with three-inch gaps between them. A ferret couldn't wiggle between the strips, which were riveted together at every point where they crossed.

The cage had a ceiling of crossed strips, too, and it was bolted onto the hardwood floor. Outside the cage, the floor retained its shine and was colored the lovely red-brown of varnished hardwood. Within the cage, the floor had been scuffed to a dead gray trough, barely wide enough to hold two flat iron bunks, riveted to the side of the cage, one above the other, and a simple toilet in the corner.

Mary thanked God she was the only prisoner in her cell.

One other such cage sat beside hers, its bunks

holding two drunk men, snoring soundly. The room had no windows and was lit by a series of electric bulbs hanging from the ceiling. The whole place smelled of bleach.

". . . and lead us not into temptation, but deliver us from evil. Amen." She moved to the first of three beads, relaxing into the rosary, and concentrating on her desire that God free her from her bonds. She said three Hail Marys, then the Glory Be, and then recited the first Glorious Mystery from memory.

She heard the scraping sound of the door to the room being unbarred. She put her rosary away in a pocket, and then the man in overalls came in, the one who had got shot at the mine. Hiram. He was alone.

She stood. "I didn't mean to shoot you."

He walked to her cage. He was more handsome than she had noticed earlier, though he held himself tentatively, like a man who expected to be rejected. He took off his hat and smoothed down the few hairs clinging to his scalp. "I know. I told them that, and they don't seem to care."

She started to touch her face, then pulled her hand away and lifted her chin. "I'm with the union. The United Mine Workers. It comes with the territory."

"You seem very . . . ladylike . . . for a union organizer."

"You would prefer a hairy goon named Moe?"

He laughed a little. Just the right amount to show her he'd rather smile than frown. "I didn't say I'd *prefer* one, but that's more like what I'd *expect*. Are you not worried about, I don't know, getting beat up? Shot at?"

"My father likely wasn't thinking about my chances of being shot when he insisted on my ladylike clothing and bearing. I think he was more concerned about doing right by the wishes of my mother, God rest her soul. But then, he was a drunk, so maybe he wasn't thinking anything at all."

"I'm sorry," the man said. "I lost my mother when I was young, myself. My full name's Hiram Woolley."

"Mary McGill. Or perhaps my father thought a good ladylike posture and dress would compensate for the disfigurement I bear in my physiognomy."

"Fizzy...?"

"*Face*, Mr. Woolley. I mean my birthmark."

Hiram Woolley looked at her face as if seeing it for the first time, and appeared surprised. "I hadn't really noticed."

"God bless you, Hiram Woolley, I believe you're telling the truth."

"I *try* to."

Mary McGill looked the man up and down. His denim overalls were frayed, his hands were callused, and even the skin of his forehead and cheeks had the leathery look that comes from years of working under the sun. "I expect you do, Mr. Woolley. Tell me the truth now, then—what are you doing in here?"

"It's my fault you're locked up. I came to see if I could get you out."

"As you promised. And it wasn't at all your fault. You spoke to the policemen, and they told you to mind your business."

"True."

"Then you came in *here*." Mary raised her eyebrows to Hiram in challenge.

Hiram put his hands into his pockets and shuffled his feet.

"Well?" she asked.

"I wondered if there was anything else I could do to help you."

"Bony thing that I am, you'd never believe it, but I eat like a horse. Always trying to put on more flesh so I look less like a twelve-year-old boy, and it never works. I don't suppose you have a pastry hidden in those overalls."

"Actually, I have a Snickers bar." Hiram produced the candy square, wrapped in cream-colored paper that crinkled when he touched it, and handed it over.

"Perfect." Mary took the bar, a little soft from sitting in Hiram's warm coat pocket. "A candy bar named for a horse, for a girl who eats like a horse."

"Named for a horse?" Hiram looked amused. "I had no idea."

Mary suddenly realized that she was enjoying the conversation. "There is something else, yes. Police Chief Fox allowed me one phone call when he brought me in, and I called the union's lawyer. And of course, since it's nighttime in Denver, no one answered."

"Will he give you another call?"

Mary shrugged. "Maybe."

"Give me the number," Hiram said. "I'll call the lawyer first thing in the morning."

"Denver two, twelve oh seven."

He repeated the exchange and number back to her. "And the lawyer's name?"

"James Nichols. And if he doesn't believe you, tell him Gil said Five-Cent Jimmy would never let her down."

"I never knew a lawyer who only charged five cents."

"You never knew a union lawyer, then. Haircuts are even cheaper."

Hiram furrowed his brow. "What are you doing here, Mary McGill?"

Mary sighed and sat down on the edge of the lower bunk. "It's true that I came here to organize the miners. And I thought I'd be doing it in the usual ways, and asking for the usual things. God knows they could use the usual things, at the Kimball Mine and also at all the others."

"Higher wages."

Mary nodded. "A better price for the coal they dig. No interest on the advances. Better rents on the shantytowns the mine companies have them living in. But also things like more safety equipment, English lessons for the men, for safety reasons, and for the families, because it's the decent thing to do, so they have a future. Stop child labor."

Hiram frowned. "I heard the kids pick rocks out of the coal."

Mary shook her head. "That's not all they do. They lead mules and carry messages and water. A lot of the mine owners will shrug and say they don't employ the children, it's the miners themselves who bring their kids down to help. So the companies technically don't violate the law yet benefit from child labor nonetheless."

"I can see that," Hiram said. "But sometimes a family's got little choice. Kids help on farms, too."

"Your son worked?"

"I taught Michael to drive when he was twelve. I needed him to run the tractor."

"You ever see a ten-year-old boy with black lung? A young man grown old by the age of sixteen, who has to roll back and forth on the floor at the end of the day to loosen up the phlegm in his lungs so he

can cough up enough coal dust and free his breathing
enough to be able to sleep?"

Hiram shook his head and looked at his boots.

"So that's why it's not enough that the mines don't
employ the children. We have to ban it entirely."

"So if a man brings his son to work, he goes to
prison?" Hiram asked.

"If he's a coal miner, yes."

"So I expect this is an idea you have to teach to
the miners."

"And I *was* teaching them. And organizing them, at
the Kimball mine and elsewhere. But then the Kimball Mine closed, and things got really bad up there."

A shadow fell across Hiram's face. "Worse than at
the other mines?"

"The other mines are still open. And since the Kimball men and their families live on company land and
get food from the company store, they're going deeper
into debt by the day."

The shadow on the farmer's face darkened. "I've seen
the miners starving. One family was trying to eat a cat."

Mary was struck by the troubled compassion in
Hiram's eye. "On top of everything else, Mr. Woolley,
the miners are divided by language."

"They're mostly immigrants."

"And Italians work best with Italians," Mary said,
"and Serbs get along with Serbs, and Chinese with
Chinese. So it's always a challenge to get them to
overlook the differences of language and food and
dress and church and pull together, only at the Kimball it all got worse."

"They picked sides." Hiram frowned. "Ammon has
the Germans. Samuel has the Greeks."

"So at the Kimball, I stopped being able to organize for wages and safety and tried to push to get
the mine back open again."

Hiram had a thoughtful expression on his face.
"Samuel and Ammon both seem to have plans for
operating the mine."

"Only they're different plans, the two can't agree,
and each man is backed by a mob."

Hiram nodded. "I'll call Five-Cent Jimmy in the
morning, and if I have to send him a buffalo head
by mail, I'll do that, too. What else?"

This strange, handsome farmer was offering to be
some kind of deputy. "Go talk to Ammon Kimball.
If he can forgive the men rent until the mine opens,
or forgive debts for food, it would be a godsend. Or
even if he could get food back into the company
store and offer the men credit on better terms, it
could be the difference between a family making it
until the mine opens, and a husband riding the rails
in search of work."

Hiram slipped his hat on. "I'll do my best. I probably should get on to Ammon's before it gets too late."

Chapter Ten

SPRING CANYON WAS A WALL OF DARKNESS RISING
to either side of them.

But for the Double-A's headlights, the sky above might
have shown them Orion or Gemini or other features of
the winter night. As it was, the truck's lamps revealed
only a pale sequence of abrupt and disjointed images.
A startled and sleepy cow. The corner of a brick springhouse. Rail fencing surrounded by sagging winter grass.
The white hindquarters of two deer, bounding away to
safety. Twice, oncoming headlights skidded past, forcing
Michael to the edge of the road.

Hiram was more than ready for a rest when he
realized that a small constellation of lights to the
right of the truck in the darkness must be coming
from the windows of Gus Dollar's shop. "Pull over."

Michael did. "You want another Coke?" he asked.

"I want to talk to the owner." Gus Dollar had craft,
and he might know if there were supernatural com-
ponents to the troubles at the Kimball mine.

Hiram clearly couldn't take Michael with him, because that would stop him from asking the questions he wanted to ask of Gus Dollar. Michael was aware of Grandma Hettie's wisdom, but Hettie had died when Michael was just nine years old, and Hiram had been careful to hide the fact that he followed in her footsteps.

He took the revolver from the glove box and carefully rotated the barrel, taking the hammer off the empty chamber, and putting it over a live round. Then he laid the pistol on the seat between them, near Michael's hand and pointed forward.

"This revolver is loaded and ready to fire," he told Michael.

"Okay." Michael's breathing sounded shallow.

"I'm leaving it with you."

"Yeah."

"Don't be excited. Don't be nervous. Nothing's going to happen."

"I get it, Pap. You're worried because of the fighting we saw today, and because you got shot, so you're leaving the gun with me. While you go in and, I don't know, talk with this shopkeeper some more. Because, clearly, the guy who sells Coca-Cola is secretly running everything and has all the answers."

Hiram ignored the barb. "Don't shoot unless you have to, but if you think you have to, don't hesitate. I'd rather have you dressed up for a jury than dressed up by a mortician. Keep the car running. I'll approach in the headlights, so I'm clearly visible. I won't be long."

He walked up to the deep porch in the bright yellow glow of the truck's lamps, then stepped up to the well-worn planks and examined the door and the front windows. He saw no posted hours, no sign saying either OPEN or CLOSED.

He saw again the strange curls of lead in the front windows, black in the light of a dimmed kerosene lantern sitting on Gus Dollar's countertop. What did they mean?

Hiram knocked, setting off a furor of barking within. Through the window he saw the two Rottweilers, bounding over each other to get at the door and sink their teeth into him.

Hiram waited for Gus.

The shopkeeper arrived. "Go on, shoo!" He chased the dogs into a back room, and then he let Hiram in. The dried mint and other herbs gave the room a pleasant odor, as did the sweet pine burning in a squat stove on the side.

"Evening," Hiram said.

"I like that," Gus said, a twinkle of a laugh in his voice. "You don't want to commit to the quality of the hour."

Hiram was caught on his back heel. "What?"

"Is it a good evening? Is it a bad evening? You don't want to say, so you just tell me it's evening." Gus shut the door. "Which I had already noticed."

"I'm sorry," Hiram said. "I was raised in a home where . . . you didn't talk about some things. I learned to listen more than I talked, in most conversations."

"Ah, yes." Gus laid an index finger alongside his nose and winked as he walked behind the counter. "I understand."

"Not just that." Hiram felt a sudden urge to explain. He felt safe here, talking with this fellow practitioner of the old arts. Gus knew the world in the same way

Hiram knew it. "My father was a polygamist. Still is, I suppose, if he's alive."

"You don't know?"

Hiram fidgeted. "He left us. When I was very young."

"Ah," Gus said. "Now I understand everything."

"What do you mean?"

"You." Gus shrugged. "You were abandoned when you were very young, so now you work hard to prevent other people from being abandoned."

"No." Hiram shook his head. "I'm just trying to do what's right."

"Hmm," Gus said. "But you are, what, forty years old?"

"Forty-four." Hiram crossed the store to stand in front of Gus at his counter.

"So the practices that were mandatory when you were a child became the oddities that were winked at when you were a young man and then the crimes that are now prosecuted, when you are grown. The world you were born into has disappeared."

Hiram nodded. "How long have you lived in Utah? You sound like you know it well."

"I was in the state as a younger man," Gus said. "And then in Colorado for many years. So as a boy you had to keep the secret of your father's other wives, as well as your . . . lore. Were they nice to you, these other wives?"

"I never met them." Hiram's eyes stung. From the kerosene smoke? "I only learned they existed late, and I never knew their names."

Gus frowned. "Did you have brothers and sisters, at least? By the same mother, I mean?"

Hiram shook his head. How had the conversation gone in this direction?

"I see. Your mother was the disfavored wife. You were kept in a corner. Perhaps hidden from the others. You were abandoned more than once, my friend. But have you met your half-siblings as a grown man? They must be easy to find, no? All with the same name. What was it, Woolley?"

"My father stopped coming around while I was still young. Later, I learned he had moved to Mexico. The other families went with him."

"To avoid prosecution. Ah, your mother truly *was* disfavored. I am so sorry to hear of your suffering, my friend."

Hiram plucked his bandana out of the back pocket of his overalls to blow his nose. He bit his tongue and managed not to tell Gus Dollar the rest of the story: after his father had moved to Mexico, his mother had spent weeks weeping, and then months staring out the front window at the road up to Salt Lake City; then his mother had disappeared, and Grandma Hettie had told him she had died, without ever identifying a cause of death, and leaving Hiram with the unsettled impression all his life that his mother's end had been dark and maybe shameful.

"Every person suffers tragedy." Hiram cleared his throat. "I guess what matters is what you do in response to it."

"And in response to your tragedy, you became a kind of knight-errant, riding around the deserts of Utah helping the poor. And a *braucher*, we Germans would say, or you English would call it a 'cunning man.'" Gus smiled warmly. "You are not a man of this century, Hiram Woolley."

"I don't know," Hiram said. "I *do* like my truck."

"So you learned to keep secrets," Gus said. "And since we know each other's great secrets now, you thought you could share something else with me. Or ask a question, perhaps."

"I only got here this morning," Hiram said. "But I'm beginning to suspect something...occult behind the closing of the Kimball Mine. Something caused the Kimball brothers to shout at each other over the heritage of their father."

"Heirs who squabble are more common than heirs who don't." Gus shrugged.

"But these men...each was convinced that the other was lying. But they weren't."

"You have a charm?" Gus's eyes gleamed.

"I carry a stone. And Samuel Kimball seemed certain that Ammon had access to some shared piece of knowledge, and Ammon denied it. Some person they both had talked with, I think. And whatever it was, it was too sensitive for either of them to speak about it clearly. Something of their father's, or something about him."

"The stone you carry...it's a peep-stone?"

Hiram shook his head. "It's a bloodstone. A heliotropius."

Gus added a smile to the gleam in his eye. "It's a shame you don't have a peep-stone. Maybe a seer stone would give you the knowledge you seek." He furrowed his brow. "Maybe the brothers saw their father in a séance?"

Hiram shrugged, feeling tired and baffled. "That might be. Some of the men think the mine is haunted. Is it possible it's haunted by Teancum Kimball, and both his sons have seen the shade? Or it might be something more like a ... document they both have access to?"

"Or you are misreading what passed between the brothers."

"Or I'm misreading it." Hiram nodded. "So this is why I've come to you. If there is something occult being done at Kimball, you might be in the best position to know it. What have you seen, Gus? What might there be between these men?"

Gus shook his head. "I'm afraid I have no idea."

"Do you know why the mine is closed?"

Gus took a deep breath. "I know enough about mining to know what sorts of things miners and their wives would like to buy, and I know *that* mostly because they ask me. I think the Kimballs have run out of money, and so they can't stock their store. It is unfortunate for them, the miners, their hungry families. I hear some have taken to banditry. All because the two brothers can't agree on where to dig."

Hiram thought about Naaman Rettig, and the offer he was being sent to make to Ammon Kimball. Might the railroad tycoon have used some means to create dissension between Ammon and Samuel? He was ambitious and driven and he wanted the land, but Hiram couldn't imagine how the railroad man could be fueling strife between the siblings. And beyond that, he didn't want them in conflict; he wanted them in agreement, and accepting his offer. Also, he hadn't seemed the type to use a hex.

Perhaps Hiram had misread *him*.

Hiram spoke in a low voice. "Maybe it would solve their problems if someone bought them out?"

"Well, you know," Gus said. "If someone bought

your farm from you, you wouldn't have to worry about farming anymore."

"But that doesn't mean I'd be interested in selling," Hiram concluded. "Of course, someone else buying the mine and investing more cash in it might mean work for the miners. So that might be a solution for the workers, even if the owners didn't like it."

"Are you thinking of getting out of farming, and digging for coal instead?" Gus smiled like an imp. "I don't think it's an easier business."

Hiram shrugged. "Just thinking. I only brought enough food for the miners for a couple of days. That mine has to start up again."

What if the railroad man *was* some kind of witch? Or one of the Kimballs was? If magic was afoot, it would serve Hiram well to prepare additional defenses. Stepping to the window, he reached up and took the bunch of bay in his hand.

"I wish I could help," Gus said with a sigh. "But I don't know what's causing all the trouble at the mine."

A dull pain throbbed in Hiram's thigh and he sucked in a sudden breath.

No, not *in* his thigh. *Against* his thigh. In his pocket. The heliotropius.

"Is something wrong, my friend?" Gus Dollar asked.

The bloodstone pulsed again.

Gus Dollar was lying to him.

The green stone was an imprecise tool. It did nothing if a person was being merely evasive. It also wouldn't tell Hiram what truth Gus was concealing, but it warned Hiram of deception.

"I hurt my back up at the Kimball Mine this morning." Hiram grunted, bringing the cluster of bay leaves to the counter. "I don't suppose you have anything I could take for it?"

"You don't mean a charm?" Gus smiled, but now the smile felt like a threat.

Hiram smiled back, and as his gaze swept the inside of the shop, he noticed things he had missed before. Lamens—metal sheets inscribed with arcane symbols—standing in discreet corners, a heavy Bible resting on a butter churn behind the door, pierced stones on leather thongs hanging as if by accident from larger appliances, the corners of a sheet of paper protruding from underneath the book of accounts, paper that looked virgin, and therefore might bear a written spell.

And in the windows, the queer twists of lead. They moved in and out of Hiram's vision as he looked at them, disappearing and reappearing again.

Gus Dollar wasn't merely a *braucher*. There was a good chance he was a witch.

"I can do that myself, of course," Hiram said. "Maybe aspirin?"

Gus produced two yellow tins of Norwich Aspirin tablets, 5 grains each. "It says take one or two," the shopkeeper said, "but for a serious pain, I'd take as many as four, and at that rate, a tin will only last you a day."

Hiram took the tablets without setting down the bay leaves. "And the herbs."

"You're going to cook?" Gus asked.

Hiram smiled as blandly as he dared. He must bluff, and bluffing was not his strong suit. "They're a good counter magic," he said. "In case I'm right about the Kimballs."

"Of course." Gus looked at the purchases. "Make it an even dollar," he said. "A dollar for Gus Dollar at Dollar's." He laughed.

Hiram laughed too, then paid, then did his best to exit without stumbling. He stepped carefully into the beams of the headlights and approached the Double-A as evenly as possible.

When he had slid into the cab and was sitting beside Michael, he took a deep breath.

"You okay, Pap?" Michael asked.

"Yes. Drive around that corner, please."

Michael drove and Hiram looked back, until the lights of Dollar's were obscured by a wall of rock and the turn of the canyon. "Okay, wait here."

"If you're heading back to burgle the shop," Michael said, "I could go for another dope."

Hiram left the aspirin and sneaked down the cold, empty road, back to Dollar's. He crept around the darkest side, where no light shone from the windows, looking for the spot where the shingled roof came closest to the ground.

It was the porch. At the far end of the wide porch from the shop's door, Hiram carefully stepped onto the planks. Earlier, the dogs hadn't barked until he had knocked, and he counted on them to have the same response now. Taking one of the rocking chairs and moving slowly to avoid creaks, he crept to the edge of the porch and set the rocking chair on the ground.

Standing on the chair's seat, he was able to reach up and touch the fringe of the roof's shingles. With his clasp knife, he cut away half of a shingle and tucked it into his coat pocket. The shingle was wooden; so much the better.

Then he replaced the rocking chair and crept back around the shop the other way. Only when he reached the truck did he realize that his heart rate was elevated, and his chest felt squeezed tightly, as if he were in the grip of a gigantic fist.

"It's me," he murmured as he approached Michael's window. "Wait just a minute while I climb into the bed of the truck."

Hiram carefully stowed the shingle in the bottom of his special toolbox, safely securing it all again before climbing down.

"Okay, Pap," Michael said when Hiram finally stood beside the cab. "I won't shoot you. But what were you doing back there, really?"

"I forgot something." Hiram hated the lie. "You wanted Coke, didn't you? I guess you drank yours." Hunger pangs twisted in his gut. He had been fasting a full day, and was ravenous. He tried not to think of the Snickers bar he'd given Mary McGill.

"Pap," Michael said, "I have a confession."

Hiram imagined the worst. "Are you alright?"

"I already drank both our Cokes. You can't leave me sitting alone in this truck with Cokes, and expect to find them when you come back."

Hiram would have laughed, if he hadn't been so shaken by his encounter with Gus Dollar. "Did you keep the bottles, by any chance?"

"Both bottles, yes I did."

"Good. Hang on to them." Hiram slipped into the passenger seat. "Let's get up to the Kimball house."

He took a deep breath as Michael put the truck into gear. Gus Dollar was a liar, and Gus Dollar had bested Hiram already twice, luring him into Gus's store and then making him bare his soul. He'd defeated Hiram's bloodstone, to boot. Only by sheer chance had Hiram put his hand on the bay leaves and learned of the deception.

Who was Gus, and what was he up to?

And what did he have to do with the closure of the Kimball Mine?

Hiram was so deep in thought, he almost didn't notice that Michael took the hill in second gear.

Chapter Eleven

THEY SAT PARKED BY THE SIDE OF THE ROAD FOR twenty minutes while Hiram worked.

He poured all the aspirin tablets into one of the Norwich tins. In the other, he mixed the tincture with his fingers, standing beside the truck. On the farm, he would have used a mortar and pestle, but he didn't carry those in his toolbox. A flashlight, balanced on the hood of the Double-A, let him gauge the consistency. Stars twinkled overhead, but no moon.

Hiram tried not to think about the cold.

Michael, wrapped up in his coat, sat in the bed of the truck strumming his Sears, Roebuck. For being the five-dollar model, the guitar didn't sound half bad. Hiram didn't know the song, but the lyric sounded risqué: *Let me be your salty dog, or I won't be your man at all.* Hiram realized he was shaking his head, and forced himself to laugh instead. He couldn't yell at the kid for not playing "My Darling Clementine" or "The Handcart Song." And Michael's love for music had given Hiram the space to prepare the cure for Ammon's boils.

If he could cure the man's boils, that might help soften his heart.

Hiram set the shovel in the bed of the truck and placed the Central Milling flour sack next to it. The company had started making their flour sacks with patterns, so women could sew dresses from the packaging. This one had golden peonies on a blue field, but no one would be making anything out of this particular flour sack, on account of the bloodstains.

"You ready?" Hiram asked.

"I guess," Michael said. "But Pap, you giving me the gun, that was serious. How much more trouble is there going to be?"

Hiram shrugged. It was bad business: railroad men, union organizers, desperate miners, starving children, and a family torn to pieces. Throw in a powerful witch who might be causing trouble, and it just kept getting worse. Had Teancum Kimball really run off with his child bride, or was he dead? If he was, did he sleep peacefully or was he out and about causing mischief from beyond the grave?

Michael burst into laughter. "And that, ladies and gentleman, is my dear, old dad. I ask a question and he ponders it for five minutes."

"We have to be careful is all," Hiram said. "This might all be over tonight. Ammon might take Rettig's offer. Or he might agree to extend credit, go easier on the men. Either way, we can go home to the farm. I expect you're anxious to get back on the tractor."

"Yay, beet farm. Two yays for the tractor." Michael wrapped his guitar up in a wool blanket and cinched it tight with ropes tied into iron rings. "Three yays, you mixing up patent medicine with your bare fingers in an aspirin tin. You know, they can send you to jail for impersonating a doctor."

"Glad to hear you like the tractor." Hiram slid into the passenger seat as Michael got behind the wheel. "I picked it out special. And I'm surprised to hear you so down on patent medicine. What do you think Coca-Cola *is*, anyway?"

"Ambrosia, sweet nectar, drunk by the gods." Michael switched on the lights. The faint orange glow showed them the white line of the road but little else. The dark claws of trees groped toward them. Boulders piled up to squelch the light, and beyond the rocks, less distinct shapes scurried about.

Hunger gnawed at Hiram's belly. Usually, he'd be asleep by this hour on a fasting day, and he wouldn't notice the pangs.

Michael didn't take the turn left into the mining camp, but kept going and took the right, up the driveway to the red house on the hill. It was a stygian corner of the valley; the cliffs were solid midnight. No stars above; just unforgiving darkness.

A greasy yellow glow came the windows of a single back room.

Michael pulled up to the front door. "Should I give him a bit of the horn, Pap?"

"Just stay in the car," Hiram said. "I'll knock."

Michael cut the engine. "Will do. I get it. The last thing in the world you want is me shooting my mouth off with Ammon Kimball."

"The thought had occurred to me." Should he warn Michael to tone down his sarcasm? He'd never been that kind of father, but maybe he was failing Michael by being too lax.

"Okay, then, Pap. I'm right here, if you need me. I'm your muscle."

Hiram pushed open the door and winced at the cold. "Good. I'm getting too old to be the muscle. Keep the lights on."

He put the aspirin tin and Rettig's manila envelope into a coat pocket. He grabbed the blood-stained flour sack and the shovel from the back of the Double-A. The dark night and the blinding effect of the headlights would hide the shovel and sack from Michael.

Hiram approached the house. No garden, no trees, no brush to entangle him. The chill perfume of the desert night came to him, sage, the rocks sleeping, a slight moisture; maybe a bit of snow would fall.

He set the shovel and the sack next to the door, and then turned to look across the canyon at the camp. Firelight twinkled across the canvas of the tents and lights glowed in the tar-paper homes. The camp was a small city, nearly as big as Helper. The barking of dogs, the mournful scrape of a violin, and a medley of human voices drifted to Hiram's ear.

Kimball must have three hundred men desperate for work, sitting idle. And at least as many women and children.

Two days of food. If that. The Greek girl, Callista, had probably already speared the cat, and if not, the creature's doom was coming. How would a cat stew taste?

Hiram went to the door and knocked, loudly.

Ammon Kimball ripped open the door. He wore sturdy work pants and a white shirt. Deep frown lines cut down from his nose and red boils spangled his throat and neck—they had been covered by plasters earlier, but now they lay bare, all swollen and shining and a few oozing pus. Ammon's breath came in snorts with a slight wheeze at the end.

"Who are you? What do you want?"

A rough kerosene lantern dangled from his left hand. His right hand gripped something out of sight in the shadow. A shotgun? A steel bar?

Hiram took off his hat and smoothed his wisps of hair. "I'm Hiram Woolley, a farmer out of Lehi. I brought groceries to the men today, before the trouble."

"What's a Lehi man doing up here?" Ammon's eyes narrowed and shifted from side to side.

"John Wells asked me to come," Hiram said. "I don't know if you know the name, but he's in Salt Lake. Your father had friends in the leadership who remember him fondly, I guess."

Ammon's head trembled slightly, and he didn't say a word.

"But I came up here tonight to see *you*." Hiram reached into his pocket and brought out the aspirin tin. "I heard you suffer from boils. That's a terrible plague, and I have a remedy here, something my grandma taught me. And I'd like to talk to you, Mr. Kimball, about...about the current situation."

"A farmer? What then, beets?" Ammon laughed. "A beet farmer shows up on my doorstep to try and talk some sense into me. And to cure my boils. Well, don't that just beat all?"

Hiram nodded. "It's peculiar. But then, I come from peculiar people."

"Come in, then." Ammon stepped back.

Hiram put the aspirin tin back in his pocket. Beside the door stood a single-shot shotgun, break-action. The house smelled of sweat, unwashed laundry, and pine wood smoke.

The sitting room was full of handmade wooden furniture: rough-hewn chairs without cushions, a long low table with uneven legs, and a couch of bare wood. A grand hutch of finer workmanship, heavy with dust, towered against the far wall. Glass doors displayed some silver and some china, but none of the finery looked recently used. A few portraits were framed on the wall, people in grainy photographs. His eyes came to rest on an old man with a beard and deep-set, piercing eyes, glaring at him from a daguerreotype. It had to be Teancum Kimball, crouched next to the entrance of the mine, angry at something. Above the fireplace hung a painting, gray in shadow.

Ammon moved to the fireplace and stooped to throw in a few sticks of split pine. The wood was dry enough to catch promptly and a fire cackled into life. The new yellow light gave Hiram a better look at the painting. It depicted a canyon, bristling with cliffs and crags, and it was done in pastel pinks, oranges, and off-white colors. On one bit of cliff were some pictographs, the markings of ancient Indians found on cliffs in southern and eastern Utah. These were black in the painting; in real life, all the pictographs Hiram had seen were white.

"Is this a real place?" Hiram asked.

"Yeah. Apostate Canyon. It's just over the ridge. You can walk it from camp, or mule it. There's a bad road that takes you there in an automobile, but you have to keep on going around the mountain and it's pretty rough. That's where my corn-for-brains brother has been camping, when he's not whipping up the Greeks into a frenzy." Ammon gazed up at the painting. "When I think maybe I shouldn't be so stubborn, I look up at that picture and I remember my brother is a smoke-addled fool. What kind of man paints a cliff wall pink, when it's really orange?"

Hiram stepped closer to the fireplace and then he saw it: a rock lying on the mantel. It was a plain stone, about the size of a baby's shoe, brown with a line of white down the middle. Firelight gleamed off the mineral—quartz?—making it prettier than it would be in daylight.

It was a pretty rock, but an ordinary one such as you might find in a streambed, while hiking. What was it doing in a place of honor, on the mantel?

Could this be a peep-stone? Hiram had never seen one, though Grandma Hettie had spoken of them often. Gus Dollar had asked whether Hiram had a peep-stone, and now that question seemed suspicious.

Something about the rock unsettled Hiram. The painting, now that he stood closer, also felt wrong. The lines of the cliff edges at the top were . . . distorted and strange. They seemed familiar.

One of the black dots of the pictographs moved.

Hiram's mouth went dry. Another of the signs moved and then another. They crawled across the painting, little black dots. Flies were on the painting. One took off in a long buzzing saunter across the sitting room, followed by another, and then a third. The flies were big, lazy, black things, a quarter inch long, big as small bees. They buzzed away from the painting and then settled back among the pictographs.

Hiram's hand drifted to his chi-rho amulet. The ringing started in his ears. He didn't smell anything yet, but it was coming, that sweet, spicy odor.

"Mr. Woolley? You okay?"

He turned. The weak light coalesced on Ammon's boils. The yellow pus glowed and the circles around the wounds darkened from red to black.

"Yeah." Hiram took in a deep breath to steady himself and focused on the other man's eyes. The ringing diminished. "I'm fine. It's been a long day, and I'm not as young as I used to be." He didn't mention his hunger; Matthew six said it wasn't a real fast if you told people you were fasting. The Lord Divine only rewarded *secret* fasting with grants of his power. "I'll take beet farming over mining. Fresher air."

Ammon nodded. "Goddamn mine. You spend a dollar to make a dime. Sorry, I shouldn't curse. I don't want you to think..."

"I'm not as sensitive as all that." Hiram had the offer to pass on, but he had also made a promise to Mary McGill. "Mr. Kimball, the men are desperate. I only brought enough food for a couple days, and the railroad won't bring in any more. After that, I'm not sure what will happen. There's only so many deer in these hills for the men to shoot. The miners are looking for a break, maybe you could extend some store credit to them, or maybe you could forgive them rent until your trouble with Samuel is over?"

"There's no food in the store because I can't buy any more food." Ammon frowned. "You think I *want* people to starve? You think I *want* my family business to fail?"

"I only wonder...is there something you could do?"

Ammon's mouth dove into a frown and his brown eyes ignited in a livid rage. "Look around, Woolley! I ain't living in style, I ain't got a wife, and I ain't got no family. All I got is a mine I'm trying to run as best I can. You want to help? Get that idiot Samuel to stand down!"

"Samuel wants to dig a new shaft." Maybe Hiram could help Ammon resolve his feelings toward his brother. Or maybe, if Ammon got worked up enough at the thought of Samuel's meddling, he'd be more receptive to an offer that got him out of the situation entirely. "Could he be right?"

A fly lit off the painting and floated through the room with a loud buzzing thrum.

Where were these flies coming from?

The skin on the back of Hiram's neck prickled.

"He thinks we should sink another shaft down valley," Ammon grumbled. "He don't understand the cost, not a bit. Also, he's taking a shot in the dark and might miss the coal entirely." Ammon fingered a boil on his neck. "We just need to follow the eastern seam, there's still coal there, and a lot of it. The Germans get it, and Sorenson does too, but Samuel and the Greeks are bent on this new hole. Damn, and then there's Eliza."

Hiram nodded. The two flies left the painting, swirled around the brown rock on the mantle, before buzzing off.

"What does Eliza want?" Hiram asked.

"Well, I would imagine you'll get around to asking her. And you'll talk to Samuel, and God bless you, Mr. Woolley if you can break up the log jam and get the Greeks to give in. And if you can't do it, I'll have to wait until they've eaten all the deer in the county and are hungry enough to give up. So no, no more food in the store, no more credit, and no breaks on the rent." Ammon coughed out a brusque laugh.

"The hauntings your brother talks about," Hiram said slowly. "Might they be connected to your father's death?"

"Hauntings." Ammon snorted. "Bullshit."

"Yeah," Hiram said. "Most likely. I'll go and talk with your brother and your sister, and see what they say. But I have one other piece of business." He took the envelope out of his pocket, feeling his heart beat a little faster. "I can't promise you'll like what's in this envelope."

Ammon stretched out a callused palm. "Every day a new bird shits in my hand. Why should today be any different?"

Hiram held the letter. "You know Naaman Rettig, with the D and RGW?"

Ammon snorted, turned away, and took a big log from the fire in one hand. He bashed the coals off a half-burned log, cracking the wood repeatedly against the stone of the fireplace. He then flung the log into the fireplace; it slammed against the wall at the back before falling onto the embers. "And does the D and RGW pay for your work, Mr. Woolley?"

Hiram sighed. "No. But Rettig asked me to bring you his offer. I was coming up the canyon anyway." He hesitated. "Would it matter to you how much money the railroad offered?"

"No!" Ammon grabbed his lantern and stomped from the room.

There wasn't any more to be said; Hiram might as

well leave. He'd failed to convince Ammon to cut his miners a break, and the mere mention of the railroad had sent Ammon into a frenzy.

He *had* learned where to find Samuel, camped out in Apostate Canyon.

With Ammon gone, Hiram couldn't resist approaching the mantel. The plain brown stone rested in shadow between two candlesticks, devoid of candles, and a music box. A blurry picture of a woman holding a baby sat in an ornate picture frame. Family knick-knacks, things of sentimental value.

Why the stone?

Unconsciously, Hiram reached between the Zippo and the clasp knife to grip his heliotropius.

That stone on the mantel must also have properties.

Ammon called to him as he reappeared in the doorway. "Mr. Woolley. You tell Naaman Rettig I'd rather dynamite every shaft of my mine than let him have it."

"I doubt he'll be surprised." Hiram moved to the front door.

"Ain't you forgetting something?" Ammon asked.

"Ah, the remedy." Hiram reached into his pocket and tossed Ammon the tin. "Put a little on each boil."

Ammon cracked open the tin and sniffed. "Rosemary and what else?"

"Rosemary, some Vaseline, a little bit of this and that." Rosemary, like bay and peppermint, warded off hostile magic. Hiram had included it in his compound to cover the possibility that Ammon's boils were caused by witchcraft.

"Why's it red?"

"This and that was red." Hiram turned the knob to let himself out.

"Why didn't you give me the letter?" Ammon asked.

Hiram turned. "You're not going to sell. Why waste time opening the envelope?"

"You're going to show the letter to my brother." Ammon's glare was dull and brutish.

"I expect he won't sign. Might not even look at it, either. Similar reasons. But then I'll have kept my promise."

Ammon stood in the doorway, not moving. His eyes went to the painting on the mantel. Or was he looking at the stone? "Look, Mr. Woolley, if you can talk some sense into my brother, I'd appreciate it. Or even my sister. If even two of us could agree, we might be able to get the mine working again. And once we get some cash flowing in, I'll be fair with the men who stayed. I'll pay back wages, as much as I'm able. But you can't get blood from a turnip. You get me?"

"I do," Hiram said. "Good evening, Mr. Kimball." He closed the door behind him and picked up the shovel. He took it and the bloodstained flour sack into the night.

Chapter Twelve

HIRAM CREPT TO THE FAR SIDE OF THE KIMBALL house, avoiding the windows of the sitting room where Ammon Kimball's lantern and low fire burned.

He grimaced at the chill air on his skin. He should have brought gloves.

Hiram put the spade into the loose sandy soil, too dry to be hardened by frost. After two minutes of vigorous work, he achieved the required depth: twelve inches. He knew the measurements, from the tips of his middle finger to mid-forearm. You couldn't carry a yardstick around with you on the farm, and it was often necessary to measure off a foot. From the flour sack, he pulled the head of a rattlesnake.

He'd killed the snake months earlier, when he'd come across it on the farm. Usually, rattlers stayed higher up in the mountains; Lehi was too marshy for their taste, but this one had gotten lost and was lurking in the weeds behind Hiram's porch. As long as you knew where it was, a rattlesnake wasn't much danger to humans, but it posed a threat to his dogs, and might harm livestock, so Hiram had duly fetched a shovel from the barn and hacked off the snake's head.

Then he had scooped the snake's head into this flour sack with the shovel, not using his hands because a severed snake's head could still bite. He'd thrown the sack into the icebox, and squeezed all the blood he could from the snake's body into a little glass medicine bottle. Before starting for Helper, he'd put both the blood and the head into his toolbox.

Snakes were useful for injuries and illness. A snake regrew its skin, it was a natural healer.

That was why the tincture was red; he'd mixed snake's blood into it. The next step, the one he was undertaking now, was key. He had to bury the snake's head near the person who was suffering from boils. As the snake's head rotted, the boils would disappear.

The serpent's flesh was still a little firm from being chilled; Hiram wanted it to thaw and then rot, quickly. Fortunately, he had a Bible verse for that. He knelt to push snake's head into the sandy soil—and his fingers struck something hard.

To be certain he wasn't placing the snake's head near something that would prevent it from decaying, he brushed aside the sand. He fished his Zippo out of his pocket and flicked it on.

And saw the grin of a human skull.

Hiram took a deep breath. The skull was fleshless, which likely meant it had been there a long time. It wasn't big, so probably not a man's. He didn't think it was Teancum's.

Nor was this a bad omen. Like attracted like, that was one of the basic hidden laws of the universe that

Grandma Hettie had taught him; it was one of the great secrets a person with the right knowledge could use to get things done. So when Hiram walked out into the garden with a rattlesnake skull in his hand, intent on burying it, the skull already buried in the garden had naturally and invisibly drawn him to it.

He shut his lighter and took several more deep breaths, smelling the Zippo's lighter fluid. The skull wouldn't impede his healing charm. He lay the snake's head atop the human skull, covered both again with loose soil, and then squatted. He touched the ground and whispered a verse from Job, chapter nineteen: "And though worms destroy this body, yet in my flesh shall I see God." In Sunday School, that verse was about the resurrection of the flesh. In the field, it was about rot and decay.

He said it three times. Then he stood, feeling fatigue and hunger dragging at the long muscles of his body. If Ammon were healed, maybe he'd be in a more tractable mood. Could Gus Dollar be the cause of the boils? For a witch, boils might be a simple curse.

Hiram made his way back to Michael in the truck. He tied the shovel into its place and wadded the flour sack into a ball in his pocket.

"Did he sign the offer?" Michael asked as they drove back down to the main road.

"No. Take a right and we'll bed down farther up the canyon." He didn't want to camp too close to either the mine or Gus Dollar's store.

"No hotel room?" Michael objected. "What about my delicate constitution?"

Hiram grunted.

About a mile farther up, the canyon opened and

the road split. To the left wound a road that looked as if it would climb over the hill to the far side of the ridge from where the Kimball Mine lay. It most likely led to Apostate Canyon. What would lie on the right hand, then? More mines? Former ranch lands?

"Go left," Hiram said.

A quarter mile farther up, they stopped at a place where the road crossed a broad patch of flat ground. Hiram found a good spot about fifty feet from the track, beside a dry creek. A stretch of sand beneath a leafless cottonwood was ideal for the tent they'd set up. There was no flowing water, but they had several gallons on the back of the truck; it was freezing, but they had the camp stove and piles of wool blankets.

They pulled on warm hats, scarves, and leather gloves, their fingers warmed by rabbit's fur. With their coats on and moving about, the cold wasn't too bad. They moved in frozen white clouds of their own breath.

They pulled their camping gear from the back of the truck, lit a kerosene lamp, and cut long branches off the cottonwood. They used the tree branches to form a frame for their tarpaulin and Hiram lugged over the hobo stove, a portable hunk of iron. A fire might warm them for a bit, but once the iron heated up, the hobo stove would do a much better job. Hiram had several big lumps of coal that would burn through the night. They would have to keep rolling over, with one side of their bodies always heating up and the other always going cold, but it would be tolerable sleeping.

While Hiram started the fire in the stove under their shelter, Michael undid his bedroll, then sat on his bedding with his Sears, Roebuck.

He started plucking, and yodeling in a low voice.

The salty dog was gone, but now Michael was singing some sort of blues drone, promising to be some woman's monkey. Hiram shook his head.

He put twigs and dry grass inside the stove as tinder, then lit it with his Zippo. He'd put it to the side of the shelter so it would vent up and out and not fill their little space with smoke.

Once the stove was started, Hiram threw the balled-up flour sack into the flames.

Michael continued to yodel, playing another blues song.

Hiram let out a sigh. "That's enough, son."

"Not a fan of Jimmie Rodgers?" Michael asked.

"I have no idea who that is. Let's just get some rest."

Michael didn't put his guitar away. "How about this one, Pap?" He then strummed a strong series of chords, which meant nothing to Hiram, until Michael began to sing: "The spirit of God like a fire is burning..."

Hiram had grown up singing that hymn, with his mother and Grandma Hettie, and on rare occasions his father. It was an early Mormon hymn, by W.W. Phelps, written for the dedication of the Kirtland Temple in 1836. Hiram loved Phelps's hymns, and often sang them to himself while working.

Michael had noticed.

Hiram sang along now in a quiet voice, quiet, because Michael sang so much better. But for the second verse, he had to raise his voice because Michael failed on the words. They sang the third verse, finishing on a pair of lines that made Hiram's hair stand on end.

That we through our faith may begin to inherit
The visions and blessings and glories of God.

Michael ended in a flourish of extra-loud chords.

"Now that's a good old song," Hiram said.

"True." Michael nodded. "But you know, Pap, some-day these new songs are going to be good old songs. And I'm sure a hundred years from now, some old-timer will be complaining about whatever new music there is about, and he'll say that the only good music is the old music. Like Jimmie Rodgers, for example."

"Undoubtedly," Hiram agreed. "But I don't think W.W. Phelps ever begged to be anybody's salty dog."

"So you're still a believer?" Michael asked. "Even after all the trouble we've seen here, the fighting, the greed, the insanity of the Kimballs, fighting each other over a mine that should be open, you still believe there's a God in heaven with our best interests at heart?"

Hiram stuck a hunk of cottonwood, its bark peeling away in dry strips, into the stove. The fine tendrils caught. "You think because we don't have everything we want in this life that God can't exist?"

Michael shook his head. "That's too easy. If I say yes to that, you'll point out that *you* don't let *me* have everything I want in life, so does that mean that Hiram Woolley doesn't exist? But I'm not just talking about natural disasters, I'm talking about general wickedness. Greed and theft and murder."

"So because there's evil in the hearts of men, we shouldn't believe?" Hiram asked.

"I guess I think that means that God isn't doing His job very well," Michael said. "If you gave me ultimate power, I'd make sure every kid got a meal. And I don't mean cat meat. And when people did rotten things to each other, I'd step in and straighten them out. I wouldn't let things lie until some final judgment."

Hiram nodded slowly. "If you went and intervened any time somebody did something wicked—which happens all day, every day—there would be no room for faith. If God wants us to develop our capacity to act in a world of uncertainty, He has to stay mostly out of sight."

"Faith, huh? So the whole point of life is to learn to do what you're told, even when no one can give you a good reason for it??"

"Doing what's right is reason enough," Hiram wished he could be arguing theology with a ham sandwich in his belly.

"And how do you know what's right?" Michael pressed. "Isn't it because someone tells you?"

"You might have a point," Hiram said. "Maybe God isn't good at His job. That doesn't mean He doesn't exist. Maybe He's busy doing other things, and so He leaves the work to us. That way we can develop not only our faith, but also our love for other human beings."

Michael jumped on that. "So what good is a God that doesn't do a perfect job? Isn't that the point of God? To be perfect? And if he's all-powerful, why can't he just *make* me love other people?"

Hiram felt that his mind was clear and his reasons sound. He also saw that Michael had far more energy than he did, and very strong feelings.

"If I answer this, can I go to sleep?" Hiram asked.

"I've been practicing a jazz tune about whoopie that I wanted to shock you with. But maybe if you answer my question, I won't scandalize you tonight."

Hiram stoked up the fire before he slid in a shoe-sized hunk of coal. Adult-shoe-sized, rather than baby-shoe-sized, like the stone on Ammon's mantel. What kind of stone would Ammon Kimball put on display? Not some lucky rock. Something with historical significance? Something that was passed down in the family? A stone the possession of which was evidence of status, or power, or blessing.

Had Teancum Kimball possessed a peep-stone?

"You know that bucket we had, the one with the crack in it?" Hiram asked.

Michael didn't quite guffaw, but he got close. "Sure, the bucket with the crack in it."

"Did that bucket work?" Hiram asked.

"Yeah, but it dripped, so you couldn't keep it full, and it'd get you wet if you weren't careful." Michael gave Hiram a quizzical look. "So the bucket wasn't perfect."

"No. And neither is the world. Neither are we. And maybe, somehow, neither is God. At least, the way we experience God isn't perfect. There's static on the radio, traffic on the road, unexpected bad weather, but it somehow works. Makes a mess, sure, but I didn't say God was clean. That's what some folks think. But in an imperfect world, God has to deal with both imperfect possibilities and imperfect people. Coal is dirty, but it burns long and hot, and on a night like this, I don't want to wake up with a dead fire. Imperfect choices, dirty possibilities, buckets with cracks."

"Huh." Michael didn't sound thoroughly convinced.

"Genesis says that God planted the garden in Eden, and Jeremiah says He was a potter. Do you know what gardeners and potters have in common? Dirty hands. Earth is dirt, Adam was dirt, you and I are dirt, and God is down here working among us."

"With a crack in His bucket."

Hiram nodded. "God is as dirty as we are, and most of the time, that's okay."

Whether he was satisfied or not—and probably he wasn't—Michael fell silent. Hiram stretched out on his bedroll, laid his head on a gunny sack stuffed full of his extra clothing, heaped blankets over himself, and tried to sleep.

The sand under the tarpaulin was soft, and it was easy to get comfortable. Hiram let sleep take him. His dreams never came into focus, but the bright pinks and yellows gave him the idea he was dreaming of Samuel Kimball's painting of Apostate Canyon. The lines kept blurring out of focus, and when he got close to it, the whole thing erupted into a swarm of flies.

A noise woke him.

He thought it was a howl. He lay next to the stove, which was glowing red hot. His chest was warm and sweating, his back ice.

He lay on the ground, listening to Michael's breath, coming in regular intervals. He was sleeping, but Hiram was wide awake. What had awoken him?

Coyotes probably. If they yipped and yowled once, they'd do it again. He sat.

Crack!

Michael snapped awake. "What the hell was that, Pap?"

Hiram kicked off his blankets. He didn't go for the lantern, and he wasn't about to throw a stick of wood in the stove. Either action would only make him more visible.

He groped for the flashlight in the sand, and couldn't find it.

"Who's there?" he called.

No answer.

Hiram stood now and stepped toward the Double-A, eyes straining to pierce the darkness.

He heard footsteps, and a sound that might be laughter. A high-pitched giggle.

"Jesus Christ, Pap." Michael sprang to his side. "It sounds like it might be people out there."

Hiram didn't comment on his son's profanity. The noises could be made by innocent hunters, or bandits, or animals. Could there be ghosts in the darkness outside his camp?

"Hello out there!" he called.

There was no answer. Innocent people would answer. His chi-roh amulet lay cool on his chest. Was it a tad more cold than usual? He reached into the gunny sack, under his extra clothes he used for a pillow, and came out with his revolver.

He heard laughter again, high-pitched, a cackle, from something that might or might not be human.

Hiram felt a shiver trace cold fingers down his spine. "Let's get to the truck." The Double-A was about twenty feet away, sitting in the weeds, with the main road another thirty feet off.

Across the dry creek the land sloped upward into pines and rocks. Could whoever was laughing be on the other side?

But then he heard the crash of branches down the creek. With no visible moon, and only a few stars peeping here and there, the sky was pitch black. The glow of the stove didn't do much, except show their position.

Hiram smelled something out of place, a vaguely fruity smell. That cackle again, staccato, high, and then crashing into a giggle. An image of a dead girl, leering with black teeth, filled his vision. In one hand, the dead child held an equally dead cat by the tail. The other gripped a cottonwood stick spear. That was Callista, with a maniacal gleam in her eye. Was it his imagination? A hallucination?

"I'm armed!" Hiram yelled.

Silence.

"We'll get in the truck and drive away," Hiram whispered to Michael. "No sense risking trouble."

Then his ears started to ring. Ringing, and buzzing, and Hiram had the sensation that flies were crawling on the skin of his arms.

And then the smell of garlic.

He heard the sound of running footsteps. "Into the truck, now!" he barked.

As they both scrambled to get into the Double-A, the smell of garlic thickened in Hiram's nostrils. He sucked in air desperately, trying not to plunge into darkness.

In the camp they had just vacated, the hobo stove crashed to the ground, spilling coals onto the dirt. In the bloody light, Hiram saw two man-shaped shadows, coming at him from the creek bed.

"Drive," Hiram muttered.

"Pap! You okay?" Michael wasn't starting the truck. Why wasn't he starting the truck?

Hiram couldn't answer, the sickly-sweet stench overwhelming him. Mustard. He smelled mustard in the garlic.

He found himself pressed against the dashboard, not sure how he got there. Then he couldn't see, couldn't hear, he could only smell and then could do nothing but slide forward into darkness.

The dead girl's giggles followed him downward.

Chapter Thirteen

MICHAEL'S HANDS SHOOK SO MUCH, DRIVING INTO Helper, that Hiram nearly took the wheel.

Given that he'd just had a fainting spell, he held back. Instead, he rested a hand on Michael's shoulder and whispered words of encouragement. "You're alright, Michael. It's okay to feel nerves after something like that, son."

Michael said nothing in return and kept his eyes fixed on the road ahead.

Hiram didn't have a charm for calming nerves as such, but he knew a passage from Isaiah forty-three, and he repeated it several times. He whispered it under his breath, probably inaudible to Michael over the growl of the Double-A, but for Michael to hear the words wasn't the point.

"When thou passest through the waters, I will be with thee; and through the rivers, they shall not overflow thee: when thou walkest through the fire, thou shalt not be burned; neither shall the flame kindle upon thee."

The scents that had overwhelmed him earlier had faded, leaving behind a bitter stink. If he thought about it, he could just find in that odor a faint olfactory halo reminiscent of picnic mustard, as if someone had broken a bottle of French's in the cab of the Double-A, and it had only imperfectly been washed out.

He realized he had dreamed. Clutching the Saturn ring, he searched his mind and found the images again. He'd raced down a desert road, calling out Michael's name in vain, as he had before. He'd also dreamed of a pit. There was no exit from the hole in the ground, and a deep voice calling a question to him over and over again.

But Hiram couldn't remember what the question was. Perhaps that was just his own fear tricking him.

"I left the stove," Michael said. "And I found the flashlight in my coat pocket."

Hiram nodded.

He took a deep breath and recited the Isaiah verse again as Michael turned onto Helper's Main Street, and the washboard rattle of the dirt road was replaced with the smooth hum of rubber on asphalt.

"Do you think we can find a boardinghouse here that *isn't* a bordello?" he said.

"I'm pretty sure we can't." Michael's face cracked into a shaky grin. "We may just have to gird up our loins and face the spiritual danger."

"'Gird up our loins' doesn't sound very good in that context."

"'Gird up our loins' doesn't sound good in any context, Pap."

"That one." Hiram pointed at a signboard that read *Boarders Welcome, Long and Short Term.* It hung on the front of a building that might otherwise have been a large brick house.

"Excellent," Michael said. "The most boring-looking front on Main Street. We shall be spiritually safe there."

"I'd settle for physically safe." Hiram shook his head.

Had someone tried to attack him and Michael in their camp? Or merely frighten them?

Who would have done such a thing? Naaman Rettig? But Hiram had been on his errand. Ammon? But he had just given the man a healing balm, and Ammon had shown him no hostility.

Gus Dollar?

And if Gus, then what was the nature of the persons . . . or creatures . . . that had invaded their camp that night?

A second sign on the boarding house said *Bufords*. Pale light shone through the first-floor windows, and when Hiram and Michael slunk into the parlor, a long hallway extended back in front of them. To the right was a door with a little sign tacked to the panels: *Mr. and Mrs. Buford. Proprietors.*

Hiram hated to do it this late, but he rapped on the door. It took several knocks, but eventually the presumptive Mrs. Buford, a substantial woman in a sleeping cap and a nightgown under a thick robe, cracked the door open and gave him a glare that could have lit coal. Through her open doorway, he saw a phone on the wall in the entryway into the Bufords' room.

Michael raised an uncertain hand. "Good evening, Mrs. Buford. Sorry to wake you."

She grunted but agreed to rent to them as long as they paid for three nights, up front.

At Hiram's request, the room was on the second

floor, the street-facing side of Buford's Boarding House. When Hiram pulled back the heavy crimson curtain, he could see the Double-A, parked diagonally at the curb between a Dodge Model KC and a bright yellow convertible roadster with white sidewalls. The room had a single bed, large enough for both of them, and a porcelain wash basin on a table beneath a tall mirror. A second mirror hung on the door. There was a slat-backed wooden chair, painted black. The water closet was at the end of the hall.

Michael hung his coat on a peg on the wall. From his pockets, he removed the revolver and the extra loader.

He showed both items to Hiram, and Hiram nodded. "Good thinking."

Michael set the revolver and the full moon both on the table. Hiram sat in the chair and closed his eyes, trying not to notice the fading stench of mustard.

Michael might be right. Maybe he should get a second gun.

"We could go home in the morning," he offered.

Michael unlaced his Redwings and set them by the door. His socks were filthy, black above the ankle with the coal dust of Kimball and red below the ankle with the native soil of Carbon County.

"We came here to deliver groceries to the Kimball Mine," Hiram said. "We could get a good night's sleep and just drive back to Lehi in the morning."

"Could we?" Michael stood in front of the wall mirror. He poured water from a jug into the basin and washed his hands and face.

Michael wasn't an especially fastidious young man. What was he really washing off his hands?

What had happened while Hiram had been unconscious? He was afraid to ask, but he had to. "While I was having my fit," he said slowly. "Did you . . . shoot anyone?"

"You mean *kill*, right, Pap?" In another tone of voice, it would have been one of Michael's witty barbs. Spoken as it was, flat and with a knife-like edge, the words hurt Hiram.

"Killing a man is a hard thing," Hiram said. "Wounding a man is also very hard. If you did either tonight, you did it because you had to, and you should feel nothing but gratitude that you and I are both alive."

Michael was quiet for a moment. "I shot at them. I don't know whether I hit them or not."

Hiram nodded. "Many men who came home from the Great War could say exactly the same words. Not knowing whether you actually hit the other fellow is sometimes the best source of comfort."

"I'm fine, Pap." Michael's voice relaxed slightly. "I don't need to go home."

"I could tell Bishop Wells with a clean conscience that I've done was I was asked to do."

"What's that phrase you like so much?" Michael patted his hands dry on a towel and sat on the bed. "The one where I tease you it's about burning up ants?"

"Magnifying your calling," Hiram said.

Michael nodded. "That's the one. Remind me what it means."

"It means . . . not just doing the minimum. It means if your responsibility is small, you can still do it well. It means carrying out the spirit of your task to accomplish great things, and not just complying with the letter of an assignment."

"Right. So tell me again that we can drive home in the morning."

Hiram's lungs felt squeezed and breathless. "I worry about your safety."

"I know you do, Pap. You worry about *my* safety, and not your own. And you also worry about the safety of all the Kimball miners, don't you? And the safety of their families? And probably even the safety of the Kimball brothers, even though they don't give a damn about you. And whether that Greek woman and all her kids are going to eat tomorrow."

Hiram thought again of Medea and Basil, their daughter Callista, and their other children. He had injured Basil—in self-defense, but Hiram felt responsible, nonetheless. What kind of man would he be if he just abandoned them?

Michael cracked a wicked grin and looked sidelong at Hiram. "Oh, and for sure you care about the union lady."

"Mary, or Gil, I guess."

"That's the one."

"I could drive you home in the morning and come back," Hiram suggested.

"That would take you all day," Michael said. "In that time, there could be another shooting up at the mine, Gil might get attacked in prison, all kinds of bad things could happen."

Hiram hung his head, burying his face in his palms, elbows planted on his knees.

"Besides," Michael added, "you'd be preventing me from magnifying *my* calling."

"You don't have a calling. You won't even step inside a church."

"I'm your driver," Michael said. "You'd probably have another fainting spell and crash the car on the drive back here, anyway. Hell, Pap, it would be downright irresponsible of me to let you try."

"You could say *heck*, you know. Other boys say *heck*."

"No, they don't."

"Two spells in twenty-four hours would be unusual." In fact, Hiram had felt on the brink of having a spell much more frequently than usual, since coming to Helper and Spring Canyon. Was that from strain? Sleeplessness? Some malign influence?

Michael just sat on the bed, looking calmly at Hiram.

"Well," Hiram continued. "What shall we do, then?"

"Get the union lady out of jail," Michael told him. "Get the mine open. Not get killed by bandits."

Also, not get trapped by another one of Gus Dollar's enchantments, whatever the storekeeper was up to. But Hiram just nodded.

Michael yawned. "I think, though, that sleep is probably the first thing on the to-do list."

"Agreed. You hit the sack, I'll go bring in the toolbox."

"Right." Michael yawned again and lay down, flat on his back. "I've heard many times that Helper's ladies of the evening are notorious for stealing shovels and water cans."

"Before today, you'd never heard of Helper's ladies of the evening."

"True. Utah is much more interesting than I ever imagined."

And just like that, Michael was snoring.

Hiram shifted Michael just enough to get the blanket over his son, then turned off the electric light.

He took the revolver with him, tucking it into the bib pocket of his overalls, and headed down to the street.

Hiram took the long steel tool chest from the back of the Double-A and carried it in both hands up to the hotel room. Once Hiram had locked the door, he lifted the top tray—with its hammer and pliers and screwdrivers and other assorted hardware—out of the chest and set it aside.

Beneath lay the chest's true, important contents. Three worn leather notebooks. A dog's tongue. Several lamens. Small sheets of virgin paper. Stones taken from the Jordan River near his farm that had natural holes in them, holes bored by the river itself, rather than by the hand of man. Two forked rods cut from the stand of witch hazel that Hiram carefully tended at the end of his farmhouse porch, and other paraphernalia.

Tools to accomplish ends, tools in their essence only very slightly different from the hammer.

Still, others would have said they were *magical*.

He looked up to make certain Michael was still sleeping.

He selected one of the lamens, an Oremus lamen, made of flattened bronze, six inches wide and eight inches long. A lamen was a written enchantment, and could be made on paper (especially virgin paper, paper of the best quality that had never been used before, and even better would be virgin parchment) or stitched into a quilt, but Hiram had a few made of metal, because he wanted them to be rugged and portable.

There was such an inscribed metal plate inside the door of the Double-A, on the driver's side. Hiram had spent an entire day figuring out how to crack that door open and fix the lamen into place, before he had let Michael drive. He'd sent Michael off on an errand first, walking to the telegraph office in town to send a message to the beet processing plant in Payson and then wait for answer. That had given Hiram the time he'd needed. The lamen in the car provided protection.

The lamen he drew from the chest now was identical to the one in the car. Hiram didn't know Latin or Hebrew, but during the Great War, he'd been briefly in London. There he'd found a copy of a volume of which Grandma Hettie had spoken highly, Reginald Scot's *The Discoverie of Witchcraft*. The old Elizabethan squire's book, to Hiram's surprise, was a screed that railed against even the possibility of magic. In attempting to expose magic to the ridicule he said it deserved, Scot recorded dozens of charms, making the *Discoverie* an excellent resource, and the closest thing to a real book of magic Hiram had ever seen complete.

It was almost as if Scot had himself been a cunning man, attempting to pass down his magical lore in disguise.

Hiram had copied it out by hand into two leather journals he'd bought on Charing Cross Road, including all the Latin. Mostly, he ignored the Latin and Hebrew and used Scot's English charms, but he had made these two identical lamens. They read, letters and crosses carefully pressed into the bronze:

Fons † *alpha & omega* † *figa* † *figalis* †
Sabbaoth † *Emanuel* † *Adonai* † *o* † *Neray*
† *Elay* † *Ihe* † *Rentone* † *Neger* † *Sahe* †
Pangeton † *Commen* † *a* † *g* † *l* † *a* † *Mat-theus* † *Marcus* † *Lucas* † *Johannes* ††† *titulus*

triumphalis † *Jesus Naserenus Rex Judeorum*
† *ecce dominice crucis signum* † *fugite partes*
adverse, vicit leo de tribu Jude, radix, David,
aleluijah, Kyrie eleeson, Christe eleeson, pater
noster, ave Marie, & ne nos, & veniat super
nos salutare tuum: Oremus.

According to Scot, Joseph of Arimathea had found
these words engraved on Christ's side by the finger
of God Himself, and anyone protected by the words
would fear no evil death, or any danger at all.

Hiram tied a leather thong through a hole punched
into one end of the Oremus lamen, and he slipped the
thin plate beneath the mirror hanging from the door.
A close observer might see the top of the thong and
investigate, but the lamen was hidden from casual view.

He wished he had one to hang in the window, too,
but he didn't have enough time to take apart the door
of the Double-A. And Michael had taken his boots off.

Hiram removed the chi-rho talisman from around
his neck and hung it in the window.

The last word of the Scot lamen, *Oremus*, meant
"let us pray." The lamen required a prayer to activate
it, so on the floor of the hotel room, the only illumi-
nation coming in through the window from the marquee of the movie theater next door, Hiram Woolley
knelt and prayed. He prayed for Michael's safety and
the peace of Michael's soul.

While he was at it, he prayed, stomach growling,
to end his fast.

Then he shut the curtain.

Thinking of Reginald Scot reminded Hiram that
Scot had a charm for rest. Standing, he spoke it over

Michael's sleeping form. "In the name of the Father, up and down, the Son and the Spirit upon your crown, the cross of Christ upon your breast, sweetest lady send you rest."

Michael's body sank deeper into the depths of the hotel mattress and his breathing became slow and regular.

Hiram looked at the bed and briefly considered going to sleep himself. His bones felt like lead, and he knew that if he could get even three or four hours of sleep, he'd feel much refreshed.

But he didn't lie down. Working with his own written enchantments had made him think of Gus Dollar's store. Specifically, he thought of the curious glyphs built into the store windows. He knew that for each planet, there was a written glyph that worked like a secret name; his Saturn ring was engraved with the sign of Saturn, for instance, in addition to bearing a signet he'd had made by a jeweler in Salt Lake City. Hiram knew the signs of the planets.

He also knew that angels and devils were said to have similar signs, and he didn't know those. But if the images in Gus's windows drew and focused the power of an angel . . . or worse, a demon of some kind . . . that might explain how Gus had so handily overcome Hiram's ordinary defensive charms, both to draw Hiram into the shop and also to loosen his tongue about his past and his secrets.

He had to find out more about the signs in those windows. And out here in Helper, with no library anywhere nearby, the only likely source of knowledge was the store itself.

Hiram removed his Harvesters. Like Michael's, his

socks were stained by alternating layers of red and black dust. He set his boots together beside Michael's, and then took his son's footwear. From the toolbox, he took a triangular bit of leather and placed it in inside the right boot. He then put both of Michael's boots on.

Michael's feet were bigger than Hiram's. The boots were a loose fit, but Hiram could walk.

Almost as an afterthought, Hiram opened the third leather notebook, which was his dream dictionary. It wasn't really a dictionary, in that it had been written by Hiram himself, and wasn't in alphabetical order, but it collected what he knew about the symbols that could occur in his dreams. He looked up images that had dogged his recent dreams:

> FLIES—*you have many enemies.*
> VOICE, UNSEEN—*denotes you will be deluded
>   by feigned pretenders.*
> PIT—*you face sudden surprise or danger.*
> RUNNING—*if you dream you run swiftly, you
>   will receive a letter.*

Did it add up an interpretation of his dreams, of driving and looking for Michael, of a voice in a pit? Not that he could puzzle out. He sighed and put the dream dictionary away in the toolbox.

Hiram put the gun and the loader into the tool chest and took the chest with him. He locked Michael into the warded hotel room and headed for the Double-A.

Chapter Fourteen

ALL THE WAY UP SPRING CANYON, HIRAM CHANTED a charm against the falling sickness, an old name for epilepsy. Epilepsy was close enough to what ailed him. "I conjure me by the sun and the moon, and by the gospel of this day delivered to Rupert, Giles, Cornelius, and John, that I rise and fall no more."

He had no idea who Rupert, Giles, and Cornelius might be, but this was the charm Grandma Hettie had taught him. He gripped the wheel of the Double-A until his knuckles turned white and said the words over and over again.

No strange smells troubled him, and he reached Dollar's.

His stomach growled audibly the entire time.

What was it he had smelled when the camp had been attacked? The garlic and mustard smells of his fainting spell had taken him eventually, but first there had been something else, a sweeter smell that reminded him of Christmas.

He stopped the car when he was still around the bend and prepared himself. He stuffed his pockets with bay leaves. He put the revolver into the bib pocket of his overalls. He tucked the leather notebooks containing his transcription of Reginald Scot into the deep pockets of his wool coat. He took a disk of wax the size of a silver dollar, imprinted with a large cross and rimmed by a ring of flowers, and held it in his hand to avoid spoiling the impressions in the wax. He made sure he had the flashlight in one pocket and his clasp knife in another, along with his Zippo and his bloodstone.

He took the bolt-cutters.

Should he make a witch bottle, or burn the shingle he'd taken? He didn't think the time had come yet for either countercharm, so he placed the two empty Coke bottles into the lower compartment of his tool chest alongside the bit of Gus Dollar's shingle, and then shut the chest into the cab of the Double-A.

He walked quietly toward Gus Dollar's shop.

The lights were out. Gus was asleep, likely. To be sure, Hiram stood on the path at the edge of the porch and recited again the charm for rest he had used on Michael. He visualized Gus, he visualized the tow-headed children, he visualized unseen and unnamed other members of the household, and he repeated it three times.

He didn't worry about the Rottweilers.

He took time to consider what he was doing. He was about to commit a burglary. He was doing it, though, because he believed Gus knew something about the closing of the mine. The bloodstone had told him as much. And since Gus had denied that knowledge, and also hexed Hiram twice, then Gus was a man of ill will.

Peace on earth to men of good will, had been the angels' song, the way Grandma Hettie had taught it to Hiram.

Also, Gus might have a connection with whoever had attacked his camp earlier that night.

"If I am sinning against an innocent man," he prayed softly, "then stop me, Lord Divine, and keep him from harm. Amen."

On the porch, he knelt and held the wax disk up to the door. On the other side, he heard the padding feet of the dogs. He spoke his charm: "I open this door in thy name that I am forced to break, in the name of the Father, and of the Son, and of the Holy Ghost, amen." Then he blew three times across the disk and into the lock.

He stood, putting the wax back into a coat pocket. When he tried the doorknob, it turned.

So Gus Dollar was not an innocent man.

Within stood the two Rottweilers. Their jaws worked vigorously, mouths opening and closing, but no sound came out. The triangular bit of leather in Hiram's shoe was the tongue of a dog, with no special words written on it and no prayer spoken; it was old and true lore that in the presence of a dried dog's tongue, a dog could not bark.

The warm air rushing from inside the store was welcome, especially as it carried with it hints of the tins of sugar and cinnamon that Gus had sitting his shelves. The sudden stab of hunger in Hiram's belly nearly knocked him down.

He knelt again and reached out to pet the animals.

Puzzled, surprised, and maybe frightened, the dogs retreated, disappearing into the back end of the shop.

Hiram stood still for a minute, until his eyes adjusted and he could make out the general outline of things in the shop: the counter, the tools, the mannequins, the washing machine.

Now for the key action, the thing Hiram most needed to do in order to stay undetected. If his guess was correct that the signs in the windows were angelic or demonic, and made Gus's magic more powerful than Hiram's, then Hiram had to destroy those signs before they undid his charms.

He cautiously moved a three-stepped stool beneath the windows and then climbed it.

For good measure, standing in Gus Dollar's window, Hiram took the peppermint leaves and stuffed them all into a pocket. Then he pushed the nose of the bolt cutters as snugly against the windowpane as he dared. Too hard, and he'd shatter the window, and he doubted the rest charm would keep Gus Dollar sleeping through a noise like *that*. Not firmly enough, and he'd have no effect.

He pressed as much as he dared, working the bolt cutter blades around the lead where it protruded most on this side of the glass and then snipped it. With a satisfying *chunk* sound, the bolt cutters bit through the soft metal.

Examining the bolt cutters' result, though, Hiram found that the sign was not completely interrupted. He applied his clasp knife to the task, gouging out additional gray twists of lead until the blade poked entirely through the window, and Hiram felt a cold squirt of air through the hole.

There. That sigil was now damaged, and its operation should be interrupted.

He moved the stool and did the same thing with the second window.

Were there other signs? Hiram checked the other windows and didn't see any. If there were painted signs, say, on the floorboard or on a wall, Hiram couldn't see them in the darkness, and of course if there were signs embedded within the walls or the door, as Hiram had done, placing the lamen of protection within the Double-A, Hiram had no way to know. But in any case, he must have interrupted *some* of Gus's power.

But what he had come here for was knowledge of what the signs meant. He studied the sigils carefully with his eye, trying to memorize the irregular curves, the curl at the one end and the arrow at the other, the way the sign seemed to creep out larger than its actual dimensions to dominate the space around it.

To be certain, he tore a scrap from the corner of an old page in Gus's account book, and with the pencil lying beside the book on the countertop, he drew the sign.

He took the nickel from Gus's revenue charm, tucking it into his own pocket. The poppet stared accusingly at him, its empty eye sockets seeming to follow him from side to side. Hiram resisted the temptation to smash the poppet flat with his fist. For good measure, he also took the Bible off Gus's butter churn and hid it on a shelf behind stacks of Henry Ford reprints of McGuffey's Readers.

Finding and fixing these little faults might keep Gus distracted.

Hiram really wanted to eat something, a cookie or a Snickers bar. He didn't. He couldn't. To steal Gus's food would be simple burglary, and a sin. Hiram's charms wouldn't work for a mere thief.

He crept from room to room, searching.

He found the dogs, lying on their bellies in a pantry in front of a wall of dried beans, tinned tomatoes, and salt crackers. They had their paws over their faces, and didn't look up as Hiram stepped past them.

He checked the windows of other rooms, but didn't see the strange glyph repeated there.

The downstairs was all store and storage, so Hiram tip-toed up to the second floor.

Around a central landing area huddled five rooms. Their doors were open, so Hiram peeped one at a time into each room. He spotted Gus, sleeping alone. There were also a couple, and a woman alone, and two rooms full of little children.

But in his squinting into the upstairs bedrooms, Hiram saw no signs of any books. No ceremonial swords or staffs, no visible lamens.

If Gus was a witch, were all his accoutrements in the store? If so, Hiram's mission was doomed to disappointment. He had learned all he was going to learn, and the curious signs in the windows would remain mysteries.

He should ask Mahonri Young. He could call from the boarding house's telephone in the morning. He could describe his sketches of the signs to Mahonri, who would be disappointed that Hiram was once again asking him questions concerning the occult, but would help, anyway.

But no, if Gus was indeed drawing arcane symbols,

then he had a dictionary somewhere, a symbols list. The signs of the planets and celestial and infernal beings were simply too complex to know by heart, unless you worked with them constantly. Gus must have at least a card, a sign list. Hiram could read that, or he could take it.

He considered the layout of the building: had he missed a secret room somewhere? To the best of his spatial estimation, all the room was accounted for.

But Gus's shop stood on high ground, far above the creek. There could be a basement.

Hiram descended again to the ground floor and retraced his steps. Here, too, he could find no space not accounted for. He looked inside the washing machine, and behind the goods on the shelves in the shop and in the storerooms, and found nothing.

Standing in the pantry beside the two Rottweilers, who still pressed themselves flat against the hardwood floor, he wondered what he could have missed. Could Gus have an office in a separate building elsewhere? But there wasn't so much as a springhouse in sight, and if you were going to keep valuable ritual gear, you would store it on your person or close to you, so you could watch it.

Could a list be taped inside one of the McGuffey Readers? Hiram didn't think Gus would risk the chance that a customer might find it. Maybe in the safe deposit box of a bank? Helper had a bank. Maybe Hiram could investigate in town in the morning.

Hiram could go out to the Double-A and get one of his forked hazel rods. Did he have time to peel it, carve it, and sanctify it as a Mosaical Rod, and then still have time to use it?

Hiram sighed. He didn't.

Perhaps he'd have to come back again and search the property the following evening. Tired as he was, and having driven the truck up alone in the dark, and standing as he was in another man's house in the middle of the night, the thought was daunting.

Then he noticed the dogs.

They lay flat. Not cringing as if in fear, and not just silent, but pressed flat to the floor.

That didn't seem like the effect of his charm.

Crouching, he grabbed one dog and dragged it aside. The dog wiggled from his grasp and immediately rushed back to lie in the same space—but not before Hiram saw the outline of a trapdoor where it had been lying.

Hiram considered his options. He had to get the dogs out of the way and keep them out of the way, and they were big enough that he could only carry one at a time. And the rooms on the ground floor had no doors to shut them in with.

He could take them upstairs and shut them into bedrooms. But that might wake the people who slept in those rooms.

Hiram picked up one of the Rottweilers. It struggled, but it didn't bite him, so he carried it to the front door of the shop and pushed it outside, shutting the door behind it. Could he do it again, and put the second dog outside without letting the first one back in? It wasn't likely. The dogs were drawn to the trapdoor.

Crossing the shop, he had a better idea.

Picking up the second Rottweiler, he carried it into the shop. There he lowered it into the drum of the washing machine and closed the lid.

Thank goodness for the dog's tongue in his boot. It kept the Rottweilers from complaining.

Hiram looked outside: pale gray light suggested dawn was approaching. Given the month, it was likely that the only reason the family was still sleeping was Hiram's charm, and that couldn't last much longer.

He opened the trapdoor and shone his flashlight down. Iron rungs descended a shaft made of red stones, mortared thickly together.

There was no more time for consideration; he sat on the lip of the tunnel and then lowered himself in. Once he was fully inside, he shut the trapdoor overhead.

A whisper of air rustling up inside the leg of his overalls gave him a moment's pause; there must be a connection below to the outside. He forced himself on, and when he reached the bottom of the shaft, he shone the light around.

He was in a square-cornered basement, all of mortared local stone. In one corner, the stones had cracked apart wide enough that a man could crawl through into darkness, and that was the source of the cold breeze. A long table filled the center of the room. Here were all the things Hiram expected to see in the house of a prosperous worker in the ancient lore: tablets and paper for creating amulets, a sword, candles and matches, wax seals, stones of various colors and sizes, and alchemical flasks and tubing about which Hiram knew nothing. Resting on wooden blocks, there was a book in the process of being assembled; virgin paper, carefully cut, was bound between two metal lamens. Hiram examined the metal plates. The first was made from a yellow metal, brass or bronze, and bore sacred

names and astral grids. That struck Hiram as a lamen
for binding or protection. It was not lore he'd mastered,
but Grandma Hettie had known such arts.

The other plate bore a series of images that Hiram
thought were astrological in nature. Curiously, the
plate was made of lead, which suggested that, like
Hiram's ring, it was Saturnine: that might connect
it with dreams, melancholy, and insight, but it might
also indicate that it was destructive in intent. The
lamen bore two short lines; one was in Latin, but
the other was in English: *Shout, for the Lord hath
given you the city.*

He knew the words. Where did they come from?

Hiram had never seen such a book, but he'd heard
about them from Grandma Hettie, and he'd read of
them: Gus Dollar was preparing a Book of the Spirits.
The thought of Gus summoning and binding creatures
beyond Hiram's craft made Hiram's blood run cold.

Ordinarily, a Book of the Spirits was used to summon and contain a spirit, and the two binding lamens
that made up the covers would trap it. But this one
was different. The brass or bronze lamen was likely
a binding charm, but the bottom lead cover? That
seemed to have been crafted to destroy something.
But what?

A city? Which city had the Lord given?

Jericho. Jericho, whose walls had tumbled down
when Joshua's men had shouted.

Hiram shook his head, not entirely sure what he
held in his hands.

While the Book of the Spirits was still half done,
there were also completed books.

He couldn't let himself be distracted. Nor could

he carry away all the volumes. And, dog's tongue charm notwithstanding, might the beast in the washing machine whine loud enough to wake its master? Sweating despite the cold, Hiram grabbed the books and flipped through them. He wasn't looking for text, but for diagrams, and not just any diagrams. He ignored astrological charts, and number charts, and esoteric alphabets, and had gone through three books and was into a fourth when he finally found what he'd been seeking: the glyph that appeared in lead in the shop's windows, one of a long series of similar diagrams, each surrounded by several long paragraphs of text in tiny gothic letters.

The words were in German.

Hiram stifled a curse.

Above him, he heard footsteps. He tucked the book, which was a small volume, into his coat pocket, and stood at the bottom of the shaft to listen.

"Boys!" he heard Gus Dollar call. "Boys?"

Hiram reached into his bib pocket and pulled out the Colt. If he had to, he could shoot Gus. Gus was no innocent man, no mere shopkeeper. Gus dealt with demons and strange craft, and he was a threat to Hiram, Hiram's son, and all people everywhere.

But killing a man was a hard, hard thing to do, and a harder burden to bear, afterward. Even when the man was a witch.

Hiram eyed the crack at the corner of the room. There was a breeze, so, somehow, that gap in the wall led to the surface.

Crossing to the split, he passed the Book of the Spirits again. He couldn't leave it with Gus. He didn't want to take it, either.

And he had already left plenty of evidence that someone had been here. He tore both lamens out of the book and inserted them into the inside pocket of his coat. With his Zippo, Hiram set fire to the virgin paper. It was a desperate move. It would certainly be noticed, and it might even risk burning the shop down. Gus was awake, dealing with his dogs, so he would notice the fire. That would prevent any loss of innocent life; the old German would have counter magic against fire.

The orange flames cast only very little light ahead of Hiram as he crawled into the crack, but his flashlight let him see his path. To his relief, in a few short feet, it opened onto a passage tall enough for him to crouch in, and he waddled forward at a reasonable pace.

Small objects struck him in the face. Insects? Flying insects, beneath the ground, in February? He swatted one against his own forehead, and when he examined it in the light he found it to be a fly as large as his pinky nail.

Fear and nausea fought for control of Hiram's stomach, and nausea won. As he finished vomiting into the side of the passageway, he heard screaming behind him.

Gus had opened the trapdoor and seen the fire.

Hiram raced ahead. In another few paces, he found himself at a fork. One passage dropped steeply to his left, and the flies seemed to swarm thickly there, boiling out of the depths of the earth. The stink of rot came with them. To his right, the passage rose; Hiram felt the breeze again, and was that daylight?

He scrambled on, and when he could see the light of morning for certain, he switched off the flashlight.

The passage opened in an oval-shaped egress bounded by stone, turned to face parallel to the canyon and hidden from the view of travelers by a large stone slab.

As Hiram stepped through exit, sudden pain wracked his entire body. He felt as if he had been cast into a fire, and he fell, tumbling down the scree at the base of the canyon wall.

Vision swimming, he held onto consciousness by a thread. Gus knew he had been there. Gus could be coming after him. Hiram lurched to his feet and raced across the canyon, keeping junipers between himself and Dollar's as much as possible. When he rounded the bend and found the Double-A waiting where he had left it, he heaved a sigh of relief.

Hiram started the truck and his incantation against the falling sickness at the same time, and drove as fast as he dared back toward Helper. He had reached Michael's alluvial fan and was dropping down toward the river when he realized that he smelled burnt herbs. Reaching into his pockets to examine the bay leaves and also the peppermint, he found it all dried and brittle, shriveled up, and scorched black at the edges, as if it had been thrown into a fire.

Chapter Fifteen

THE SUN SHONE DOWN ON HELPER BY THE TIME Hiram reached Main Street. He didn't want Michael seeing him, and he was too anxious to wait any longer, so he pulled over in front of a restaurant that was clearly closed, its curb empty. There he cracked open Gus Dollar's book.

If he'd hoped that during his drive down Spring Canyon, the text would be miraculously transmuted from German to English, he was disappointed.

Of course, there were plenty of Germans up at the Kimball Mine, and one of them might help Hiram read the book. Or for that matter, there were Germans at other camps, in Spring Canyon or in the other canyons around Helper. There were probably German-speakers living down in Helper, running a restaurant or working in the department store.

Only Hiram had no desire for Carbon County's German community to be talking about that strange traveler, the demonologist Hiram Woolley. If word got back to Bishop Smith...Hiram preferred not to think about the consequences.

He found the sigil in question quickly and double-checked that he had the right one by comparing it with his own sketch. Hiram had learned a smattering of phrases as a Doughboy, and he looked for them now. He found *isst*—wasn't that *is?* But then here was *ist*—were they two spelling for the same word? He looked for *gut*, and *schlecht*, and *kann*, and *muss*, and found none of them. He gave up, but in searching for words he knew, he found two words, appearing several times each all in capital letters on the page with the glyph in question, and, as far as he could tell from a quick page-flipping, appearing nowhere else in the book.

MAHOUN.

SAMAEL.

Hiram didn't know the lore of demons. You didn't have to know such lore to cast devils out; you needed it if you wanted to summon and command them, and Hiram emphatically did *not* want a demonic ally. That made you a witch or a sorcerer.

Still, he thought he knew the name *Samael*. Samael was a demon, a fallen angel. He didn't remember whether he'd read the name alongside such names as Semyaz and Azrael in the apocryphal books like 1 Enoch, or if perhaps Grandma Hettie had told him the name in one of her rocking-chair sermons, but he was confident he knew the name.

Curious that *Samael* and *Samuel* were so similar. Coincidence?

Mahoun, though...nothing.

The sigil was the sign of a demon, Samael, with

Mahoun maybe being another name for him. Or could they be names for two different demons? Why would Gus Dollar want such a sign? To summon the being? To channel its power? To command it?

Some combination of all of those?

A drunk staggered into the side of the Double-A, startling Hiram out of his train of thought. The sun's height in the sky told him that more time had passed than he'd planned.

The Denver lawyer might be available.

He reparked the truck in front of the Buford's Boarding House and went inside. It was morning and the smell of bacon frying and coffee dripping filled the place. To ward off the worst of his hunger pains, he grabbed a handful of mints from a crystal dish in the front hall and choked them down, almost without chewing. They were sweet, they pushed back against his hunger, and the mints had the added benefit of sweetening his stale breath.

He knocked on the Bufords' door.

Again, the woman answered and this time wore a turban. Slippers fuzzed her feet. "You again. Out late. Up early."

He winced shook his head. "I'm so sorry, ma'am. Could I possibly use your phone?"

"That'll be a nickel."

Hiram produced the coin. She let him inside the entryway where the phone was connected to the wall and snatched the coin out of his hand. "Make it quick. And keep the door open. If you come any farther into my room, my husband will give you the what-for." She retreated.

He unhooked the receiver and placed it to his ear.

He spoke into the transmitter attached to the ringer box, tripping over his own tongue with the sudden flood of saliva stimulated by the mints and the smell of the bacon. When the operator asked for the exchange and number, Hiram gave her the number for B Y High.

A secretary answered, which was unsurprising, since the one telephone in the building was in the central office, but she quickly brought Hiram's friend to the phone.

"Mahonri Young."

"Mahonri, it's Hiram." Hiram hesitated. "I have a...a strange question."

He listened to Mahonri's deep breath and exhalation.

"What kind of strange?" Mahonri asked.

"Well, I'm not in jail, if that's what you're worried about."

The joke brought a laugh from Mahonri, and then a touch of relaxation to his voice. "Okay, Hiram. Fair enough. What do you want to know?"

"I'm looking for any information you can give me on two names. They might be old angel names, I think."

"Angels?" Mahonri pressed.

"Or something like that."

Mahonri hesitated. "I don't expect I should hope you need this information to teach Sunday School."

"I don't want to tell you why I want the information," Hiram said. "And you don't really want to know."

"I don't want to know," Mahonri agreed. "But I do want to know that you and Michael are safe."

"We're safe," Hiram said, probably too quickly. "Except I'm not so sure I'm safe from Michael. He's as aggressive and sarcastic as ever, and no closer to finding faith. And now he's taken to cussing."

"Maybe he'll find God through cussing," Mahonri said. "He wouldn't be the first, and I believe that's the *traditional* route for Catholics. What are the names?"

Hiram gave him the names *Mahoun* and *Samael*, spelling them both out. He then told Mahonri that the easiest way to contact him back was to send a telegram to Buford's Boarding House.

"I'll get back to you," Mahonri said, and hung up.

Hiram contacted the operator again.

"Denver two, twelve oh seven," he said when the operator came on the line, and then he waited.

"I heard that!" Mrs. Buford called from the other room. "Another five cents, Mr. Woolley, if not ten!"

Hiram called back, "Yes, ma'am."

A few seconds later, a woman's voice came on the line. "Law office of James Nichols, esquire."

"I need to speak to James Nichols."

"Is it about an existing matter?"

Existing matter? "I'm not a client."

"If you could just give me a few details as what the nature of the matter is, I'll know how to direct your call."

Hiram felt that privacy was being invaded, his or maybe Mary McGill's. "Please direct the call to James Nichols."

"Please tell me the nature of the matter, sir." The woman's voice had become frosty.

The nature of the matter? What *was* the nature of the matter? Hiram was exhausted. A mine was closed, two brothers were fighting over which direction to take the mine, and stirring up ethnic tensions in the process. A union organizer was being held for a bogus crime, a pride-ridden railroad magnate wanted to use

Hiram as his messenger boy, and a beloved shopkeeper appeared to be summoning or planning on summoning demons, for a purpose Hiram couldn't imagine.

What *was* the nature of the matter?

"Sir?" the woman's voice shook him back to the present.

Hiram cleared his throat. "I need to talk to Five-Cent Jimmy. It isn't for me, it's for Mary McGill. And Gil said Five-Cent Jimmy would never let her down."

"I see," the woman said. "You should have said that in the first place."

"I was trying," Hiram offered weakly, but the *click* on the other end of the line told him he'd already been transferred.

"Jimmy," came a man's voice.

"Gil told me that Five-Cent—"

"Yeah, I heard that. What's happened to Gil?"

Hiram told the story as he understood it.

"Sorry, did you say that she's being held by the city police? City of Helper, Utah?"

"Yes."

"And was she arrested in the city? Of Helper, Utah? Jeebus, what kind of name is that?"

"It comes from the railroad locomotives," Hiram said.

"What?"

"No," Hiram said. "She was arrested in one of the mining camps. They're outside the city."

"Okay," the union lawyer said. "So this is a pretty basic jurisdiction problem. Cops behaving badly, think they can get away with it because they're in a small town. They won't know what hit 'em."

"That sounds good," Hiram said.

"Tell Gil to sit tight, I'll be there late tonight with

the writ. First thing tomorrow, she'll be out, I guarantee it. And if they move her before that, give me a call again, will you?"

Hiram nodded, and then realized that Five-Cent Jimmy wouldn't hear the nod. "I will."

Jimmy hung up.

Mrs. Buford marched up with bacon grease flecks dotting the front of her robe. "That was two phone calls."

Hiram dug into his pocket, and produced a second coin for Mrs. Buford. He left her room and the woman slammed the door. When her turned to climb the hotel stairs, he was facing Michael.

Who was in his dirty socks.

Hiram froze. The book full of demons' signs and names felt very heavy in his coat pocket, as did the two metal lamens he'd taken from Gus's basement workroom.

"I'm disappointed," his son said.

"What do you mean?"

"When I discovered you'd accidentally walked off wearing my boots, I hoped you had at least gone to get pastries or something. You can understand my disappointment at learning that all you're doing is making a telephone call."

"Mary McGill's attorney," Hiram said. Had Michael heard his conversation with Mahonri, too?

"Yeah, I heard the whole thing. The door was open. You know, many men get awkward when talking to a girl. Leave it to you to get all mumble-mouthed when talking to a girl's *lawyer*."

"I was telling you yesterday, I'm not a ladies' man."

"On the other hand," Michael said, "*for once*, you

can't ask if I'm wearing my boots. Because *you're* wearing them."

"Sorry." Hiram retreated to a couch in the parlor, relieved that Michael hadn't mentioned Mahonri, Mahoun, or Samael. He sat and began unlacing the Harvesters.

"You have to remember that my feet are bigger than yours. That means that I *can't* wear *your* shoes."

Hiram stood and handed Michael his boots. "Now I can tell you to put your boots on. There are people I want to see in town. Eliza Kimball, for one."

"After we get some pastries?" Michael took a seat and put on the boots. The moment the right boot was laced up, Hiram felt easier.

"Pastries would be good," Hiram said. "Bacon would be better." He turned to the exit.

"Pap," Michael said.

"Yes?"

"*Your* boots are still up in the room."

Hiram grinned, blushing. Good, he'd retrieve his boots as well as the Oremus lamen he'd hid behind the mirror in their room. He wanted all the protection he could get.

Chapter Sixteen

AFTER BREAKFAST, HIRAM AND MICHAEL KNOCKED on Eliza Kimball's door in the Hotel Utah.

She opened it and stared. Hiram, caught off guard by the long, withering look, could only stand and endure it. Eliza had intense brown eyes sunk deep into a face that was smooth and youthful, other than faint crow's feet and a maze of wrinkles around her small mouth. She once might have had Ammon's coal-black hair, but now it was flecked with gray, tied back in a bun. Her dress and her small hat were both black.

Hiram had known actual nuns in France, but, on the score of severity, Eliza Kimball outnunned them all.

"So you're the Mormons who've been causing trouble."

Michael let out a noisy breath. "One Mormon, and one believer in science. Raised by Mormons, though."

Eliza stood unmoving in the open doorway. "I saw you two at the mine, and I confess that I was curious. Now that I've had a better look...good day."

Hiram found his mind blank.

"We have a letter you should see, Mrs. Kimball," Michael said.

God bless Michael.

"*Miss* Kimball." The woman corrected like a nun, too. She shifted her stare to Michael. "You're a bold young man, telling me what I *ought* to do. I can't have two men in my room alone. My standing in this part of the world is already so very uncertain."

"We could talk in the lobby," Michael suggested. "But I'm not sure you would want anyone listening in on our conversation, seeing as it involves financial matters."

Eliza tried to smile, but her mouth got stuck halfway. "Calling my bluff."

She stepped aside and waved them in.

"Thank you, Miss Kimball," Hiram said.

The sheets on the bed were tucked in tight and the bedspread arranged perfectly. The room had just enough space for the desk and a wash basin squeezed against one wall. The wallpaper matched the lobby's, gold swirls on brown. Standing against one wall was a large rectangular object wrapped in brown paper.

Like maybe a framed painting.

The place had a vaguely feminine odor, rose water perhaps, but mostly it smelled of the central heater's dust.

"You can sit on the bed," Eliza said to Michael. "And your father can take the chair."

"I'd feel better standing." Hiram removed his hat and ran his fingers across his scalp. "In the presence of a lady."

"I'd feel better if you did what I told you."

Hiram sat. He ached all over.

Michael sat, and Eliza closed the door.

"The letter," Eliza reminded them.

Hiram blushed, then gave it to her.

"Letter opener. There's one on the desk." Hiram swiveled and presented her the brass blade. She flicked open the envelope, saw the letter's heading, and threw it back at Hiram. The envelope struck his chest and fell to the floor.

"Tell Naaman Rettig the answer is no, from me, from my brothers, and from my deceased father. And even if my father's shade were in the D and RGW's pocket, we would not agree to throw our land to those vultures." She brandished the letter opener with white knuckles.

Hiram bent to pick up the envelope.

"You didn't even read it," Michael said. "What if Rettig offered you a million dollars?"

Eliza pointed the letter opener at him. "My father made that very mistake, choosing money over happiness. The mine, always the mine. Do you know what we did before he decided to sell his soul for coal?"

"Ranching," Hiram muttered.

Eliza snorted.

"You know, there are still cattle up in that canyon today," Michael said.

Eliza glared at Hiram like a hawk at a rabbit. "My earliest memories are of feeding chickens and milking goats with my mother, and riding horses into town, when Helper was nothing but a post office and a general store. Now the place reeks of debauchery, and the cliff above cringes."

"That's not a cringe." Michael smiled. "It's a bit of

Cretaceous sandstone leftover from an eroding edge of the Wasatch Plateau."

Eliza's piercing gaze flashed with anger. "Young man, you need to learn your place."

Michael's smile turned wicked. "Would that place be on the reservation?"

Eliza hissed. "You should show your elders more respect."

"Please forgive us our rough manners." Hiram stepped in. "We're just farmers, and a little uncivilized in our ways. Miss Kimball, the men at the mine need work. I make it, what, three hundred men? Maybe as many as a thousand people? The mine has to be reopened. Surely, you can see—"

Eliza cut him off. "See what? See that the mine has caused my family nothing but trouble? It broke up our family, killed Samuel's mother, and drove everyone away. The unrest of 1903 ruined my father's soul. He had been a gentle person who loved feeding horses from his hand, and he became a tyrant who would hold a man's children over his head to deny him three cents a ton. And as much as a struggle as it is to discipline the children of Connecticut, they never force each other into starvation."

"Why return?" Hiram asked. "To rebuild the family ranch?"

"To set things right." Eliza stood tall above them, her spine straight as a flagpole. "To give my brothers a third option. Samuel wants to dig a new shaft because he's scared of bogeymen, and Ammon is maniacal that the east seam will be the richest yet."

"*You* want cows," Michael offered.

Eliza nodded. "And peace."

"I'm not sure Samuel's wrong about the bogeymen," Hiram murmured. He instantly regretted it.

"You can't be serious," Michael said. "Either of you."

Hiram winced.

He found himself fingering his Saturn ring and looking at the wrapped rectangle. It must be a painting. He remembered the pinks and oranges of Samuel's desert landscape hanging over Ammon's mantel, the same images that had returned to Hiram in dream.

"*I* am serious," Eliza said. "And you and your father have nothing to say about any of this. Your part in this is not clear at all."

"We came to bring the miners food," Hiram said. "Only a couple of days' worth, it turns out."

"I heard that." Eliza's dark eyes glittered. "And yet now you seem to be a pawn of the railroad."

"The beets we brought won't do a thing if we don't address the real issue," Michael said.

"And ham," Hiram murmured. "And beans and flour."

"We have to get the mine back open," Michael continued. "You might need a dozen hands to ranch, but there are hundreds of men in the camp who need work. To eat."

"That is none of my concern." Eliza lightly stuck the point of the letter opener into her palm.

Hiram cleared his throat. "Is that one of Samuel's paintings?"

"It is."

Hiram couldn't stomach the cruelty of her gaze, and he let his eyes drop. "Can I see it?"

"Art aficionado?"

Hiram shrugged.

"What's your name, child?" she asked Michael.

"Michael. But I'm seventeen years old, so if I can't call you 'Mrs.' I think you can't call me 'child.'"

Eliza nodded. "That's fair."

"And my father is Hiram. He's single. And good with farm animals."

Hiram choked.

"Michael, will you help me with the painting?" the woman asked.

Michael stood and held the frame upright. Eliza sliced open the top and peeled away the paper to reveal a painting that was dementedly framed. Warped wood painted the color of rust met at irregular angles to form a rectangle that was approximate at best, and spangled with black feathers. The nails themselves were corroded and bent, and a line of staples ran up along one side of the frame like a suture, holding nothing together.

Eliza stood to the side and gestured at the painting. "My brother is obsessed with Apostate Canyon, and the rocks and caves there. He's working as a WPA artist, now, because of his obvious talent."

It was a companion piece to the painting in the Kimball parlor, with the same array of colors. The shape of the cliffs portrayed in pink and orange bothered Hiram, causing something beneath the surface of his mind to itch.

This painting too had pictographs on the canyon walls, but there were no flies. Hiram saw figures of men, surrounded by beasts with antlers. But they didn't look quite right.

Some of the antlered beasts had only two legs.

A chill trickled down his back and the hairs on his arms stood up. Maybe Samuel had harried them in their camp. His madness could be the result of some dark league, some magic that had shattered his mind. But why would he bother Hiram? Were Samuel and Samael in league? Was it stupid to find a connection in the similarity of those names?

And then Hiram recognized the lines of the ridge. He pulled the hand-copied sign of Mahoun or Samael from his pocket and held it up in front of the painting. He compared the rough sketch to the line of the cliff in the painting...

They matched perfectly.

"Are you an artist, Mr. Woolley? Or a critic? Have you been rendered dumb by my brother's gift?"

"I visited Ammon in the red house," Hiram said. "There's a painting like this above the mantel. Your brother paints good, I'll give him that."

"Paints *well*," Eliza corrected, just as Hiram was realizing his mistake.

"Come on, Pap," Michael put in. "You have to get your grammar right. We're in the presence of higher education here."

Eliza scorched him with her eyes. "If you speak well, young man, society might overlook the color of your skin."

Hiram winced.

Michael chuckled slowly, a sound like the purr of a mountain lion. "I'm sure that if I spoke with your impeccable style, the bigots of the Earth would overlook my melanin."

"Melanin?" Eliza frowned.

Michael jerked two thumbs at his own chest. "Melanin! This boy reads *Popular Science*. Yes, prejudice would be a thing of the past if only we recipients of ethnic disdain would make use of our adverbs more correctly. Or is that correcter? Correctlier?"

Eliza, stared for several seconds, her mouth open. Then she cleared her throat and let the painting relax against the wall. "Our business is at an end. You will return to Rettig and let him know our ranch is not for sale. And I'll wish you both a good day."

Hiram and Michael stood. Eliza stepped into the corner, giving them an exit.

Michael nodded. "We don't work for Rettig, Miss Kimball. All we really want is to get the mine back open. Thank you." He left the room.

Hiram hesitated in the doorway. "Miss Kimball, I apologize. Sometimes his passion exceeds his self-restraint. I've tried to... give him guidance."

"You should try harder," Eliza said coldly.

"I will." Hiram swallowed. "But I was wondering about a stone on the mantel in your family home. A plain brown stone with a line of quartz through the middle. Not very pretty, but it was right there, in the parlor, as if it was important. What can you tell me about that?"

"A stone?" Eliza's voice was cool.

"Yes, ma'am, a stone. Maybe it was your father's, or maybe it's Ammon's, but I thought it was striking that such a plain rock should sit in such a place of honor."

Hiram felt keen discomfort, locking eyes with the woman.

Eliza blinked first. And nodded. "Samuel talked about a stone. Father mailed it to him, apparently just before he disappeared. Maybe it was something Father found in the mine, a memento for his son. How *that* stone would come to be on Ammon's mantel, I can't imagine. As far as I know, in any case, it's just a rock."

"So your Father mailed it to him? And Samuel came back because of it?" Hiram asked.

"Samuel came back to paint the West, paid by the WPA. Someday art collectors around the world will be glad President Roosevelt gave artists the work."

Teancum Kimball had mailed his son Samuel a stone and then disappeared. Samuel had then returned to his family home. But then, how did the stone wind up on Ammon's mantel and not with Samuel out in the desert? Might this have something to do with the argument the two brothers had had at the mine opening? Maybe the stone had come with a letter, and the letter contained the information about the mine that Samuel was so confident that Ammon also knew?

Or . . . the stone was a peep-stone, a seer stone, and Samuel had had visions in it, and he believed Ammon had had the same visions. Had he given Ammon the stone?

Hiram would have to go to Apostate Canyon to ask Samuel directly.

"Thank you for your time." Hiram put his hat back on and left.

Michael was waiting for him at the end of the hall.

Hiram sighed. "Could you be a little less . . ."

"Caustic? Sarcastic? Opinionated? Clever? No, wait . . . brilliant?"

Hiram frowned.

"Probably not," Michael said. "Did you and Eliza Kimball have a moment? Is she going to be my new mother?"

Hiram guffawed, slapped his son on the back, and headed for the truck. "Come on, son, let's go to jail."

"Ah, the union lady." Michael followed Hiram down the hotel's stairs. "Is *she* my new mother?"

"I don't think you should expect to have any new mothers," Hiram told him. "But it's my fault she's in jail, and I'll do whatever I can to get her out."

"Like call her lawyer," Michael said.

"Yes."

Or employ more unusual means.

Chapter Seventeen

THE DOUBLE-A'S ENGINE REFUSED TO TURN OVER. When Hiram pressed the starter, it made no sound at all. He checked the key and the spark and tried again. Both he and Michael tried the crank with the throttle half-down and the ignition started. They inserted the metal arm into the socket in the front and spun the arm up, but the engine stayed dead.

"The good news," Michael said, "is that you just want to go to the jail next, and that's about two hundred yards down the street."

"Helper's a small town." Hiram made a face. "But if the truck won't start now, it probably won't start in an hour, either."

"Well, you've tried all the tricks you know."

"But I haven't tried all the tricks that the guy at Conoco knows."

A long whistle from a train shrieked and the city seemed to shake from the cry. Hiram took a deep breath; the train sound was *not* the whistle he had heard in the canyon. Hiram turned to lope down the street and Michael quickly caught up.

The man working at the Conoco had long arms, greasy hands, and a cheerful smile. A shock of red-orange hair peeked out from under his forest-green cap. Hiram checked the name embroidered on his shirt.

"Good morning, Bert. My Ford Double-A won't start. I'm thinking it's the spark plug, because I don't get any noise at all when I hit the starter. It's parked in front of the Hotel Utah. Can you walk up and take a look at it, or do we need to get it towed here?"

The mechanic looked up from the engine of the car he was working on. "I'll get to it in about half an hour. You can just leave the keys right there on the table."

Mary McGill woke to the sound of the door opening.

The drunks in the adjacent cell had been let out as they had sobered up, each receiving a lecture about the importance of savings and sobriety, and maybe it would be a good idea to let their wives control the spending. She had been dozing and dreaming of receiving just such a lecture herself when the door groaned open, and she sat up.

Police Chief Asael Fox entered first, swaggering across the room on his bowed legs. Behind him came the tall farmer, Hiram Woolley. Fox walked right to Mary's cage and grabbed it. "This gent here says he's got a message from your lawyer."

Mary stood. "I'm glad you've let him in."

"He also admits he ain't a lawyer himself. So I think I might just sit right here and listen while the two of you talk." Fox pressed his florid face to the strips of the cage. There was something wrong with his appearance, but Mary couldn't quite figure out what.

Hiram Woolley looked flummoxed.

"That's very generous of you, Chief," Mary said.

"How do you figure it?" Fox frowned.

She realized what was strange about his appearance. Where he gripped the cage with his right hand, Mary McGill saw a thumb and, opposing it, four fingers. But where he gripped with his left, there were a thumb and *five* fingers.

Six digits on his left hand.

"When I appeal my conviction," she said, "my attorney, Mr. Nichols, will show the judges in Salt Lake City how I was denied my right to the assistance of counsel, because when he sent his agent, Mr. Woolley, the police chief insisted upon eavesdropping."

Fox stared with beady eyes. "That ain't a thing."

"Sure it is," Mary said. "It's in the sixth amendment to the U.S. Constitution." She was no lawyer and couldn't have recited all the constitution's amendments, but she knew this one. "You know, in the Bill of Rights? The first ten amendments?" Without meaning to, she held up her hands, palm out, and wiggled her ten fingers at the policeman.

Fox hissed like a snake and leaped away. He glared at her and Woolley both as if he were considering just beating them with his nightstick then and there. Hiram Woolley gazed back coolly, and the policeman backed down.

"Fine!" he called over his shoulder as he retreated. "I'll just go get myself a cup of coffee. That means you got fifteen minutes, at most!"

"Maybe you should be a lawyer," Hiram Woolley said when the policeman had shut the door.

Mary curtseyed. "When this country has the laws its people deserve, then I'll hang out a shingle and speak at the bar. Until then, I have more urgent things to do."

Hiram nodded and said nothing.

"So you spoke to Jimmy?" Mary prompted him. "As I suspected, the police chief has not let me have another phone call."

Hiram suddenly looked flustered again. "Maybe I should have written it down. Jimmy says there's a problem with . . . jurisdiction, maybe? And he's on his way with a writ right now. He says hold on, no later than tomorrow morning you'll be out. If he's driving all the way from Denver, I guess he must value you highly."

"He might be taking a train." Mary smiled. "But he didn't say hold on."

"No?"

"No, he said *sit tight*. Didn't he?"

Hiram chuckled. "He did. I guess you know Jimmy."

"This isn't my first jail, and it isn't the first time Five-Cent Jimmy has come to fish me out of hot waters. Does that shock you, Hiram?"

"No," he said.

"So I'll sit tight."

He shuffled his feet. "I'm a little worried. Jimmy told me to keep an eye on you, in case they moved you."

"Where would they move me? There are only ten buildings in this town."

"I don't know," Hiram said. "But I guess if they're willing to arrest you when they have no legal right, you being outside of town at the time, they might be willing to do other things they have no legal right to."

"I don't want to say anything that will wound your tender heart," Mary McGill said, "but it wouldn't be my first *beating*, either."

"This is going to sound odd," Hiram said, then stopped.

"Go on," Mary told him. "I just noticed that the police chief has eleven fingers. Whatever you have to say can't be odder than that."

"It might be." Hiram reached into the pockets of his coat and produced two items: a cheap copper ring and a large dried leaf.

"What is that, mint? How adorable. You've come to propose marriage, and you're offering me tea as a dowry."

Hiram Woolley blushed. For a moment, Mary wondered whether she might want to spend more time with this Utah farmer, in a more romantic environment.

"Before I go any farther," Hiram said, "promise me you won't mention these things to my son."

"Does the boy despise tea?"

"You're teasing me, but I'm serious. This is between you and me."

The flustered air had fallen away, and Hiram looked as solemn as a priest.

"I promise," Mary said.

He handed her the leaf through the cage. "You'll see writing on that sage," he told her. "Those are the names of the twelve apostles."

"Ah, which twelve?" she asked. "I spent the better part of my youth at St. Francis Xavier Academy for Females in Chicago, you see, and I know that there's more than one list."

"I prefer John, where possible, only John doesn't

have a list of the twelve apostles. So I followed Matthew. Because, you know, Matthew was a tax collector, and that's kind of like being a lawyer."

Mary laughed, then caught herself. "You're serious."

"Very." Hiram nodded. "If it comes to an appearance in court, will you promise me you'll put this leaf in your shoe? Under your right heel, if possible, but in your shoe."

"You want me to wear a leaf listing the twelve apostles when I go to court."

"Under your heel. In your shoe."

"My God," Mary said. "You're a witch."

Hiram grimaced. "A witch is what you call someone who means harm. I mean you no harm, Mary McGill."

Out of shock, or tenderness for the open-faced farmer and his tough, timid ways, Mary found herself taking the leaf. "I'll wear the sage to court. And I won't mention it to the boy."

"And here's the other thing." He nodded and held up the copper ring. It had a rough inscription that read † ACHIO † NOYA †.

Smart comments flooded into Mary's mind, and she bit them all back, giving the farmer time to explain himself.

"This ring helps a person escape from prison," he said. "It will help *you*."

"Magic words?" she managed to ask without laughing.

"A special name of God that Joshua used to defeat twenty-two kings and make the sun stand still."

"I don't remember Joshua's ring from when the nuns told me the story."

"Not everything was passed down in the Bible." His gaze was so solemn and so vulnerable, she took the ring.

"How does the magic work?" she asked. "Does it turn me invisible, or help me slip through the bars?"

"I dislike the word *magic*," Hiram said. "People expect that magic means you fly, or you can catch bullets, or you throw around balls of fire. Most charms are much subtler than that."

"Okay." Mary nodded. "How does this charm work?"

"Wear the ring," he said. "You'll get out of this jail."

"I'll get out... because Jimmy will show up with the writ?"

"Maybe," Hiram said. "Maybe the ring will stop Jimmy from getting a flat tire, so he gets to you in time. Or maybe it will make the judge better disposed to your case. Or maybe it will make the police chief change his mind and let you go. Or maybe it will cause an earthquake, and you'll walk out of the ruins of this building."

"Like St. Peter." Mary smiled modestly. "The nuns told me that one, too."

"Will you please wear the ring?"

"I'll wear your ring, Hiram Woolley," she said. "I can see you have faith in it, and didn't Jesus say that if you had faith like a grain of mustard seed, you could move mountains?"

At the word *mustard*, a shadow flitted across Hiram's face, but then he smiled. "That's exactly right."

She put the ring on her finger. "Two charms together should do the trick, don't you think?"

Hiram nodded.

Mary smiled. "And where are you off to now, then?"

Hiram took a deep breath and blew air out through loose lips. "Now I have to go figure out what's wrong with my truck."

✧   ✧   ✧

Hiram and Michael walked back to the car in silence.

Mary McGill's questions had Hiram thinking. Did he know a charm that would get the car started?

He knew plenty of healing charms, and healing charms were flexible. You could take a hex for warts and apply it to blisters, with a few changes. A charm that eased the pain of a broken arm could relieve the pains of childbirth, with some word substitutions.

Could he adjust one of his healing charms to heal a car?

But surely, it was a dead sparkplug, and Bert from Conoco would have it replaced by now.

Only when they reached the Double-A, they found Bert sitting behind the wheel, turning the key and pressing the starter in vain, with an expression of frustration on his face that mixed in large quantities of bafflement and was quickly mounting toward rage.

"You changed the sparkplug, I guess," Hiram said.

"This is the second plug I put into your truck, mister, and it still ain't turning over. I checked all the connections, they're good. I tried to crank her up until I nearly broke my arm. I can't figure it out."

Hiram felt a cold fist wrapped around his heart. "Let me look."

Under the hood of the Double-A, everything appeared in order. But when Hiram lay on his back in the street and scooted beneath the truck, he found what he'd been looking for: a scrap of paper, stuck to the bottom of the engine with wads of chewing gum. He pried the paper and the gum off and tucked it into his pocket as he stood.

"Alright, I'll figure this out, Bert. How much do I owe you?"

"Not a thing. I didn't get it to start."

"Can I give you fifty cents for your time?" he suggested.

"Only a fool would say no."

With Bert walking back to the Conoco with two new quarters in his pocket, Hiram climbed into the back of the truck and opened his toolbox. "Stay in the truck, will you?" he called to Michael. "I have to take care of something."

"Is that *something* finding another mechanic?" Michael climbed into the cab. "Perhaps a . . . *lady* mechanic?"

"Sort of." Hiram dug into his tool chest and found the bit of wooden shingle from Gus Dollar's roof. He touched the brass plate and the lead lamen he'd taken from the old man's basement workshop, shaking his head. *The Lord hath given you the city* . . . what wall did Gus Dollar want to bring tumbling down? He shut the chest again and hopped down.

Then he picked a restaurant—the letter in the front window read MANDURINO'S and its front door was open—and stepped inside. As he walked, he examined the paper he'd taken from the underside of the truck. It was a written *Sator Arepo* charm:

SATOR

AREPO

TENET

OPERA

ROTAS

Someone had hexed the truck. Not just anyone but, it seemed clear, *Gus Dollar* had hexed the Double-A. He had overcome Hiram's defenses to do it. The lamen in the truck's door should have blocked the spell, or if not that, then the two chi-rho amulets he and Michael carried—one around his neck, and the other in Michael's boot.

Was Gus simply a stronger magician than Hiram?

Or had Hiram compromised his craft? Had he failed to keep a chaste and sober mind, so that his defenses failed?

Mary McGill? Did his attraction to the union organizer render him unchaste? But surely, no.

And what about Gus? He had vandalized Gus's shop, convinced he'd been justified, and then he'd stolen from the man.

Had he been wrong to do so?

Had he exposed himself and Michael to danger by wronging Gus?

And what else did the charm consist of?

He gave the hostess a friendly smile and walked back, as if headed to the restrooms. Instead, he stepped into the kitchen.

There it was, the big pizza oven, with an open mouth and with burning wood lining the inside. Hiram tore the sheet of paper right through the *Sator Arepo* grid, balled it up, and threw it into the flames. Then he tossed in Gus's shingle, too.

Burning thatch from a witch's roof was a good counter magic. Gus had no thatch, but the shingle should work.

"Thou shalt not suffer a witch to live," he murmured, and, "I am Gabriel, that stand in the presence of God." Gabriel was the archangel who had dominion over flame.

He watched a few moments to be certain that the

paper and the shingle both took fire, then turned to leave.

"*Ma tu, che ci fai qui*?" a big-chested man in striped trousers and an apron yelled at him.

"Thank you." Hiram left the kitchen.

"Wow," Michael said when he reached the truck. "Again, you let me down with the food. You go into a pizzeria and don't come out with pizza. Shakespeare couldn't write a worse tragedy."

"I must disappoint you profoundly." Hiram climbed into the passenger side of the cab.

Michael shook his head. "You didn't bring the lady mechanic, either. But I know you're doing your best."

Hiram laughed. "Try starting the truck now."

Michael pumped the clutch and pressed the starter. The Double-A coughed into life.

"Let's fill up the tank and the gas can at the Conoco," Hiram suggested.

Chapter Eighteen

ON THE DRIVE UP SPRING CANYON TOWARD APOS-
tate Canyon to see Samuel, Hiram debated internally.
The lamen in the door of the Double-A had failed to
protect them from Gus's curse.

If they got in a wreck, it would also fail to protect
Michael from injury.

By the time they'd reached Dollar's, Hiram had
come to a decision.

"Stop the car," he said. "Wait for me here."

"Coke?" Michael asked.

Hiram felt thirsty, too. So Gus had restored his
poppet-charm and was once again besting Hiram.
There was probably no way harm could come of a
couple of Cokes, as long as Hiram himself chose them
out of the icebox, so he didn't get doctored drinks.

"Okay," he said.

Hiram turned the knob of the front door with a
heavy and conflicted heart. Making amends was the
right thing to do, both because the Bible taught that he

should, and because his defenses would only have power as long as he was worthy. Also, he didn't want to have Gus Dollar interfering in his activities anymore. And short of burying the hatchet with the man, he worried he'd be constantly engaged in a running battle of hexes.

And Hiram didn't *know* that Gus was working evil. He might have the German book for instruction's sake, or to satisfy his curiosity, rather than for the purpose of summoning anything.

Hiram couldn't let fear stop him from doing what was right.

The two Rottweilers saw Hiram, but rather than bark, they broke into a cowed whimper and slunk out of sight.

Gus Dollar stood behind the counter, frowning. "I gave your boy a free Coke."

Hiram nodded. "That was kind. And I repaid it by stealing from you. I'm sorry."

"And destroying my property."

"I'll pay the damages."

"I don't want you to pay the damages. I want you to explain yourself."

Hiram sighed. "I'm trying to get the miners back to work. And I thought . . . maybe . . . you were involved in the closing of the mine."

"And now you think it's someone else instead?"

Hiram hesitated. "I think you know something about it. Something you don't want to tell me."

"Those idiots Ammon and Samuel Kimball can't agree what to do with their mine. If they wreck it and the mine shuts permanently, you understand that I lose a third of my livelihood. Why in God's name would I do that?"

"I guess that's right," Hiram said. "But what do

you know about the closing? What is it that you aren't telling me?"

Gus sighed. "The Kimball family is under a malign influence."

Hiram wrapped his hand around the egg-shaped stone in his pocket. "A witch?"

"Something older. A demon that lives beneath the earth."

Hiram thought of the crack in Gus's basement room. "And you're in league with it."

"No!" Gus's voice was firm. "No, I use my lore to protect myself against it!"

The bloodstone was inert.

"Do you know how to overcome the demon?" Hiram asked.

"I wanted to defeat it with a Book of the Spirits," Gus said. "You destroyed that."

"I'm sorry I did that." Hiram didn't offer to return the two lamens he had taken.

"I'm sorry I spooked you with my books," Gus said.

Hiram was tired, and his thoughts meandered more than he would have liked. "I also got spooked by you charming me."

"What, the customer lure? I diabolically seduced you into coming into my store, so I could give your son a free Coca-Cola?"

"That isn't all. You also got me talking, made me share a lot of private things."

Gus Dollar nodded. "I apologize. But consider it from my point of view. I am the only practicing cunning man up here in these hills. Yes, I sell Cokes and sewing needles and washing machines and canned beef, but you know what else I sell?"

"Cures," Hiram guessed. "Scryings. Love charms."

"And all the usual things. So when you showed up, and demonstrated you had some craft, I had to know more. Were you going to be a competitor? Were you going to reveal my secrets?"

"What charm did you use?" Hiram asked. "It was effective."

"And also simple." Gus held up his hand, revealing a silver ring with a sapphire.

Hiram didn't need to see the sign that must inevitably be engraved on the ring, likely on the inside of the band, or its embedded signet, perhaps cupped in Gus's palm. "Jupiter."

"Cast by myself, with a stone I selected myself from the mine, all things done during the reign of the Jovial planet. *You* wear a Saturn ring. I see the signet: a man riding a dragon, with a sword in one hand and an egg in the other. Are you a dreamer?"

"Sometimes." Hiram thought of his dreams of driving along the road, looking for Michael, and tried to dismiss them from his mind. Hadn't his dream dictionary suggested that he was supposed to receive a letter today?

"The *Picatrix* warns any man who would wear the ring of Saturn to beware eating the flesh of ducks and entering into any shadowy place."

"Duck isn't a large part of my diet." Hiram didn't want to think about shadowy places, or about the fact that he hadn't read the *Picatrix*. He knew the name, but it was an old book, such as you might find in Latin or Egyptian, and very rare. "Jupiter isn't the only influence you channel in this place."

Gus hesitated. "Yes, the seals in the windows."

"Is that the demon influencing the Kimballs? Samael? Mahoun?"

Gus nodded. "But not by my doing. I put those seals into the windows to protect myself. To protect myself and . . . maybe to channel a little power."

Hiram frowned. "That's a dangerous way to operate, Mr. Dollar."

Gus removed his glass eye and rubbed a knuckle into the empty socket. Then he sighed. "Look, this place. You're from Utah Valley, aren't you?"

"Lehi."

"Big freshwater lake there. Good fishing, there's the Provo River, all those fruit trees. It's a nice place to farm. One of the best in the state."

"I don't understand your point." Hiram put a hand into his pocket and wrapped his fingers around the heliotropius. It was cool and inert.

Gus Dollar sighed. "*This* land, on *this* side of the mountains, is different. It's dry and hot and hard. There is wealth under the rocks, but it only comes to the surface with a great sacrifice of sweat and blood. You've seen the strange stones, down by Moab?"

"The arches. Yes."

"A geologist will have a neat explanation for those arches. Ancient inland sea, wind and water erode the stone into patterns that only look strange, but are completely comprehensible when you understand their true nature. A neat explanation, but nonsense."

"I guess you favor a different view."

"Strange complex patterns that are completely comprehensible when you understand their nature?" Gus's eyes gleamed. "Of course, I do! This land was made by angels, my friend, and their signs are written upon its face."

"I've heard people call it 'God's country.'"

Gus laughed bitterly. "Wrong angels. No, there are angels here, trapped beneath the stone, but they are outcasts, rebels, sinners, angels who have become devils. *Theirs* is the strongest influence that can be channeled here in the Wastes of Dudael. Yes, I take measures to protect myself, and yes, to feed my family, to make my business prosper, to bring me the kind of affluence that lets me give your son a free Coca-Cola, I dare to channel that power as well."

Hiram thought he knew the name *Dudael*, too, but he let it lie. Was Gus insane? Likely not. Was he misled about the nature of the powers he sought to deal with? Maybe.

But the bloodstone lay still in his pocket.

"This is why you have the opening in your basement," he said.

"Power comes up through the hole. As long as my signs were in place, the angel itself could not pass." Gus leaned forward to look Hiram in the eye. "It would be very, very bad if the angel got out."

Hiram wanted to kick himself. "I put your family at risk when I damaged your seals." No wonder his charms had stopped working.

Gus shrugged. "And yourself."

"A fallen angel," Hiram said. "You think that's what's at the root of the trouble in the Kimball family."

"Of course, it is."

Hiram shook his head. "Look, I'll be candid. I don't like what you're doing. I think it's a mistake. I think you're going to get yourself hurt really bad, and maybe some of that hurt will come down on your children and grandchildren."

"Maybe," Gus agreed. "And the hurt is more likely, if you destroy my protective wards again."

"I guess that's a fair point. But I have to ask you some questions."

"Do you wish to lay the tongue of a frog on my chest, to be certain my answers are true?"

In fact, Hiram very much liked the idea of doing just that. But he shook his head. "I've got other ways."

"Your stone."

Hiram gripped the heliotropius. "Are you causing Ammon and Samuel to fight?"

"No."

The bloodstone lay still.

"Are you trying to close down the mine?"

"No."

The stone gave Hiram no warning.

"Did you put a Sator Arepo charm on my truck, to stop it working?"

"Of course, I did. You burgled my shop. I wanted to stop you from coming back up the canyon."

True. Hiram sighed and took his hand from his pocket. "I've brought your book and I'll give it back to you."

"You mean the one you stole, of course, and not the one you burned to ash."

"I said I'd pay for the damages."

"You couldn't afford them, beet farmer. I forgive the debt."

Hiram laid Gus's German book on the counter. "I couldn't read it, anyway."

Gus nodded. "A little language skill goes a long way, in this trade. Do you know any Latin?"

"Just English," Hiram admitted.

Gus left the book on the counter, untouched. "If you're looking for a way to open the mine, have you considered divination? I assume you haven't *dreamed* an answer, or you wouldn't be accusing me."

"You mean like sieve and shears? I'd need two people to work that charm, and I don't have two people I can confide in."

"We could do it now," Gus said.

"You and I couldn't. You need two people in addition to the charm-worker, two people who have no interest in the outcome."

"You and I *alone* couldn't," Gus agreed. "But with my two grandchildren we could."

Gus was right. The two tow-headed children he'd seen running around the shop would be perfect. But he had to be careful. Could he trust Gus fully? Gus was powerful, and at the very least was willing to *channel* the energy of dark powers.

But Gus had shown good will, admitting his sabotage of the truck and his use of the fallen angel's sign, and also forgiving Hiram's destruction of his Book of the Spirits. Gus might genuinely want to assist Hiram.

And in any case, Gus's intentions were irrelevant, if he could help Hiram marshal the resources for sieve and shears.

Hiram would simply have to be certain *he* was the one doing the asking.

Hiram nodded. "I'd be grateful for your help in giving it a try."

"Children!" Gus bellowed. "Greta! Dietrich! Come help your Opa Gus for a moment!" The two children scrambled into the store like beads of water on a hot skillet, hissing and bouncing off each other. Gus leaned in Hiram's direction confidentially. "They're twins. And there is magic in twins."

Hiram nodded. Christ, some accounts said, was a twin, Thomas being his double. And James and John were known to be twins.

"Come over here, children," Gus instructed Greta and Dietrich. "Come stand on these chairs, we're going to play a funny little game. The game is to see how long you can hold a sieve without dropping it."

"Hold a sieve?" The girl picked up the circle of tin with the mesh bottom.

"That's easy!" The boy snatched the hoop from his sister.

"Hey!" the girl protested.

Gus smiled at the two. "We shall see. The great trick is that you must hold it with a pair of shears."

Gus set up the divination and Hiram considered the questions he would ask. When investigating a theft, sieve and shears was used to ask who the guilty party was. Here, the parties all seemed guilty, so he must ask a different question. What he really wanted to know, as he thought of Teancum Kimball's three children, was which one he needed to persuade.

Maybe then Gus would help him protect the mine and the Kimball family from Samael.

Gus wedged the blades of the shears around the rind of the sieve, the sieve hanging underneath the shears. "Now," he instructed the children, "when I say *begin*, you must try to hold it. But you must hold it only by pressing just your middle fingers here...and here. Understood?" The children nodded. To Hiram, Gus said, "Will you do the speaking?"

Hiram took a deep breath and knelt. "Yes."

The children put their fingers on opposite sides of the handle and pressed, holding the sieve suspended in the air. "Begin." Gus stepped back.

"By St. Peter and by St. Paul, and by the sons of Zebedee, if it's Ammon whose heart must soften all, turn about shears and let sieve fall." The line about the sons of Zebedee was improvised, and aimed at capturing the magic that is inborn in twins. It ruined the rhyme, but Hiram felt that was a good trade.

The sieve didn't budge.

"By St. Peter and by St. Paul, and by the sons of Zebedee, if it's Samuel whose heart must soften all, turn about shears and let sieve fall."

The sieve held. Greta and Dietrich smiled like cupids.

"By St. Peter and by St. Paul, and by the sons of Zebedee, if it's Eliza whose heart must soften all, turn about shears and let sieve fall."

Nothing happened. The children smiled.

Hiram looked at Gus and the German shrugged.

Hiram was at a loss. "By St. Peter and by St. Paul, and by the sons of Zebedee, if it's all three Kimballs' hearts that must soften all, turn about shears and let sieve fall."

The sieve abruptly twisted, slipped sideways from the grip of the shears, and struck Hiram in the chest before falling to the floor. He stood.

Gus, who had been waiting and watching the shears intently, snatched them from the air before they could hit anything.

"I won," Dietrich said.

"No, I won," Greta said. "You slipped, I felt it."

"You were both very good at this game," Gus said.

"So good, I believe I must award you each an animal cracker as a prize."

"I want a monkey!" Greta clapped her tiny hands together. "The monkey is cute!"

"The hippo is biggest!" Dietrich snapped his mouth open and shut in imitation of a hippo. "I want a hippo."

Gus gave his grandchildren animal crackers and Hiram stepped back, lost in thought.

All of them. *All* of the Kimballs needed to soften their hearts. With Ammon and Eliza, he'd accomplished *nothing*. Could Samuel be different? Could Samuel be the key?

"Thank you," he murmured.

"Are you and I friends again?" Gus asked.

"I don't think we're enemies," Hiram told him. "Maybe later you can help me protect the Kimballs."

Gus nodded. "Or maybe the Kimballs are safer if they move away from this place."

Feeling numb, Hiram headed for the truck.

Chapter Nineteen

MICHAEL DROVE THEM PAST THE KIMBALL MINE, and then up the winding road and the left fork. Before starting up the track that skirted the mountain to get to Apostate Canyon, they stopped at their previous campsite. The hobo stove was still there, cold and lying on its side.

Hiram and Michael loaded the stove into the bed of the Double-A and kept going. The truck bounced along the road, jostling over exposed tree roots, chugging up over shoulders of slickrock, and screaming down the other side. At one point, Hiram had to get out to soften the slope of a stone shelf by piling additional rocks to build a ramp for the truck.

For all that Hiram was sweating and his muscles beginning to ache, though, Michael grinned like a cat on the hunt.

"You can't be enjoying this, son. If we break an axle or open our oil pan, it's a long walk down."

"Ease up, Pap, this truck is indestructible and I'm the best driver there ever was."

Hiram sighed.

They finally topped the ridge. Descending into the canyon on the other side by an easier road, they saw a clearing below sharp cliffs that ran from pink to a chalky white. In the clearing lay scattered squared-off red boulders like forgotten dice from an interrupted game, and among them a camp, with firepit, tent, and even easels.

It took an hour to make the descent and by that time the sun was starting to sink behind them. The lengthening shadows brought an anxious itch between Hiram's shoulder blades. He didn't relish the idea of being out in the desert at night, exposed to another ambush.

The interview would just have to be to the point.

Hiram wanted to see Samuel's paintings, try and suss out the strange lines of the ridge, and ask Samuel about the stone on the mantel. Also, Hiram wanted to know more about Samuel's plan to drop a new shaft. Where had that come from? If Hiram was right, and the brown rock was a peep-stone, had the *stone* shown him the location for the new shaft? And why would a WPA painter care about the mine he'd run from so many years before?

He'd mention the D and RGW offer, though not until the very end.

Michael turned up and drove until he had to stop in front of two gargantuan rocks blocking the way. A narrow slit between them allowed access into the clearing beyond.

They got out of the truck; Hiram brought the revolver.

"Samuel Kimball?" Hiram hollered. "My name's Hiram Woolley. My son and I have come to talk with you."

A crow cawed in the distance. A breeze mussed a stand of pinyon pines.

"Come on." Hiram went first.

He had to turn sideways to edge his way through the crack and he had memories of the trenches, when a shell would hit close enough to collapse the wall, and you'd have to wiggle your way through the debris and the bodies.

He remembered such a collapse, when Yas Yazzie had run out of ammunition for his rifle, and had seized a dead lieutenant's Colt M1917. The six bullets in that revolver had been the difference between life and death that day, when Yas had shot the first three German soldiers over the wall and the others had turned back. He'd saved the platoon and kept the weapon, scratching his initials into it.

Of course, the Colt hadn't saved Yas in his final battle, two months later.

Hiram carried that same revolver now. He swallowed a few times, shook a drop of sweat from his nose, and finally made it to the other side.

And into a different world.

The air on this side smelled of pine, charnel house, and dust. Hiram hoped there wasn't a human corpse in the camp.

Easels stood everywhere, a couple dozen at least, some with paper flapping against their clips and others bare. One had a rotting crow strapped to it, the wings spread wide and the bird's skull showing through the rot. Another had mice nailed to the wood. Flies abounded, but not the fat flies Hiram had been seeing for the past two days.

On one canvas, Samuel had incorporated a dead

cat in his painting and it dropped maggots across the drawing of the pink cliff faces. Scrawled indifferently across the canvas and the feline corpse alike was the name SAMUEL, in red paint and confused letters.

Or was that *SAMAEL?*

Hiram couldn't be sure.

Cow bones lay stacked in piles. A campfire smoked beneath a tripod and a boiling kettle, but Hiram smelled nothing that reminded him of food, and had no interest in seeing what might be cooking.

A neat tent, with square shoulders formed by freshly cut pine poles, stood a few paces from the cooking pit. The sun threw long shadows within and behind the canvas structure, and Hiram half expected something awful to rise out of those pockets of darkness.

He wrapped his wool coat tighter around him.

"Holy jeez, Pap. What's this guy's problem?" Michael had made it through the crack and stood next to him.

"He's an artist, son. It's why I don't want you to play the guitar too much."

"Real funny."

It was a good joke, but Hiram's stomach was twisted in knots.

"Samuel Kimball?" he called.

No answer.

"Keep your eyes peeled, son." Hiram walked up to an easel with a complete painting, but this wasn't of the landscape, though it had similar colors, pinks, creams, a little red of the sunset. Instead of a cliff face, it bore the image of a man, with a full beard and black dots for eyes. Hiram waited for a moment for those eyes to sprout wings and buzz off, then relaxed when they stayed put.

Hiram stepped closer to the painting. It reminded him of the daguerreotype he'd seen of Teancum Kimball. Below the man's forest of a beard someone had pinned a letter in rough handwriting.

February 13, 1933.

Dear Samuel,

Enclosed is a stone. It's a dear thing to me and it's guided me through the more fertile parts of this wilderness. The stone assures me now that you will understand. I don't suppose you'd come home. I'm making another deal of thirty years that might change things. It might not turn out right because it's so easy to get lost down there. Either way, Ammon will need his people. God knows, few enough of us have survived.

You might not love me, but we're family. Family should stick together.

Love,
Your father.

P.S. Don't talk to Eliza about this letter or the stone. She wouldn't understand.

Michael read it alongside him. "Another thirty-year deal? And where's he going to get lost . . . down in Helper?"

Hiram didn't say a word. His intuition was itching and if he kept quiet, that itch might turn into answers.

"The mine," Michael said. "Maybe you can get lost down there in the mine. Maybe it was a thirty-year deal about some new seam. Or he bought new equipment, modern drills or whatever. But, Pap, how can a stone guide anyone? Is this like Urim and Thummim stuff? Or the Leporello?"

What was the easy answer here, that neither opened Hiram to mockery nor led down to a conversation of Grandma Hettie's occult lore? "Yes. Like the Urim and Thummim. And you're thinking of the Liahona."

"I'm pretty sure a Leporello is something. Anyway, a guy asking for information out of a rock is obviously nuts."

Hiram shrugged, pondering the note. Another deal of thirty years? A guiding stone—well, that pretty definitively explained the rock on Ammon's mantel, at least. It *must* be a seer stone. And apparently Teancum had seen in a vision in the seer stone itself that he should send it to Samuel. Had Samuel given the stone to Ammon because of a similar vision? Was it because of visions in the peep-stone that Samuel was convinced he must sink a new shaft to save the mine, and believed that Ammon had the same knowledge? Did Samuel have reason to think that Ammon had used the same peep-stone?

And who or what was giving the Kimballs visions through their seer stone? A benign power, as Teancum Kimball seemed to have thought? Or something more wicked, something such as the fallen angel Samael?

And Michael's initial question remained. Was Teancum referring to the mine? Did he send his son the seer stone and then go down the mine, trying to make a deal but fearing he'd lose his way?

A whistle broke Hiram out of his reverie. He was far too far from the train tracks for the sound to be coming from a train. He shook his head.

Tripping down through the scree at the base of the ridge came a man with black hair and round glasses over his sunken eyes. Samuel Kimball.

Samuel was carrying an easel and a satchel hung off a shoulder. His palette was attached to the satchel by a piece of string and paint spackled his pants with every step.

He bounced into the camp and put his easel down. "You come to arrest me, sir?" His hands fluttered around his chest.

Samuel must be right around thirty. Hiram remembered someone telling him that Samuel's mother had died giving birth. Did that have something to do with Teancum's deal?

"My pap here is a farmer," Michael said. "I'm his driver. And future scientist."

"I remember you," Samuel said. "Henry Furry?"

Michael laughed, coughed, and choked.

"Hiram Woolley. Are you out here painting for the WPA?"

"I am, sir. I am." Samuel set up his easel, showing them his painting.

A shiver went through Hiram. It was a close cousin of the two he'd already seen, the same ridge, the pictographs, and the symbol that came together in the rough outline of the landscape. Hiram pivoted where he stood, examining the ridges surrounding the camp. None of them resembled the glyph he'd copied from Gus's window at all, or Samuel's painting. To be sure, Hiram slipped the scrap of paper from his pocket and compared.

Samuel was imposing the sign in Gus's window on the landscape, over and over again in all his paintings.

Why?

The pictographs in this painting weren't of men battling beasts, but of a cyclone tossing bodies in three directions: two men and a woman, with lines for a dress. Beneath the three lay an outline that looked like the head of a snake, or a lizard.

Samuel threw out his hands. "Sir, the air is alive, can you feel it? This is Apostate Canyon, the canyon of the great rebel. I have fallen away, and yet I am reborn. You, Indian brave, can you feel it? You must. Your kind were born in the heart of the desert."

"Not *my* kind," Michael said. "I grew up in a house by the lake."

Samuel lurched forward. His glasses glowed in the light of the setting sun, and Hiram couldn't see his eyes. He'd behaved oddly before, when he'd faced off with his brother at the mine entrance, but here, in his camp, he seemed stranger still.

Samuel's fingers gripped Hiram's arm. "You know. You're a special one, I know it. And other…things… do, too. The spirits of the canyon, fallen away, to find freedom. They have a purpose for you. I have seen it!"

"In the stone?" Hiram gripped the painter's shoulder.

Samuel ignored the question. He lifted Hiram's hand and pressed his lips to it. "You've come to help me. You've come to show Brother Ammon the error of his ways. The mine is emptied out, cursed, and haunted. It is the valley of the shadow of death, and no man should tread there without fear. But I know where to find coal! The wise response to the current crisis is to dig a new shaft. I've seen what Kimball Canyon can become, what we can all become. Please, Mr. Furry, please."

Samuel seemed to be echoing what Gus had said

about fallen angels, and gave the impression that he was being fed his information through the seer stone. If Gus was right and the Kimballs were under Mahoun's influence, did that mean the demon was speaking to them through the stone?

As gingerly as he could, Hiram extricated his paw from the young Kimball's grip.

Michael looked coiled, ready to spring.

"Samuel, how do you know you're right?" Hiram asked. "Is your father's stone guiding you?"

The painter stepped back and hissed. "You've heard about the haunted mine tunnels. If you've talked to Sorenson, you have. But he doesn't believe. Dimitrios, Stavros, they understand."

Another shiver slid a cold finger down Hiram's spine. "I don't have a side in this. I just want the men in the mine to make some money, get out of debt, and get their families food. Greeks and Germans and all the rest. Maybe you, Ammon, and Eliza can all sit down, and I can be there, to help you all hash things out."

Samuel reached into his pocket and got out a cigarette. In his pocket, he found a match, which he lit with the flick of his thumb. He sucked in the smoke. "Maybe you don't understand, Hiram. I thought you might. But you don't."

"You were close to your sister, weren't you?" Hiram asked.

The smell of the cigarette hit Hiram; whatever Samuel Kimball was smoking, it wasn't tobacco.

Samuel relaxed, sucking some from his cigarette. "Eliza loved my mother, begged her to escape with her, during the riots. She never had much use for me. I killed my mother."

Michael stood a few steps back, arms crossed over his chest and eyes wide.

"You didn't kill your mother, Samuel," Hiram said. "She died in childbirth. It happens a lot."

Elmina hadn't even made it *that* far.

Samuel blew out smoke. "It only had to happen to me once. My sister, half-sister really, took me in. I was grateful for it, but she was never warm to me."

"I bet if you talked to Dimitrios and the other Greeks," Hiram said slowly, "you could convince them the mine is still viable. Or at least, that you should finish mining the last of the coal in the eastern seam before dropping a new shaft. And then they could get back to work, get paid. We could bring in a priest, maybe, to put the men's minds at ease. There's a Catholic church in Helper. St. Anthony's, I think."

"You should leave, sir. The road back is rough. I've disappointed you, Mr. Furry, I feel sorry for that. I can't capitulate. Ammon will have to bend to the will of heaven. And Eliza will be irrelevant once Ammon sees the truth."

Hiram sighed, regretting that he had ever agreed to help Naaman Rettig. "The railroad has made an offer to buy the mine. You wouldn't be interested in a deal like that?"

Samuel stubbed out his cigarette and tucked it back into his pocket. "The D and RGW will never have our land. Not while a single Kimball is alive. We are sacred guardians."

Hiram glanced at the pictographs on the painting and that cyclone, killing what had to be Ammon, Samuel, and Eliza. To defend the lizard's head? *Not while a single Kimball is alive.*

Though if they all died, Naaman Rettig might get his deal.

Or would another Kimball relative appear to be guided by the stone on the mantel? Teancum had had four wives, that Hiram knew about. Apparently, many of the children had died young, while the wives themselves had fled. Could there be further living half-siblings? Or cousins?

But Hiram had a more pressing question. "Your name, Samuel. Have you ever seen it ... with a different spelling?"

"Sam," Samuel said instantly. "S-A-M. Also S-A-M-M-Y. But that are kids' names, and I'm a man."

"Never S-A-M-A-E-L?"

Samuel looked at Hiram with big eyes, then started to laugh. He held his belly and kept laughing, laughed so hard he fell to the ground. And still didn't stop laughing.

Hiram left without ceremony. He and Michael returned to the truck; with Michael driving, they headed back over the ridge. The boy was quiet, and didn't seem to enjoy the tricky driving nearly as much as he had on the way in. Night fell while they were still atop the ridge; they had to slow to a crawl.

When they started down the other side of the mountain, Michael finally broke the silence. "He's crackers. Full-on Saltines, or what are those new ones you like, the ones that taste like butter?"

"Ritz."

"He's Ritz crackers. And he's convinced the Greeks that his crackers taste good. Like salty butter. And magic rocks? Please."

Hiram took a deep breath. "Maybe you're right."

But what had *caused* Samuel to lose his mind? Or what was *causing* his madness now?

Rattling along the narrow crest of the ridge, the truck sputtered and died. Hiram guessed they were half a mile from their camp of the previous night.

Michael tried the starter again and the truck sat dead.

Damn Gus Dollar. While Hiram had been foolish enough to make amends, Gus had done something to the car again.

But making amends didn't make Hiram a fool. He'd gone in, as a Christian, turning the other cheek. And it was only because he was Christian that he had any power. And Gus had been forthright, hadn't he? And Samuel had seemed to corroborate Gus's words.

Hiram and Michael climbed out of the Double-A and into the cold. "Anyway," Hiram said, "I hope you've learned something about the dangers of art."

"You already told that joke, Pap. We might be sleeping in the truck tonight, you know. There's nothing but rocks around us. Besides, shouldn't you be lecturing me about the dangers of giggle-smokes?"

"No," Hiram said. "You're not that stupid." The warm car felt good against the chill.

Michael opened the hood while Hiram went for the kerosene lantern and the crank.

He had only taken two steps when he heard a high-pitched staccato laughter.

Chapter Twenty

"GET IN THE TRUCK, SON." HIRAM CREPT TO THE back of the Double-A, the revolver heavy in his hand. They'd broken down on a shelf of rock, out in the open. The moonless night sky wouldn't help, but at least it was clear.

More laughter and then a howl, but Hiram wasn't sleepy this time; he was awake and ready for them. His hand was steady and his weapon loaded.

Michael got into the truck and tried the starter again. Nothing happened.

A gunshot rang out and the whine of a ricochet rang across the top of the ridge.

More of the shrill laughter, like a cougar or a woman screaming.

Hiram wiped sweat from his brow and took deep breaths. His nose caught a strong mélange of scents drifting across the high ridge. No garlic or mustard, but there was the juniper, and the faint musk of desert animals, the oil and gasoline smell of the Double-A, and that same fruity smell he'd smelled the night before.

A Christmas sort of smell, like oranges and spice. It had the underlying alcoholic smell of a perfume or cologne, and then Hiram realized where he'd first smelled that scent.

The Greek miner, Dimitrios, had worn it.

At the mine entrance, the first time Hiram had entered Kimball.

Rettig had made a comment about knowing what went in the camp. Was Dimitrios his spy? Or could the Greek be following Samuel's orders here?

He didn't think Rettig and Samuel could be allies— Samuel seemed too unstable to be in league with anyone.

"Get down and stay down," he whispered to Michael.

The boy obeyed. Hiram crouched behind the truck's body.

Touching his chi-rho amulet, he chanted a prayer he'd learned from Grandma Hettie. The original was in German, one of the long list of prayers she had memorized as a girl out of a book by some Pennsylvania fellow named Hohman, but Hiram knew no German, so he'd gone ahead and learned the English version.

"I conjure thee, bullet or blade, whatever is injurious or destructive to me, by every prayer of the priest, and by him who brought Jesus into the temple and said, a sword shall pierce through thine own soul, that thou suffer not me, a child of God, to suffer. Jesus. Jesus. Jesus, Lord Divine."

At each mention of the Lord's name, and again at *Lord Divine*, Hiram crossed himself. Hopefully, he'd repented sufficiently of his wrongs against Gus Dollar that the prayer would be effective.

Then he waited.

A minute later, he saw four figures coming up the rocks. In the starlight, Hiram couldn't make out their faces.

The first of the figures, a short man who seemed to be all torso, reached the hood and went around to the driver's door, on the same side where Hiram squatted.

"Hey!" Michael yelled.

The door squeaked open, and Hiram attacked. Grabbing Shorty's throat, he smashed the fellow's head into the side of the truck. He crumpled, muttering something to himself about biscuits.

The next fellow came at Hiram, and he was enormous. Something in the shape of his head was familiar; it was narrower than it should be. Hiram pistol-whipped his attacker in the face and heard bone crunch. Big Man dropped, and Hiram hoped he hadn't killed him.

Hiram had taken two down, good work, but not good enough. And where were the others?

The third attacker appeared out of nowhere, grabbing Hiram and throwing him up against the truck. He had the stink of sweat on him. He clocked Hiram, a good blow to the nose, and Hiram felt his blood gush down his lips.

And then he felt a pistol in his gut. "Gotcha, pal," Sweaty grunted.

Hiram pushed back, and Sweaty slammed him against the truck again.

Sweaty's gun made a loud *clack*. That metallic noise was the sound of the semiautomatic pistol's action jamming.

Grandma Hettie's charm had worked.

Hiram threw a knee up and caught Sweaty in his nethers. It was a cheap move, but better than blowing the man's head off. Sweaty sagged to the ground like a split flour sack.

Hiram spun and raised his revolver at the fourth man, who had to be Dimitrios. The miner stood in his cloud of cologne, hands raised. He was dressed in black and his face was darkened.

"Dimitrios Kalakis! I squeeze this trigger, and you die. Do you understand me?"

Shuffling sounds came from behind him, and Hiram couldn't afford to be ambushed. He stepped sideways, keeping the Greek covered.

Sweaty still lay on the ground, clutching himself, but Shorty was up on all fours and muttering. "Goddamn farmer saw us coming, and I said for us to wait until they camped, but the Greek, he said we should get it done . . ."

"Shush," Hiram said.

Dimitrios puffed out his chest. "Shoot! We Greeks, we are invincible. Do you know the story of Achilles? He was covered in fire that melted any spear that attacked him—"

"Except for his heel," Hiram said. "And a blow to his heel killed him. Only I'm thinking you may have an Achilles forehead."

Dimitrios sucked in breath and his surprisingly high-pitched voice fell silent. He'd been the one laughing.

Of the four men, Dimitrios was the only one who spoke with a foreign accent. Then it struck Hiram who the big man was. He'd been the tough working the door at Naaman Rettig's suite, the man with no neck and the sides of his head shaved.

"Mr. Kalakis," Hiram said, "does Samuel Kimball know you're working for Naaman Rettig?"

"No," the miner admitted.

Hiram kept watch out of the corner of his eye. He hoped he hadn't killed Big Man. He hoped he wouldn't be forced to kill any of them.

"And what would your wife think about you doing this?" Hiram asked. "I'm an innocent man. My son is in the truck. He's seventeen years old, and he's scared silly because men in masks are attacking us!"

"Hey," Michael muttered.

"And for what?" Hiram continued. "So you can drive me out of town? Don't you remember that I'm the one who brought food to camp just yesterday?"

Dimitrios said nothing.

Hiram turned on the dwarf. "Does your mother know what you do for a living? Does she know you're a two-penny bravo for a railroad bandit with the ethics of a cornered rattlesnake?"

"No," Shorty said. "And that's low, talking about a guy's mom. I'm a bona-fide employee of the D and RGW."

"And yet, your mother says rosaries, praying that her son is a good man. Keep in mind, I have six shots, there are four of you. I earned medals as a marksman in the Great War, and I shot a hell of a lot of Germans on colder, darker nights than this." That was a straight run of lies on Hiram's part. "I'll kill at least two of you before you can even stand up."

Shorty and Dimitrios Kalakis both raised their hands in surrender.

Hiram prodded Shorty with the toe of his boot. "Tell me your name."

"Tyson Gibby."

"And the big fellow over there?"

"He's Frank Johnson."

"Mr. Gibby, could you check to see if Frank Johnson is still breathing?"

Gibby crept over to the big man.

"You'd better tell me your name, too," Hiram said to Sweaty.

"Lemuel Hanks," he muttered.

"Good work, Pap," Michael called from the truck.

Hiram took a deep breath. "Turn on the headlights, would you?"

Lemuel Hanks sat up. "You should've been dead. I've had that heater for ten years, never jammed on me once. You're a lucky man. And as for my wife or my mother, I don't have either, so don't try that stuff with me."

"The Lord Divine has saved you and me both from committing murder," Hiram said. "Assuming Frank lives."

The charm had worked. Hiram's repentance had been acceptable. *Blessed are ye, when men shall revile you, and persecute you*, that was one of the Beatitudes. Hiram had turned the other cheek. He had resisted unnecessary violence, he had spared the lives of his attackers.

And the Lord had given power to his charm.

But that didn't mean the truck would start now.

"He's breathing," Gibby said, "but he's out cold. Hey, Lemmy, help me drag him some. That usually wakes 'em up." Then in a lower voice, "I had an uncle who drank something awful, and he'd get so gassed he'd fall down . . ."

Gibby and Lemuel Hanks lugged the unconscious giant out into the glow of the Double-A's beams.

The three men stood uncertainly, looking at Hiram. Now that he had some real light, Dimitrios's single eyebrow stood out even with the black on his face.

Michael got out of the truck. "Do you believe in ghosts, Dimitrios?"

The Greek shrugged. "Maybe, I do."

"But the phantoms running the ridges up here—that's been you, all along."

Dimitrios looked down at his feet. "We frighten the people."

"Because Rettig told you to?"

Dimitrios nodded.

"But tonight you tried to attack me," Hiram said. "Rettig told you to do that, too?"

The Greek nodded again.

"What about the ghosts?" Hiram pressed the Greek. "Really, do you think the mine is haunted? The eastern seam has a ghost?"

Dimitrios opened his mouth and closed it twice before he found the words he wanted. "I have never seen a ghost, but other men swear to it. But the railroad man pays me a good pay to do what Samuel says and report to him. And since Samuel promises me Bill Sorenson's job, this is a very good work for me. Samuel says the mine is haunted, and I say, yes, sure it is. Once the railroad owns the mine, that will be better for everyone. We can all go back to work."

Hiram nodded. So Rettig had had an inside man. He tasted his own blood in his mouth, from his bashed nose. He spit.

"Dimitrios, this is what's going to happen. You're going to go back to the camp, talk with the Greeks, the Chinese, the Japanese, and whoever else you can, and tell them that there is more coal in the eastern seam, and until that coal gives out, you're going to mine it. You all need to bury your differences with Ammon and the Germans."

"They won't listen. They're scared."

"Well, you're going to try," Hiram said. "There is coal in the eastern seam, isn't there?"

Dimitrios shrugged. "I think maybe."

Hiram felt tired; he had to go down the mine. He had to confirm the presence of coal there, and he also wanted to look for evidence of Samael. If there was a fallen angel under the earth, was it even safe to open the mine again?

Which meant that he had to find out quickly.

Hiram continued. "Even if there's a whole city of coal down there, you're done, Dimitrios. You're going to take your family, and you're going to leave the camp. Do you understand me?"

The Greek nodded. "What of my debts?"

"I'll worry about that." Hiram wasn't quite sure where he'd get the money, but he wanted Dimitrios out of the picture, for his sake and for the miners'.

Frank sat up and shook his head.

Hiram felt a huge relief at the sight of Frank moving. "As for you three, you're going to go back to Rettig, and you're going to tell him I spared your life. I could have killed all of you, but I don't want trouble. Also, tell him the Kimballs won't sell. At any price. He needs to quit trying. It's your job to convince him of both."

"Why should we?" Frank asked.

"Aw, knock it off, Frankie," Gibby said. "He could shoot us now, but he hasn't."

"That all may be," Lemuel Hanks admitted sourly. "But the boss don't quit. And I don't see him quitting because I tell him to."

"We'll try, Mr. Woolley," Gibby said. "Hanks, you fool, shut your gob."

"Mr. Gibby, call your mother tomorrow and tell her you love her." Hiram shifted his gun barrel to cover Lemuel Hanks. "And you, I think you should find yourself a good woman. It'll settle you down, and if you eat right and drink less, you might not sweat so much."

Lemuel Hanks grimaced. "I'd rather die."

"Yes, but I don't want that," Hiram said. "I'm letting you go, unless you force me to do otherwise."

"I ain't forcing you," Hanks said.

Hiram pointed across the ridge. "I think that's your most direct route back to Kimball and Spring Canyon. From there, you just walk downhill."

Frank got to his feet, wobbling. Gibby and Hanks had to take an arm each to steady the big man. Together with the Greek, they took the direction Hiram indicated.

Hiram let a long breath, put his revolver back into his bib pocket, and then got out his bandana. The cold night had already congealed his blood to his lips and chin. It took some wiping, but he got most of it off.

"For the record, I wasn't scared silly. Or even scared amusing." Michael walked to stand in the glow of the headlights. Then he laughed. "You pulled the hammer back, as cool as a cucumber, and said, 'I think you may have an Achilles forehead.' And that's Henry Furry, he has ice water for blood. Damn, Pap, that was a close one."

Hiram took a deep breath.

"Don't curse, son."

Time to get the truck moving.

Hiram kicked himself for letting his guard down, and for giving Dollar back his book. The man had fooled Hiram.

Again.

But the bloodstone hadn't warned Hiram of any attempt to deceive. Either Gus Dollar's magic had been too strong for him . . . or Hiram had asked questions the old *braucher* could easily evade.

Had Hiram, in fact, returned Gus's book to him because Gus had hexed him?

Or was Gus wrong about his being the only magician in Spring Canyon? Had some unknown witch hexed Hiram's truck this time?

Or had Samael done it?

Hiram felt exhausted. He rubbed his eyes with his knuckles. "Okay," he said to Michael, "let me take a look."

He slapped at a fly buzzing in his ear, and missed. Flies in February. It wasn't right. He heard a distant whistle, piping on the cold wind. Hiram winced. A bad taste filled his mouth and it wasn't just blood. Things worse than men were about.

Chapter Twenty-One

HIRAM CIRCLED THE TRUCK WITH HIS FLASHLIGHT, hands going numb from the cold; he was looking for evidence of Gus Dollar's new curse.

He found it on the rear bumper, in the form of a single word, repeated three times: NEMA! NEMA! NEMA!

It was written in thick red characters. Crayon? Or lipstick? And what was *Nema?* Another demon's name?

Several flies buzzed into his face, and he waved them away.

Spitting into his bandana, he erased most of the writing in a few long strokes Then, with smaller, fastidious motions, he wiped out the last traces.

Then he stood. "Michael, I have a question that's going to sound strange."

"A strange question from my Pap! What is the world coming to?"

"You know, when you're grown, and you've figured out what you want out of this world, son . . . I'm going to miss your acid wit."

"Don't worry, Pap. I'll keep cracking jokes, so you don't feel deprived." Michael puffed and waved in front of his own face. "What's with these flies? They have the body of a *musca domestica* but are the size of a *tabanus trimaculatus*. Either is strange when it's this cold."

Hiram didn't get sidetracked. "While I was in the store this evening, did anyone approach the car?"

"You mean, when you forgot to get more Cokes? Yeah. I said hello, but she performed a strong Jenny Lindow impression and just ignored me. And then she picked something up off the ground and went inside."

A tall blonde woman. Dollar's daughter? While he had been talking with Hiram, Dollar had sent the woman out to put a hex on Hiram's truck. Or at least, to prepare the Double-A for Gus's hex.

Had Gus kept Hiram in the shop with the sieve and shears only to allow the curse to be placed?

"Dammit," he muttered.

"That's right, Pap. Dammit."

What was *Nema*?

Hiram brushed flies from his face. "Try the starter again."

"Nothing," Michael called back.

Hiram needed to do more. He'd already burned a shingle from Gus's roof, but he had the Coke bottles.

Hiram climbed into the back of the truck and threw open his toolbox. He had to move the brass and lead lamens, and at the sight of the lead one, he wondered again what wall Gus Dollar was trying to bring down. He snatched up a Coke bottle. He also grabbed a bundle of steel sewing needles wrapped in a swatch of cloth and a wad of modeling clay. It was only when he went to replace the upper tray in the chest and found he was unable to do it without trapping flies inside that he realized just how thick the cloud of insects was around him.

Flies. In February.

Flies, like he'd found in the tunnel below Gus Dollar's shop. Flies, like he'd encountered in Apostate Canyon.

He knew a charm against flies. It involved burying the image of a spider beneath the house you wished to protect from them, and was useless to him here. He slammed shut the tool chest and jumped to the ground, full can of gas in one hand and an empty Coke bottle in the other.

Fire was the most basic defense against evil. If he didn't know what was attacking, and didn't know who had sent it, the most useful thing he could generally do was make a fire. Fire was the lightest element, it chased away darkness, and the sun's fire nourished the earth. Fire was primitive man's oldest weapon against the wolf. In the Book of Daniel, God had saved Shadrach, Meshach, and Abednego *in* and *by* fire.

"Keep trying!" he called to Michael.

The flies were thick enough to nearly blind him now. He shoved the bottle into a pocket and lurched off the side of the road, looking for wood. He nearly impaled himself on a dry branch, and when he dragged it back onto the road, he found he had brought almost an entire juniper tree, dead and shriveled.

It would do.

Something moved out in the darkness, ahead of him and on the road. Hiram tossed the bush to the dirt in front of him and sloshed gasoline onto it.

"I am Gabriel," he muttered, "that stand in the presence of God."

He heard the crunch of footsteps, slow, heavy, and deliberate. At each step, the buzzing of the flies reached a crescendo just as the foot seemed to strike the ground. And after each crescendo, the total sound of the flies increased in volume and pitch.

Could this be Rettig's men, returning to harass Hiram again? Big Frank Johnson, making heavy footsteps?

But the footfalls were too loud. And there were the flies.

Hiram's heart raced.

He struck a spark with his Zippo—only to have the flame snuffed by a phalanx of flies, so densely-marshaled that they might have been a hand.

A second attempt met the same fate.

The steps drew nearer.

Hiram knelt, smelling the gasoline reek like an overwhelming cloud. He struck the Zippo's flint a third time—and before flies could knock it away, the juniper burst into flame.

Hiram fell back onto his shoulders. His face hurt, seared by the fire.

In the darkness and among the flies, he heard an angry shriek that resembled a train's steam-whistle more than the cry of an animal. The buzzing of the flies lessened.

"Pap! Pap, are you okay?"

"I'm okay! Keep trying!" Hiram spat flies from his mouth.

He didn't hear the engine turn over, so Hiram had no choice. He pocketed the Zippo again and removed the bottle. He made sure his back was turned to the Double-A so Michael wouldn't see what he was doing, and then he unbuttoned the fly of his overalls and carefully filled the Coke bottle with his own urine.

Grandma Hettie had explained to him the theory of the witch bottle one day when he had found a cracked glass bottle in the stone fire ring out behind the barn. The idea was that the bottle represented the bladder of the witch who was attacking a person, and the witch bottle would deliver sharp pains to the witch's bladder that would force an end to the witch's magical attack.

The flies' buzz rose in intensity, and Hiram again heard the crunching of enormous feet in the cloud. He set the Coke bottle carefully aside, grabbed the gas can, and sloshed a jet of petrol over the fire.

The *WHOOSH!* of the resulting flame felt like it might have obliterated his eyebrows, but the flies eased off. Seeing a fallen log beside the road, Hiram grabbed it and dragged it across the flaming juniper.

Then he returned to the bottle. Holding the bottle in his left hand, he bit three fingernails off his right hand and spit them into the bottle. If he were defending another person against the witch's attack, he'd use that victim's urine and nail trimmings. If he had more time, he'd add hair and other similar ingredients, but he was pressed.

He took the bundle of needles out of his pocket and dropped them into the bottle.

He thumbed in the wad of modeling clay to close up the Coke's top.

Footsteps crunched closer.

Was that the outline of a man in the cloud? Could it be Frank Johnson, after all?

But no—the silhouette suggested a man who was eight feet tall, with impossibly broad shoulders.

His hands occupied, Hiram drew on another expedient to push back the threat. "And the angel of the Lord appeared unto him in a flame of fire," he called, "out of the midst of a bush!"

The fire of Hiram's burning bush rose higher, and again he heard the whistle erupt into a terrible, injured wail that faded into a whistle.

If he wasn't killing the thing out there, he was injuring and angering it.

Could it be Samael? Mahoun? *Nema*?

Could Gus Dollar have been telling the truth? Could this be one of Lucifer's fallen angels, living out here in the Wastes of Dudael, in the hills above Helper, Utah? Had the witch summoned it and was he now controlling it?

Had Hiram himself let the thing out of its cave?

Nema, he suddenly thought. *Amen*, backward.

Nema! Nema! Nema! was amen, three times, backward.

Hiram realized what Gus's curse was, and how he could push it back.

He set the witch bottle in the fire. Activation of the witch bottle required that the urine inside be brought to a boil.

Hiram staggered off the road three times. Each time he grabbed the nearest sizeable piece of wood he could find, sloshed it in gasoline, and added it to the fire, nestling each new log as close as he could to the bottle, building up the fire there so as to be sure the liquid inside was exposed to the maximum possible heat. Each time he added wood, he shouted, "Thou shalt not suffer a witch to live!"

"Pap! Pap!" Michael was invisible to him, obscured by the flies.

"Hold on!" Hiram spat more flies out of his mouth. They were bigger than raisins and they wiggled on his tongue, causing him to gag and choke.

He emptied the gasoline on the fire, jumping back to avoid getting burned again. Then he threw the gas can into the back of the truck and lurched to the window of the cab.

"What the hell is with all these flies?" Michael asked. "And are you shouting something?"

"Shouting at flies." Hiram forced a hollow laugh. "It's like we stumbled onto a bobcat's lair, isn't it? Only it's a nest of flies. I think the fire is killing them. I'm going to get under the hood now, and I need you to keep hitting the starter until it takes."

"Got it, Pap."

Hiram lifted the hood. He couldn't see the bottle, but he trusted that it would boil any second. If he hexed Gus Dollar, that might break his curse on Hiram's truck. Now he needed the thing out in the darkness to stay away until the engine turned over.

Hiram had never had occasion to curse anyone. But he understood that one element witches used to curse their victims was the recitation of scripture, backward.

Especially the recitation of the Lord's Prayer, in Matthew, chapter six.

Hiram would counter the hex by reciting the prayer forward. "Our Father which art in heaven, Hallowed be thy name..." The familiar words tumbled from his mouth.

The truck hadn't yet started.

Footsteps—the creature in the swarm was approaching again, and Hiram groped for any Bible verse dealing with fire. "And after the fire," he shouted, "a still small voice!"

The flames rose again, but the flies only got thicker. He whipped through the Lord's Prayer a second time. He could hear Michael cursing inside the truck. The many hours he'd spent with Grandma Hettie, memorizing not only individual verses—what she used to sneer at as the "five-minute Sunday School technique"—but also whole chapters, and long sections of scripture, were paying off now, inside a swarm of flies and under attack by an unseen beast.

But he was drawing a blank on his efforts to think of another useful passage about fire. There were the three children, but the account said *furnace* over and over.

When would that witch bottle boil?

He heard an enormous bellow directly behind him. If not fire, then light.

"In the beginning was the Word!" Sweat poured down his face and dripped from his body. "In him was life; and the life was the light of men."

The fire vamped again. A sheet of dead flies struck the windshield of the Double-A like limp black hailstones, bouncing off and piling up on the engine block.

He sang the Lord's Prayer again, picking up speed and pitch, without missing a syllable. "Amen!" he shouted.

The truck's engine turned over.

"Pap!" Michael shouted.

Hiram slammed shut the hood of the truck, trapping ten thousand flies inside and sending another ten thousand bouncing into the dark night.

Something grabbed him from behind. Hiram looked down and saw a hand clutching the hip of his overalls. It was gray and scabby and four times the size of a man's hand, with three fingers and a long thumb. A nail like a tent stake sprouted from the end of each digit, yellow and jagged. A smell that mixed the dry scent of dust, the cloying iron reek of blood, and the sweet, fertile stink of rotting flesh swept over Hiram from behind.

This was not Frank Johnson.

Hiram placed both Harvesters against the side of the truck and kicked, flinging himself backward. He and the thing fell together into the flies and struck the sand together, and the creature felt as if it stretched, as if Hiram had fallen back onto modeling clay, or a water balloon.

Hiram scrambled to his feet as quickly as he could, pulling the revolver from his bib pocket.

"Pap?"

A vast shape rose up from the swarm, too quickly for Hiram to see any detail, other than a face with too many mouths.

He fired the revolver at the thing. It staggered back, and he fired a second time, and then a third.

The sweet smell of crushed garlic filled his nostrils.

Oh, no. Not now.

He leaped onto the passenger-side running board of the Double-A, steadying himself with his left arm inside the vehicle.

"What the hell is that, Pap?" Michael yelled.

"Drive!" he yelled back.

The thing loomed up again in the swarm of flies and Hiram fired at it as Michael punched the Double-A into gear. The truck had a high center, which let Michael take it off the road and around the bonfire as Hiram fired twice more. The next pull of the trigger clicked the hammer down on an empty chamber.

Michael stomped on the accelerator and the truck burst out the far side of the cloud of flies, and into the cold February night.

Chapter Twenty-Two

"PAP, WHAT WAS THAT?"

"Watch the road!"

Michael jerked his eyes back around to look at the road as Hiram switched out the empty cylinder for the loaded full moon.

"You're avoiding the question! What was that thing out there? And why were you shouting Bible verses?"

Should he lie?

Should he tell Michael, his skeptical and progressive son, that he was a cunning man?

"I don't know," he said finally. "It was about the size of a bear, but I couldn't see it clearly for all those flies."

Michael cursed long and hard. Hiram didn't object.

As the Double-A rattled around the winding desert road and back down toward Spring Canyon, his hands shook beyond control. He reloaded, carefully put the revolver into the glove box, pushed his shoulders back against the truck's seat, and took deep breaths.

Turning his face out the window so Michael wouldn't hear, he chanted his charm against the falling sickness. He sucked in cold night air, and that seemed to help.

"I don't think I'm going to sleep tonight," Michael told him. "Holy shit!"

Hiram's heart was pounding, and he was grateful for an opportunity to change the subject. "Look, this cussing thing," he said. "Maybe, in this case, just say *shit*. Then you sound like a farmer."

"I sound like some other profession when I say *holy shit*?"

"That makes you sound...Italian. You know, I don't mind if you say words that are rude, but I don't want you to say words that offend God."

"Which god, Pap?"

"Come on, Michael."

"How about Ganesh, the elephant-headed Indian god?"

"Fine, also don't offend Ganesh."

Michael drove in silence for a moment. "How should I swear if I want to sound like a high-priced and extremely successful lawyer?"

"I'm pretty sure they never curse."

"Somehow, that doesn't feel right to me."

"Besides, you want to be a scientist." Hiram smiled. "Take us back up to the mining camp, please."

"I guess we'll try out the no-sleep thing for real, then."

Lawyer. Hiram could have kicked himself. Had Five-Cent Jimmy come with his writ and gotten Mary McGill out of jail? It was a long drive from Denver.

Hiram had more pressing things he needed to do at the mine. Hiram couldn't get the words of Teancum's letter out of his mind. *It might not turn out right because it's so easy to get lost down there.* Was the ghost of Teancum Kimball frightening miners, Teancum who had descended into the mine and not emerged?

Or was there, after all, no ghost, but only a demon? A demon that was now possibly on the loose because Hiram had destroyed Gus Dollar's binding charms. If the demon attacked them, it might attack others, and that would be Hiram's fault.

Hiram needed answers. He thought the mine would have them.

The lights of Kimball came into view as the Double-A rounded a bend in the canyon.

"Take us to Bill Sorenson's house," Hiram said.

"What do you think it was? That thing up there?"

Hiram didn't answer for a while, his mind scrambling after a fitting response. "It could have been a bear. Or, I suppose, a bad man, though it seemed too big for that."

Michael fell quiet.

What was the boy thinking?

Michael parked the Double-A next to the foreman's tidy home a few minutes later. Light shone inside, as it did in a few buildings elsewhere in the camp and in the big house at the north end of the canyon. "Are we staying?"

"I think so. Come inside with me."

"Are we going down the mine? You know, it's easy to get lost down there."

"*I* am," Hiram said. "You...you need to try to sleep."

They got out of the truck, and Hiram knocked on the foreman's door.

Bill Sorenson answered it in a sleeveless white

undershirt and cotton pants, blustering before the door was fully open and shaking the rolled-up newspaper. "Is dere a problem with de mine, dat you knock on my door so late?" Then he recognized Hiram and his face softened. "Ah, you dere. Come in."

"Thank you." Hiram stepped inside. "I'm sorry to call at this hour."

"It's nothing. You know, de men are proud and dey might not want to say anything to you, but you done a real good turn here. And if deir wives knew you were in my house, well, it ain't dat dey're less proud, but dey're less stupid, and you'd get a lot of thank-you kisses."

"Aha," Michael said. "Now I see why we came back."

"I'm glad to help them," Hiram said. "And I'm hoping you'll be willing to help *me*."

"You name it," Sorenson rumbled.

"I'm hoping you'll take me down the mine tonight."

"*Ja, ja*, I can sure do dat. Don't you want to wait until morning?"

Hiram suddenly felt exhausted. He had barely slept the night before, and the effect of the last two days' physical exertion, adrenaline, and fear abruptly piled on top of him like a mountain collapsing. Also, he was starting to get hungry again. "No, I want to do it now. Though if you have a slice of cheese or a crust of bread I could eat, I'd be grateful."

"Exciting," Michael said. "Do I get to carry the gun?"

Hiram meant to ask Sorenson if Michael could stay in his house, but the Dane beat him to it. "No way, young man. Dat mine is barely safe for grown men with deir wits about dem."

"Pap," Michael objected.

"Nope, I'm de foreman here, my decision is final."
Sorenson seized Michael by the wrist and slammed
his rolled-up newspaper into the boy's open hand. "I'll
give you dis, dough. It's enough weapon for any man."

"Great, and I can read the news." Michael unrolled
the newspaper and looked at the headlines. "From
1932. The *Helper Journal*, our local informant. Hey,
that guy Roosevelt won. Who knew? But what will
poor Hoover do now?"

"Just keep reminding yourself," Sorenson said to
Hiram. "Men with dumb kids wish dey had smart ones."

"I remind myself of that every day," Hiram said.

Mrs. Sorenson appeared in the kitchen door, wrapped
in a nightgown and carrying a blanket. "The boy can
relax here on the sofa, and hopefully get a little sleep.
There's milk in the icebox, and I baked a pan of sweet
rolls."

"Like my mudder made," the foreman said. "Only
better."

"Don't let *her* hear you say that!" Mrs. Sorenson
wagged a finger.

"If my sainted mudder is following me around in
her afterlife, she's got much bigger concerns dan de
fact dat I think she made de *second*-best smorkager
since de world began."

Mrs. Sorenson kissed her husband on the cheek as
he shrugged into a long coat and shoes.

"Mmm, smorkager," Michael said. "It sure *sounds*
delicious."

Bill Sorenson lumbered back into the kitchen and
returned shortly after with two bottles of water and
three sweet rolls piled on a plate. Was the mine
that deep, that they needed to carry drinking water

with them? Hiram wolfed down the rolls, and then he and Sorenson exited the house, shutting the door behind them.

"Hold on just a moment." Hiram climbed into the back of the Double-A, opened his tool chest, and took out two long pieces of chalk and an unpeeled witch hazel rod.

"I'm going to do something that looks strange," he warned Sorenson. "I ask that you not mention this to Michael."

"Look," Sorenson said. "In my work, I've known men from every country under heaven, and I learned dis. Every man's got his own weird bullshit. You don't bodder me about *my* weird bullshit, I won't bodder you about *yours*. And I won't tell your son anything."

"I like your philosophy," Hiram said. "It's possible my bull is weirder than yours."

He carefully peeled all the bark off the rod with his fingers, revealing the soft white wood beneath. In an ideal world, he'd have soaked it in nightshade and dried it; in an ideal world, he'd also have something personal to Teancum Kimball to wrap around the rod.

This was not an ideal world.

He sang as he worked, and he held a prayer in his heart. Without specific words, his prayer was that he would find Teancum Kimball, or evidence that would tell him more about Teancum Kimball's fate. His song was Psalm 130, to a melody Grandma Hettie had taught him.

Out of the depths have I cried unto thee,
O Lord.
Lord, hear my voice: let thine ears be attentive
to the voice of my supplications.

If thou, Lord, shouldest mark iniquities,
O Lord, who shall stand?

There were other psalms that were appropriate to sing over a Mosaical Rod, but the one beginning *out of the depths* seemed appropriate in this situation. On the rod, he slowly carved three crosses, then the name TEANCUM KIMBALL, then three more crosses.

Hiram stuck the chalk into a pocket. "I'm ready."

"Dat ain't de weirdest bullshit I ever seen," Bill Sorenson said as they climbed up the slope toward the mine opening. "Not by a long shot."

Hiram didn't ask for details.

Walking up the hill, Hiram saw his own breath in a white cloud and felt the skin of his face slowly freezing. He thought he saw the shadow of a man detach itself from the mine opening, slip to one side, and disappear again into the trees. But he might have imagined it.

In a rectangular stone building just below the mine opening, they got helmets. "You ever work with a carbide lamp before?" Sorenson asked.

"Show me how."

Hiram followed Sorenson step by step through the process of lighting the brass lamps. They opened a port in the top of the lamps by swinging a little gate horizontally, and filled the lamps' upper reservoirs with water from their bottles. Then they screwed the lamps open through the middle, revealing lower reservoirs. Into these chambers, they scooped dusty gray pellets like gravel, screwing the lamps back together afterward. They pushed long levers on the top of each lamp from OFF to ON.

"Calcium carbide," Sorenson said. "Makes a chemical reaction with de water. You feel de lamp getting warmer already, *ja*?"

"I do," Hiram agreed. "Will the light start automatically?"

"No, de reaction just puts out a flammable gas. Now, you cup your hand over de dish here, and hit dis little guy, just like a cigarette lighter."

They both struck their igniters, and two fierce white flames sprang into being.

The flames threw a long white light, but they stank infernally.

"Aren't there flammable gases down there?" Hiram nestled his lamp into place on the front of his helmet, then put on the helmet. He put his fedora on an empty peg.

"*Ja*, dere are. Mining ain't for chickens, son."

The Dane went to two big yellow rectangular boards nailed to the wall. Rows of hooks covered both; one was full of brass chits while the other was empty. Sorenson took a chit with a number on it and moved it from the "OUT" board to the "IN" board. "If dey wonder where I am, dey will see dis and know I'm down below." He transferred another chit with a "V" stamped on it. "Dat is for you, my do-gooder friend. If dere is a cave-in, dey know to look for two bodies."

They approached the mine entrance by a trough cut straight into the hillside, lined left and right with mortared stone that looked just like the stone of the mine buildings. Straight up the center of the trough ran railroad tracks. Beneath their feet and the tracks lay a rough scree of stone and dirt, studded with many chunks of coal. Where the hill rose steeply and the trough cut into it, becoming an actual tunnel, a concrete lintel lay over the opening. In large capital letters, cut an inch deep into the concrete, were the words KIMBALL MINING CO. ✮ 1891.

Down the slope from them, the long wooden tipple blocked their view of the highway and the eastern sections of the camp. The large building where rock was sorted out of the coal screened out a lot of light and made the mine entrance much darker than it would have been.

Here at the gate, the air was warmer. The dirt immediately at the opening and to either side was free of snow and the soil was relatively dry.

"Hold on one moment," Hiram said.

A correctly prepared Mosaical Rod should lead its user to find whatever it had been prepared to seek. Usually, that was water, though Hiram had heard of more than one prospector using such rods to try to find gold or silver. Hiram was looking for Teancum Kimball, either missing or dead.

But a Mosaical Rod should also answer questions, and especially questions relating to the purpose of its creation.

He gripped the rod loosely in both hands and let the pointing end rest a couple of feet above the ground. Sorenson watched, making no comment.

Hiram started with a couple of test questions. "Is my name James?"

Nothing happened.

"Is this the Latuda Mine?"

Nothing.

"Am I standing here with Vilhelm Sorenson, the foreman of the Kimball Mine?"

The pointing tip of the rod dipped sharply, pulling Hiram's hands down with it.

Sorenson raised his craggy eyebrows, visible to Hiram in a gray penumbra at the edge of his vision, but said nothing.

"Is Teancum Kimball in the Kimball Mine?"

Nothing.

Hiram felt a sharp pang of disappointment. Where had he gone wrong? Maybe the presence that haunted the mine wasn't Teancum Kimball. Maybe the old man had run off to Mexico, like Hiram's father, abandoning his family to their daily struggle.

Hiram sighed.

Bill Sorenson cleared his throat. "Can we find Teancum Kimball by going into de Kimball Mine?"

The rod dipped down.

Sorenson chuckled. "Okay, den. You heard de rod."

On the way in, they passed a tin advertising plate, rusted over its lower third, advising the miners to chew Copenhagen smokeless tobacco.

Within the mine, the air was warmer still. The tunnels were tall at first. Sorenson pointed at the chiseled rock. "When de coal was dere, dey called it *high coal*," Sorenson said. "Dat means dat you can mine it standing up. At first, before I was here, it was all high coal, de work was easy. But you can see here, de high coal is all mined out."

Hiram swept the Mosaical Rod from side to side, careful to hold it loosely in his hands, so that if it moved, he'd feel it easily, and also so that any movement that occurred would be due to the rod, and not due to involuntary muscle contractions in Hiram's hands.

The tunnels gave opening to galleries, long rooms wide enough to hold dances in.

They passed beaten, rusty metal carts, not much larger than large wheelbarrows, standing on the railroad tracks. The mine was supported by beams climbing the walls and across the ceiling, but also by half-length railroad ties stacked in pairs in alternating orientation, creating rough wooden columns that held up the ceiling.

Sorenson slapped his hand onto one. "Dese are called cribs."

Affixed to the cribs hung brief signs in multiple languages. Many were in characters Hiram didn't know, that could be Greek or Chinese. In letters he recognized, he read one that said NON FATEVI MALE.

"Latin?" he asked. Wasn't *fata* a word that meant something like fairy? No bad fairies?

"Italian," Sorenson told him. "Dese are all safety warnings. Dey say 'be careful.'"

"None of them are in English."

Sorenson laughed. "None of my boys read English. Half of 'em don't read deir own language. Maybe you heard dis already, but dey call Helper 'de town of fifty-seven varieties.'"

"Like the beans?"

"*Ja*, like de beans. Like beans in a can, me and my men."

They walked through the galleries and passed shafts exiting left and right. Hiram continued sweeping the road as he moved. Hiram wished he'd brought a pocket watch, and thought they might have walked half a mile.

Sorenson pointed out tunnels that were only four feet tall. "Here you see where dey found de crawler coal. Same kinda coal, burns just as good, only de seam is shorter. You gotta do de work sitting on your bum, or on your knees. De work is harder, de pay ain't no better."

"You could still dig a taller tunnel."

"*Ja*, but den you do more work to get all de extra rock out. Dat's no good. But you see dat? Dis is de eastern seam, and dat's coal." He pointed at a wall of black rock. "Dat's good coal, dat can be mined, everybody knows dere's good coal down here, only de crazy Kimballs got to sort out deir heads."

Samuel Kimball had said the eastern seam was petering out? Was he simply mad? Or under the sway of Mahoun?

As he spoke, they passed an opening that was boarded over. Hiram swung the Mosaical Rod past the opening, and the rod tugged downward. He tried it again, and a third time, and each time the rod clearly signaled that he should go down that passage.

"Mr. Sorenson," he said. "Is that boarded off because it's dangerous?"

"*Ja*, sort of. It's boarded off because it ain't de mine."

"What?"

"*Ja*, in a couple of places, de Kimball mine ran into old caves. Dat ain't de mine. It's a maze down dere, you can get lost, easy, so we boarded up to keep de boys from wandering off and getting lost."

It might not turn out right because it's so easy to get lost down there.

"That's where I have to go." Hiram brushed a fat fly away from his face.

The insect lazily drifted off him and through the wooden slats. In the enclosed space, trapped under all the rock, the buzz sounded like a sawmill.

Chapter Twenty-Three

SORENSON THREW A COILED LENGTH OF ROPE OVER his shoulder, and then they ripped off two of the planks boarding up the side passage.

The walls in this new passage were rougher, with the jagged look of a chasm torn open by an earthquake fault. The planks supporting the ceiling, as well as the beams overhead and the stacks of short railroad ties, were nonexistent here.

"Something's wrong with my eyes," Hiram said.

"Tunnel vision." Sorenson laughed. "It's just because of de way de carbide lamp works. It shines most brightly in a line straight ahead of you, and your eyes focus on dat line, but dat means dey adjust to dat brightness, and everything else looks dark."

"Can I do anything about it?"

"You can avoid looking straight ahead. Den your eyes will adjust to de darkness some. Or you can just get used to turning your head to where you want to look every time."

"But never at another person's face."

"*Ja*, very good, you have just avoided de number one reason a man gets his lights punched out on de first day of de job. Look ahead, and down, so if you meet anudder man, your light is on his feet."

They followed the crack down. Five feet wide, seven feet tall, it was a rough passage created by the Earth itself. Sorenson lumbered ahead, slouching and half-leaping from one stone to the next. It was a steep and long descent, choked with boulders and wet with seeping moisture that trickled down one wall and disappeared among the rocks at their feet. Hiram saw it all a few square feet at a time, with the entire periphery of his vision filled with darkness.

And again, a distant sound.

"If we meet another man down here, though," Hiram said, "he won't be a miner."

"Right," Sorenson agreed. "He would be an outlaw, or a lost hobo who got stupid drunk."

"You've seen outlaws?"

"Oh, sure, from time to time. De biggest was back in de early days, when old Teancum Kimball ran dis place. You know de name Butch Cassidy?"

"Butch Cassidy mined coal?"

"No, but he robbed a coal company. Pleasant Valley Coal Company, at Castle Gate. Dat's north of Helper, up in de canyon. About forty years ago, Butch robbed de payroll. Dat's why even today, every mining company in Carbon County pays its payroll on a different date every month, and dey choose de date at random. De foremen draw cards, or roll dice, or stick a pin in a calendar. It makes it harder for payroll robbers to plan."

"How do *you* pick the day?" Hiram asked.

"I got a bag of poker chips with numbers written on 'em. I pull chips out of de bag. Maybe I should switch to using de dowsing rod, eh?"

"Using a dowsing rod requires a chaste and sober mind. A prayerful heart at all times. I find it helps to fast often."

"Can you use a dowsing rod if you drink?"

"I think it *helps* not to drink."

"Okay, den I'll leave de dowsing rod to you and I'll stick to de poker chips."

At the bottom of the chasm, they entered a wide, oblong chamber. To their left, the floor gave way to a pool of water, punctuated by strawlike stalagmites reaching for the unseen sky. On the right side of the chamber, three different passages broke the cavern wall, two descending and the third boring away into darkness on the level.

"Spare de rod, spoil de child." Sorenson laughed raucously. "Come on, Woolley, pick a trail for us."

First, Hiram chalked a clear, large arrow on the cavern floor, and a second on the wall, pointing back up the way they had come, along with an estimate: *200 yds to mine.*

Then he held the Mosaical Rod and paced sideways down the chamber, facing rightward, swinging the rod back and forth to give it the chance to indicate which of the three passages would help him find Teancum Kimball.

The rod didn't indicate any one of them.

He tried it a second time, and then a third.

Nothing.

"I think you broke de rod," Sorenson said.

Hiram examined the Mosaical Rod. His carvings all seemed intact, the wood otherwise unblemished. His eyelids were heavy, fluttering perilously close to sleep as he huddled over the witch hazel.

Hiram brushed at his face. Flies? Or was he seeing things? He was sweating copiously, though the air was cool, and he was so tired that every time he shut his eyes, he was afraid he'd fall asleep standing.

"Unless, of course," Sorenson added, "de rod wants us to take a swim."

Hiram snapped back to full wakefulness. Standing, he walked in a slow half-turn on the shelf of rock—there.

A definite tug on the rod, and when he repeated the turn in reverse, the rod pulled again.

"Oh ho," Sorenson said with a chuckle. "Dis is interesting."

Hiram tilted his head down to look into the water. He felt a cool breeze on his neck, and a faint tickling sensation. In the water, small white things that might have been fish or salamanders scurried along at the edge of his view.

"Does anything...dangerous...live in these waters?"

"Not dat I know," Sorenson said. "But den, I never walked around caves like dese following a dowsing rod, so I'm learning all kinds of new stuff about de world."

Hiram took his bearings again with the rod, made another chalk mark on the stone, then stepped into the water. It was deeper than it appeared from the surface, and he sank immediately up to the middle of his thigh.

"Oh, dat's cold." Sorenson lurched into the pool beside him. "Hey, are you hearing a buzzing sound? Like bees?"

"Yes." Hiram stopped, and something like a crayfish, but totally white, crawled over his boot. "Are you armed?"

"I got a knife. In my experience, if I don't carry a gun, de boys are less likely to bring a gun to talk to me when dey're angry."

"What about for defending yourself against criminals?"

"*Ja*, well, dat's why we pick a random payday."

"I've got a revolver."

"You keep it. I'll use my knife. We'll both look really silly when we get attacked by de big white swarm of cave-bees."

Hiram pushed ahead, crossing the water. When he got closer, he saw that, where the cave wall had appeared to him to drop down into the water and end the cavern, it in fact stayed above water, and there was a two-foot tall space between the water and the ceiling, over a passage moving forward. Holding the revolver and the Mosaical Rod above the water to keep them dry, he crouched and waddled along the submerged passage.

Something slimy felt its way briefly up one leg of his overalls. Shuddering, he shook his foot and dislodged it.

He felt a tugging at his ankle. Was that a rise in the pitch of the buzzing?

But no, the tugging was only water current, and in two more steps, he had passed it, and then the ceiling rose, and in two more steps he was able to stand.

Sorenson shook himself dry like a bear with a fresh salmon in its jaws. "Give me a coal mine any day. For one thing, de mine has supports to keep up de ceiling. Here, I don't know." They both looked up, and saw that they stood inside a chimney-shaped hollow. An exit from the chimney to Hiram's right hinted at unknown further passages. "Maybe de rod will warn us of a cave-in."

Hiram laughed at the joke, but only for a moment.

"Shout," he murmured. "For the Lord hath given you the city."

"Dis ain't no city."

Hiram didn't know any charm for bringing down a wall, not the wall of a city or the wall of a cave. Such hexes existed. They were in books like Henry Cornelius Agrippa's, or the *Picatrix*. They were books Hiram had never read, and most likely never *would* read, since they were written in Latin.

But Gus Dollar read those books, and owned them. He'd created a lead lamen with quotes from Joshua on it. Was it possible Gus wanted to cause a cave-in of the mine? Yet he'd truthfully said he didn't care about the mine. Then again, these caves were below the mine.

Gus had said he was making the Book of Spirits to defeat Samael.

Climbing out of the water onto another dry shelf, Hiram found himself looking at a chunk of stone. At first, due to its blunted edges and slick appearance, he took it for a lumpy stalagmite. After a moment's observation, he realized that it couldn't be natural. For one thing, the walls here were of reddish stone, and the rock in the center was nearly white, marked by black streaks.

Also, the stone was shaped very distinctly like a lizard's head. Hiram clearly saw eyes, and the ridge of a brow; the great flat top of the stone, like the upper surface of an altar, lay behind the reptile's eyes.

As in Samuel's painting.

Only the lizard's head seemed to have three mouths.

And then Hiram realized that the streaks were stains.

"By *Gud*, de rod was right. Look dere."

In the corner of the chimney, slumped against the wall of the cavern, and beside a foot-wide horizontal crack in the stone, lay a corpse.

The body was a man's, and it was dressed in Sunday best, though wearing a mine helmet much like the one Hiram had on. Its long-bearded face was twisted in an expression of horror, which Hiram could read clearly, because although the flesh had rotted away and the eye sockets gaped wide, the body's skin and hair were intact. The skin had a bluish tint under the carbide light, but Hiram recognized the face.

"Teancum Kimball," Hiram said.

In the crook of one arm lay a collapse tangle of small bones, under a skein of desiccated skin. A lamb?

"*Ja*, I'd know dat old bugger anywhere. You want to . . . check his pockets or something?"

Hiram *did* want to search the body. What was he looking for? Some indication of witchcraft, maybe. Some sign of intent, a hint that it was Teancum Kimball who had ultimately caused all the trouble at the mine. Some sign it might be Teancum's shade speaking to his sons through the peep-stone, lying to Samuel, and hardening Ammon's heart. If Hiram could do something as simple as lay Teancum's body in a grave and bless it, for instance, he'd be thrilled to do it, to bring an end to all the conflict.

First, he marked the floor with chalk.

"I should have brought a blanket or a sack," Hiram said. "I don't think we can carry him out."

"If we do dat, he falls apart."

Hiram knelt. He set the revolver and the Mosaical Rod to one side. The buzzing sound was definitely louder. Gingerly, he patted down the corpse's pockets, finding keys and a billfold, which he took.

"Ffffffffffff . . ."

Hiram nearly fell over, pulling away.

Had he heard the corpse speak?

"What's wrong?" Sorenson asked.

Hiram felt too silly to answer. However, if Teancum Kimball's spirit wanted to speak to him now, the easiest way to find a solution might be to listen.

Slowly, he leaned in over the corpse's open mouth. Turning his ear to the corpse meant that his tunnel vision reduced the entire cave to a single spot of bare stone wall, a few feet across. He imagined the body lurching forward to bite him, but that was ridiculous nonsense, the lurid sort of thing you would read in cheap magazines.

"Teancum," he whispered. "Talk to me."

A column of flies exploded from the corpse's mouth. It struck Hiram in the face like the kick of a mule, knocking him backward. He struck the altar under one shoulder blade and fell to the ground, reeling. Flies banged off the reflecting disk of his carbide lamp, and he smelled the bitter stink of burnt insect.

He managed not to lose his helmet.

"Jesus!" Sorenson shouted, flapping his arms to drive the flies away. The foreman staggered back to the water's edge. "Come on, Woolley, we'll do dis anudder day, bring a big basket of flypaper with us."

Lying nearly on his back, propped on his elbows, Hiram peeked into the crack. What he had taken for darkness, he now saw consisted of swarming flies. Was this the locus, the epicenter? Had he stumbled into some kind of flies' nest?

Scooting around to point his lance of light into the crack, he looked for more. Eggs? Larvae? A way through?

He saw mouths. Mouths with jagged teeth, and white slug-like larvae dripping from the mouths like slobber. Three mouths, all set in the same gray, scaly face.

Hiram threw himself backward. His helmet slipped and he grabbed it, burning his hand on the carbide lamp. He searched for the revolver and the dowsing rod, but his sight was hampered by tunnel vision. He managed to get his hand on the revolver, but felt the rod skitter away from him into the darkness.

An arm burst from the crack. It was huge and gray, and it jostled Teancum Kimball's corpse to one side. Hiram leaped back into the water, managing to avoid the talons. His breath came in short gasps made shallow by fear and by the chill of the water.

"Dis way, Woolley! Duck!" Bill Sorenson grabbed Hiram by the shoulder and pulled him backward and down. Hiram stared at the crack, seeing the many-mouthed face once more before the dropping ceiling obscured it, and the reptile-head altar with it.

He and Sorenson dragged each other to their feet on the stone shelf on the other side, and Hiram was hyperventilating. Light speared his eyeballs, and then his vision went dark, a blackness pierced by a dull red sun that illuminated nothing.

"Woolley!" Sorenson slapped him across the cheek. "Woolley, get hold of yourself! What was dat thing?"

"I can't see!"

"Your helmet's on backward, and you looked into my lamp. Here." Sorenson adjusted Hiram's helmet, and he regained a narrow tunnel of vision, though now it was marred with bright red circles.

He whirled around to look at the submerged passage. Flies were swarming out, and the size of the swarm grew from moment to moment.

"Run now!" he panted. "Later, we talk!"

Sorenson responded by pushing Hiram ahead of him along the shelf. They followed Hiram's chalk marks. Hiram ran to the chasm, and then scrambled as quickly as he could over the boulders, slipping where they were wet and picking up a few bruises in the process. Sorenson stalked behind him.

The buzzing sound grew louder as he went.

"You're with me!" he shouted every minute or so.

"*Ja!*" Bill Sorenson shouted back.

Finally, they came to the planks barring off this chasm, and Hiram turned to run for the surface.

"Wrong way, Woolley!" Sorenson against grabbed Hiram, this time by the neck, and dragged him through the high coal tunnels, stumbling and nearly tripping over and over on the mine-cart tracks, until they burst out into the cold night air. Then he let Hiram go, and they both staggered down the stone-lined trough and out onto the hillside of Kimball Canyon.

Hiram turned and shone his carbide light into the mine opening. He saw nothing.

"What was dat?" Sorenson asked him, panting.

"Do you hear the flies?"

"No. Do you?"

"No." Hiram took deep breaths, steadying himself, trying to get control of his breathing. "I don't know what that was. I didn't get a good look." He straightened his back, raised his helmet, and ran his fingers through his hair over a scalp slick with sweat.

"Did you find what you wanted?" Sorenson asked.

Hiram considered the question. The presence of Teancum Kimball's corpse in the cave suggested that he had mailed Samuel Kimball his seer stone and then deliberately gone down into the tunnels, as his letter had seemed to indicate. He had gone dressed well, and carrying a small animal. Had he known he was going to die? Had he gone down there to face something?

The thing behind the flies?

Mahoun, Samael? The fallen angels of the Wastes of Dudael, as Gus had said? Gus claimed he wanted to defeat the demon—had Teancum done down into the caves to defeat Samael? No, he had gone down to make a thirty-year deal.

But first he'd sent the peep-stone to his son, the stone from which Teancum thought he received guidance.

Guidance from whom, or from what?

Hiram needed to take a good look into the seer stone.

"Can you check on Michael for me?" He handed his revolver to Sorenson, grip first.

Sorenson took the Colt. "Something comes for your boy, don't worry, it'll have to come through me first."

"And then just wait at your home for me to join you? I have something else I have to do, over at the

Kimball house, but I'll be along shortly. And, Sorenson ... Bill ... if you see Ammon, don't mention me
coming around. And with my son ... maybe ..."

"*Ja*, of course, and I won't tell your son nothing.
Holy Jesus, I won't tell my wife nothing. But be
careful, Hiram. Dese things that you have to do ...
dey frighten me." Sorenson chuckled, a bass rumble.
"Hey, de mine ... maybe it's haunted, after all, like
Samuel says."

Hiram smiled. "How do I turn off the lamp?"

"De *on* switch," Sorenson said. "You turn it to *off*."

Hiram extinguished his carbide lamp and gave the
helmet to Sorenson. He retrieved his fedora from the
mine building, and he moved both their chits from
the "IN" board to the "OUT" one. He then headed
north across the canyon, toward the big house.

Chapter Twenty-Four

HIRAM HAD BECOME ACCUSTOMED TO THE WARMER air within the mine; the February night pierced his flesh and sank into his bones. His feet, damp from the water of the cave, froze immediately. He walked faster and huddled into his Army coat. Smoke from fires hung like a fog over the shanties.

He paused by the light of a window to rifle through the billfold he'd taken from Teancum Kimball's body, finding only a few ragged dollars. What kind of thirty-year deal had Teancum attempted to make with the fallen angel? And, since it was 'another' deal, did that mean he had made a previous thirty-year deal? The answers to his questions might have died two years earlier with Teancum himself.

Or had Teancum *become* the demonic fly creature?

Gus Dollar might have the answers, but Hiram couldn't test the truth of Gus's words unless he knew the right questions to ask the man.

Hiram pocketed the billfold and felt the keys he'd retrieved from Teancum's body. One should fit the lock of the Kimball house. That would save Hiram the task of working a charm at the door, and such a match would also confirm the identity of the corpse.

A man in a thick wool sweater and a hat pulled down ambled past Hiram. He wore a red bandana over his face, and Hiram recognized him from the scuffle at the mine gate. He stared intently down an alley as he walked past. Perhaps he was looking for a lost dog?

Hiram raised his hand in a silent greeting.

The masked fellow stopped and looked at Hiram.

"Evening," Hiram said. The ordinary politeness sounded strange in the wake of the evening's events.

The masked man nodded and walked on.

Hiram jogged down the hill and across the road. He approached the Kimball house past the spot where he'd buried the snake head and found the human skull.

What might the skull have to do with Teancum's planned bargain? Or had Hiram stumbled across the remains of some prospector, or a Ute hunter who had lost his way and died in this canyon, perhaps long before the house was even built?

The stone on Ammon's mantel had to be a seer stone. As a mere rock, it had no value, but a peep-stone could grant true visions which had a worth beyond price. If Teancum Kimball possessed such a stone, he might well have sent it to one of his sons as a gift, especially if he were approaching a meeting that might result in his death. Such a stone could have shown Samuel where to dig a new mineshaft, and it might even have directed Samuel to then place the stone back in his family home . . . perhaps with the intent that Ammon would then look into the stone.

But *whose* intent? The intent of the stone? Teancum's

intent? The intent of someone who had created the stone, or a power that was connected to it?

Could the stone have guided Teancum to his death? Could the stone have told Samuel one thing, and then Ammon another, setting them at odds?

Or could the stone be giving them true visions in a difficult situation? Could the Kimballs be failing to heed the guidance of a true messenger?

Hiram shuddered. This was really not what he had expected when Bishops Smith and Wells had asked him to deliver groceries to out-of-work miners.

He sneaked around to the front of the house.

He didn't want Ammon to catch him breaking in. "In the name of the Father, up and down," he chanted, "the Son and the Spirit upon your crown, the cross of Christ upon your breast, sweetest lady send Ammon Kimball rest." He repeated the charm three times, then stepped onto the porch.

There he paused. He was an honest man. Wasn't he? And yet here he was, breaking into someone's home for the second time in as many days. When had he become a burglar?

And breaking into Gus's home had deprived Hiram's charms of power.

Only, he had tried to speak with Ammon openly— as well as with Samuel and Eliza. And they weren't willing to budge. Could he wait until morning, and try to talk to Ammon again?

But Hiram doubted Ammon would be any easier to deal with now. He had called Samuel a thief, presumably for having their father's seer stone in his possession, even though it seemed that Teancum himself had sent Samuel the stone.

And besides, Hiram wasn't going to take anything from Ammon. He just needed to look at the stone, and confirm it for what it was. Ammon wouldn't be harmed.

Hiram chuckled, but his chuckle split into a sob.

"Lord Divine, if what I work here is sin, I beg thee to look on my heart with mercy and forgive me. But also, don't let my charms fail, and don't let me get caught. Amen."

It felt like a burglar's prayer, but at least it was honest.

He felt inclined to add, "And a special blessing on the Markopoulos family, Medea, and Callista, and help heal Basil's leg, but keep him from the temptation of banditry. Amen."

He stepped to the door and tried the key; a perfect fit.

He opened the door, the hinges whining. Closing the door produced more squeaking, and he clenched his teeth. Door shut, he waited to see if Ammon came down, forcing himself to count to a slow one hundred.

No light, no sound, no Ammon.

He probed in the darkness to see whether the single-shot break-action shotgun was by the door. It wasn't. Ammon might sleep with it under his bed. For use against burglars, presumably.

Burglars like Hiram.

But the house was quiet.

Hiram was grateful for the cloudless night, the stars, and the bare windows. He slunk across the front room to the mantel. A handful of coals glowed orange in the fireplace, but not enough to illuminate more than two feet in front of them. Hiram took off his hat.

The brown stone was only a dark shape. If it was a seer stone, Hiram might see visions. But visions sent by what power? Hiram half-hoped he was wrong, and that the stone was just a rock.

Hiram steeled himself.

He picked up the rock. It was cool to the touch. It didn't feel evil, or good, or spiritual, or powerful at all. The stone felt like a stone.

Hiram placed the stone in his hat.

He took a minute to listen again to the quiet of the house. Nothing but silence.

Hiram lowered his face into his hat.

The effect was immediate and overwhelming.

The quartz strip in the rock ignited in a blinding light that hurt to look at and he felt his body move. Vertigo seized him, as if he were flying, and a strong wind beat at his face.

A Bible passage bubbled up into his mind: chapter seventeen of Matthew, the first few verses. *And after six days Jesus taketh Peter, James, and John his brother, and bringeth them up into an high mountain apart. And was transfigured before them: and his face did shine as the sun, and his raiment was white as the light.*

Hiram knew, and felt, that he stood in front of the dying fire, faced buried in his fedora. Yet at the same time, he was standing beside himself, head up, gazing upon both his own body and the shape of a beautiful man, legs, arms, torso, head, and a face that was both indistinct and sharp. Light came from the man's body. Looking right at the figure, he couldn't make out any details. Shifting his gaze, he saw in his peripheral vision features well-proportioned and without blemish.

He and the angelic man stood atop a high mountain, clouds and light around and below them. As long as his eyes rested upon the man, Hiram could see him and the rocky landscape, but when he shifted his eyes slightly, all he saw was Ammon's furniture and shadowy walls.

Greetings, Hiram Woolley, of Lehi. I bring thee glad tidings.

Hiram's heart pounded. Something bothered him, in the back of his mind.

"Greetings, spirit. I stand ready to hear your words," he whispered.

Thy heart is troubled by the suffering of the Kimball family and their endeavors to excavate the treasures of the earth. The time of weeping will soon be over. I shall remove a keystone from the vault of the earth, and the blessings of wealth and prosperity will return to this valley.

The voice came from everywhere and nowhere.

"What is my role, messenger?"

Many are called, but few are chosen. Thy labors here are completed. I bid thee to return to thy home.

Hiram took a deep breath. Everyone wanted him to leave, including Rettig and his ruffians. At first, Rettig had seen Hiram as someone who could help him bring the Kimballs over to the railroad man's side. Word must have gotten back to Rettig that none of the Kimballs would sign, so hurting Hiram would make him just another victim and throw a scare that no one was safe in Spring Canyon. Or maybe Rettig had come to fear that Hiram would unite the Kimball family *against* the railroad man.

And of course, Michael had provoked Rettig.

Hiram saw his situation with Rettig so clearly now. Could this be a true vision of an angel? Did God want Hiram to leave?

"I can't go until I see the mine operating again," Hiram said. "The food I brought is running out." Medea Markopoulos, whose husband Hiram had run over, would starve. So would her children.

Wouldst thou argue with me? The voice in Hiram's mind rose to a thunderous roll. *Where was thou, when the morning stars sang together, and all the sons of God shouted for joy?*

The shining man was quoting scripture. That was as should be—when angels showed up, to Mary in the New Testament or to Brother Joseph in upstate New York, they quoted scripture.

And then Hiram realized what bothered him. The other piece of any true angel's introduction was *fear not*. Hiram feared, and the angel had not tried to allay his fears at all.

Was it a false spirit?

Could this, after all, be Mahoun or Samael? Could a fallen angel or a demon or a monster have pitted the Kimball brothers against each other, and was the same being now attempting to trick Hiram into leaving?

And if the spirit spoke deception, why didn't his bloodstone warn Hiram? But Gus Dollar, with his Jupiter ring and his Samael glyphs, had already proved that the bloodstone could be defeated.

"I don't mean to be difficult," Hiram said. "But I was sent to get these men fed. I brought them food, but men need to eat more than once. Tell me how I can soften the hearts of the Kimballs . . . Ammon, Samuel, and Eliza."

This is my work, and not thine. Go home, cunning man.

Hiram knew a way to test angels.

"Spirit," he said. "I understand. Take a grip from me in sign of our covenant." He reached out his right hand, both the physical hand in Ammon's drawing room and his spiritual hand atop the cloud-shrouded mountain.

He hoped the spirit wouldn't notice his fingers trembling.

The shining man regarded Hiram coolly.

Dost thou not fear to be struck down, as was Uzza when he dared to touch the ark of the Lord?

"What have I to fear from my Father's servants?" Sweat poured down between Hiram's shoulder blades.

So be it. The blinding white figure reached forward. Diamonds seemed to sparkle on its ethereal skin as it reached out to touch his physical body.

Hiram drew his spirit hand back. "Liar."

An angel of heaven was a creature without flesh and bone, and knew it, and would never try to shake hands with a human being. Any spirit that would attempt to touch a person bodily was a deceiving spirit—a fallen angel, a demon, or a ghost.

It was time to end the interview. Hiram tried to remove the hat from his face and couldn't. He tried to turn his feet and step down from the high mountain, and couldn't do that, either.

What is this treachery?

Hiram grunted from the exertion of will, but he couldn't move his body. He couldn't get his face out of the hat.

I will repay thy trickery with death.

Hiram felt cold fingers around his heart, and his vision began to blur. Parts of his consciousness drifted into silence, as if the memories and personality of Hiram Woolley were being wiped off of a chalkboard.

But not thy death, cunning man. I will wield thine own hand to visit horrors upon thy kin!

His own hand? Kin? What kin did he have?

He had no kin.

He was floating, a mote in a cosmic sea.

Alone.

But he wasn't alone.

Michael. The fading parts of Hiram's mind snapped back into clarity.

The demonic being was threatening Michael.

Thy son, the man-child!

The thing knew his thoughts.

"I will call upon the Lord," Hiram cried, shouting the words of the psalm at the top of his voice, "who is worthy to be praised: so shall I be saved from mine enemies!"

He couldn't take his face from the hat, but he managed to slap one clumsy hand to his chi-rho amulet.

The mountain disappeared. So did everything else, and Hiram stood in darkness, his body freezing with cold sweat. He whipped the hat away from his face, panting, and found he could see nothing. Blindly, he dug the seer stone from his fedora and managed to grope his way to the mantel again. He set the stone there awkwardly, on the lip of the wood.

Hiram gasped, shuddering to get air in and out of his lungs. He was making way too much noise for a burglar. Nausea hit him, his legs buckled, and his stomach boiled. Closing his useless eyes, he drew in deep breaths until his belly calmed down.

Finally, he opened his eyes. Tracks of light blurred his vision, and he blinked and blinked until tears stung his eyes and he could see again.

The seer stone was not divine. A malign creature gave visions through the stone. It had given Samuel false visions, and it must have given false visions to Ammon as well. The creature, fallen angel, ghost, demon, or monster, wanted the Kimballs to fight.

Hiram couldn't leave the stone in the house.

He was also loath to touch it again.

Hiram climbed unsteadily to his feet. He got out his green bandana, stained with the blood from his nose and the crayon or lipstick that had been used to write on the Double-A. That seemed fitting. He wrapped the stone up in the cloth and then pocketed it.

He left the house.

He wasn't sure whether the stone's spirit was the same entity as the fly demon, and whether either of those was Mahoun or Samael, but it seemed likely that they were all one and the same.

And the creature had threatened Michael.

He broke into a ragged run, racing across the dark valley back to Bill Sorenson's house.

Chapter Twenty-Five

MICHAEL DREAMED OF FLIES. EVERY SO OFTEN, HE heard a *bang* against the side of the house, or a *crackle* on the street. At each noise Michael started, but then nothing happened, and he'd wonder whether he'd heard anything, after all. Sleeping on the hard sofa against the wall of Sorenson's small house wasn't easy, but he tried to force himself.

The front door slamming shut finally woke him. Bill Sorenson stood alone in the door with the Colt revolver in his hand.

"Eh, you're awake. Oh *ja*, your fadder will be here soon. He's just got some udder work keeping him for a bit, at de big house. You want a beer, boy?"

"No, thanks." Michael sat up. He wasn't sure why he declined the beer. It wasn't like his pap was around to enforce the rules. It was only beer, home-brewed by Sorenson, so it probably wasn't even very strong. Or maybe that meant it would be stronger. Michael wasn't sure.

Regardless, he passed.

Within a year, he'd probably move away from the farm, and the world was full of beer. No rush.

"Water, though," he said. "Or a Coca-Cola, if you have it."

The cold night air sneaked in through the tar-paper walls of the Sorensons' house, and Michael squeezed to the end of the sofa, as close to the stove as he could get.

Why had his father given Bill Sorenson his revolver? Michael knew the weapon, and if he hadn't, those initials scratched into the barrel were a dead giveaway.

Images of swarms of flies came into Michael's mind when he shut his eyes. He tried to keep his eyes open.

Behind those flies, he was pretty sure he'd seen a man. An enormous man, the size of a bear, but a man. And his father had shouted Bible verses at the man. The whole thing was odd. There had to be scientific explanation for the flies. Maybe a cow had collapsed near a hot springs and the carrion had drawn the insects. Maybe there was a thermal vent somewhere in the canyon that kept flies alive through the winter.

Sorenson brought him water in a large beer-stein, holding a second stein for himself. Michael could smell the sweet, hoppy scent of the beer. Sorenson had changed into a shapeless gray flannel shirt and trousers, and wore the revolver tucked into a length of rope holding up the pants.

Sorenson threw more coal into the stove, then sat on the other end of the sofa from Michael.

Michael drank most of his water in one long series of gulps. "Is my pap talking with Ammon Kimball, then?"

"*Ja.*" The Dane seemed deliberately nonchalant. "I guess dey had a meeting."

"In the middle of the night?"

"Haven't you noticed dat de Kimballs are crazy? Mad bastards, all of dem. I stuck with Ammon because he seemed less crazy dan Sam, but now I don't know."

"Maybe you stuck with Ammon because you could do the most good for the men that way," Michael suggested.

"No." Sorenson belched. "I don't care too much for de men. De men don't get paid, dey can just hop on de train and go find a job in Salt Lake or Denver. No, I don't give a damn about dem."

"I don't believe you," Michael said.

Sorenson shook his head. "No, it's de families I care about. It's de families dat don't eat when de man don't work, it's de families dat get left behind when a man goes to ride de rails. So if Joe's a good worker and just needs a little help, and he's got a family, *ja*, den I'm dere to help him. Every time."

"You should go into politics," Michael.

"No, politics is full of rotten bastards dat say dey want to help, but dey really just want to take all your money and you go to hell. No, I want to really help de people, and I tell you what, so does your pap."

Michael felt pride. His pap had some strange old beliefs, but he really wanted to help the poor. *The widows and the fatherless*, as Hiram Woolley himself might say.

Again, something thumped against the wall. Maybe a mule had wandered up and was butting against the house? Or kept falling and standing up again? Probably not. It wasn't a tree. No trees that close to the building. Then what was it?

The stove was heating up with the extra coal; Michael stood and walked close to the door, where he could feel a little cold air rushing in around the edges of the doorframe. Should he get his guitar from the truck? He could entertain himself, and maybe Sorenson would like to hear a little Jimmie Rodgers or Charley Patton.

Sorenson stood to get himself a second glass of beer, and Michael decided he was too tired to play.

"You have a radio, by any chance?" he asked.

Sorenson shook his head, filling the stein. "De miners' families don't have a radio, do dey? So we don't have a radio."

As he settled in to drink his second glass, Sorenson launched into a monolog. Michael could barely follow a long story about how Sorenson had been hired by Teancum because he knew how to get men to work, especially when the work was hard and the conditions dangerous. Sorenson had done it before, for the D and RGW up at a place called Soldier Summit, before he'd lost two fingers, burned off when a boiler exploded. Michael heard about Bill Sorenson's growing up on a ranch, and breaking horses, and chasing girls.

Michael longed for the mercy of flyless sleep. It didn't come.

Mrs. Sorenson appeared during the story. She pulled a kitchen chair close to the stove and sat there, working at needlepoint. She was a big woman with a wide face, though her eyes were small and merry and she moved with a lot of energy. The constant motion of her fingers and needle was a bit mesmerizing.

Fragments of his experiences over the last two days filtered in and out of Michael's consciousness. Samuel's camp had been an excursion into bizarre territory, and yet, the truck breaking down and starting again felt weirder. What exactly had his pap done that had restarted the truck? What was the thing that had attacked them? Rettig's toughs might be the least strange thing Michael had seen since coming to Helper.

But the swarm of flies? In February, with snow on the ground?

Grandma Hettie would have had an explanation for all this stuff. She had died when Michael was nine, a year before he lost his mother. If Grandma Hettie wasn't actually a witch, then she was someone who knew an awful lot about old folk magic, and seemed quite convinced that it worked. She'd tried to explain to Michael that everything had a spirit, and some spirits were ghosts and some were demons and some were angels, and that you had to watch out for the movement of the planets, and a black cat was bad luck, and that with the right stick, you could find buried treasure, if the spirits didn't take it away first.

As a small child, he'd thought she was kidding, telling him stories. But he'd realized one day when he'd twisted his ankle and the first thing that Grandma Hettie did was make the sign of the cross over it that Grandma Hettie really believed.

It was quaint and old-fashioned. Michael could imagine a day when the superstitions of the past would fade away, and scientific theory would be applied to all improve aspects of life. Tell me about a ghost? Prove it, empirically. Any axiom about god, ghost, or devil should be backed up with strong evidence or abandoned. Otherwise, it was all fairy stories, the bogeyman under the barn, and Jesus walking on water alike.

His pap might believe in silly things about God, but he genuinely wanted to do right. So Michael was proud of him, and happy to be his driver. When he went off to college, he knew he would miss their long drives, their banter, and even the good work they did together. Hiram wasn't just bellyaching about people being out of work, he was doing something to help.

Sorenson was in the middle of a story, something about a couple of Comanche stealing his horses, when he was growing up in Oklahoma after immigrating from Denmark, and how other boys made fun of his accent.

Thump.

"Do you hear that?" Michael asked.

Mrs. Sorenson's whirring fingers and the sound of the needle piercing the cloth on her lap was all they heard.

"Hear what?" Sorenson's eyes were red-rimmed and runny.

"You don't hear that?"

Sorenson shrugged and then took up where he left off, saying something about how Quanah Parker respected the courage of a man who asked for his horses back.

Michael's large drink of water had run its course through his system, and he now had a more urgent concern than likely-meaningless noises in the night. "If I have to answer the call of nature, do you have an outhouse?"

Sorenson gave him a wavering stare, opening one eye. "Call of nature? I don't understand."

"I have to . . . take a piss," Michael said.

The Dane chortled, his eyebrows shaking like jelly in an earthquake. "*Ja*, dat's how de miners say it! It's out back, I'll come with you."

Michael jumped to his feet. "I haven't needed help in the outhouse for years."

"I told your fadder I'd watch you." The grogginess fell away from Sorenson's face.

Michael help up a hand, backing toward the door. "You can watch, but watch from far away. Like, maybe from right here."

He slipped out the door, shutting it before Sorenson could follow him.

Outside, the wind blew strong. Passing around the house, Michael heard another *thump*. He took in a great big breath. After being inside the closed, hot room, the cold air felt good on his skin and in his lungs. The outhouse was about twenty feet away in an empty space like a lane between homes. Windows glowed with a muted light from a few of the other houses. The air was thick with the cold and the settling smoke of coal fires.

He went to the corner of the house. He heard something else now, a scratching sound followed by the thump.

Scratch. Scratch. Scratch. Thump.

What the hell? He wished he had his father's revolver.

A shiver ran up his spine and lodged in the base of his skull as an uneasy tingling feeling. He imagined Samuel, smoking marijuana and swinging a dead cat by the tail. Maybe he'd come to pin something more human to his horrid easels. Or what if Rettig's men were back?

Or what if there were really ghosts, come up from the mine?

All just stories. He'd soon see the empirical evidence. That was the only scientific thing to do.

Michael peered around the corner of the Sorenson house.

Lying on the dirt was a dog, a big, shaggy beast. It had three legs, and when it scratched itself, it fell off balance and its back foot struck the Sorenson's house. The mutt would get upright, then scratch itself until it fell over and hit the wall again.

Scratch, scratch, scratch, fall, then *thump.*

"Michael?" he heard Bill Sorenson calling from behind him.

Michael stepped forward, getting away from Sorenson. His movement surprised the animal. It leapt to its three feet and growled, showing teeth, hackles up, and tail straight back.

Michael wasn't a stranger to dogs. He crouched down and pretended to pick up a stone. He stood and cranked his arm back as if ready to throw. The dog went loping away toward the mud street in front of the house in a stutter step, two back legs working and the one front leg hopping along.

Michael dropped his arm. Just a dog.

Something struck the back of his neck; something small and moving fast, and the pain was fierce.

Michael slapped his neck, trapping something. A wasp? Buzzing filled his ears. Another sting in the palm of his hand, and more stings on the neck. He spun. Insects swarmed over him, drowning out the light, rushing down his shirt and even into his pants, biting him everywhere they found exposed skin.

He yelled and threw himself against the wall, trying to smash the swarm with his body.

"Michael?" Sorenson's voice sounded remote.

Something emerged from the shadows. For a mad

moment, Michael thought it was the dog. This dark thing came forward, and he'd seen it before. It was broad-shouldered, but had the tapering waist of a man, rather than the bulk of a bear. Its skin was the color of mottled ash, and there was something wrong with its face.

Mouths. It had three mouths.

Michael backed away, but his feet got twisted under him.

He crashed forward onto his belly. The man—it had to be a man, what else could it be?—sank a knee into his back. Michael felt his hair pulled back and then his face was smashed into the ground…over…over… over. He was surprised he didn't hurt, just experienced a dull feeling of his head being pummeled into the dirt. The stinging hurt more, and the awful feeling of the insects inside his clothes, scuttling around on his skin to find fresh flesh to eat.

Michael vomited, then gasped in coal smoke. A tingling started in his right foot and then his whole leg seemed to be on fire. His face smashed into his own vomit. He heard a *pop* above him, saw a flash of light, maybe?

Or were those stars?

His foot hurt. It was like someone had stuck a hot coal in the heel of this boot. But he was already so dizzy, and hurt, and scared. The world went black.

Bang!

Michael woke up in surprise and in pain. Where was he?

Bang! Bang!

Gunshots. From inside the Sorenson house.

A pause. Scuffling inside the house. A final shot.

Doors of other houses flew open.

Michael staggered to his feet. He wiped the half-dried sick off his face and brushed away the dirt. His skin burned.

He went to the window. Inside, Mrs. Sorenson lay on the floor in a widening pool of blood, her needlepoint clenched in a dead fist. The left side of her head was missing. On top of her lay her husband, part of his scalp hanging off his head. Most of the scalp, however, was gone, exposing white bone, and his flannel shirt was soaked in blood.

On the floor beside them lay Pap's revolver.

Yelling, and the pounding of feet.

Michael's head throbbed.

The thing that had attacked Michael—no, the man, it had to be a man, his eyes had played tricks on him—must have killed the Sorensons. But instead, it might look like Bill Sorenson had killed his wife.

Or worse . . . like Hiram Woolley, whose revolver lay on the floor, had killed them both.

Or *Michael* had.

Men stomped by, not noticing Michael in the shadows. They went busting into the house, hollering. At first, the shouting was in languages Michael didn't know, but it gradually shifted into English.

"God in heaven, that's Bill Sorenson! Shot his wife! Shot himself?"

"I don't believe it. Look at the scalp. Who takes scalps?"

"That truck, it's the Mormon. And he have an Indian with him, don't he?"

"That gun, it have something on it, scratched on the barrel."

"An *H* and a *W*. Hiram Woolley. *Ja, das stimmt*, that gun is the farmer's."

"Yeah, but who is Y.Y.?"

"The other fellow must be Y.Y.! The dark guy who was with him!"

"Where is he? Where is that Indian? I bet they did it. I bet they working for Samuel and the Greeks! Make us believe it was suicide . . . but no, not Bill. Bill never!"

"Them strangers were for Ammon and you Germans!"

"No, the Indians, that Indian, they hate us white-skins. I seen the movies!"

Michael felt every slam of his heart in his aching head. He couldn't breathe.

A hand touched his shoulder and he started—but it was the Greek girl, Medea. She crouched beside him, her homemade spear in her hands. Maybe it was the way the light from the Sorensons' cast shadows across her face, but as he looked at her, Michael thought she looked like she might be his kid sister.

She jerked her head, indicating an open alley beyond the outhouse. Michael climbed to his feet and ran.

Chapter Twenty-Six

SOMETHING WAS WRONG IN THE CAMP. THERE WAS too much noise for the middle of the night, and it seemed to be centered around the Sorensons' house. Hiram made his way cautiously through the shadows of the tarpaper shacks, cold sweat chilling his face. He sprinted up the slope and took a back way that threaded the narrow lanes between homes. He had to duck laundry lines, laundry buckets, and washboards, along with shovels, picks, axes, and other tools.

Hiram crept up through an alley on the other side of Sorenson's place. Miners had pulled their cars around to shine their lights on the big Dane's house, lighting the bare lanes on all sides. Two Ford Model Ts very nearly boxed in the Double-A. Hiram sneaked closer, staying in the darkness. He caught snatches of conversation in broken English.

Police were on their way. The Mormon's revolver. Sorenson shot his wife and then shot himself. No, that farmer shot them both. Ghosts from the mine might have driven them all crazy. Now the Dane believed, God rest his soul. No, it was the Mormon's Injun friend. Killed the Danes, took their money, and left. No sign of the Indian, but they found tracks leading away. Wasn't the Injun, it was the Mormon. You knew how they are. Probably wanted Sorenson's wife, and then shot them when they wouldn't go along.

Hiram had to rest for a minute while relief opened his lungs again. His son was alive.

He and Michael might both be in trouble with the law, and poor Bill Sorenson. Poor Eva. Bill had promised he'd protect Michael, and had died doing so. Hiram felt gratitude and sorrow, and then apprehension. Without the foreman, the strife in the camp would surely get worse.

Had one of the miners killed the Dane? Had Rettig ordered it done? Had the demon in the mine followed Sorenson home? That might make his death Hiram's fault, and Hiram found his eyes filling with silent tears.

Could Hiram show his face in Kimball, suspected by the miners, hunted by the police? And where was Michael now? Alone in the freezing wilderness and on foot, since the Double-A sat empty in front of Sorenson's house. Surely, he must be heading for Helper.

If Hiram could get to the truck and get away, he might be able to find Michael on the road. He'd have to hurry, before the police arrived—he didn't want a high-speed chase through the canyons.

The Model Ts might try to follow him.

But Hiram had learned a car-disabling charm from Gus Dollar.

The miners were clustered around the doorway, chattering breathlessly. Some of their women stood among them, arguing and waving fists, while others pulled children away from the Sorenson's house, stuffing them back into their own homes.

Hiram crept up to the back of one of the Model Ts and took a piece of chalk from his pocket. He scratched three words across the back bumper: *Nema, Nema, Nema*. Was this blasphemy? But he was only trying to escape, to rescue his son. And he didn't know the Lord's Prayer backward, so he'd say it forward and hope the Lord Divine would give life to his charm.

To his curse, that is.

Hiram whispered the prayer and then repeated the process with the second Model T.

He then drew in a deep breath. This next piece was going to be risky. *Lord Divine, help me start this truck.*

He shambled up to the Double-A, head down to hide his face, counting on the darkness to help him. Slipping into the truck with as much nonchalance as he could, he flipped up the spark, turned the key, gave the clutch a couple of pumps because of the cold night air, and hit the starter.

The truck rumbled to life.

"In the truck! The Mormon!"

Hiram slammed his foot onto the gas pedal and the Double-A shot forward. He swerved around a mustached Greek man and then took a sharp turn. He felt the truck lurch to the right and he wasn't sure his wheels were touching earth. Spinning the steering wheel, he got the vehicle onto the ground again, only to have the Double-A lurch and nearly topple over the other way.

He fought the truck into submission and he made it

through the shacks and out of the camp. The Model Ts didn't follow him—his curse had worked.

His first curse.

And he'd learned it from Gus Dollar. The thought sobered Hiram.

Hiram slowed as the Ford Model Bs of the Helper police raced past him going the other way. Then he raced toward Dollar's, where he skidded onto the main Spring Canyon road. He longed to give the Double-A real gas, to keep ahead of those Model Bs with their V-8 engines, but he kept himself in check. If Hiram died in a ditch, he did Michael no good.

But it wouldn't be long before the miners told the cops that their prime suspect was on the lam and that they'd driven right past him.

He found a rough side road, little more than a dirt track, and he pulled off, going up enough distance to get out of sight. He parked the truck and crept down to the main road to wait.

All the sneaking, breaking in, and acting in a generally guileful manner didn't sit right with him. What he'd told Michael turned out to be true. It was a dirty world, and even if a man only wanted to do good, he'd likely get his hands filthy.

Soon, the Model Bs raced by again. They wanted to catch him before he reached Helper and the highway.

And if they beat him to the mouth of the canyon, they could put up a roadblock and trap him. Or could he drive out some other way? Some of these other tracks must go over the ridges and out. Samuel must have some other way in and out of Apostate Canyon—he couldn't pass his family home every time, could he?

Hiram wearily shuffled up to his truck. He hadn't

really slept in two nights, and he felt fatigue now in every muscle, but especially in his eyelids.

He backed up the Double-A, did a dozen-point turn, and rolled carefully down to the road. He turned. The headlights caught the dust still swirling from the police cars.

The police might not set up a roadblock, especially if he went soon. They might chase off in the direction they imagined he'd gone. Plus, there didn't seem to be that many police in Helper. Did they really have the manpower to set up a roadblock anywhere?

Maybe they would get the Carbon County Sheriff involved.

Hiram drove slowly, searching for a sign of Michael.

A smell filled his nose, of strong garlic and sugar, sweet, spicy. His vision tunneled in, more tightly than it had in the mine. His heart thumped like a toad flopping over. "Rupert, Giles..." What was it? He couldn't remember his charm against sleeping sickness, he was just too tired.

He tried to stop the truck, get it to the side of the road, to his left, because to the right was a precipice. If he went over that, he wouldn't be walking away.

He aimed for a patch of dark green on the left side of the road. He was reasonably sure he'd pointed the truck in that direction when he lost consciousness.

Mary McGill winced when the morning sun pierced the clouds and struck a white wall of Spring Canyon, forcing the glare into her red and white Model A Ford. Her eyes stung and she blinked.

Were the tears filling her eyes the result of the light, or the events of the night before?

The evening had started out promisingly enough. Five-cent Jimmy had shown up in his best suit, wrinkled, with his gorilla arms and his necktie all out of control, just in time to drag Mary into the Helper Justice Court. To Mary's delight, Jimmy had made Police Chief Asael Fox look silly. Jimmy would fight on him on every front: acting beyond Fox's jurisdiction, censurable behavior, borderline criminal, and of course Jimmy threatened a civil lawsuit against the department if Mary wasn't released immediately and left alone.

Mary hadn't thought about the sage leaf under her heel until later, and then mostly to consider with bemusement the possibility that maybe, in some way, it *had* helped.

Jimmy left immediately—business in Salt Lake City, he'd said.

Mary had stopped to eat at the Chop Suey. A woman named Yu Yan, whose husband worked at the Kimball mine, told her that Bill and Eva Sorenson had been murdered. The prime suspects, she had whispered, were the Mormon do-gooder and his Indian friend.

Mary had laughed that off as obvious nonsense. Still, a part of her had wanted to rush up to the mine immediately, but she had given in to her desire for a bath and a real bed.

In the morning, feeling rested, and strengthened by a bellyful of coffee and bacon, she had headed up Spring Canyon.

On the outskirts of the Kimball camp, a flash caught her eye.

Mary slammed on the brakes. Dust flooded past her. When it cleared, Mary saw thin legs sticking out from under a low Juniper a few steps from the track, and the hem of a blue dress.

Her heart hammered. She willed those legs to move, but they lay still.

Mary left her car, trying to control her breath. The images of dead children she'd seen before, suffocated in a Chicago tenement, drained bloodless in a sawmill, crushed under a fallen tree, flashed into her mind.

"Please, don't," Mary whispered. She crunched quickly across the gravel.

The child, a young woman, really, lay under the evergreen bushes. Bruises covered her arm and legs as well, but the worst were around her throat—huge, mottled, purple marks, with torn skin. Big hands had strangled her.

Flies crawled on her face.

The girl held a long, sharpened stick in her hand, like a spear.

Mary recognized her—her name was Callista, and her parents were Basil and Medea.

Mary had to tell Bill Sorenson.

No, he was dead.

She slipped into her car. She'd tell Ammon Kimball. That big red house had to have a telephone. And if not, there was Gus Dollar's store down the canyon.

But leaving the body felt like sacrilege. Mary got out, took a tarp from her trunk, and covered Callista Markopoulos's small body. The flies rose up as she whispered Hail Mary after Hail Mary.

Chapter Twenty-Seven

HIRAM WOKE UP WITH HIS FOREHEAD PRESSED into the steering wheel of the Double-A. When he raised his face to peek above the dashboard, a bright yellow sun low on the horizon burned his eyes.

His ears buzzed, and it wasn't from flies.

He was almost certain.

He'd rammed the Double-A into a stand of junipers. Looking around, he saw now that he'd made it a hundred yards from the road.

How long had he been passed out?

He was lucky, but he didn't *feel* lucky. A fainting spell gave him no rest, so he'd missed two nights of sleep. He was afraid to stay where he was, but he was also afraid to be on the roads—there were few enough of them, it would be an easy matter to block off, say, one road up to Utah Valley and one to Price, and he'd be trapped.

Even with the small number of officers Helper had. If he were trying to escape, he'd do it by mule.

He shook his head, trying to clear fog from his brain, and partially succeeded.

He didn't want to escape. He wanted to find Michael.

Michael was alive. He was a smart boy, and no miners would have caught him.

But the thing in the caves might have Michael. Or Gus Dollar might have taken Hiram's son, to punish Hiram for escaping from his second curse stopping Hiram's truck and to continue to raise the stakes in their grindingly slow duel. Or the Helper police might have taken Michael, to warn Hiram away from interfering in their persecution of the union organizer, Mary McGill, or as a suspect in the Sorensons' death. Or Rettig or his thugs . . .

Hiram jerked himself awake—the sun had moved higher in the sky. He'd slept a bit, though he still felt exhausted. He willed his limbs to begin taking action.

He took his second unpeeled witch hazel rod from his tool chest; he could find Michael with it. He peeled off the rind, taking deep breaths to keep himself awake, then cut the three crosses.

And for a name? After consideration, he slowly carved MICHAEL YAZZIE WOOLLEY on the rod. Because there was room, he also carved both Michael's parents' names: YAS YAZZIE and BETTY YAZZIE. Then, after a long hesitation during which he almost nodded off, he added his own name: HIRAM WOOLLEY, and his wife's, ELMINA WOOLLEY.

He sang as he worked, the same song over and over, to a Grandma Hettie tune. Psalm 130 didn't feel quite right, or maybe Hiram didn't like using it to look for Michael because only a few short hours earlier, he had used it to go looking for Teancum Kimball, and had found the man a corpse.

He chose Psalm 67 instead, just the first two verses, and focused the prayerful desires of his heart on finding his son: "God be merciful unto us, and bless us; and cause his face to shine upon us; Selah. That thy way may be known upon earth, thy saving health among all nations."

He crawled slowly over the driver's seat of the Double-A. His hair and Michael's were very different, and no one other than the two of them had driven the truck. No, wait, there had been Bert from Conoco. Hiram closed his eyes, trying to picture the color of Bert's hair, and had to snatch himself back from the brink of sleep again.

Red hair. Bert was a carrot top.

Hiram found several long, thick, black hairs on the back of the truck's driver's seat. They had to belong to Michael. He made a very thin cut into the soft wood of the hazel rod, inserted the hairs, and then let the still-green witch hazel spring back into place to pin the hairs. For good measure, he tied them in a knot.

This would not be efficient; he couldn't operate the Mosaical Rod while driving. He fed several test questions to the rod, getting satisfactory results, and then steeled his stomach.

"Is my son Michael alive?"

He nearly wept when the rod dipped, indicating *yes*.

It remained only to find him. Find him, and, if necessary rescue him.

He swung the rod, looking for Michael, and got a tug informing him he needed to drive farther up Spring Canyon.

He drove half a mile, hid the truck, tried again, and got the same result.

He was coming close to Gus Dollar's store. Hunkering low over the wheel—to be invisible? for cover, in case Gus shot at him?—he drove *past* the store and around the corner. When he could park the truck discreetly, he tried the rod again—and it told him to go back down the canyon.

Gus Dollar. It had to be.

Gus had his son.

He fumbled in his tool chest for his dried dog tongue and slipped it into his boot. He'd walk in the front door and didn't care if the dogs barked, but the tongue should keep them from biting him, too.

His clasp knife was a stupid weapon, but it had a locking blade, and if need be, he could cut with it.

He shook himself. No, that was a terrible idea. He'd confront Gus and demand the storekeeper release his son.

But, in the case of last resort, and truly dire need…it was strong counter magic to make a witch bleed. If he needed to overcome some last spell of Gus's, he didn't have to kill Gus, he only had to bleed him.

The clasp knife might be enough.

For good measure, he took the bronze Oremus lamen that had hung behind the mirror in their hotel room, tucking it into the inside pocket of his coat.

Mosaical Rod in hand, Hiram marched up onto Gus's porch and threw the door open.

The Rottweilers scattered.

The dowsing rod in his hand burst into flame. Dropping it to the floor of the shop, Hiram stared at the branch: the carved letters and symbols stood out briefly in blazing letters, and then they were gone as the entire hazel rod was engulfed in fire. Within seconds, the wood disappeared, leaving a trail of ash.

The floor itself remained unmarked.

Clutching his burned hand, Hiram stared into the shop. There was no sign of Gus Dollar. Behind the counter, on two high chairs, sat the twins, Greta and Dietrich. They weren't the sliding drops of mercury they'd been before. Now the pair sat still and smiled at Hiram, perfect, flawless smiles, like ten-dollar dolls from the Sears, Roebuck catalog.

Hiram's eyes shot to the lead signs of Samael, or Mahoun, in the front windows. Not only had they been restored, they had been painted over in a garish red paint. Dollar's now flaunted its wards, or association, or whatever it was, to the world.

Only it was a world no longer prepared to see the message that was being clearly published.

"Opa Gus told us you would be back," the children said together.

Hiram shook his head. He'd have sworn they'd just spoken together, mouths perfectly synchronized.

"You're the sieve and shears man," they added. They raised their hands, and their fingers glistened, as if slick with oil. Their nails and fingertips were blackened. Dipped in soot?

The hair on the back of Hiram's neck stood up. The children had been normal, happy, healthy-looking children the two times he'd seen them before. What had happened? What had Gus done? "Where's your Opa Gus?"

"Not here. No one's here but us."

Hiram could take Gus's grandchildren. That would be fair, and he could trade them to Gus to get his son back.

"Your mother?" Hiram asked.

"No one but us, sieve and shears man."

But that would be kidnapping.

But Gus had done it first. As Gus had pushed Hiram to perform counter magic by charming him first, and as Gus had forced Hiram's hand, making him commit burglary.

And something seemed wrong with these children. Maybe the old man had ensorcelled them somehow. He'd be rescuing them from Gus.

Hiram shook his head. He wasn't thinking clearly; that might be fatigue and the lingering effect of his recent spell, but it could also be Gus. Gus had influenced Hiram before, with his Jupiter ring and his other charms.

Did Gus *want* Hiram to kidnap his grandchildren?

Was Gus *trying* to get Hiram into trouble?

"Michael!" Hiram yelled. There was no answer.

He wheeled around the ground floor, crying out. "Michael!"

Silence, but for the low whimpering of dogs.

He climbed the stairs. If Gus simply shot Hiram now, he'd tell the Helper police—or the Carbon County Sheriff—that he'd interrupted a burglary in process, by a man who'd already burgled him once, and that would likely be the end of the investigation. Gus would be within his rights.

For that matter, the police might think Gus had shot the Sorensons' murderer.

"Michael! Michael?"

The second story was empty.

He turned to go downstairs and the twins stood at the top of the stairs, smiling at him.

"We told you," they said.

Hiram shivered. He wanted to lock the children in one of the upstairs rooms so they'd stop following him, but he didn't dare. Instead, he rattled downstairs as quickly as he could and entered the pantry.

The Rottweilers lay pressed to the floor on the trapdoor. Hiram grabbed each by its collar and walked back to the storeroom. The front door was open, as he'd left it, and he heaved both beasts out onto the porch, shutting the door behind them.

The twins stood watching him when he turned around.

"You shouldn't hurt the dogs," they warned him.

"The dogs are fine," he said. "Have you seen my son Michael? I'm just looking for my son."

"We haven't seen any boys here today." They continued to speak in perfect timing together. Unless Hiram was just imagining it. His head hurt. "Are you going to look in Opa Gus's secret room now?"

"What do you know about your Opa Gus's room?"

"What do *you* know about it, sieve and shears man?"

Hiram wished he'd locked them upstairs. But the Mosaical Rod had shown Michael to be here at Dollar's.

Hadn't it?

Or had Gus tricked the rod?

Or had Hiram, in his fatigue and hunger, made a mistake?

He dug into his pocket and found two quarters and a dime, setting them on the counter. "I need ten Cokes. Will you count out ten Cokes from the ice box for me? And two Snickers bars."

They stared at him, but then turned to the red icebox in the corner and began to fetch his Cokes.

Hiram rushed to the pantry. Yanking up the trap-door, he looked down into darkness. He pulled his flashlight from a pocket and shone it down, illuminating the ladder rungs and the stone wall of the descending shaft.

"Michael?"

Nothing. But his son could be tied up and gagged, or unconscious.

Or dead.

Or Gus Dollar could be waiting down there with a loaded shotgun.

Gritting his teeth, Hiram climbed down. Sweat trickled between his shoulder blades, and he felt a breeze blowing on the back of his neck. Fear made him drop the last few feet, landing unsteadily on his Harvesters. He whipped around, half-expecting to be blasted into oblivion.

The room was empty.

The crack in the corner of the room was gone.

Hiram's heart pounded.

He paced around the room to be sure, angry and mournful that his rod had been destroyed. He pushed at the stone in the corner where there had been a crack—under the glare of his flashlight, the wall there looked like a different color, and the mortar seemed fresh. He shone his light closer; the mortar was wet and had a reddish hue to it.

This, perversely, was reassuring. He wasn't insane, he wasn't imagining that there had once been a crack, and now it was gone.

There had been an opening, and Gus had bricked it shut.

He pounded on the stone. "Michael!"

No answer.

He went back to the ladder and looked up. The faces of the twins looked down.

Greta held an iron in her hand. In both hands, Dietrich held a heavy black skillet.

Hiram pressed his chi-rho amulet to his chest with his left hand and sprang up the ladder as quickly as he could with one hand. As he climbed, he shifted himself left and right.

The iron struck him on the left shoulder. Hiram grunted in pain, but he held tight to the rung, and pushed himself higher.

"Did that hurt, sieve and shears man?"

The pan struck him on his back. His feet lost his grip and he hung briefly over the shaft, scrabbling to get a grip. Then he dragged himself up and into the pantry.

The children stared at him with cold eyes.

Damn Gus Dollar.

The Cokes and candy bars stood on the counter. Hiram ignored them for the moment and rushed outside. He charged up to the boulders and scree behind the store, looking for the sheet of stone that screened the outside entrance into the caves that connected into Gus Dollar's workroom.

And most likely into the mine as well.

He found the stone and climbed around it, grabbing his flashlight and preparing to deal with the spell he expected to find on the cave mouth—but this opening, too, was bricked up. Bricked up, and dirt and pebbles had been piled over it to conceal it.

"Michael!" He pounded on the stone.

Nothing.

He staggered back to the store and saw a second automobile parked in front, a red and white Ford Model A. On the porch stood Mary McGill. She wore a different dress under a stylish jacket, this one a beige color accented with a maroon scarf. A brown overcoat hung from her shoulders. She stared at him with a pale face and haunted eyes.

"You don't look well, Hiram Woolley."

"Sorry to say, Miss McGill, but you don't, either."

The woman clenched her jaws and nodded. That was strange.

Had she heard about Sorenson's death? Did she blame Hiram? "I bet you're thirsty."

She raised her eyebrows at him. "Pardon me?"

"You stopped here because you were starting to feel warm and thirsty, and thought you might get a drink."

"Well, I *am* thirsty. But I also came here to try to use the phone."

"I just bought ten Cokes," Hiram said. "I'll give you one."

"I'll need something far stronger than that," Mary whispered. "Someone has murdered a child up at the mine."

Chapter Twenty-Eight

HIRAM FOUGHT SORROW AND ANGER AS HE CARRIED the ten Cokes in an apple crate he'd taken from behind Gus's counter toward Mary's car. He'd already wolfed down the Snickers bars, which took the edge off his hunger but also made him feel nauseated. Looking over his shoulder, he saw the two tow-headed twins, staring at him from the front window of the shop. They pressed their oily, soot-marked fingers to the window and smiled dreadfully.

Bewitched by Gus?

Or by the thing in the caves? Gus was evil, but Hiram's real enemy was the fly demon, Mahoun-Samael. He'd have bet his farm that the demon was the same entity he'd seen in the peep-stone.

It was the demon that was manipulating the Kimballs.

Had it killed the Greek girl?

Fear spiked Hiram's heart. If the fly demon had killed Callista, had it found Michael as well? Had it killed his son or dragged him into the pit? He recalled his dreams... searching for Michael, the empty roads, the voice booming out of a bottomless pit.

The fear threatened to kill him. His only sanctuary was prayer. *Lord Divine, if it be thy will, bring my son to me. And please, let it be thy will. Amen.*

"Sheriff's deputies are coming up to retrieve Callista's body and ask questions." Mary opened the car door.

"Callista?" Hiram felt his heart stop.

"The murdered girl is named Callista Markopoulos. You shouldn't be anywhere around here. Word has it, you're a suspect for Sorenson's murder."

Hiram set the crate into the back seat. He looked; the twins were no longer in the store window. His stomach ached. "Do you want to ask whether I'm guilty?"

Mary laughed, and it was a bitter sound. "Hiram Woolley, I *know* you're innocent. But it sounds like you should be taking your ring back. You might just need it." She handed him the copper ring of escape.

He slipped it onto his finger; for him, it was a pinky ring.

"Let's talk in my car. It's cold out here." Mary got behind the wheel.

Hiram sat in the passenger's seat. He pulled his eyelids down with his fingertips. "I met the girl's family." He didn't mention his run-in with Basil on the road nor how the man got his leg broken.

He'd wounded Medea's husband, and now her daughter... was it Hiram's fault?

Mary sat behind the wheel. "I told Ammon Kimball," she said. "He called the police. He didn't offer to help the family, though."

"He won't." Hiram had to find Michael.

They lapsed into silence.

Finally Mary broke it. "Thank you, Mr. Woolley. Both the ring and sage leaf seemed to work. Here I am, free."

Hiram was glad for the change of subject. "Five-Cent Jimmy showed up?"

"He did," Mary replied, "and he worked his own special magic. When Jimmy tipped his hat on the way out the door, I'd swear Asael Fox wet his trousers."

"Jimmy sounds like a good friend to have." Hiram was glad Mary had escaped, but he had a hard time focusing on her freedom.

"Well," Mary said, "if you get yourself tossed into the can, be sure to wear that ring. It may summon him. And do you know who came to the hearing, bold as daylight, and sat in the back grinning?"

Hiram tried to organize his reeling thoughts. "Ammon Kimball? Gus Dollar?"

Mary McGill snorted, blowing air. "The D and RGW Director of Carbon County Operations. The railroad man, Rettig. Filthy thug didn't even try to hide his involvement."

"You think..." Hiram concentrated. "You think Fox put you in jail because Rettig told him to."

"Yes, I do. I think he's making some kind of play for the mine, and I complicated things, so he wanted me out of the way."

Hiram tried to follow the logic all the way through. "He could still buy the mine if the men working there were organized."

"Yes, but it'd be worth less, because he'd be paying the men more."

Hiram thought about the three railroad thugs and Dimitrios. Rettig wanted *him* out of the way, too. "I'm sorry."

"For what? You aren't Naaman Rettig. Oh, but I'll make that little bastard sorry, I will. Once I'm done with the mine, I'll start riding the D and RGW back and forth from Denver to Salt Lake, and I'll organize every last porter, and get them to ask for better wages, and the firing of Naaman Rettig."

Hiram managed to crack a smile. "I bet you will, too."

"And I bet you'll help Medea Markopoulos."

Hiram nodded. "I will. But I need help, myself." Hiram wanted to explain the situation calmly, but it was complicated, and suddenly he found himself babbling. "My son is missing. He was at Sorenson's house when Sorenson got killed, and I haven't been able to find him."

Mary frowned, sighed, and let her sarcasm slip. "What, you didn't try a charm?" Then she saw the expression on Hiram's face. "Ah, I'm sorry. You *did* try a charm."

"Other powers interfered," Hiram said. "I have enemies."

Mary glanced over and tried to find a smile. "I'm sorry for teasing. You must be worried sick. I want to vomit, myself. I feel so powerless. Tell me how I can help."

"A ride?"

"I'll be your chauffeur, Mr. Woolley. Let's go find your son."

Hiram's heart was heavy. "This will sound odd, but . . . can I bring along my tool chest?"

He hid the Double-A by driving it into a depression screened by junipers and a jagged pile of red rock. Mary followed and waited on the main road as Hiram shifted his toolbox into the trunk of her car. Moving the toolbox, he thought about the lead lamen, with its reference to Jericho. Surely, Gus intended to use it to collapse the mine.

To defeat the demon.

But that didn't mean that Gus was on Hiram's side.

Hiram hurt, the ache of sleeplessness as well as the pains he'd acquired being bruised in the cave, waylaid by bandits, and attacked with ironmongery. At Mary's suggestion, he hunkered down on the floor of the car's back seat, ready to cover himself with a ratty wool driving blanket in case they passed anyone.

A wave of fatigue washed over him so hard, he almost fell asleep immediately. "Guess I better drink a Coke. Or two."

"I thought you people weren't supposed to drink coffee and Coca-Cola," Mary said.

"Well," Hiram said, "there's more gray area than that."

He downed one bottle of cola immediately, setting the empty bottle neatly on the back seat, then held the second to nurse it.

"What's your son's name?" Mary McGill asked over the front seat, once she had started the Model A.

"Michael."

"He's the young Indian man I saw up at the mine, right?"

"Practically a man."

"What led you to adopt an Indian?"

Again, they were talking about nothing. It felt like

a layer of icy normality lying over the top of a cold, wet abyss of horror. "His father and I were in the Great War. Yas was my best friend over there. He survived gas, and German bullets, and French girls, and army food. He was the toughest man I ever knew. He was a dreamer, he was very sensitive to things of the spirit. He talked about meaning and the gods and truth with an earnestness you never see, these days. And then he got killed by..."

By darkness itself, he didn't say. By fools worshipping dark old gods, trying to salvage bloody national lines and pride.

"Anyway," he continued, "his wife died in the Influenza Epidemic. It hit Indians pretty hard, I guess. But their baby son survived. It took a lot of talking to the tribal elders, but they finally let me adopt him."

"You're a good man, Hiram Woolley."

"I aim to stand before the judgment bar and say I tried, with a clean conscience. I guess I can't do much more than that."

"Where would Michael go?"

...*if he's still alive.* She didn't say them, but Hiram felt the words hanging in the air.

He considered. He'd driven up and down Spring Canyon already. He'd tried a charm, and it seemed to have led him into a trap. Anyway, Michael hadn't been where the Mosaical Rod had indicated. Hiram doubted Michael would stick around the mine, or Kimball Canyon at all. With Sorenson dead, there were no friendly faces there. So he'd head back to town. Maybe to Buford's. The boarding house was so warm and comfortable that Hiram regretted he hadn't taken at least a little nap in that large bed.

Hiram found himself drifting to sleep, Coke notwithstanding.

"Hiram?" she tried again.

"Town, I guess," he said. "Just hopefully not one of the brothels. *Ooh-la-la.*"

"Town it is."

Hiram watched the canyon walls spin slowly around the windows above him as Mary McGill turned the Model A about. He found the motion of the car hypnotic, so he grabbed another pair of Cokes.

He needed to find Michael, but there were other things he had to do, as well. If Michael wasn't dead or held prisoner by Gus Dollar—Hiram shuddered at both possibilities—then he was probably fine. He was smarter than Hiram, and he should be able to handle himself.

"Why do you think you're getting blamed for Bill Sorenson's murder?" Mary asked.

"I have a revolver. It belonged to Michael's father, Yas. Well, really, it belonged to an officer, but that fellow died and Yas used his gun to save the platoon and then everyone figured the gun should belong to Yas. He gave it to me when he died." Hiram was babbling again; he tried to focus. "Last night, I gave Sorenson my weapon so he could protect Michael with it. And then Sorenson and his wife were both murdered."

"With your gun."

"I think so. Anyway, my gun was there, and some of the miners blamed me. Or my son."

"Callista wasn't shot. She was strangled." Mary's voice became subdued. "Her body was crawling with flies."

Hiram nearly vomited.

Mary was silent—expecting a response? "I don't have any good answers."

"Things aren't going to improve at the mine," Mary said. "Dead kids have a way of making even sane people crazy."

The mine. The Kimballs. Ammon, Samuel, Eliza. If he wasn't at Buford's, might Michael have gone to Eliza? Michael knew where her hotel room was. Other than Eliza and Naaman Rettig, Michael didn't know anyone in Helper.

Eliza. The seer stone in Hiram's pocket suddenly felt heavy, and seemed to burn him through several layers of fabric. Eliza needed to be warned. She'd need to be persuaded, too, because when he told her what he knew, she would scoff.

She might not scoff at the machinations of Naaman Rettig, though.

"We need to go see Eliza Kimball," he said. "It's a long shot, but Michael might have gone to her."

"The sister. Where is she staying?"

"At the Hotel Utah. We'll want to be careful, because Naaman Rettig is staying in the same hotel."

"I know the place. It has a back stair. In a manner of speaking."

Hiram was drifting into a warm sea of mindless sleep when the car jolted to a halt, shaking him awake.

"Lie down, cover up, and hold still," Mary hissed.

He took the last sip of Coke and obeyed. He huddled under a blanket that smelled like engine oil and sweat and it cut off Hiram's air, but he lay still as a lump of coal in the back seat and waited.

A brief silence ensued.

"Hello, Miss McGill."

The voice belonged to G. Washington Dixon. Shanks.

"What's the problem, officer? I was going to drive up to mine, after hearing about the Sorensons, but then had second thoughts." Mary kept her voice even and cool.

"So you know about the murders," Shanks continued. "But we also found a girl. Not sure who done it yet, but it looks like it might be that feller who came and saw you twice in the hoosegow. Woolley."

"I don't believe that," Mary said.

"Nor do I," Shanks exhaled loudly. "Chief Fox and the railroad do, though."

The railroad? Rettig.

Mary tsked. "Surely, after getting chastised by the judge last night for exceeding his jurisdiction, Chief Fox doesn't want to go arresting anyone up Spring Canyon this morning?"

"Nope," Shanks said. "We're just helping out the Carbon County Sheriff today."

"Any other suspects?" Mary asked.

"Not one," Shanks said. "The fellow's gun is all we have, so even if he didn't do the killing, we need to talk to him. The girl...wasn't shot. I won't say more. Only that you should stay away for a bit, ma'am."

"So I should restrict my organizing activities to the other mines?"

"All these canyons are close enough, I figure you should probably stay in town for a few days. Get a hotel room, try the food at the Chop Suey. We got three movie theaters in Helper, you know, and a bowling alley."

"You're practically Coney Island. Well, as you can see, Sergeant Dixon, I'm headed down the canyon.

As it happens, I have business in town, for today at least. I can't guarantee I'll stay down there. The spirit breatheth where he will, you know."

Hiram heard a metallic thumping that suggested that Shanks was pounding on the roof of the Model A. "Alright then, you drive safe."

Hiram waited until the car was in gear and traveling down the road again before he pulled the blanket away from his face and spoke. "I think you quoted John chapter three," he said.

"Ah, well, you wouldn't quite recognize the words, would you? You're stuck in your silly little King James translation, while I learned from the lovely, lilting phrases of the Douai. Deeply poetic, not afraid of the Virgin Mary like your English protestants were, and of course, rigorously checked against the Vulgate."

"I don't really know what you're talking about," Hiram admitted. "But the version I know says the wind bloweth where it listeth."

Here they were, talking about nothing again. But it felt like a breath of fresh air in the cloud of death that enveloped them.

"What's *listeth*?" she asked.

"It means *wants*. Old-fashioned. So I guess that means the same as your version. But I'm not sure about the wind and the spirit."

"Well, you know," Mary McGill said with a sigh. "Nuns."

Chapter Twenty-Nine

HIRAM KEPT LOW IN THE BACK SEAT AS THEY DROVE through town and eased down an alley toward the Price River.

His thoughts danced erratically. The demon had killed twice—three victims in total. The mine still had to be opened, but the urgency of Kimball's starving families faded by comparison with the murders. For that matter, Hiram was convinced the demon beneath the mine was the same entity as the luminous person he'd seen in the seer stone, which likely meant that the demon had been manipulating the Kimballs all along.

Rettig and his thugs complicated the situation.

Gus's presence complicated everything even more. Did he truly want to defeat Samael? But if that was *all* he wanted, why not recruit Hiram as an ally, rather than manipulate and sabotage him? And Michael seemed to have disappeared near Dollar's store.

And there remained the divination by sieve and shears, and what it had told Hiram—that he needed all three Kimballs' hearts to soften.

Mary stopped behind the Hotel Utah, pointing out a fire escape up the back. If Michael wasn't there or at Buford's, Hiram didn't know where else to turn. He had failed to find Michael, even with the Mosaical Rod, and having used up his supply of witch hazel, he couldn't try again. He could drive back to the farm and peel more branches off the bush he carefully cultivated at the end of the porch, but that would be a whole day lost.

He could turn himself in, if only to get the police's help to find his son, but Shanks had confirmed that Chief Fox was in the pocket of Naaman Rettig. He feared what the Helper City Police might do if they got their hands on either Michael or him.

Could he turn himself into the Carbon County Sheriff instead, who now seemed to be involved? But if Chief Fox was working with the sheriff, what did the sheriff think of Hiram?

He turned to Mary. "While I go visit Eliza, could you swing by Buford's Boarding House and see if Michael is there? Also, I'm expecting a telegram."

"And you think the police might be watching the boarding house for you."

"I do." He handed her the key. "It's the second floor, the room facing Main Street. Of course, they might be watching for you, too."

"Don't worry," Mary said. "If Chief Fox sees me, he'll think of Five-Cent Jimmy and run. Hopefully."

Hiram let out a shaky breath. "Let's meet back here."

Mary mock-saluted. "Sir, yes, sir. Just be careful. It would be a shame for you to end up in the Helper jail when I have only recently been released."

Hiram tried to put a brave face on his exhaustion.

"Don't worry. I know the right names of the twelve apostles."

He stopped at the trunk to retrieve the wax disk from his toolbox, then jumped and pulled the swinging ladder down. He climbed up the fire escape quickly.

On the second floor, he wasn't taking any chances. He pronounced the single line of his charm, blew three times across the disk of wax into the window latch, and then raised the window.

The hotel's second-story hallway was empty. Hiram walked down to Eliza's door. Knocking before sending up from the lobby might upset her, but Hiram couldn't afford the niceties. He rapped on the door three times.

From inside he heard, "Who's there? What is this?"

He knocked again, not wanting to say his own name too loud.

He remembered his hat and removed it. He was smoothing his hair down when the door opened.

He might have caught Eliza Kimball by surprise, but she was fully dressed in her mortician's black, and her hair was pinned to her scalp.

"I'd appreciate it if you let me in," he said. "I imagine it's not strictly Emily Post, but I'm in need."

She let the door swing open and Hiram slipped inside. He turned and found Eliza staring him square in the eye, an astonished expression on her face. "And now you can explain yourself, Mr. Woolley."

Michael wasn't there.

Hiram gripped his hat in both hands. "My son is missing. Has he contacted you in any way?"

"No." Eliza shrugged. "Has he been missing long?"

Hiram shook his head. He swallowed hard, his

mouth dry. "Also, ma'am, there's something else. Since I'm here, I want to talk about your family situation. About the mine. You may struggle to believe it, but there is an evil at work, here."

Her eyes iced over. "By *evil*, do you mean greed and foolishness? Because if you mean the *occult*, Mr. Woolley, the conversation ends here."

Hiram reached into his pocket and eased the seer stone out of his bandana—he preferred not to show Eliza the bloodstains—and took it out of his pocket. "You remember that I mentioned a stone, the last time I was here? This stone belonged to your father, and he mailed it to Samuel. Samuel put it back on the mantel for Ammon to use."

Her eyes dropped. "It's a simple rock. How does one *use* a rock?"

"Your father looked into it, and he saw something. Look, I know you're not a believer, but you were raised by believers. You know what this is."

The line of Eliza's jaw relented, slightly. "I know what it is."

"I think Samuel looked and saw something. Ammon too. You might be the only living member of your family who hasn't taken a turn."

"If you're suggesting I should look into that stone, stop right now." Eliza Kimball's upper lip curled into a sneer.

"I'm a believer, Miss Kimball. And I've looked into the stone, and I've seen what's in there. It isn't pretty. It appears to be an angel of light, but..."

"Stop."

Hiram took a deep breath. "Yes, ma'am. But I want you to remember the things your father believed, and the kinds of men your brothers are, and I want you to believe that your brothers are both ... well, if you can't believe they're controlled by an inhuman evil that appears as an angel, can you believe that they're mad? Can you believe that an old family madness has taken your brothers, Eliza? Can you believe that the best thing for you right now is to help me make peace between you and your brothers?"

And soften all their hearts.

It was a long speech for Hiram, and he'd forgotten to call Eliza by her surname.

"Give me the stone."

Hiram felt a chill run up his back. "I don't want you to look."

"I'm not going to. You want my help? I'm going to help you, by throwing the stone into the river. It will end the madness."

Until someone else found the stone. "No ..."

"That's my family's property," Eliza Kimball said curtly. "You can give it to me, or I can call the police. There's a policeman standing in the lobby, within earshot." She glared at him. "Or are you willing to overpower me and rob my family?"

Hiram felt numb. He wanted to keep the stone, because it was dangerous. He had felt the shining person reaching into his own heart, and only his chi-rho amulet had saved him. He considered jumping out the window and racing down the fire escape, but then the police would be chasing him for two reasons.

And besides, if stealing from Gus Dollar had made Hiram's charms misfire, what would stealing from Eliza Kimball do?

Perhaps, after all, the seer stone would be safest

with Eliza. Her secular education and her pride might mean that the stone went straight into a shoebox and stayed there.

Or straight into the Price River.

Hiram took a deep breath and handed over the peep-stone.

"And now you may leave," Eliza said.

Mary McGill walked into the open back door of the boarding house, holding her dress up to keep it from the mud, hands trembling.

Hands trembling, and mind full of the image of two dead feet, poking out from under a juniper.

And here she was, aiding a fugitive and trying to help him find his missing son. Yet in her heart of hearts, she knew Hiram Woolley was innocent, and Mary McGill had never run from trouble.

Buford's Boarding House was warm and Mary smelled tea and toasted bread in the parlor. A policeman with big knuckles and a heavy forehead stood in the ground floor hallway, looking at Mary. After a moment, his eyes widened and he turned his head away.

She managed not to laugh.

The upstairs hallway was unoccupied. Mary let herself into Hiram's room. She moved carefully and she stayed away from the windows. The room had simple furnishings and no sign of Hiram's son.

But there were two envelopes lying on the hardwood floor, just inside the door. Curiosity about the farmer's affairs nearly got the better of Mary's manners, but she managed not to look inside the envelopes. She did see a note written in a neat penciled hand on the outside of one envelope.

Mr. Woolley,

A boy came twice from the Western Union with messages for you. I tipped him three cents each time. I expect to be repaid.

Sincerely,
Mrs. Buford

Mary took the envelopes, locked the door, and calmly walked out of the boarding house, nodding at the policeman on the way.

She sat in the car for fifteen minutes, watching a train slowly pull out of the station and roll up toward Price Canyon through the fogged windshield of her Model A. Two Model Ts pulled up just before the train began to move, disgorging men gray with coal dust at the residential end of Helper. Mary watched them jump onto flatcars and climb ladders to get atop boxcars, riding the rails toward Salt Lake and points west.

Miners. Fleeing Helper.

Hiram abruptly opened the car door and sat down. His face was bright red and he brought the smell of the cold river in with him.

"Michael wasn't with Eliza Kimball," he said. "Did you have any luck?"

"No sign of your son. I'm sorry. And you owe Mrs. Buford six cents." Mary handed over the envelopes.

Hiram grabbed a Coke from the back seat and drank half of it in one sustained attack. He plucked out the messages and scanned them. Mary saw the Western Union logo at the top.

Mary wanted to ask about the messages, but she kept quiet. When Hiram felt like sharing, he would. She started the car to get a little heat in and waited.

Hiram's face was gray and he sat still, staring up at the white cliff looming over Helper.

Mary fidgeted. She took a deep breath and straightened her back.

Hiram looked at her, and the bleakness of his expression caught her by surprise. "You should read this. Both of these, I suppose."

He handed her the two telegrams.

Mary read the two messages, each typed in capital letters beneath the heading of a Western Union blank. The first read:

YOU ARE HEREBY DIRECTED TO COME HOME. WEVE HEARD RUMORS OF INAPPROPRIATE BEHAVIOR INCLUDING WITCHCRAFT. WILL MEET YOU NEXT SUNDAY AT YOUR CHAPEL TO HEAR YOUR REPORT AND DETERMINE WHETHER DISCIPLINE IS NEEDED. I AM YOUR FRIEND JOHN

When she looked up from reading, Hiram laughed softly. "It could be worse. They don't direct me to turn myself in to the police."

"They don't know Michael's missing."

Hiram nodded. "The other one is from a librarian friend of mine."

Mary read the second:

ACCORDING TO THE TALMUD SAMAEL IS CHIEF OF ALL THE SATANS. CANT FIND ANYTHING ABOUT A MAHOUN.

MAYBE MASTER MAHAN FROM BOOK
OF MOSES. HIRAM WHAT ARE YOU
DOING. MAHONRI.

"What is a *mahonri?*" she asked.

Hiram laughed.

"That's my friend's name. Mahonri Young," he said. "He's concerned I'm mixed up in a bad business."

"And are you?"

"Yes," Hiram said. "And maybe worse than I thought. So now might be a good time for you to tell me to get out of your car, and for you to drive away."

"I can't have it on my conscience if you're arrested. Not after you helped spring me. And if I can't fix the entire world, perhaps I can help repair this little corner of it. Now, I don't remember the nuns telling me about a Book of Moses. Does Mahonri mean Exodus?"

Hiram shook his head. "No, it's one of the extra books Mormons use."

"And is Master Mahan one of the Satans in the Book of Moses?"

Hiram was slow to answer. "Master Mahan is a sort of title, I guess. It means someone who has learned to kill for gain. To convert human life into wealth."

Mary snorted. "Well, that's Ammon Kimball. And it's Naaman Rettig. A lot of people turn human life into money."

"I guess so." Hiram smiled. He shot her a glance. "So this talk of devils doesn't trouble you?"

She shrugged. "My catechism was clear, Mr. Woolley. There are evil forces in the world, and it's my duty to fight them. I must admit, I had assumed the conflict would be metaphorical."

"If only it were," he said wearily.

"What do we do now?"

"Set it right." He clenched his jaw. "All of it."

She didn't ask where they would go next. They sat. Chief of all the Satans?

Mary laughed before she could stop herself. "Well, it seems you have trouble on every front, physical as well as spiritual. Setting it right is going to take some work, but I'm game."

"Good."

Then the man said nothing more for a long, long time.

Chapter Thirty

HIRAM SAT WITH MARY MCGILL IN HER MODEL A beside the Price River, the engine running. She must have installed a heater; Hiram felt warm air blow on him. Clouds cast shadows across the stretch of dirt behind Helper where they were parked.

"Gus Dollar. I've got to make Gus bleed," Hiram muttered.

Mary blinked. "What? That is a bit shocking. Do you mean the storekeeper?"

"Was I speaking out loud?" Hiram's own voice seemed to echo to him from far away.

"Let's pretend you didn't just say that. How many of those Cokes did you have?"

Hiram rested his face in hands. His whole body hurt. His eyes hurt. He couldn't go to sleep. "Ten, minus however many are left."

"There's *none* left. Sweet Jesus! And how many do you *usually* drink?"

Hiram shook his head, still cupped in his fingers. His hands were shaking like leaves in an August

storm. "I don't drink a lot of Coke. Or coffee anymore, either. I just can't fall asleep right now. I've got
to find Michael, first of all, and then the rest. The
bishopric can't recall me now."

"They don't know you've read the telegram."

Hiram shifted in the passenger seat. The engine heat
dried out his nose and the windows were steaming up.
"But they don't know. They're wrong, they've been told
lies. I'm not down here working as a cunning man."

"What's a cunning man?"

"You would say a wizard, I suppose."

"You're not?"

Hiram shook his head. "I'm just...doing the things
that I know work. And I...sometimes the things that
work look like magic. Anyway, I'm not working. I'm
serving. Religion, pure and undefiled, that's what James
says. Widows and orphans, that's what I'm trying to
do. Why would they object to that?"

"I don't really know your people," Mary said. "But
it's my sense they don't object to the *what* so much
as to the *how*."

"You mean if I just used false arrests and lies and
threats and guns to solve my problems, like everybody
else does, that would be acceptable?" Hiram heard
the bitterness in his own voice.

"I think your Mormon bigwigs just want you to stop
what you're doing here and go back. *Report*, it says."

Hiram clenched his hands into fists to stop them
from shaking. "I can't, in any case. I can't leave
Michael. I won't."

"You're going to get caffeine poisoning and end up
with a permanent case of the jitters, if not dead of
a heart attack."

"The thing under Gus's shop is behind the murders. Gus . . . is involved somehow." And, despite the fact that Gus Dollar had repeatedly bested Hiram, Hiram liked his chances with Gus better than his chances with the demon.

"Gus is the shopkeeper?" Mary asked.

"Yes."

"Who's in his basement?"

"Not who, but what. And it's not his basement, it's the . . . cave under his basement. The cave under the mine."

"The old German fellow? With the glass eye?" Skepticism tinged her voice.

Hiram remembered that eye rolling toward him across the store counter. In his mind, it seemed to be rolling toward him again now, only it was vast, a huge sphere of glass that had been cut out of the mountain without hands, and was going to crush Hiram Woolley flat.

"Yes, him. I've got to hurt him."

Mary gripped the steering wheel. After a moment, Hiram looked up and found her looking at him with a queer expression.

"Hiram . . . you didn't kill them, did you? The Sorensons? The girl?"

Hiram pressed his face against the cold glass of the window. "No, Mary, I . . . I'm exhausted. And I . . . I don't know what caffeine poisoning is, are you serious about that? But I don't feel good, and my son is missing. And the police want me, and I'm innocent."

"But you want to hurt an old man."

"He's not . . . he's not just an old man. He's a witch. And he's connected with something that's much older than he is. Something to do with the mine." A fallen angel, as Gus himself had said, living in the Wastes of Dudael? "I think he might be in league with the killer. If not, I think he'll know how to stop whatever killed Callista."

"Something much older?" she asked. "Is that the *what* in the basement?"

Hiram hesitated. "It's a demon."

"You seemed so kind when you visited me in the jail," Mary said slowly.

Hiram drooped.

Mary's voice was breathless. "Now you seem like a madman, or just a hair shy of mad."

"I don't mean I'm going to *kill* Gus," he said. "I don't want to kill him. I don't want to kill anybody. But I need to *wound* him."

"Are you hearing yourself? You *need* to wound an old man?"

"He's a witch. And he's better than me, he's been beating me at every turn." Hiram felt his eyes soften into tears, but Mary's face only looked horrified. "He lured me into his shop, and then he forced me to open up my heart to him. And then I think he tricked me into coming back, and burned my Mosaical Rod, and his grandchildren nearly killed me."

"His grandchildren. With what, guns?"

"An iron. And a skillet."

Mary frowned. "I'm on your side, Hiram, but . . . what kind of grandchildren are we talking about here?"

Hiram looked down at his knees.

"Jesus, Mary, and Joseph, are you telling me they're *little children*?"

"There's something wrong with them. They seemed

normal before, but maybe he's bewitched them, too. I didn't hurt them, even when they tried to kill me. We can go back to the shop, you'll see them, they were healthy as can be when we left, evil, grinning little monsters."

"I'm all for battling Satan and all the demons, but I don't have a fight with Gus Dollar," Mary said. "Or his evil, grinning grandchildren. Is it possible you're so tired and so jooked up on Coca-Cola, you're actually hallucinating?"

Hiram shook his head. "Do you want the mine reopened? Do you want to stop Callista's killer? That thing has murdered three people—do you think it's finished?"

"You think Gus Dollar will help you?"

Hiram considered the question. "No," he said. "Clearly he won't. But Gus knows things he isn't telling me, and I want to know what before I have to face the thing in the pit. And I have to put an end to his hexing me before I can trust anything he says."

Mary folded her arms across her chest and took a deep breath. "Utah," she muttered. "McClatchy warned me."

"Please," Hiram said. "I don't want to kill Gus. Drawing blood from a sorcerer who is bewitching you is a strong counter magic."

"It's a recipe for chaos. If everyone thought every bit of bad luck they had was to be blamed on their ugliest neighbor, and the best way to fix it was to go break that neighbor's nose, society would fall apart in an afternoon."

"True." *That's why we need cunning men,* Hiram thought but didn't say. Cunning folk were needed so that people could resort to other kinds of defensive charms first, when there really was a witch involved.

Mary McGill shook her head. "I can't believe this tale of demons, Hiram. Your sage leaf with apostles on it—maybe that worked, and maybe it didn't. But I can't be party to you getting to the ring with an old man, not when your reason for doing so is monster under the bed."

"Under the general store." Hiram rubbed his eyes. "Will you turn me into the police, then?"

Mary seemed to consider the possibility. "No. Not yet, anyway. But this talk of monsters and madness has given me a different idea."

Hiram was almost afraid to ask. "A different idea?"

"Samuel Kimball," she said. "He's lost his mind. Might he be capable of murder in his state?"

Hiram said nothing.

"Maybe madness runs in the Kimball family," Mary said. "Maybe violence does, too."

"Teancum Kimball had a number of children die young," Hiram said slowly. Was it possible that Mary was right, and that he wasn't thinking clearly?

"I'll see how far back the *Helper Journal's* records go," she continued, "and what I can learn about the clan that may shed light on the murders. If you can calm down, I'm happy to have you come with me. Michael will probably show up on his own, and if the police find him, I'll call Jimmy Nichols."

But no, Hiram had seen the demon. He couldn't go spend time in a newspaper office, trying to find out how Teancum Kimball's children had died.

His limbs sank against the car's seat like lead bars. "I guess our paths part here. Good luck in the records."

"Whatever demons you're wrestling with, Hiram Woolley...real or metaphorical...I hope you conquer them."

"Mary..."

But she had iron in her eyes, so he stepped out of her car, removed his toolbox, and watched her drive away.

Hiram stood in the leafless trees above the river, considering his options.

What was Gus's connection with the fly demon Mahoun? He likely wanted to summon and control it, using the Book of the Spirits Hiram had destroyed. Or he already controlled it, and he wanted to channel its power to summon and control something greater. Hiram had heard tales from Grandma Hettie about witches who had begun by dominating and binding earthly and infernal spirits with the goal of summoning more celestial beings.

The stories ended badly, at least the way Grandma Hettie told them. Summoning was not the business of mortal man; devils were too dangerous and tricky to work with, and angels deserved better treatment.

And why did that Book of the Spirits include a lamen designed to bring down walls?

To stop the demon, Hiram needed to find out the truth. And that meant he needed to get information from Gus Dollar that he was certain wasn't distorted by a charm.

Time to bleed Gus.

Hiram rode a stolen donkey up Spring Canyon.

He was wanted for murder, so a little borrowing of a farm animal wouldn't weigh too heavily in the scales. He picked a donkey rather than a horse for its dependable gait, and also because it reminded him of Balaam, in the Book of Numbers.

There was magic in an ass. Hiram could use any angel's warning he might get.

He borrowed the donkey and its saddle from a stable beside an adobe bungalow on the north end of Helper, underneath the stark, staring face of the white cliff. He also took a thick wool serape and a sombrero, to disguise his appearance. The sombrero went on right over his fedora.

From the same stable, he took a bullwhip.

As he crossed the river, a blast of wind scoured out of the canyon. The sky had grown cast-iron dark, and now the cutting front edge of a snowstorm rushed along the Price River and slammed into Helper. The force of the gale very nearly drove Hiram and his donkey off the railroad-tie bridge and into the waters. The serape, over his army coat, kept him comfortable, but his fingers froze in his gloves. He worked his digits to keep the blood flow going and longed for thicker socks.

Once he'd crossed the river, he cut away from the road. The wind was less once he was no longer directly before the canyon, but the snow fell thickly, obscuring the ground.

He used Spring Creek as his guide, and every bit of greenery he could as his shelter. When any cars were visible, he stuck to the trees, waiting for solitude to cross from copse to copse.

The donkey wasn't lazy, and once pointed in a direction tended to keep going in a straight line, so Hiram dozed. Fading in and out, toolbox clutched to his lap, he dreamed. In between dreams, in waking moments, he remembered his earlier dreams, of searching for Michael in vain and of a booming voice in a dark pit.

A gust of freezing wind, throwing snow, blew him awake.

He'd managed to reach Dollar's with the sun low in the sky and a storm coming on fast. Hiram checked the canyon for traffic, found none, and crossed the river. He unsaddled the donkey and picketed it to a fallen log within reach of many tufts of grass, poking up from the snow and standing up bravely to the stiff wind.

"You stay here." He stroked the beast's neck and shoulders. "I'll get you home."

He climbed up a steep bank to the edge of the road, toolbox in one hand and whip in the other. He was about to step into the tall grass on the other side, approaching the store, when he heard the tell-tale rattle of Utah's most common venomous snake. It was an irregular rasp, that started slowly, shook into full rattle, and then trailed off. The snake was barred with interlinked diamond shapes all along its body, and its head was an evil wedge-shape.

In a snowstorm in February? The snake should have been hibernating in a pit somewhere.

But if flies, why not snakes?

The rattler raised its head, twitched its tail. Hiram retreated. Circling counterclockwise to get out of that snake's territory, he walked toward the store again—and again heard a rattle.

He leaped back. Could it have been the same snake?

But no, looking left, he saw the original snake still, lying in a lazy S-shape across the snow.

Taking no shortcuts, this time he walked fifty feet to his right, and again started forward.

A rattler lunged at him from the tall grass. Only its eagerness, or its irritability, made it miss; it attacked from far enough away that Hiram saw it, and was able to shuffle aside. Darting forward, he grabbed the rattlesnake by the tail and flung it far to his right, near the base of the ridge.

Gus Dollar had surrounded his store with rattle-snakes.

Chapter Thirty-One

THE SNAKES WERE IMPOSSIBLE; THEY DEFIED nature's common-sense rhythms.

Gus had summoned them.

No problem. The Bible was full of charms for snakes.

Headlights flashed past Hiram, briefly throwing his shadow up against a wall of yellow rock.

He turned and saw one of the Helper Police Model Bs turning with the winding of the canyon's road. Clouds darkened the sun as it settled down behind the western ridge, but there was still enough light to make out the words HELPER CITY POLICE.

Was there enough light for the driver to have seen *him*? Police Chief Fox might or might not have jurisdiction in Spring Canyon, but he could still slow Hiram down by arresting him. Or beating him up.

The car stopped.

Hiram turned to run, and a fierce rattle reminded him that he still had a snake problem. Only he wanted to address that issue with a clear mind and heart, and not in a fear-pumped panic.

He turned and jogged the other direction, away from the store.

But had they seen him already?

He crouched behind a lone juniper tree, peering through its dark green screen.

Police Chief Asael Fox stood beside the car and scanned the canyon. Hiram's heart, already driving over the speed limit, took a ninety-degree turn and hit the brakes.

He tried to hold perfectly still.

Fox's sergeant, Shanks, was down along the bank of Spring Creek, looking at something.

The donkey. They had found the donkey.

Would Chief Fox and his sergeant now set about looking for the thief?

As if in answer to his unspoken question, Chief Fox walked in Hiram's direction.

Hiram lowered himself onto hands and knees, checked visibility, and then lowered himself again, onto his belly in the snow. Thank goodness for the serape and his gloves. His toes, though, were ice.

"The snakes," he murmured to himself. "Not toward the snakes."

If he crawled on his belly into a rattler, he'd take an immediate bite in a very painful and dangerous location.

"They shall take up serpents," he murmured, "it shall not hurt them." It was the simplest of charms for a snake. He hoped it was enough, and he repeated it several times.

He hoped the snakes were all behind him.

He dragged himself a hundred feet without to rising to check his progress or look at the policemen. Once he was curled behind two dead tree trunks leaning against a crumbling yellow rock, he levered himself up onto his feet and cast an eye in their direction.

The police chief had turned southward, paralleling Hiram's own path. Had he seen Hiram? No, he was looking at something in a tangle of gambol oak. From Hiram's position, it was clearly a faded old canvas tarpaulin, once stretched out by a traveler as a tent. To Chief Fox, it must appear to be a man in a serape.

All Fox had to do was cross Hiram's path, and the man would see his tracks in the snow.

Where was Dixon? Either in the car, or with the donkey, in either case, unseen in a twilight that grew darker by the second.

With the chief coming this direction, Hiram dared head the other way, toward Dollar's.

He started with a phrase he had memorized from Reginald Scot: "I conjure you, O serpents, in this hour, by the five holy wounds of our Lord, that you not remove out of your places, but that you stay."

The five wounds were the wounds of Christ, the manner in which the serpent had wounded the heel of the seed of Eve, bringing to its climax God's great curse on mankind. The threat Hiram was making to the snakes was their heads would be crushed, as God had warned in Genesis. He filled his heart with a prayer and focused his will on directing the snakes to remain calm.

He wished he had an amulet against snakes. He touched the chi-rho and the protective bronze Oremus lamen in his coat pocket, but their power was weaker for being broad.

Also, the old German witch had beat Hiram before.

As he neared the place where he had nearly been bitten before, in his best estimation, he tried another charm. This one came directly from the Bible, and it was the most triumphant serpent-verse he could think of: "And he laid hold on the dragon, that old serpent, which is the Devil, and Satan, and bound him a thousand years."

He shed his gloves and reached inside his shirt to touch the iron of the chi-rho talisman directly, and at the same time grasped the heliotropius with his bare fingers. He had never heard that the heliotropius had power against serpents, but it was supposed to purge poison. And if poison, why not venom? And if it would purge venom, might it also drive away creatures that bore venom?

His fingers were numb from the cold and felt like ice against his chest. Snow was beginning to pile up on the sombrero and the shoulders of the serape.

Hiram heard the rattle of a snake in the darkness, but it was slow.

He repeated the Scot incantation, and the verse from the Book of Revelation, and watched very carefully where he placed his Harvesters. He stepped forward slowly, and again . . . and again.

And there was the first snake. It sat coiled directly ahead of him, looking at him with its treacherous beads for eyes, tongue flicking slowly in and out, rattle shaking from side to side.

But the rattle's movement was slow.

". . . bound him a thousand years," Hiram said, focusing his will and his prayer on this snake in particular. It wasn't easy. His hands shook, his temples were beginning to throb—was that the cost of the intense concentration, or part of the caffeine poisoning Mary had warned him about, or from the cold?

He couldn't feel his feet.

Hiram locked eyes with the snake. If he could walk past this one, he could walk past them all.

And if this one bit him, he would turn and run, and Chief Fox would throw him in jail.

"They shall take up serpents, and it shall not hurt them. They shall pass by serpents, and not be seen."

He eased his left foot forward, placing the Redwing boot firmly on the soil beside the rattlesnake, and very definitely not on top of it.

He eased his weight forward onto his front foot.

He kept his gaze locked on the snake's eyes, weirdly visible to him in the gloom. The snake turned its head as Hiram leaned into his step, and then moved his other foot forward, shifting weight onto that boot . . .

And then he was past the first rattlesnake.

He took a deep breath. Dollar's was perhaps a hundred yards ahead, barely visible in the growing darkness. How many more snakes could there be in a hundred yards?

Mary McGill wanted to kick herself. Hiram Woolley wanted to assault an old man. The farmer had turned out to be . . . what? A wizard? A madman? A murderer?

None of those words felt right, though.

Hiram said things that sounded crazy, but he didn't seem insane. He seemed humble, and hard-working, and self-sacrificing.

And scared.

She approached the newspaper office, just off Main Street.

When she explained what she wanted, the old man standing in the door of the nondescript brick building frowned. "We don't generally open our archives to the public."

He was thin and bent as a question mark. A green eyeshade, like a bank teller's, caught light from the street, casting a green splotch on his face. It made him look like a goblin—that and his large nose and pronounced ears.

"I'm not the public." Mary smiled her most ladylike smile, trying not to wince at the knowledge that the old man was looking at her birthmark and feeling revulsion. She fought to keep her hand away from her face.

Hiram Woolley might be nuts, but he'd been a gentleman.

"You aren't Helper City government, and you aren't Carbon County. I know all *those* people. Are you someone down from Salt Lake City, then?"

There was nothing for it. "Mr. . . . Bowen, did you say your name was?"

The goblin creaked his assent.

"Mr. Bowen, how do you feel about protecting the rights and improving the quality of the working man, here in Helper?"

"Ah, you're *that* kind of not-the-public. Well, you can't unionize the *Helper Journal*," Bowen said. "There aren't enough of us. Most days, it's just me."

"I mean the miners."

"Oh, yeah, well, those poor devils. Why didn't you say so? Come on in."

Ten minutes later, she was looking at a row of four filing cabinets squatting beneath a precarious stack of manila folders. Bowen was setting text at a Linotype machine in the corner, and on a card table between them stood an open bottle of whiskey and two paper cups.

"Where did all this come from?" she asked.

"Paper itself is only three years old. Most of this comes from the city's archives," Bowen said. "They were going to throw it out, and I asked if I could have it instead. I can use it for background, you see, and research, and archive photographs. In a pinch, I can fill in a few column-inches with a *Remember When?* feature. It's not official records, it's all the other stuff they had sitting around in their shelves. There's maps in there, and photos, and handbills, and paintings, and sketch books, and half a dozen journals. I was looking for a photo the other day and I found a shopping list written on the back of a receipt from Lowenstein Mercantile. There are boxes of letters and postcards and telegrams that couldn't get delivered for one reason or another, so they ended up at the city. Someday, we'll get a proper museum. God help the poor bastard who has to run it."

Mary McGill was an organizer of people, not of objects. Another person, confronted with a heterogeneous stack of materials, would have spent many hours segregating the various papers and volumes and photographs into stacks of related material, for more easy digestion.

Mary just started at the top and dove in.

She found several photographs of Naaman Rettig near the top of the pile, which made them recent.

They were thought-provoking, so while Bowen was looking the other way, she pocketed them.

From handwritten journal accounts and letters dated from the nineteenth century, she got a picture of Teancum Kimball's life and dealings. Each of his three surviving children was born to a different mother. References in a picnic flyer seemed to suggest Teancum's marriages were at least partially overlapping, and that no one at the time batted an eye. For a polygamist, that seemed like a small family, and in newsletters and old announcements, she found multiple references to Kimball family stillbirths.

Teancum Kimball's children had mostly died at birth. She couldn't get to anything like a comprehensive count, digging through papers and jotting down notes in a dogeared memorabilia book, but north of twelve deaths, at least.

She found no suggestion, though, that Teancum had killed the children, or that he was insane.

Letters made it clear that, in the decades when Teancum had begun building his family and his ranch, he was loved by many, and hated by many more. He gave employment, and he acted as a local spiritual leader—Mary read more than one letter expressing some parent's gratitude for the healing of their child by Teancum Kimball, with his famous gift of the laying on of hands. She also found handwritten records of prophetic blessings Teancum pronounced on others, promising long life, wisdom, a good marriage. or success in business.

Odd. Not Mary's culture. Still not madness.

On the other hand, she found letters of complaint. Teancum had come into a valley that was already occupied by various kinds of settlers. On the basis that he was acting under the direction of Salt Lake City and its Mormon leadership, Teancum ran many of those others out of town. For immorality, or violating local custom, or criminal allegations—Teancum as local patriarch seemed consistently to end up as prosecutor and judge both, and no accused person came out vindicated. Without access to the land records, Mary couldn't see the details, but it seemed clear that Teancum at least sometimes ended up with their land, all clustered around what would eventually become his mine in Spring Canyon.

Mary generally didn't side with the landed classes in her heart, but in this case, the landed victims were prospectors, small farmers, or local businessmen. For instance, there was a Lohengrim Zoller, who had run a general store in the 1860s and 1870s, right where Teancum had eventually built his house.

And then in 1881, Lohengrim Zoller simply disappeared, and Teancum Kimball scooped up his land and added it to his holdings.

She found an old daguerreotype that seemed to show Teancum Kimball and Lohengrim Zoller together. They stood at the center of a line of women and men at a barn-raising. She knew the men were Kimball and Zoller because the surname of each person in the image was penciled in a neat script below them. Kimball had the fierce, sunken eyes of a vulture and stepped toward the photographer with one foot, as if he were about to attack. Lohengrim had hair that stood straight up, as if a micro-tornado were sucking it toward the heaven at the moment the plate was exposed, and two eyes that didn't point in the same direction.

Two eyes that didn't point in the same direction.

Mary McGill checked the date of the photo on the back. Penciled in ink that had faded to a dull tan color was the year *1881*.

She looked at the image of the two men again.

What had Hiram Woolley said about Gus Dollar having a connection with ancient things?

"No. It couldn't be."

Chapter Thirty-Two

RATTLESNAKES LAY COILED IN THE SNOW EVERY
fifteen feet, all the way to the store. Hiram looked
them in the eye, repeated his chants, moved slowly,
and was very, very careful not to step on a snake.

They were coiled in even greater number in the
flat gravel around Dollar's, and Hiram found himself
trying to look two or three snakes in the eye at the
same time. His legs shook and sweat poured down
between his shoulder blades.

"You there!" Asael Fox called, behind him.

Hiram kept walking.

"In the poncho!"

He was only a few steps from the store. Snakes
slithered back and forth atop each other underneath
the porch. Snakes sat coiled on the rocking chairs,
gently shaking their rattles back and forth and waiting for Hiram.

Bang!

There was no way the police were shooting at him.

They didn't know for sure who he was, and even if they did, he was walking slowly up the canyon, not resisting arrest. They must be firing at the sky to get his attention.

Unless Gus had somehow bent their minds.

He turned his shoulders slowly, curious to see what the policemen were doing. The two men were running his way, jogging across the grass-speckled white field. The flurry of falling snow was thick enough that their Model B appeared only as a dim and distant glow behind a crystalline curtain.

Asael Fox was closer, but Shanks had longer legs and was catching up.

"Stop!" Hiram yelled. "Snakes! Stop!"

And then Fox shrieked and staggered backward. He screamed again, and then began firing his pistol over and over.

At the ground.

He'd been bitten. Sergeant Dixon was coming to help him, and the colored man might be the next victim, but Hiram couldn't do anything for them.

He stepped up onto the porch, conscious of the snakes tangled up with each other beneath him. A fat rattler shook its tail languidly in the space immediately in front of the door. Hiram tried to lock eyes with the creature as he slowly shrugged out of the serape. Folding the wool to double thickness and meeting the snake's gaze, he tossed the serape forward, covering the snake.

Hissing angrily, the snake uncoiled to slither out from under the blanket, but it didn't attack Hiram—it just crept a few feet to one side and coiled up again.

The lights were out in the store, but now that he

was on the porch, Hiram could tell that the door was cracked slightly open. Also, he could see that a coiled rattler hung on the doorknob.

Gus Dollar was expecting him. Hiram threw aside the sombrero.

With the toe of one Harvester and the end of his toolbox, he pressed at the door, very close to the hinges. It swung inward. The snake hanging from the knob hissed but didn't so much as shake its rattle as Hiram Woolley slunk past it and into Gus Dollar's shop, mayhem on his mind.

He stopped, letting his eyes adjust the darkness. Outside, the shooting had stopped, but he was afraid to devote any more of his attention to Fox and Shanks. Crisp wind blew in through the door, throwing wet flakes in all directions.

Hiram had come to wound Gus Dollar.

He held the bullwhip coiled in his right hand. With a whip, he could strike from fifteen feet away. Also, he could cut a man's skin open with it and make him bleed, with almost no risk of accidentally severing an artery.

He didn't want to kill Gus.

"You've come thinking I will give you back your child." The voice in the darkness was Gus's, and Hiram realized with a start that the shopkeeper was standing behind his counter.

"That's part of it," Hiram agreed.

"I pissed blood, you bastard," Gus said. "You made a witch bottle."

"You hexed my car. I had no choice." Hiram set his toolbox on the floor.

"So I did." Gus chuckled. "You know, in England

they didn't burn witches. They hanged them, like they hanged other criminals. And mostly they didn't punish them for the act of magic, they executed them for the crimes they committed *using* magic. A witch would be hanged for murder or theft, not for witchcraft as such."

"Are you threatening to hang me, Gus?"

"On the contrary, I'm trying to understand your intent. Have you brought that rope to hang *me*, or merely to tie me up and force me to talk?"

"What rope?"

"I saw you in vision before you arrived, farmer. You can conceal nothing from me."

"I don't want to kill you, Gus. I *do* want my son back, among other things."

"I don't have him. But maybe there's something else that you want."

"If you don't have my son," Hiram asked, "why have you summoned a field of snakes?"

"Because I knew you were coming. And I knew you hated me. You burgled my shop. You vandalized my property. You terrified my innocent grandchildren. You are *getting in my way*, Hiram Woolley."

"If I hated you, I'd have done something to those grandkids of yours."

"No, you wouldn't have. Never." Even in the darkness, Hiram could see that Gus was shaking his head. "You're not that kind of man, Hiram. You would rather die than hurt an innocent. I admire that."

Hiram felt sick. Had his scruples doomed Michael? If he had been willing to kidnap Gus's strange grandchildren, would Michael be with him now? "You're going to tell me now that your grandchildren are there behind the counter, all hexed up again, and I shouldn't shoot because I might hit them."

"No. I sent my family away. I only . . . used my grandchildren in that fashion because I was desperate. I don't want them hurt, just like I don't want your son hurt. Besides . . ." A note crept into Gus's voice that sounded like delight. "Besides, I *know* that you don't have a gun."

"You killed Sorenson." Hiram's voice shook like his hands.

"No."

"What about Callista Markopoulos? What about Teancum Kimball two years prior?"

"No. I killed none of them. Shall we try the sieve and shears?" Gus sounded much calmer than Hiram felt. "Book and key? Clay balls? I dislike the Kimballs. They drive business away from my store. But I like the miners."

"And you hated Teancum. I don't know quite why, but it has something to do with what happened when the mine ran into the natural caves under the ridge, and they boarded the cave openings up, years ago."

"That was a long time ago, and before my time," Gus said. "I've only been here about fifteen years."

Hiram felt a pinch in his thigh.

He hadn't been thinking about his heliotropius, assuming that every word Gus Dollar said was a lie or at least misdirection, so the stone's warning twinge caught him by surprise. He'd meant to wound Gus first and then ask him questions, but the snakes had distracted him.

But the bloodstone seemed to be working.

And of all the things Gus had said, he'd lied about the caves being discovered before his time.

"Did you hate Teancum Kimball?" Hiram asked.

"No. I barely knew the man. I didn't hate him."

Another pinch.

Hiram shook his head. He was sleep-deprived, anxious, and jittery. Had he misunderstood?

"When did you first move to this area?" he asked Gus.

"Nineteen twenty."

The stone pinched Hiram a third time.

Gus's lies were clear. But that also meant that he'd been telling the truth when he'd said he hadn't killed Sorenson, the little girl, or Teancum.

"Do you know where my son is?"

"I don't. I believe he lives."

The stone didn't pinch him. Hiram asked, "Why did you build your store over the cave opening?"

"What have you got in your pocket?" Gus shot back. "Hyacinthus? Chalcedony?"

"Heliotropius."

"Ah, the rain-bringer. So your beet farm prospers, no doubt. And are you famous?"

"What's your involvement with the mine closure, Gus?"

"You never answered my question, Hiram. Are you going to hang me? This is the west, after all. It seems appropriate. The beams in my shop might not do very well, but you can find tall cottonwoods down by the creek that will serve as fine gallows."

Gus had something bulky in his hands. Was it a rifle? Hiram shifted slowly to his left, trying to get a better look. As Gus turned to follow him, more light struck Gus in the face.

His eye was missing.

Hiram shuddered. He imagined Gus hiding the glass eye under the seat of the Double-A, and then following all Hiram's movements without effort. Hiram didn't know a charm that would do that. Might Gus?

"What do you call that thing?" Hiram asked.

"The angel? Do you not have lists of angels' names to consult? Ah, perhaps not. You did, after all, steal *my* list. And apparently you couldn't read it."

"I returned it. I'm a farmer, not a magician."

"I call it *the Beast*, mostly," Gus said. "Some names are not meant to be spoken too often out loud."

"And if I spoke its name?"

"It might come. Like it came to the camp last night."

"But you're not ready, are you?" Hiram asked. "You're not in league with that thing, you're in thrall to it. And you're trying to break out. That's what the Book of the Spirits was for. You want to summon and bind it."

"I was in thrall once. I'm a stronger magician, now," Gus said. "I know two of the Beast's names, and I have the knowledge to bind it. To bury it deep under the ground."

"Mahoun," Hiram whispered. "Samael. Your Book of the Spirits was meant to crush . . . the Beast . . . underground." He thought for a moment. "So that you could take its power forever?"

A cold wind blew in through the open doorway, slamming the door against the wall. Hiram felt a fly creep across his face, a huge insect the size of a marble. He brushed it away with his left hand.

Feeling was returning to his feet.

"Don't be a fool." Gus raised his arms slightly. Hiram saw that the object the shopkeeper held was his ceremonial sword. "Find your son and leave. I don't wish to harm you, and you can do nothing to stop the Beast. You would be mere food to it. Food that it might eat very, very slowly."

"You gave it your eye," Hiram said. "That's why you have a false one. Long ago, when you first encountered it, you made a bargain with that thing and the bargain cost you an eye. What does the demon give you in return?"

Gus shrugged. "What do you bargain for? Wealth, power, the adulation of men, the satisfaction of the lusts of the flesh. But the demon only gives its blessings for thirty years."

"What did old man Teancum give it? When you were younger and first knew him? I know you knew him."

"His children."

Hiram frowned. "Ammon, Samuel, and Eliza? They live."

"The others died the day they were born. These three live on borrowed time, concessions to their mothers. The bill is due now, and the Beast is coming."

The bloodstone lay inert in Hiram's pocket, and his heart was heavy with dread.

"And my appearance worried you," Hiram said, "because you feared that I might make a bargain with the demon, and upset your plans."

Gus said nothing.

Hiram heard a car engine outside. Headlights blazed in through the shop windows, and then the car pulled to a halt. He heard the soft, scaly sound of a hundred snakes sliding out of the way and the crunching of heavy feet in snow.

"Last chance," Hiram said. "I'm not here to hang you, but I *will* hurt you. How do I stop the Beast?"

"You know enough."

Hiram shook out the whip.

Gus frowned. "That's not a rope."

Hiram whipped the shopkeeper in the face.

Gus shouted, incomprehensible words that might be German. He raised his sword defensively.

"Thou shalt not suffer a witch to live!" Hiram whipped him again, *crack*! And again. In the headlights' glow, he saw a curl of blood across Gus's forehead, and something... something else that was off about the shopkeeper's face, though Hiram couldn't quite put his finger on it.

Gus dropped the sword with a loud clatter.

"You should have left the beets and gone home, farmer!"

Gus fumbled under the counter. A gun, no doubt. Thank heaven he was having trouble putting his hands on it in the darkness.

Hiram heard steps on the porch. He grabbed his toolbox and melted back against the wall, trying to make himself invisible in the shadow of three mannequins in Sunday dresses.

The shadow that loomed through the door and across Gus was misshapen. It was tall, but also unnaturally broad in the shoulders, and its head seemed to be a giant, neckless mass. The wood of the porch bowed down and protested against the weight.

Hiram grabbed the chi-rho talisman.

Gus hissed. In his hands, he held a sawed-off, double-barreled shotgun.

"Helper City Police!" Hiram recognized the voice of Sergeant Dixon. His shadow was distorted because he held the unconscious police chief in his arms. "Put down that gun, unless you want to spend the rest of your life in prison!"

Gus eased down the weapon. Shanks hoisted Asael Fox onto the countertop. "Whisky, right now!" he shouted. "The chief here's been bit at least three times, but maybe more. I gotta find all the bites and get the poison out."

Gus grabbed a bottle and opened it. Pressed against the wall in shadow, Hiram heard the sound of cloth being torn, and then the slosh of liquor poured over snakebites and a blade to sterilize them.

He wanted to help, but he couldn't go to jail now. As Shanks bent over his chief's leg and began sucking venom out of the first of the wounds, Hiram slipped out the front door.

At the side of the police Ford, he hesitated. He couldn't do *nothing at all*. Taking the heliotropius from his pocket, he tucked it behind the cushion of the back seat. Surely, that was where Chief Fox would ride down into Helper. The stone purged poison, so it must might against snake venom, too.

Hiram trod carefully, but the snakes were gone. Maybe in biting Chief Fox, they had dissipated their force.

He found the donkey easily; it was braying from discomfort from the snow and pulling at its picket. Hiram realized that he knew a charm to cure the bite of a scorpion, a charm that involved a donkey.

He reflected briefly on the words he knew and how they would have to be adjusted. Leaning close to the ass and cupping his hand over his mouth as if sharing a secret, he whispered into its ear: "God enacted everything, and everything was good, but thou

alone, snake, art accursed, thou and all thy brood."
He thought of Police Chief Fox, wished recovery for
the man, and crossed himself three times. *"Tzing,
tzing, tzing."*

What to do now?

He would have to deal with the demon and the
mine, but Hiram's first obligation was to his son.
Michael was alive, at least as far as Gus knew. If
Michael was alive, the boy would probably try to find
his way to Helper.

Hiram climbed onto the donkey.

Chapter Thirty-Three

HIRAM CREPT INTO THE BUSHES ALONG THE RIVER behind Buford's Boarding House. Underneath the bare willow branches, the air was cold and wet. The Price River was nearly invisible in the blast of snow crashing out of the canyon; twice, Hiram found rocks and crossed the icy water without getting wet.

Hiram was exhausted and now also saddle-sore. The ride down on the donkey's back had been an endless trudging into a wet, invisible curtain of snow.

The donkey had seemed considerably less bothered than Hiram, and once Hiram returned the sombrero, serape, and beast to the stable, had pushed its nose placidly into its feed trough.

Hiram had put the bullwhip, coiled up, inside his toolbox. The whip had Gus Dollar's blood on it now. Leaving that blood lying around carelessly might give some unknown third party a tool for influencing Gus, and if Hiram kept it, he thought he might find it useful.

Too tired to carry his toolbox anymore, he set it in

the snow at his feet. He wasn't sure he could make his way back into the room at the boarding house. He needed to rest for a second.

The trees on the river didn't offer him any cover, but the thick bushes did, and Hiram hunkered down. He felt thwarted, baffled, and sad. He'd rarely been in more trouble in his life, and his failures troubled his heart. Evil was powerful. Had Hiram done a single thing to slow its progress here in Helper?

An unexpected voice made him jump.

"Pap!" Michael was crouched next to the thick stump of a dead cottonwood on a square of snow-covered riverbank. "I figured you'd come back to the boarding house."

Hiram stumbled through the undergrowth and squatted beside Michael. He took off his wet gloves, shoved them into a pocket, and squeezed his son's hand. "Thank God you're okay."

"Your fingers are cold, Pap."

"You should feel my toes."

"Mine, too." Michael's teeth chattered.

They needed to get somewhere warm. Hiram eyed the backs of the houses fronting on Main Street, wishing the snow wasn't blocking so much of his view. Maybe he should take Michael back to the donkey's stable. "What happened?"

Michael nodded. His face was dirty, the filth swirled into curious patterns by the flakes of falling snow. His coat and jeans were caked with mud. Thorny weeds clung to his coat, each sticker a tiny shelf catching snow now, and his hair was plastered to his skull. But Michael's eyes were bright. "I took off after Mr. Sorenson ... after Mrs. Sorenson." Michael swallowed hard. "I didn't hurt them. I got knocked out by some-thing. And there were flies."

"Was it..." Hiram thought carefully about his question. How much had Michael seen? "Was the killer a man?"

Michael hesitated. When he spoke, he sounded dis-tant. "I'd have sworn it wasn't, last night. It seemed... like a monster, Pap. But it was dark, wasn't it? And I was tired. I'm not really sure what I saw."

Michael was talking himself out of his own eyewit-ness, and Hiram was inclined to let him do it. "How did you get down here?" he asked his son.

"I walked," Michael said. "It was easy. Just kept going downhill."

Hiram grunted his appreciation. "Quite a feat, still. You're a regular Flash Gordon."

"Pap, please."

"What, can't I be proud of my son?"

"Yeah, but Buck Rogers is the real thing. Flash Gordon is a total knock-off."

"Buck Rogers, then." Hiram dropped his son's hand. "Maybe it's time to go home, Buck. Admit failure and get out of town. I got a telegram from Brother Wells. Said as much."

Michael looked away into the wall of snow sur-rounding them and shivered. Then he looked back and met Hiram's eyes. "What's in my boot, Pap? It's what saved me from the demon, wasn't it? That was no man that killed the Sorensons."

Hiram retreated before his son's stare.

"We could get a taxi," Hiram said. "The truck is up in Spring Canyon, and I bet we could get a taxi to drop us off there." The plan might be totally insane, either for the slick state of the road or for the possibility of interception by police, but Hiram had to say something to change the subject. He also wanted to get Michael out of the storm.

"Dad," Michael said.

The word stopped Hiram cold. "Yes?"

Michael latched onto his arm. "No, Pap, we're going to talk, really talk. I spent a whole night and then a whole day sleeping in bushes or wandering through the canyons. I hid in trees, I drank snow. All that time, I thought about every weird thing that's happened over the years, and the strange things I've seen this in the last two days. I knew Hettie was a . . . well, she liked to say *cunning woman.* I didn't think you were . . . but you are, aren't you, Pap?"

Hiram felt Michael's hand like a weight on his arm. "You don't believe in magic."

Hiram turned to walk away, but Michael tightened his grip. "I know I've teased you about Grandma Hettie, but last night, when that thing grabbed me, well, that was empirical evidence of something. I don't know what. I bet you do. And I didn't use the word *magic.*"

Hiram forced himself to look into his son's face. "Think about whether you really want answers to these questions. I wanted to keep you safe. I've always wanted to keep you safe and do the right thing. And I didn't want you to . . . I don't want you to . . ."

"Don't want me to *what?*" Michael's eyes, shadowed pits in the thin light drifting from Main Street, bored into Hiram.

Hiram couldn't reveal his own fears and self-doubt. His heart was in his belly, and he'd broken into a cold sweat. Michael knew.

"You don't want an old-fashioned life, son. You want to go to college and do great things, become a scientist, or a lawyer, in some city somewhere. All I have to offer is farming and old folklore."

Michael shook his head. "You're changing the subject. What don't you want me to do?"

"Leave," Hiram admitted.

Michael was silent.

"You will someday, anyway. I mean, you're old enough, and that's the way of the world. But I don't want you to run away, because you find me... ridiculous... wrong."

Michael took a deep breath. "I was nearly killed last night. The Sorensons *were* killed. The thing that killed them was big, like a bear, and it came in a swarm of insects. I believe it's the same creature that attacked you and me up on the ridge. You fought that monster by lighting a fire and shouting the Bible at it. And you got the truck started. If I'm not mistaken, you did it with a *Coke bottle*. So what killed the Sorensons? What, Pap? You know, don't you?"

Hiram's jaw trembled. "If we leave now, if we don't talk about this, we can go back to our old, normal life. If you push me, if I tell you these things, your life will never be normal again."

Michael grinned. "Normal? We were never normal. Not when Mom and Grandma were alive, and less since they passed. I've got too much melanin for the girls of Lehi and I shoot my mouth off. And you, Pap, you were born at least a century late. What a pair we make."

"Buck Rogers and... who's Buck's pal? Ming the Merciless?"

Michael coughed. "Pap, no. But maybe you can be Dr. Huer. That's kind of a match, Dr. Huer knows stuff, like you know stuff. Only you have to say *Heh!* a whole lot more."

"Heh!" Hiram would always be an outsider, with men like Smith watching his every move. Having Michael for a son didn't make him less of an outsider, because Michael, too, stood on the outside. But Michael knew his secrets—or at least, the headlines—and the world hadn't ended.

"I love you, Michael."

"I love you too, Pap. And...I respect you."

Hiram hugged his son.

He then straightened out his arms and looked into Michael's face. "The creature covered in flies is... I'm not sure. Best to think of it as a demon, maybe. But it's old and it's dangerous, and it's behind everything...the murders, the mine closures, the Kimballs' fighting. Ammon and Samuel both looked into their father's seer stone, and that demon used it to manipulate them. Hand me your boot."

Michael did. In silence.

Hiram pried the heel off with his clasp knife. He shook the secret compartment and a second chi-rho amulet fell into his palm. "That's a talisman that is good for defense against enemies. I wear one, too, around my neck. It's not perfect, but it's strong protection. Another one, or something similar, anyway, is nailed into the door of the truck. This sign is the chi-rho—its influence may be what saved you from the fly demon. And it's why I always wanted you to wear your boots."

His son's eyes widened. "Wow."

"I told you," Hiram said.

"Did you think I was in danger?"

"*Life* is danger." Hiram put the amulet back into the boot and hammered it into place by slamming the heel against an adjacent tree trunk. "At first, I figured I'd tell you about it when you were older. Then I kept putting it off, and I saw how you laughed at Grandma Hettie behind her back. Then, at some point...I figured if you didn't know about the spirit realm, you might grow up to live a normal life. Somehow, in the big city, the need for lamens and bloodstones and amulets seems less pressing."

"Lamens? Amulets?"

Hiram laughed and removed the bronze Oremus lamen from his pocket. He gave it to his son. "This is a lamen. Hold on to it. I'll explain later."

Michael pushed his fists into his eyes. "I can't believe this. Only I *can*. It's why we drive around the state when we're not planting or harvesting, isn't it? You're not just helping the poor, are you? You're also demon hunting."

"The poor need more than one kind of help," Hiram said.

The wind picked up, and the branches that were already rattling began to sound like machine-gun chatter. Both he and Michael shivered.

Michael thought in silence for a few moments. "Samuel must be behind the demon. His camp was right out of the scary part of Dante. And he was crackers. Is the shopkeeper at Dollar's the witch?"

Hiram nodded. "A powerful witch. He knows more than I do, and he has better tools. Samuel? I don't know, I think Samuel's a victim. But with everything going on, police after us, the evil of the demon, murders ... I think we need to get out of town. I've been called home. It wasn't just the Sorensons. The demon murdered Callista Markopoulos."

"Callista?" Anger and sorrow flashed across Michael's face. "We can't leave, Pap. I don't care if I go to jail. And if this thing killed that girl, it could kill again."

"I will stay." Hiram knew he had to. "You should go home."

Michael touched Hiram's shoulder. "The Kimballs don't stand a chance, not without you and your magic." Michael rolled his eyes at the word. "Cripes, I can't believe I just said that."

"Maybe don't call it *magic*."

"Hexes. Charms. The occult. Lore. Wisdom. Special skills. The police are going to be useless against that thing, Pap. Unless someone calls in the Army, it's up to you."

Hiram nodded. "But you can go home."

"I'll stay." Michael's eyes blazed. "I owe it to Callista."

What had passed between the Greek girl and his son?

A car crunched through the back alley, sliding slightly in the snow. It had driven around from Main Street and now pulled to a stop not far from Hiram and Michael. It was Mary McGill's Model A, with Mary at the wheel, and no sign of anyone following her.

She stepped out stood beside her car, smoking a long cigarette, and she looked right at the river where Hiram was.

And then a second woman stepped out, from the other side of the car: Eliza Kimball. Eliza walked stiffly around the car to stand beside Mary.

"Hiram!" Mary called. "Pretty sure I saw you down here! And if there's someone in there who isn't Hiram Woolley, come out slowly, with your hands up! I have a gun."

"Just in case," Hiram told his son, "let's put our hands up." They stepped out of the bushes and into the headlights.

"Mr. Woolley!" Eliza called. "I owe you an apology, and I need your help."

Hiram lowered his hands, feeling a little foolish, but Mary smiled at him. "You don't need to apologize for anything."

"I did not behave well toward you when last we spoke," Eliza said. "Please forgive me."

"Forgiven," he said.

Neither of them mentioned the seer stone.

"I went to the big house," Eliza continued, "to speak to Ammon. I found blood and crow's feathers on the parlor carpet, and my brother gone. I fear Samuel has taken him or killed him or both!" Eliza was visibly trembling. "I don't know to whom else to turn. The men at the mine don't like me, for obvious reasons. As for the police," she gestured at Hiram, "I have been warned they are in the pocket of Mr. Rettig and the D and RGW."

"They are," Hiram said.

"Remind me to tell you something else about Naaman Rettig," Mary murmured.

Hiram felt Michael's arm around his shoulders. "Looks like we have work to do, Pap. Do we know a charm to deal with kidnapped brothers?"

Chapter Thirty-Four

SNOWFLAKES GLISTENED IN THE HEADLIGHTS OF the Model A. The wind shook the trees where they stood and made it hard for Hiram to think.

"Did you find evidence that Samuel is mad?" Hiram asked Mary.

"Not in the records," she admitted. "Don't you think the kidnapping is evidence enough?"

Hiram wanted to believe that Samuel, distracted and dazed by the substances he smoked, was innocent, but he had seen the man's art...including the animal corpses. More than that, he was under the influence of the seer stone's demon. "If Samuel has taken Ammon, I believe I know where they are."

"Samuel's camp?" Eliza looked distracted, her expression torn. Shattered by fatigue and trauma, much like Hiram, no doubt.

"The mine." Hiram looked at Michael. The boy had accepted that his father was a cunning man with surprisingly good grace. Could Hiram throw him into the presence of the demon...or Gus Dollar? But was it any safer to leave him behind? The monster had come out the mine to kill. It might not be in the mine now. "Or rather, the caves below the mines. We're going to need help."

"Are you going to call out the National Guard to stop a crazy drug addict from hurting his brother?" Mary asked.

"I wish I could get the National Guard." Hiram laughed weakly. "Or even a halfway decent elders quorum. There are at least two exits out of the caves, and maybe more. I want them blocked off when I go in."

"In case Samuel gets away." Eliza smiled ruefully.

"Yes. Or Gus Dollar, if he shows up. And also, I'd rather that uninvited people not break in on us."

"Like the police." Michael grinned. Was he enjoying the idea that his father was an outlaw? Hiram resolved to look more closely at the pulp magazines that Michael was always reading. And this Buck Rogers fellow.

"Gus Dollar!" Mary didn't shout, but the sudden energy in her voice felt like shouting to Hiram. "That reminds me, I want to show you this old daguerreotype. This is why I came looking for you. I found it in the files of the *Helper Journal*. They inherited a bunch of the city's old documents, and you need to look at this one."

Hiram almost snapped at the organizer. He had no time, he was hunted, he was exhausted and cold. But he held his tongue. "Show me."

The storm had taken a break, no wind, no snow. The headlights of Mary's car lit the yellowing image Mary pulled from her purse. It was of a row of men, and one of them was clearly Teancum Kimball; he matched the old daguerreotypes in the big house, and

Samuel's painting, and even the shrunken features of the corpse. Also, his sunken eyes were echoed in the features of all three children.

"Is this your father?" he asked Eliza, to be sure.

She nodded.

Another looked just like Gus Dollar. At his present age, with his straight-up hair and his not-quite-symmetrical gaze.

"Eighteen eighty-one," Mary said.

"Fifty-four years ago." Hiram frowned. "Could this be Gus's grandfather?"

"As far as I can tell on short notice," Mary told him, "there was no one named Dollar before about 1920 living in this valley. Not Gus, and not a father or an uncle or a cousin. I haven't checked the city records, though, and of course even that may or may not record the presence of any given person. I mean, if he owned *land*, he would probably show up."

Gus had given his eye to the demon. Could this possibly be Gus? If Teancum Kimball had made a thirty-year deal with the demon that ended in 1933, then Gus's deal would have had to have taken place earlier.

Something niggled at the back of Hiram's mind, and he couldn't quite figure out what it was. Something about Gus's eye.

"This is Gus Dollar," Hiram said.

Mary whistled. "But that would make him ... mathematics was never my best subject ... old."

"One million," Michael said. "One million years old. That makes him a dinosaur. As I suspected from the start."

Hiram's heart sank. So Gus had known Teancum, because Gus had been here in Spring Canyon, fifty-odd years ago. He'd made his deal with the demon then, and when his time was up, his place had been taken by Teancum Kimball. And now Gus was back, to master the demon once and for all.

Hiram should have killed Gus when he had the chance.

Mary took the picture back.

"The miners will help us rescue Ammon," Michael said.

Hiram wasn't sure. "What if they think I'm the murderer? Bill was good to them, he was their champion."

"You're their champion now, Pap." Michael shrugged. "Besides, you have the world's most honest face. People believe you when you tell them things. Even, let's face it, really weird things."

Mary McGill threw Hiram a surprised glance. "So...he knows now?"

Hiram nodded.

"Yeah, I know," Michael said. "Not quite sure *what* I know."

"But you *do* have a good face," Mary told Hiram.

"You could have been the world's most successful insurance salesman. Or banker." Michael grinned. "Hey, it's not too late, if this year's beets are thin."

"It's going to be a good harvest," Hiram said.

"Let's go," Michael said. "Can we take the truck?"

Eliza stood still, snowflakes piling up on her dark hair. Her brother's kidnapping had curbed her tongue.

"Sorry, Hiram, your big truck is too conspicuous," Mary said. "But four will fit in my car."

"As long as I can stop carrying this toolbox around." Hiram nodded.

"I can drive," Michael said.

"Are you assuming I can't, because I'm a woman?" Mary challenged him.

"I'm just saying I'm probably better. Not because you're a woman, but because I'm really good at driving cars."

"You know, I drove myself out here. All the way from Denver, Colorado, and I didn't wreck my car once. Had a flat tire outside Green River. You know what I did?"

"Swooned?"

"Fixed it."

Michael nodded. "You got me."

"Ride in the back," she told him. "With your father."

"I need to grab something first." Hiram put his toolbox inside the car's trunk. He tucked the two stolen lamens—the brass plate for summoning and the lead for collapsing a wall—into his inside coat pocket.

After a moment's thought, he put the bloodstained whip into one the largest pockets, too.

Michael still had his bronze Oremus plate.

Hiram climbed into the car and huddled under the blanket. "Keep me awake," he said to Michael. "Kick me now and then or something."

But Michael didn't kick him. Hiram gripped his Saturn ring in his clasped hands and promptly fell asleep, rocked to sleep by the battling rhythms of the car's engine and the wind's blast.

Mary McGill's Model A jerked to a stop, bouncing Hiram awake. Tattered fragments of a dream escaped him—a maze of tunnels, an enthroned demon before whom Hiram had prostrated himself, and an object buried beneath the throne that Hiram would not quite see.

He needed to consult his dream dictionary.

"You should wake him up now," Hiram heard Mary say.

"I'm awake." Hiram physically pried his eyelids up with his fingertips and then pulled back the blanket. Cold night air blasted his face and neck, which helped shake him to alertness. He could only see thirty feet, for the blasting snow.

His hands shook and he felt nauseated, but if his path crossed the path of a bottle of Coke, Hiram resolved to drink it immediately.

"Pap," Michael said. "The miners are here. I . . . I think they're waiting for you."

Hiram unfolded himself out of the Model A's back seat. His joints hurt, and when his booted feet touched the frozen soil, he felt as if someone was pounding his soles with a mallet.

The miners stood under the imposing structure of the silent tipple. There was Hermann Wagner, the German leader with his blocky head, and all the Germans with him. There were the Greeks, other than Dimitrios Kalakis, lined up behind the miner who always wore a bandana on his face. There was a scattering of Chinese and Japanese and Italian miners too, and they all held weapons. They had ax handles and spades and several even held rifles, but they weren't standing against each other, and they didn't hold their weapons as if they were about to attack.

They stood as if waiting, and when Hiram gingerly climbed up the hill to meet them, a welcoming murmur rippled through the mob.

Hiram straightened his back and tried to look the men in the eye. He wished he had a stone for eloquence, or a gift for it. Instead, he just looked every man in the eye he could and spoke plainly.

"I expect some of you think I'm a killer."

"Did you murder Callista?" The voice that asked was a woman's voice, so Hiram turned, looking for Dimitrios. To his surprise, the voice came from the red-bandana man; the miner pulled the bandana down, revealing a woman's face that Hiram knew—Medea Markopoulos.

Hiram managed not to stare.

"I didn't kill her." Hiram met her gaze.

Her eyes burned with rage, but tears streamed down her cheeks.

"Did Samuel Kimball kill my daughter?" Medea asked.

"I . . . I don't think so." Hiram met Mary's gaze. "But I can't be completely certain."

Medea nodded.

"I didn't kill the Sorensons, either. The last I saw of Bill Sorenson was after he took me down into the mine last night."

"*Ja*, we know." Wagner jerked a thumb at one of his Germans. Hiram recognized the man as the foul-smelling miner who had tried to shoot Samuel Kimball. "Paul saw you."

There had been a witness? "Did you see who killed the Sorensons?"

Paul shook his head. "But I saw Sorenson take you down into the mine, and bring you back up again."

Medea sniffed and cleared her throat. "I believe Hiram Woolley."

"*Ja*, we do, too," Hermann Wagner added.

There followed a round of general nodding and

affirmation noises. Hiram took a deep breath; a weight he hadn't realized was there had lifted from his chest.

"How did you...? Did you know I was coming?" he asked.

"I received a note from Samuel Kimball," Medea said, "telling me to guard the mine to stop you from coming in. Or rather, the note came for Dimitrios, and made its way to me."

"She's the Head Greek now," the club-footed Greek said, as if Hiram needed the explanation. "She a woman, but she smarter than us blockheads."

The Greek with the bad foot bobbed his head. "I'm Stavros."

"I received a similar message from Ammon," Hermann said. "And we got to talking. The food you brought is gone, and Herr Sorenson is dead. We are hungry and tired. Then we remembered what Mrs. McGill said, that we must work together to get the Kimball brothers to behave, and not fight each other when the Kimballs tell us to."

"The Kimballs have been..." What should Hiram tell the miners? "They haven't been themselves. I think they're going to come around, but the reason they asked you here was to stop me from trying to... fix the situation."

"Is that who's got the missing carbide lamps and helmets?" Medea asked. "Is it the Kimball brothers, down in the mine?"

"It is my brothers," Eliza said. "I'm Eliza Kimball. Let us go down into the mine, and we'll set the situation right."

"You certainly look like Teancum's girl," Stavros said.

Medea cast a narrowed gaze on Eliza.

"I need a little more help than that." Hiram sighed. "I need all the entrances watched. If anyone tries to leave—Ammon or Samuel or anyone else—I need you to hold them for me. Can you do that?"

"We will all help," Wagner said.

Medea nodded. "I'll do more than watch."

"So will I," Mary said.

"There are two more mineshafts, higher up on the hill." Hermann Wagner gestured up at the ridge above Kimball Canyon. "We can bottle those up, easy."

"What about the caves?" Paul said. "I know where there are a couple of cracks in the rock. I'm not sure, but I think they connect into the mine tunnels."

"And there's at least one near Gus Dollar's store," Hiram added. "If the shopkeeper is there, make sure he doesn't leave."

The miners floated several other locations that needed to be watched to completely bottle up the underground complex. Then they broke up into squads of four to five men each and scattered to the various openings.

Hermann stayed at the main opening, with Paul and Stavros. All three had rifles.

The German miner with a large neck goiter and a bright red waistcoat volunteered to accompany Hiram and his party. Eliza objected that the mine tunnels were narrow, and the German bellowed in response, "Den ve go in zinkle file!" He shook a pickaxe in both hands. "My name is Valter," he said to Hiram. "I apolochize for any earlier rudeness."

Medea didn't say a word, and she didn't leave Hiram's side. A blade appeared in her hands, the same sword Hiram had seen in her home. The weapon had a curving blade like a scimitar, narrow near the hilt and broader near the tip. That and her denim jeans and bandana around her neck made her look like a Janissary dressed as a cowboy.

"Why did you hide your face?" Hiram asked her. "Wouldn't Dimitrios know who you were, anyway?"

"When my Basil got injured," the woman explained, "I had to take his part. All the Greeks knew who I was, but I wore the bandana so the Germans and the others wouldn't give me trouble."

"I'm glad to have you." Hiram checked his inside coat pockets and felt the two lamens from Gus Dollar's Book of the Spirits. He had not recovered the heliotropius from the back seat of Police Chief Fox's cruiser. He handed what he hoped was a protective lamen to Mary. "Will you carry this? In a pocket, or wear it on a string?"

"From the man who wrote the apostles on a sage leaf and sprang me from jail? Yes, I will." Mary smiled, but took the lamen. She tucked it into the inside of her jacket. "It's heavy."

"It's made out of brass, I think." He didn't mention the lead plate in his own pocket, the Saturnine one with the astrological markings, the text from Joshua and the words he couldn't read. The lamen that—he thought—was designed to collapse the caves below the mine.

Hiram realized he should have stopped at the Double-A to pull his other protective lamen from the door. Too late.

Hiram took his chi-rho amulet from his neck and offered it to the Kimball sister. "Eliza, would you wear this?"

She shook her head and stepped away. Hiram felt embarrassed.

He offered the amulet to Medea and Walter both. Walter shook his head and Medea snorted, so Hiram put the talisman back on his own neck.

Turning to Eliza, he asked, "When you were a child here, did you ever learn to ignite a carbide lamp?"

"It's been a long time." Eliza's voice was dull, as if she were very tired. "Perhaps you can show me."

"One last thing," Hiram said. He quickly thumbed through the pages of his dream dictionary. There was nothing for either *king* or *throne*, but he did find one apparently relevant entry:

> UNDERGROUND—*if you go underground and you are not digging, it denotes your early death.*

Chapter Thirty-Five

THE CAFFEINE HAD LEFT HIRAM'S SYSTEM. HE WASN'T shaking anymore, and his heartbeat was regular, and he didn't want to vomit. On the other hand, he struggled against an urge to lie down in a mine cart and fall asleep. Once the affairs of the Kimball Mine were set right, he'd sleep for a week and eat for a month.

First, he had to rescue Ammon from Samuel.

Medea and Walter had moved various chits to the "IN" board. Then they'd entered. Coming in out of the snowstorm, the mine's warmer air was a relief.

"Samuel!" Hiram called ahead of them in the darkness. With the bright carbide beams and their noisy footsteps, there was no way his party was going to surprise Samuel, in any case. "It's Hiram Woolley! Your sister's with us. Don't do anything you'll regret!"

But was there anything a drug-addled maniac like Samuel Kimball would regret?

Hiram wished he had a way to know where the demon was. He wasn't sure whether he preferred the idea that it was on the surface and therefore wouldn't attack them in the mine, or in the mine and therefore wouldn't kill innocents on the surface.

He led the way, Eliza Kimball to one side, Mary and Michael following, and the two miners bringing up the rear. He had no trouble finding the cave entrance with its removed boards, and the six of them crawled down the bottom of the boulder-choked crack and onto the flat stone shelf beside the waters, following Hiram's previous chalk marks.

Mary bent over to gaze into the pool. "Ugh, it's full of little white things. Fish and insects and snakes. Why are they so white?"

"They don't need pigment," Michael said. "They've never seen the sun, not their whole lives. I read that in *Popular Science*."

Hiram looked down the three passages he hadn't stepped in before. Might they be exits? Or might Samuel have taken Ammon down one of those tunnels? But he didn't think so.

Hiram wished he had another hazel rod. "I don't think they've gone down any of those passages."

"Why not?" Medea held her sword up and to one side of her body, as if she were a warrior, entering a hostile castle. She looked competent and controlled; Walter, by contrast, nervously swung his pickaxe around with one hand as if he were strolling in the park and the pickaxe were a parasol. Hiram worried he'd hit someone.

In his other hand, at Hiram's insistence, the German carried a gas can.

"Samuel?" Hiram called, turning and facing over the water.

No answer.

"Follow me." To Michael, he said: "Stay close behind me."

Then Hiram stepped into the water.

The shock of its temperature took him by surprise; he had forgotten how cold it was. At every step, the knobby texture of the walls presented a new landscape. His eyes, tightly focused by the carbide beam, interpreted those changing shadows as movement, and he continually turned his head one way and then the other, trying to find the sources of the flitting and swooping motions in his nearly-blind peripheral vision.

He wished he had his revolver.

Hiram climbed out of the pool and onto the shelf of stone with the lizard-head altar. The sound of water sluicing from his clothing and splashing all around him was loud. He wouldn't hear anyone or anything approach over that racket, he thought, but then Eliza climbed out of the water after him and was even louder.

Ammon and Samuel Kimball both sat against the wall, beside the mummified corpse of their father. The two men both stared at Hiram with expressions of horror, and then he realized that they couldn't see him, due to the power of the carbide beam.

"It's Hiram Woolley," he said.

"The witch!" Ammon gasped.

"No." Hiram sighed.

But then he realized that both men sat with their hands tied before them, and more rope knotted around their ankles. "Wait a moment." He raised a hand in warning to his friends behind him.

"So it will come to a confrontation here, will it?"

A beam of light snapped on in the darkness. It shone in Hiram's face, blinding him. He held his hands up and still could see nothing but flashes of light. He knew the voice, in any case.

It belonged to Gus Dollar.

The beam came from waist height, so it was a flashlight, not a carbide lamp. It was still plenty powerful enough to blind Hiram, whose sight was already squeezed into tunnel vision by the effect of the carbide lamp on his helmet.

"It doesn't have to come to any more confrontation, Gus," Hiram said. "Let the Kimballs go. Walk away."

"You haven't come alone." Gus hissed. There was a brief silence. "You brought a warrior maiden and a jolly dwarf, I see."

"I decided I wanted reinforcements," Hiram said.

"You are a tricky old man after all," Michael added.

"I should have bound you. I would have bound you, only he stopped me."

Who was *he*? How would Gus have bound Hiram?

"What do you mean, have me arrested?" Hiram asked. "You certainly don't want a judge of the Helper Justice Court to come look at the charms and hexes in your shop and try to figure out what they mean."

Hiram shifted slightly to one side, and the beam came out of his eyes. He still couldn't see a damn, with all the blazing suns of red and green that splashed across his vision and swam in circles.

"I can see through your eyes," Gus said. "I know you think I'm pitiful, and my best weapon has been taken from me, but I've come down here to bring you to heel."

With his tunnel vision and the light in his eyes,

Hiram had no idea what the others were doing. At least one of them was moving—he heard the sound of shoes scuffing on the damp stone of the shelf.

"If you can see through my eyes," Hiram quipped, "you're seeing nothing at all."

He heard squirming and whimpering noises. At first, he took them for Samuel, but then he realized it was Ammon who was wiggling and crying.

"I don't need the book," Gus said. "I've brought you here with another gift, a little tender piece of bait. You can't resist the offer of a deal, but now you've stepped inside my circle, and you are mine."

A tender piece of bait? That was the strangest imaginable way to characterize Ammon Kimball, and not much better a description of his brother Samuel.

Hiram swung his face down on a hunch, looking at the top of the lizard-head altar.

A small sphere sat there, glistening.

Flesh.

An eyeball. That was the bait.

"You're not talking to me," Hiram said out loud.

Gus Dollar hadn't been talking to Hiram at all. Who had Gus been addressing?

The skin on Hiram's neck crawled.

Was the demon present?

Gus laughed, a shrieking whoop that ended abruptly in air being sucked in through his teeth. "You're a sideshow, farmer. Your death here is incidental and irrelevant."

Hiram snapped his head back in Gus's direction. The beam of his light caught the shopkeeper in the face. Scabbed whip marks slashed down from his forehead to his chin. For an instant, Hiram felt bad for whipping the man. Then he felt revulsion. Gus retained his glass eye, but the socket which had recently housed an eyeball of flesh and vitreous liquid was now empty.

Gus had sacrificed his second eye. As bait.

The demon had to be present.

Eliza laughed, but it was a deep laugh, below baritone, below bass, a rumbling laugh like the sound of a mountain shifting from one foot to the other. A cold wind gusted from her as she laughed, and Hiram heard a buzzing of flies that rose in crescendo to a shrill whistle.

"Pap..."

Hiram grabbed in the darkness and found Michael. He dragged his son behind him, trying to put himself between the young man and either of the two dangerous figures they now confronted. Hiram grabbed the whip—it was his best weapon.

He wished he could see better.

"WHAT THEN, ZOLLER?" The voice rippling out of Eliza was titanic. Hiram turned his light to face her in time to see flies erupt from her mouth with each syllable. The skin of her face and arms bulged and rippled as she moved, as if she had too many muscles underneath. Or as if there were a swarm of flies inside her, trying to escape. "I GAVE YOU THIRTY YEARS OF PROSPERITY, AS PROMISED. WERE THEY NOT ENOUGH? WILL YOU BIND ME NOW FOR ETERNITY?"

Hiram heard muttering in Greek and German both.

In English, Mary whispered, "Holy shit."

"You allowed Teancum Kimball to run me off my land!" Gus yelled.

"YOU HAD HAD YOUR PROSPERITY AND YOUR TIME WAS UP! YOU CANNOT BIND ME!"

"I already have," Gus said. Hiram turned his light to Gus Dollar's face and saw the shopkeeper shift posture. He pulled a sword up in front of him, the ritual blade Hiram had seen earlier in the shop. "I have summoned you to this place, and now I will slay your vessel of flesh, and transfer the power of your spirit to *me*."

"FOOL." The Beast-Eliza waved an arm at Ammon and Samuel, slumped against the stone. "*I* SUMMONED *YOU*. I BROUGHT YOU ALL HERE TO FEED UPON! TEANCUM KIMBALL DELIVERED HIS OTHER SPAWN IN PERSON. I WILL TAKE THESE LAST THREE AS HIS FINAL OFFERING."

Gus's voice jumped in pitch. "I command you in the name of *Elay Adonay* to submit!"

Hiram shuddered. Invocation of any of the Divine Names was dangerous. An unworthy man who attempted it would fail, and if he was unworthy enough, might be destroyed.

Eliza laughed. She turned toward Hiram, who got a split second's view of Eliza's face. Flies swarmed her eyes, nostrils, ears, and open, leering mouth. "THANK YOU FOR DELIVERING MY STONE TO THE WOMAN."

Eliza punched Hiram. That single blow tossed him and Michael both across the chamber. He narrowly avoided the altar, with its gruesome little deposit, and fell to the stone beside Teancum Kimball.

His helmet rattled away, across the stone. He dropped the whip.

Climbing onto all fours, Hiram looked into the crook

of Teancum Kimball's arm and realized that the man wasn't carrying the skeleton of a lamb—the skeleton belonged to a very tiny human baby.

Michael yelped.

Hiram gagged, tried to vomit, and failed. Of course the Beast had found a child to kill during its rampage. It had developed a taste for it devouring Teancum Kimball's babies.

"You killed my daughter!" Medea howled.

Violence erupted into the cave, but Hiram saw it only through the crazed and shifting window afforded to him by the crossing beams of the various carbide lamps. Medea leaped forward with her scimitar swinging, and at the same time, Walter lunged and swung the pickaxe.

Eliza attacked with fists that swelled to the size of milk bottles, black masses of flies flowing like tar. Her first blow struck Walter in the face. His neck exploded, the goiter throwing a dark wave of blood across the chimney. Her second caught Medea in the stomach, and the miner dropped her blade into the water and fell to all fours.

Gus shouted in Latin, or maybe Greek.

Scrambling, Hiram found his helmet and got it back onto his head.

Eliza stepped into the water, flies bursting from the orifices of her face at the chill touch, and she towered over Medea. The miner coughed and retched into the water, helpless.

Hiram threw himself into Eliza's path. "No!"

Eliza swung a punch at him, and only a wild, last-second duck brought him beneath a blow that might easily have brained him. He fished in the water, feeling several slimy things with his fingers and the back of his hand before he found the sword's hilt.

He raised the weapon in front of him.

"You will serve me!" Gus shouted.

Hiram meant to swing the sword at Eliza, but hesitated. For all that flies now swarmed her, she had a woman's form, and not the form of an enemy.

Eliza struck him, knocking him into the water. He dropped the sword and floundered, feeling he had too many limbs until he realized he was tangled up in Walter's corpse.

Gus was still chanting.

Eliza stepped forward. She swelled to twice her normal size. She raised enormous talons over her head for a killing blow. Was she aiming at Hiram or at Medea?

Fire sprang up behind Eliza and the Beast howled in surprise.

Gus's spell? But no, there was Michael, with the gas can. He'd lit the back of Eliza's dress on fire. The flies swarmed angrily as they escaped her body.

But as the flies exited, the sound became less and less the bellow of a wounded ogre, and more and more the shriek of a terrified woman whose body is on fire.

The flies swarmed densely, cohering into a dense, humanoid shape between Hiram and Eliza. He couldn't save her unless he moved the monster.

Standing on wobbly legs, Hiram raised his right arm to the square, elbow bent, hand up, like a carpenter's square, an ancient sign of true alignment, blessing, and oaths. And he shouted the secret name of God.

Not *Jehovah*, the silly sub-Latin English spelling of the King James Bible. Nor yet *Yahweh*, the more fashionable pronunciation that Mahonri had learned from reading those books of Biblical scholarship, and that he used when he wanted to put on intellectual airs.

Hiram used the secret pronunciation of the Tetragrammaton that Grandma Hettie had taught him. It was the only one of the Divine Names that he knew. She had whispered it to him in a closet and made him whisper it back to her until he got it right. And she had told him only to pronounce it in dire need, or else in a wind so strong it would whip the word right out of anyone's hearing, or else when passing the vital pronunciation on to an apprentice of his own.

Hiram shouted the name of God and the fallen angel Samuel, Mahoun, Master Mahan, the Beast of many names—flinched.

Five times, Grandma Hettie had told him. No demon can stand in the presence of the Tetragrammaton spoken five times with authority, by a person with a chaste and sober mind.

Was Hiram worthy? He risked failure and his own destruction.

He didn't see any other choice.

He stepped forward, keeping his right arm square, and shouted it a second time, and now the Beast darted to one side. It roared, taking shape in the cloud of flies, and tore at the sides of its head with its own talons.

Hiram wanted to keep shouting the Name, to drive the Beast out of the world for good.

But Eliza was on fire.

With the Beast to one side, he leaped forward. He tackled Teancum Kimball's only surviving daughter, pain from the fire searing his arms.

The fire splashed left and right, some of it spreading across the surface of the water and some of it still clinging to Eliza Kimball as Hiram dragged her from the pool and threw her to the stone shelf. His helmet gone again, he would have been blind but for the light of the fire, on Eliza and on the stone shelf.

He ripped his coat off and slapped it down on Eliza, patting out the flames. Remembering the lamens, he grabbed the lead one from the coat pocket. He saw the whip lying beside Eliza, and picked it up, as well.

Medea joined Hiram and together they dragged Eliza to her feet.

"Mary?" Hiram asked.

Michael pointed; the labor organizer had cut the bonds on the Kimballs' wrists and was grunting, trying to pull them to their feet. Of the six of them, she was the only one still wearing a helmet with a lamp. The beam of her lamp bounced around the cave as she moved, both giving light and baffling Hiram's vision. Shadows and flies swarmed.

The Beast lunged at Hiram, and he snapped the whip at it.

It was an awkward attack, and the Beast grabbed the bullwhip, a hand clearly visible within the swarm of flies. Then the misshapen, multimouthed face appeared, and it yanked the whip from Hiram's hand. Hiram backed away and the demon laughed.

Then it stuffed the leather into one of its open maws.

And laughed.

"Run!" Hiram yelled.

But the Beast turned around and advanced on Gus. The shopkeeper screamed in Latin and held the ceremonial sword up in front of him, but the demon didn't slow down. Something had gone wrong with Gus's charm.

But what?

"Run!" Hiram pushed Michael into the water first, with Eliza's elbow in the boy's grip. The Kimball heiress muttered dazed gibberish. "Help her get through!"

Mary and Medea followed, each dragging one of the Kimball brothers. The men stumbled, limbs probably cramped or asleep from having been tied up.

Hiram grabbed the gas can and checked that its cap was screwed on tight. He followed last, backing along the submerged tunnel by feel and watching Gus Dollar and the Beast. He was the only witness when Gus shrieked in rage and flung his blade to the ground.

The whip, Hiram realized. The whip with Gus's blood on it. The demon had eaten Gus's blood, and Gus's hex had failed.

Exploding into a swarm of flies, the Beast fell on Gus.

Chapter Thirty-Six

BACKING THROUGH THE TUNNEL, HIRAM SLIPPED. He plunged into the icy water and lost his grip on the sword. For unreal moments he floated at the bottom of the pool, the icy tendrils creeping into his blood.

His dream dictionary had warned him of an early death.

But a beam of light from behind him crossed the stone, illuminating white creatures like scorpions and glinting off the fallen blade.

Hiram grabbed the sword, pushed himself to the surface—and smacked his head against the tunnel ceiling.

For long seconds he could see nothing, and he didn't know whether he had blinded himself with the blow to the head, or whether the last carbide light had gone out.

"Pap!" A gentler beam crossed Hiram's path.

A flashlight, held in Michael's hands. Mary, Medea, and the Kimballs huddled behind him. Medea stood

375

in front of them with her sword in hand, rage in her eyes; the others looked terrified.

Hiram staggered onto the rocky shelf below the boulder-strewn crack leading up to the mine. Three other tunnels branched off from the chamber, and his enemy could come out of any of them. If only he could close every passageway, including the one out.

"The lead lamen," he said. "Joshua brought down the walls of Jericho. Gus came down here to fight the demon with a sword, but his original plan was to bury it under rock."

"Pap?"

"The lore is beyond me, but he was going to kill the monster and . . . absorb it. Eat its soul. It's the other lamen!" Hiram pulled the lead plate from his pocket. "Give me some light."

Michael stepped close and shone his beam on the lead plate. "Pap, you hit your head."

Hiram chuckled. "True. But I think I know what Gus was trying to do. He wanted the Beast's power, so he planned to trap its spirit in his Book of the Spirits, but destroy the body."

"And that . . . bit of plate there?"

"It's image lore." Hiram looked into his son's shadowed eyes and made a noise that was half-laugh and half-sob. "I'm sorry, I know this is all too much."

"Pap, we should run."

"We will." Hiram jabbed a finger at the writing on the plate that he couldn't read. "What does that say?"

"*In nominee patris et filii et spiritus sancti*," Michael said. "Is that Latin?"

Mary McGill shouldered her way between them. "*In nomine*, not *in nominee*."

"It's Latin?" Hiram said. "Nuns?"

"Nuns," Mary agreed.

"Teach us the pronunciation," Hiram said.

She said it twice, Hiram repeating it the first time, and Hiram and Michael both following along the second.

Medea stared at the passage back into the altar chamber.

Michael pulled them back on task. "Pap?"

Hiram held up the plate. "The English quote is from Joshua six, about Jericho."

"Joshua fit the battle." Michael grinned. "I can play that one on guitar."

"Shout," Hiram said, "for the Lord hath given you the city. And what shall we shout?"

"The Latin prayer," Mary said.

"And that will bring down the cave behind us, and trap the thing inside."

"It . . . will?" Michael furrowed his brow.

"It should." Willpower should not be a part of any charm. The magician didn't impose his will on the universe, the magician acted in accordance with known laws, or else the magician asked God.

In either case, faith was essential.

"It *will*," Hiram said.

"The cave *will* collapse," Michael emphasized. "It has to."

Hiram tousled his son's hair. "Back to the mine." He gestured to boulder-stuffed chasm that led upward. "As fast as you can and say the Latin words as much as you can. Shout them!"

"Anything else?" Michael asked.

"If you get to the mine, and you can find it in your heart . . . pray."

Michael hesitated, nodded, and scampered up the crack. He dragged Eliza with him. The black-clad teacher from the east was now scorched black of complexion and her hair was burnt short. The stink of fire hung about her, and she moved as if half-asleep.

"*In nomine patris,*" Mary McGill said, "*et filii, et spiritus sancti.*"

"Louder," Hiram said. "Shout!"

"Mr. Woolley."

Hiram turned to find Ammon and Samuel Kimball. Both men were pale and shivering. How much had they seen? And what had their fragile minds allowed them to remember?

Samuel looked more rational than he ever had. "I'm sorry," he said simply.

"I'm sorry," Ammon echoed his brother.

"Up the rocks with Miss McGill," Hiram said. "She's going to be chanting Latin. Whatever she tells you to shout, shout it with her."

"I stay with you," Medea told Hiram, her voice flat.

The two brothers clambered up the rocks, awkwardly echoing Mary's clipped and precise Latin syllables.

A hideous roar rang out. It seemed to come from low along the icy pool, but also from two of the tunnels that opened onto the shelf. The Beast had fed, but it was coming for them.

Hiram and Medea retreated up onto the lowest of the rocks and Hiram splashed some gas down to create a thin barrier. As he lit the gas with his Zippo, he looked up and saw flies swarming from all three tunnels opening onto the shelf, and from the submerged tunnel as well. A wall of flame rose between him and the flies, but he knew it wouldn't last.

He shouted. *"In nomine patris et filii et spiritus sancti!"*

Kneeling, he wedged the lead lamen down among the boulders at the base of the crack. This was not a charm he was master of, but he thought that images written to bring down walls and cities—and mines— had to be buried inside the walls to be effective. In his dream, too, something had been buried beneath the demon king's throne.

Had he dreamed of the lamen, then?

The Beast lumbered toward Hiram, and for a moment he feared he would be flattened.

But the Beast reached the line of fire and stopped. It opened all three mouths of its eyeless face and leaned back, gaping skyward. With a sound like a horrific belch wrapped around a high-pitched whistle, three columns of flies exploded out of the Beast's maws. Hiram smelled rotten meat. As the swarms grew in size, the Beast's body dwindled, until it had disappeared entirely, and there was only the swarm.

But the swarm stayed below the flame.

Hiram raised his arm to the square and shouted the Name.

"Up!" Hiram shouted at Medea.

"Look!" She pointed below the swarm.

A pile of blood and torn flesh, and splintered bones like a demented game of pick up sticks, lay beneath the swarming flies. For a moment, Hiram wondered what it was, but then he saw the glint of a glass eye nestled in with the gore and the shattered remains.

His stomach turned. He was lucky it was empty.

"Go!" he cried.

"You go!" Medea pulled Hiram past her and sent him scampering up the rocks. He climbed breathlessly, swooning from lack of air and from effort, and had to stop to catch his balance and avoid dropping the gas can. "Lay down more fire!"

Looking down, he saw the beast re-form and lunge at Medea.

The miner was not a trained swordfighter, but the Beast had killed her daughter. She hurled herself at the Beast with such ferocity, slashing and howling, that the Beast stepped back.

Then she turned and raced toward Hiram up the chasm.

He lay down a second line of gasoline across the boulders, a little thicker than the previous one. He thought he had enough for one more wall.

The Beast bounded up on Medea's heels. She leaped from one giant stone, over the gasoline barrier, to another just as Hiram touched flame to the gas.

Whooosh! Fire leaped up, blinding Hiram.

The Beast roared but fell back.

Hiram shouted the Name at it again. It hissed and roared but didn't fall back.

"*In nomine patris et filii et spiritus sancti!*" Hiram yelled, resuming his dogged upward climb with Medea at his side. He was careful not to get his hands or feet wedged between rocks. "*In nomine patris et filii et spiritus sancti!*"

Near the top of the chasm, maybe fifty feet from the mine entrance, he saw Michael, Mary, and the others. They were shouting too, but Hiram didn't sense the slightest evidence that the cave was about to collapse.

Was Gus's hex a failure?

Had Hiram misunderstood the lamen? Was it the will of God that he fail? Was his faith too weak?

Or was he not pure enough? All charms, but especially the spells of the high court magicians, were said to depend on the magician's personal purity. A chaste and sober mind. It was one of the reasons why Hiram fasted, and tried to keep his heart free of enmity toward any.

And if he wasn't pure enough to make the lamen work, would the use of the Divine Name also fail him?

He paused his ascent and glanced up again. Medea stopped with him. Did the *others* have insufficient faith, or purity?

And specifically, they should all be as pure as possible with respect to the operation at hand. He remembered abruptly his divination by sieve and shears, with Gus Dollar and his grandchildren. Hiram had asked whose heart must change.

The answer had been: all the Kimballs.

He shouted at the Kimballs. "Ammon! Samuel! Eliza! You have to forgive each other! Forgive each other, or this won't work!"

They stared at him.

The Beast leaped over the dying flames and galloped up the chasm, its grey misshapen form shrouded in the buzz of countless flies. Hiram stopped and laid down one last line of gasoline. Twenty-five feet above, the others were yelling the Latin words, but Hiram feared the words were useless.

"You *must forgive* each other!" he shouted.

He knelt to put fire to the gasoline.

The Zippo slipped from his fingers.

Medea watched the lighter click against the stone. She cursed in Greek and leaped down the chasm to the face the Beast once more.

Hiram fumbled for the lighter. It had slipped down into a crack, and he had to stretch to get his hand down there. Something cold and dry touched his fingers and retreated, and he imagined horrible things that might eat his hand or inject him with venom.

But he grabbed the lighter.

"Medea! Come back!" He crouched again over the line of gasoline, ready to light it when the Greek woman rejoined him.

Medea struck at the Beast, and Hiram saw that she was doing no real damage. Its skin was uncut and its movements were unslowed. Then Medea turned to race up the crack, and the Beast grabbed her by the ankle.

Hiram raised his arm to the square once more and shouted the Name. Before he could shout it again, the monster swung Medea through the air, splattering her skull into fragments in a single blow against the stone wall.

Hiram felt faint. The Beast seemed to fade away into the distance and then pulse closer into his view again, and Hiram sucked in cool air, battling to stay conscious. A faint smell struck his senses, spicy and sweet.

"Pap!"

The Beast was racing toward him.

Medea had followed her daughter into death, there was nothing Hiram could do for her. But Medea's other children still lived, as did her husband, and so did Hiram's son. He lit the gasoline.

The Beast threw itself into the flames this time, but they drove it back. It wasn't the heat at work—a man could have jumped through the flames—it was the light and sacred power in the fire itself. It was the power of Gabriel.

Hiram hurled the gas can at the Beast. Flames licked around the open stubby neck of the can as it bounced off the creature's shoulder, and then Hiram shouted the Name again.

The Beast shrank and hissed, but then roared at Hiram. A column of flies shot from its open maw, slamming into the flames. Thousands of charred flies fell dead onto the stones and the fire burned on, keeping the thing trapped.

That conflagration wouldn't last much longer.

Shouldn't the Name be hurting the Beast more?

Was Hiram not worthy?

"Mary!" he shouted. "Get Michael to the surface, warn the miners! Eliza, Ammon, Samuel, I need you to stay. We can stop it."

Mary looked pale, but she nodded and they ran. Michael took the flashlight with him, leaving the flames the only light in the chasm.

Hiram scurried up to where the three Kimballs stood, trembling and staring, on a flat boulder the size of a double bed. He grabbed Eliza and shook her, shocking alertness back into her eyes.

"Eliza!" he shouted. "Samuel! Ammon! No heart is completely pure, but your hearts have been corrupted by that thing. It gave you all false visions, like it gave your father. If we are to have any chance at all, *you must forgive each other now!*"

Ammon broke first. "I'm sorry, Samuel," he said. "I'm sorry, Eliza." Then he dropped to his knees. "I didn't know the power I was serving, but in my heart,

I knew I was wronging you. I forgive you, and I ask you to forgive me."

Standing above the man, Hiram noticed that he had no visible boils.

The Beast bellowed, and is if in response, Eliza threw herself on her brother's neck in an embrace. "I'm sorry I judged you! I'm sorry I gave into curiosity and looked into the stone! I'm sorry I tied you up and brought you down here! It wasn't me, but also it was! I'm sorry! I forgive you! Forgive me, Ammon!"

Samuel stood, a glazed look on his face.

Hiram could guess what might be causing the youngest Kimball's daze. "Samuel, are you on reefer right now?"

Samuel shook his head, but the motion was a shocked one. Hiram had seen it before, on the fields of France.

He took Samuel's hand and wrapped an arm around the younger man's shoulders. "Come on," he said. "I'll help you. But your sister and brother are kneeling. Let's kneel together."

Woodenly, Samuel fell to his knees. "You were never really my brother and sister," he began.

"Please, Samuel," Hiram begged. "Forgive them."

The light disappeared as the gasoline burned itself out. They were plunged into unforgiving darkness.

Hiram heard a roar and the scratching, thudding sound of the Beast resuming its climb up the crack.

"Please," he said.

"I forgive you," Samuel said. The words were simple, but they sounded sincere.

"Now one more time. Say the Latin words with me, and believe that we will be fine. *In nomine patris et filii et spiritus sancti.*"

A roar so close, the Beast might have been standing on Hiram's shoulder.

The stones beneath his feet shifted abruptly and began to give way.

Hiram took in a startled breath and heard the others do the same. "This way!" He grabbed in the darkness and found a hand—he wasn't sure whose. Placing his other hand against the wall, he groped his way up in stygian blackness. The stones beneath his feet shifted and trembled. "And keep chanting. Shout! *In nomine patris et filii et spiritus sancti!*"

Their pronunciations were no better than Hiram's, and Hiram was pretty sure that his was terrible.

"Is that a light?" Eliza asked.

It was. It was a flock of lights, rushing toward them from the mine. They ran forward to meet the lights, still chanting.

"*In nomine patris et filii et spiritus sancti!*"

The earth shook. The Beast roared. It sounded in the darkness as if it were only inches from Hiram's face.

At the boarded entrance into the mine, Hiram stopped to look. The others scrambled past him and into the arms of the miners. Behind and below the Beast, Hiram saw sudden flame and heard the deafening crack of an explosion in a confined space. Had one of the carbine lamps abandoned below ignited some subterranean gas? Or was the lead lamen simply doing its work?

A shadow lunged up to block his view of the flame, roaring and whistling.

Then the Beast's bellowing was whipped away and buried in a cacophony of crashing stone. The boards were sucked into the cave and the ground beneath

Hiram's feet shook. Finally, a chunk of stone larger than the Double-A crashed into place, sealing off the natural cave.

When Hiram could see, he saw the dirty faces of the miners of the Kimball Mine. He found he was whistling, and when he recognized the tune, he laughed out loud in shock and relief.

It was "Joshua Fit the Battle."

Chapter Thirty-Seven

HIRAM EMERGED FROM THE EARTH WITH MICHAEL, Mary, and the Kimballs, escorted by a brigade of miners.

They were met by blinding lights. The wind had stopped. Dust from the cave-in danced in shifting whorls with slow, fat snowflakes that seemed almost warm, and as Hiram stepped into the light, he heard a cheer.

The light came from headlights—three cars, at least.

A hand gripped Hiram's shoulder from behind, and Hiram heard a man's voice he didn't know. "Hiram and Michael Woolley, you're under arrest for the murders of Vilhelm and Eva Sorenson."

"Sergeant Dixon?" Hiram asked, but the voice didn't sound right.

"My name's Jefferson. Deputy Sheriff of Carbon County. I'm taking you to Price."

Hiram nodded.

"What are you talking about?" Michael snapped. "We had no reason to kill those people!"

Ammon coughed deeply, a painful sound just to hear, and spat a black wad into the snow. "It wasn't them, Deputy. The night of the murder, both Hiram and his son were at my house. I was showing them an old stone of my father's. It couldn't have been them."

"I spent all day yesterday with you." The deputy sounded irritated to the point of anger. "You couldn't mention this earlier?"

Tears cleared the dust and light from Hiram's eyes enough that he could see the man's face, weathered and tired. A hard-working policeman's face.

Ammon shrugged. "I was distracted. I had family business to attend to."

"Mr. Woolley is innocent." Eliza looked surprisingly dignified, with her dress scorched and burned. "As is his son."

Samuel's glasses were a sight to see, covered in dust and now collecting snow. "I also want to go on record vouching for them. You don't, don't...want to fight us on this, Deputy. We employ a lot of men in this canyon."

Samuel still sounded dazed, but he was lucid.

Mumbling a baffled apology, the deputy retreated.

Sergeant Dixon grabbed Hiram by the other shoulder. "Pretty sure you left this in my car." The policeman pressed a small object into Hiram's hand.

His bloodstone.

"Thanks," Hiram said. "How's Chief Fox?"

"Damnedest thing," Shanks said. "Got bit by a whole bunch of snakes in the middle of a February snowstorm."

"Damnedest thing," Hiram agreed.

"Best I can figure is the storm somehow knocked

open a nest in the valley and woke a bunch of 'em up. I've seen enough root doctoring to guess that maybe it was that stone sitting in the back seat of the car that saved his life. Anyway, the chief ain't dead, but he's taking a nice long rest."

"Does that leave you in charge? Chief Dixon?"

"Acting Chief Dixon at most. And your gun..."

"I guess the county sheriff has it?"

"I'll get it back to you. Where did you say your farm was?"

"Lehi," Hiram said.

Hermann Wagner tottered forward, head swinging from side to side, followed by Stavros, whose foot made him lurch forward in stutter-steps. "So is the mine back open?" Wagner asked.

"It is," Ammon said. "We'll work carefully, and we'll seal up any natural caverns we encounter."

The thought made Hiram nervous, but he believed the Beast was destroyed. They'd better conduct a divination of some kind, before Ammon resumed any digging.

"We'll dig the eastern seam," Samuel said.

Eliza Kimball nodded. "We'll get started clearing out the shaft in the morning. Ammon will have to act as foreman, for now. Miss McGill, perhaps you will stay for a while?"

Mary's face was red from cold and exertion. "Me?"

"The miners might like someone to give them advice, as we get our operations started again." Ammon paused. "I think I could use a little advice, too."

"As long as you're taking advice," Eliza said, "I advise a corral of horses, a few pigs, a few cows, and of course, a chicken coop."

"As soon as we can afford them," Ammon agreed.

"If nothing else, Samuel might need something to paint other than rocks."

His brother laughed.

Hiram couldn't help but smile.

Mary met Hiram's gaze. "And you, Mr. Woolley, our business isn't quite finished. If you're quite finished with the mine, I'd like a word."

Hiram blushed.

Ammon approached him and put out a hand. "Before he left, Dimitrios Kalakis said you were going to pay his debts to me. I've come to collect."

Hiram squinted at him even as he took his hand. "I believe Mary is going to argue my case. Good luck with that."

Ammon slapped him on the back and his laughter rang out across the valley.

The next morning, Hiram left Michael sleeping in their room at the Buford Boarding House. He had one little errand to run, and his son's sarcasm wouldn't help him.

Frank Johnson stood in front of the suite at the Hotel Utah with his arms crossed. Bruises clouded his face, both his eyes were bloodshot, and a narrow bandage pasted his nose into place. "Up early, Woolley?"

"Out late, Frank?" Hiram asked.

"What do you want?"

"I'd like to talk with Mr. Rettig."

Frank hesitated, but opened the door.

Sitting at his elevated desk, Rettig had his gloves on but his shirtsleeves rolled up. In front of him lay correspondence and an open book of maps. The office smelled of sweat.

Hiram stood behind one of the chairs with the legs sawed short.

"You." Rettig looked like he wanted to snarl. "Word has it that the Kimballs have become such a loving family, any chance I had of buying their mine is gone. Does that make you feel good?"

Hiram grinned. He'd slept, and he'd managed to get a few peanuts into his belly. "That makes me feel pretty good," he admitted. "You know what makes me feel even better?"

Rettig hesitated. "You'll tell me, of course."

"Buying the mine would have benefited the D and RGW, because you would have got cheap coal. You would have been the hero, so promotions and bonuses for you."

"So what?"

"So you weren't content to take that shot alone, were you?" Hiram reached into his pocket and produced just one of the photos Mary had given him the night before, when she'd asked for a word alone. The picture showed Naaman sitting at a table with several men in suits, smiling. "You had to have a second angle, another way to benefit."

"That photo proves nothing," Rettig said.

Hiram handed the photo over. "I don't aim to prove anything. What that photo shows is you meeting with the owners of the Latuda mine. I have others like it, of you at other operations."

"So what?"

"Here's what I think happened," Hiram said. "You cut yourself a side-deal, a couple of years ago, when the Kimballs were just starting to fight. You bought in to some of the coal mines yourself, personally.

If you could buy the Kimballs out for the railroad, great, you're a hero at the D and RGW. But if not, the Kimball mine shuts down, and all the other mines get to raise their prices because there's not as much coal. So you get personally rich, though the D and RGW's costs go up. You'd have been cheating the railroad you work for."

Naaman Rettig scowled.

"So you'd have been happy if the Kimballs accepted your offer. But failing that, you wanted to add to the chaos and fear and stop the mine from reopening under any circumstances. It's why you sent your men around to scare people."

"Self-dealing and corporate chicanery? My men roving the countryside? You can't prove any of that," Rettig said again.

"I guess I probably could," Hiram told him. "But I don't want to. I just want you to know that I beat you. I beat your plan to buy the mine, and then I beat your plan to shut it down. You have a good morning, Mr. Rettig."

"Damn you, Hiram Woolley."

"Damn you right back."

Hiram left. On his way out, he nodded at Frank Johnson. "I'd find a different boss if I were you."

Later, after Hiram had paid his bill at Buford's, and he and Michael had eaten a pile of breakfast, they walked to the Double-A, parked beside the Price River. The smell of the water mixed with the scent of coal smoke and wood smoke from the houses and the trains.

They'd retrieved the truck the night before from

where Hiram had hidden it, and it sat under a sky, dazzling blue, shining down on a snow-capped landscape. The truck wasn't alone. Other cars were there, as well as a gang of people. Mary was present, as were a few of the miners, including Hermann Wagner, Stavros, and the odoriferous Paul.

Eliza stood at the rear of the company.

"We came to say goodbye," Mary said. "And to thank you. You are something, Hiram."

He shook her hand and blushed.

Stavros limped forward. "Mr. Woolley, we don't know exactly what you did. But we thank you for it. My wife, she made a little candy for you."

"And I have some *Käsekuchen*." Hermann Wagner offered him something pie-shaped and wrapped in a gray kitchen towel.

Other miners came forward with gifts. Most gave Hiram and Michael food, but a few had brought him coins or a little folding money.

From miners who had just been unemployed, the gifts were generous.

Hiram thanked them all. Then he shook his head. "I feel bad for Walter and Medea. Without them, we wouldn't have made it out. Especially Medea. Are their families going to be taken care of?"

He thought of Callista, and her father who had taken to banditry, and now might be lame for life.

"*Ja*," Hermann said. The others bobbed their heads. "We'll take care of their families. We of the Kimball mine local will take care of our own."

Hiram said a silent prayer for the fallen, including Vilhelm and Eva Sorenson.

He gave Mary one last little smile.

She drew near and handed him the brass lamen. "You'll need this more than I will."

Hiram stuck it into his inside coat pocket. Feeling awkward, not knowing what to say, he squeezed her hand and stepped back.

Her reaction was to smile more brightly.

Eliza handed Hiram a heavy object, wrapped in paper. "I got curious, and I looked into the stone. I shouldn't have." Her face was pale and she had dark circles under her eyes. "We want you to take this and keep it safe."

Hiram took the stone. "Curiosity is natural. You didn't do anything wrong. The Beast did those things."

She smiled, for just a second, gratefully.

Hiram raised a hand. Michael said his goodbyes, and the pair drove away in the Double-A.

Hiram sat back and closed his eyes. He'd sleep, Michael would drive, and hopefully there wouldn't be much conversation.

They were going up the slope, up toward Soldier Summit, when Michael broke the quiet. "I gave Mary our address. I figure you could use a pen pal. I think you might be sweet on her. Am I wrong?"

"Not . . . *wrong*," Hiram said, eyes closed. "But."

"So why didn't you kiss her?"

"It wouldn't have been appropriate."

"Nuts with what's appropriate. Come on, Pap, Mom's been dead for six years now. It might be time to find someone who's sweet on you. And you definitely were sweet on her. You squeezed her hand and everything. Wow."

"Hmm."

Michael didn't take the hint and kept talking.

"Okay, so can you give me a summary of the more supernatural problems at the Kimball Mine? I can't believe I just used the word 'supernatural.'"

"I have more guesses than knowledge, son."

"Well, I have less than guesses. Share."

Hiram took a deep breath. "The Beast...let's call it that. I hope it's been destroyed. I won't know until I make another Mosaical Rod."

"Okay."

"I guess that over sixty years ago, Gus lived here, and went by the name Lohengrim Zoller. And he met the demon under the earth—maybe he came here because of the demon, I don't know—and he struck a deal with it. For thirty years, the demon made Gus prosper. Maybe the demon also taught him magic, I don't know that, either. But when Gus's time was up, the demon made a deal with a new person."

"Teancum Kimball," Michael said.

"Teancum Kimball. And I guess that must have been right around 1903, when there were riots in the mines. So maybe the demon had something to do with the riots—it caused them, or it used them to run Gus off, or it stopped the riots when Teancum made his deal."

"Teancum gave the monster his children. All of them. And Gus gave them his eyes." Michael shuddered.

"Gus left," Hiram continued, "but he didn't stay gone. He came back around 1920, and somehow, Teancum didn't recognize him."

"I'm going to go out on a limb," Michael said. "Gus used a charm."

"Seems likely. And Gus was sensitive to the possibility that I might have a seer stone, so my guess is that the Beast gave the peep-stone to whoever made a deal with it. So Gus probably had the stone in his day, and then Teancum. And then Teancum gave it to his children."

"I want a peep-stone," Michael said. "Or at least, I want to look in one."

"Someday." Hiram considered. "My guess is, at the same time Teancum was trying and failing to talk the Beast into renewing their deal, the Beast manipulated him into sending the seer stone to his children. My guess is the Beast planned to strike a deal with Samuel or Ammon."

Michael clutched the wheel, keeping his eyes on the muddy road, blanketed with snow from the storm the night before. "So, demons, huh? How can people not know about this?"

"Many do," Hiram said.

Many others, though, were taught not to see the evidence. Or were taught to disbelieve at all costs. Or talked themselves out of belief to preserve their own worldview, or belief in their own innocence, or in the superiority of their way of life.

"Are you going to teach me the hocus-pocus?" Michael asked.

A very good question.

"Maybe if you let me be for the drive home, I might show you a thing or two. But most charms only work for a person with a chaste and sober mind. You sure you want to walk that path?"

"Chaste *and* sober? Jeez." Michael laughed.

Chapter Thirty-Eight

HIRAM HAD PUT ON HIS CHURCH CLOTHES FOR THE interview.

It was the chapel in Lehi, early on Sunday morning before meetings started. Hiram sat on a wooden chair in a classroom, trying not to put his hand into his pocket to hold his bloodstone.

Bishops Smith and Wells sat on similar chairs facing him. The radiator hissed like a dragon, and Hiram was sweating. Outside the building, a cold snap had hit, and it wasn't going to get above freezing, but inside it was an oven.

The walls were white plaster. The only decoration they held were two framed pictures, one a painting of Jesus knocking at a garden door and the other a photograph of Heber J. Grant, the President of the Church. It shouldn't have bothered Hiram that Grant's picture was slightly larger and hung a bit higher, but it did.

The place smelled of furniture polish and prayer,

and every sound started an echo that hid within it the hint of a hymn.

He had on his white shirt, which he had pressed, but which had nevertheless become very creased on the drive to the chapel. His slacks had a hole in the seam on the right leg, and his shoes, he realized, could have used more polish. At least his bolo tie was straight.

Bishop Smith sat with his fingers steepled, dressed impeccably in a brown suit and fashionably wide tie. John Wells wore a smaller tie and a waistcoat, with his jacket over the back of another chair.

"What on earth caused you to become embroiled in a murder?" Smith asked. "You were sent there simply to deliver groceries to the Kimball miners, yes?"

"Yes," Hiram said. "And I delivered them."

Both counsellors waited for more, Smith frowning, but Wells with a relaxed smile.

"Well?" Smith asked.

Hiram shrugged. "I guess I think I told you everything."

"Except why the police considered you a suspect in a murder investigation," Smith said.

"I let the man borrow my gun," Hiram said, "so it was on the scene when he died. As far as I know, that's all there is to it. I'm not a suspect anymore."

"Did they find the killer, then?"

Hiram shrugged. "You could ask the Carbon County Sheriff."

"And the witchcraft?" Smith asked.

Hiram shook his head. "I'm no witch."

Smith pursed his lips in thought.

Two weeks had passed since Hiram and Michael had driven away from Helper. Planting hadn't started yet, but Hiram was ready—the tractor was all tuned up and he'd checked his stock of fertilizer and seed.

Hiram had cut a Mosaical Rod with all the names he knew for the Beast and interrogated it about the Beast's fate. Satisfied that the being was dead, or at least would not be found again by the Kimball Corporation's miners, Hiram had telegraphed a discreet all-clear signal back to Ammon.

Ammon's response telegram had told Hiram that Dollar's was boarded up and the family gone. Where were they now? The daughter knew some craft; she'd sabotaged Hiram's truck. And the grandchildren had seemed perfectly delightful...until Gus had hexed them.

Michael had written Mary. He had better penmanship than Hiram and was far better with words; also, he had a lot to say, and Hiram didn't.

She hadn't written back.

On the other hand, Hiram *had* received a package from the Carbon County Sheriff's Department. In it was Hiram's Colt, cleaned and smelling of gun oil. Hiram was glad to get it back.

He scratched his chin, comfortable in the silence.

President Smith, though, finally cleared his throat. "The times are changing, Brother Woolley."

Hiram nodded. "Every day."

"We're getting organized. We've learned from our best stake leaders how to get storehouses together, and how to manage collective effort. Have you heard about the Welfare Program the Pioneer Stake runs? And the L.D.S. Business College has set up a Women's Sewing Center. We're going to lick this depression, and we're going to do it as a people."

"President Roosevelt would be proud," Hiram said.

Smith snorted. "We're going to do it like Henry Ford. We're building a machine, and it will take care of our people the world over. We're going to get a real organization in place. And there won't be room for men like you in it."

Hiram considered. "Farmers, you mean?"

President Smith's face turned sour. "I mean men who buck the system. Men who can't take orders. Men who so flout the public conscience that they're accused of serious crimes. Men who dowse and consult familiar spirits."

Nostrils flared, Smith stood and left.

"He's a good man," John Wells said after a brief silence.

Somewhere in the building, a choir had begun rehearsal.

"He's a good *organization* man," Hiram agreed. "He does what he's told and gets others to do the same."

"I knew a beet farmer once," Wells said. "He had a hundred sugar beets, and he had a shiny new John Deere that took care of the patch. It plowed and it planted, it weeded and it watered and it harvested, and it did very well by ninety-nine of those beets."

"Hmm."

"But there was the one beet that the combine couldn't reach," Wells continued. "And so my friend the farmer had to go out himself, to weed around that beet, water it, and keep the worms away. It look a lot of labor, but the one beet turned out just as well as the ninety-nine. Do you think my friend the farmer did right to give that beet special care?"

Hiram snorted. "I think you have no idea how to grow sugar beets."

John Wells gave a Hiram a nod. "Let Bishop Smith build his machine. It will care very well for the ninety and nine. And you and I, my friend..."

"We'll go after the one."

"We'll go after the one."

"Ammon Kimball had a seer stone. Or, really, it was Teancum's." Hiram blurted the words out. He had to say something.

John Wells nodded slowly. "A seer stone?"

Hiram nodded. "But a seer stone that was connected to... a demon."

"I suppose if I were to find such an item," Wells said slowly, "I would think it was safer in the hands of someone who believed in its power, than being given to a bureaucracy that found it to be an embarrassing piece of history, best forgotten."

That was the end of the conversation. Outside the door, Wells turned right and Hiram walked left, to where Michael waited beside the Double-A.

The next morning, Hiram rose early and cut a length of witch hazel from the bush at the end of his porch.

Michael would sleep the morning away if permitted, and on this morning, unusually, Hiram would let him do just that.

After fortifying himself with a glass of buttermilk and a couple of hardboiled eggs, Hiram opened his toolbox. From the lower compartment, he removed the peep-stone, still wrapped in paper. He didn't know whether the stone had any value other than contacting the Beast, so he preferred not to touch it.

To prepare the Mosaical Rod, he carved into it the usual crosses and the Tetragrammaton. He recited a passage from Helaman out loud as he worked: "Whoso shall hide up treasures in the earth shall find them again no more, because of the great curse of the land, save he be a righteous man and shall hide it up unto the Lord."

He pocketed his blessed knife from the tool chest as well.

Then he walked out to the south forty, the Mosaical Rod in his hand, the mud under his feet frozen in swirls. Later in the spring, once planting started, there would be hired men out and about at this hour. All Hiram saw was a lone hawk circling overhead.

He walked swinging the Mosaical Rod from side to side and waiting for it to guide him. Gradually, dipping to indicate direction, it led him to the spot.

He drew an X into the dirt with his dagger, then walked back to the farmhouse, only to return to his X with a pile of split wood on the back of the Double-A. Above him, the Wasatch Mountains were crystalline ramparts, still white with snow over their gray rock and the dull brown of the gambol oak in their winter clothes. The snow on the peaks would stay until July, or maybe August.

Hiram got a fire going. He was grateful for the warmth himself, but also he needed to thaw out the ground before he dug. On top of that, fire was the element of intelligence, it was ruled by Gabriel, it undid enchantments, and so forth.

The fire was essential.

Hiram wasn't completely sure what spirit or angel moved the cache on his farm. Robin Goodfellow, whom Eva Sorenson had fed milk to? Grandma Hettie? A Ute medicine man who had once lived on the land? An angel who served the God of heaven?

Elmina?

Hiram's mother?

He wasn't sure who helped him, but he knew what worked. The helpful spirit, whoever or whatever it was, moved the box around, so no one could unearth it, either on purpose or by accident.

As the fire did its work, Hiram thought again of the hex he'd used to tumble down that wall in the mine. It was image magic, far beyond Hiram's lore. Hiram hadn't even been able to read the lamen without help.

Hiram's skills were woefully inadequate.

How could he possibly teach Michael?

How could he fight the demons of the land, as John Wells wanted, and keep the people safe?

Hiram took a deep breath.

He let the fire burn to coals and then waited for those coals to become ash. Sinking a shovel into the dirt beneath, he dug until he unearthed a box made of flat stones cemented together. On those stones he'd scratched every warding symbol he knew.

He should definitely learn more symbols. He should get books.

Where would he even do that?

He pulled the stone box out of the warmed, muddy ground and then knelt in front of it.

The vault's stone lid squeaked when he lifted it off. The things inside—a skull with horns, a glass bauble, a black candle, a hand of glory—were here for safekeeping. The chest kept them out of the grasp of those who might misuse them.

Which, in the case of some of the objects, was anyone who would touch them.

Hiram placed Teancum Kimball's seer stone inside

and then replaced the lid. Locking it felt good. Burying it again felt even better.

Would he ever show Michael the contents of the chest? It depended on the kind of life his son wanted. Part of him hoped Hiram could pass along to his son Grandma Hettie's special skills. Yas Yazzie's ways had not been so very different, after all. Another part of Hiram wanted his son to learn the sorcery of the chemistry lab and the occult language of academic publishing.

There were other evils than demons to fight in this world.

He said another prayer to the Lord Divine. He knew that even as he finished, the guardian spirit of the stone chest was whisking it away. No one could casually stumble across the items Hiram guarded, not now, and not ever.

A voice echoed across the bare, wintery landscape. Michael stood on the porch, waving.

Hiram waved back.

He drove back to the house.

What would he say to Michael, if the boy asked why he'd been out on the back forty with a shovel?

Hiram sighed.

"Cambias has achieved a feat of world-building: an expansive, believable setting with fascinating aliens, compelling mysteries, and a rich sense of history."
—*Bookpage*

"Far-flung adventure . . . Cambias offers up an entertaining coming-of-age novel filled with action and surprises. His aliens are suitably non-human in mannerisms, attitudes, and objectives, and his worldbuilding suggests a vast universe ready for further exploration. Readers . . . will find this hits the spot."
—*Publishers Weekly*

And don't miss:

THE INITIATE

HC: 978-1-9821-2435-9 • $25.00 US / $34.00 CAN

If magic users are so powerful, why don't they rule the world? Answer: They do. And one man is going to take them down.

"Cambias' energetic prose and grim take of the idea of a secret wizard community should please most urban fantasy readers."
—*Booklist*

NORTH AMERICAN HISTORY

WITCHY EYE
by D.J. BUTLER

Sarah Calhoun is the fifteen-year-old with a bad eye and a
natural talent for hexing, and all she wants is to be left alone.
At the Nashville Tobacco Fair, a Yankee wizard-priest tries
to kidnap her. Sarah fights back with the aid of a mysterious
monk named Thalanes, who is one of the not-quite-human
Firstborn, the Moundbuilders of the Ohio. It is Thalanes who
reveals to Sarah a secret heritage she never dreamed could
be hers. She embarks on a desperate quest with Thalanes
to claim this heritage, hunted by the Emperor and a legion
of dark creatures. If Sarah cannot claim her heritage, it may
mean the end to her, her family—and to the world where she
is just beginning to find her place.

PB: 978-1-4814-8311-7 • $7.99 US / $10.99 CAN

───────────────────────────

"[A] unique alternative-history that is heavily influence by urban and
traditional fantasy and steeped in the folklore of the Appalachians. . . .
Fans of urban fantasy looking to take a chance on something with
a twist on a historical setting may find this novel worth their time."
—*Booklist*

"Excellent book. I am impressed by the creativity and the depth of
the world building. Dave Butler is a great storyteller." —Larry Correia

". . . intricate and imaginative alternate history with a cast of characters
and quirky situations that would make a Dickens novel proud."
—Kevin J. Anderson, *New York Times* best-selling author

───────────────────────────

WITCHY WINTER
HC: 978-1-4814-8314-8 • $25.00 US / $34.00 CAN
PB: 978-1-4814-8379-7 • $7.99 US / $10.99 CAN

WITCHY KINGDOM
HC: 978-1-4814-8415-2 • $25.00 US / $34.00 CAN
PB: 978-1-9821-2466-3 • $8.99 US / $11.99 CAN

Available in bookstores everywhere.
Or order ebooks online at www.baen.com.